Trade, Integration and Institutional Reforms in Latin America and the EU

Roland Eisen
Alberto M. Díaz Cafferata
Ángel Enrique Neder
María Luisa Recalde
(eds.)

Trade, Integration and Institutional Reforms in Latin America and the EU

PETER LANG
Frankfurt am Main · Berlin · Bern · Bruxelles · New York · Oxford · Wien

Bibliographic Information published by the Deutsche Nationalbibliothek
The Deutsche Nationalbibliothek lists this publication in the Deutsche Nationalbibliografie; detailed bibliographic data is available in the internet at <http://www.d-nb.de>.

ISBN 3-631-55348-X
ISBN-13: 978-3-631-55348-0
US-ISBN 0-8204-9948-X

www.peterlang.de

Table of Contents

Preface

The Sixth Arnoldshain Seminar
Córdoba, República Argentina
March 14-18, 2005

Globalization and the expanding information and communication technologies (ICT) as well as the processes of enlargement of Mercosur in South American and of the European Union, demand an effort from national economies to adapt to these global changes and uncertainties about the future, enforcing institutional changes and structural reforms.

Economists must be able to understand these processes to formulate strategic scenarios and to ask how far do the institutions and forms of intervention contribute to favorable outcomes.

This Seminar is part of an ongoing endeavor of academic cooperation between the Universidad Nacional de Córdoba (República Argentina), and the Johann Wolfgang Goethe-University Frankfurt am Main (Germany), but is open to everybody interested in comparative economic studies.

A main intellectual and institutional challenge for the organizing universities from Europe and Latin America has been, starting in 1994, to open academic channels towards mutual knowledge and understanding. The driving interest on both sides of the ocean has been to help develop from academic exchange, an articulated perception of the ways in which social and economic life, and the opportunities for human development, are being rocked by the rapid and profound changes happening around the world that are the sign of our historic time.

With this inspiration the stated objectives of such cooperation are to foster and improve comparative research on the effects of globalization and in the field of economic integration, with a special emphasis on the EU and Latin America, as well as to encourage international and interdisciplinary research cooperation.

In this regard, the Arnoldshain Seminars were conceived to provide regular opportunities to meet for discussing the different research perspectives and policy implications.

It is worth mentioning that a new step in this direction is the creation under way of the International Association for Comparative Studies in Economic Integration.

The international perspective provided by the Seminars alert about a number of aspects. One is the powerful transformation forces and the limits of the globalization process. Another one is the presence of both winners and losers between countries and multiple dimensions of distributive effects at their interior. Also, the difficulties to incorporate the uncertainties about the forces driving the future of the international economic system and balance of power in a development strategy.

This complex of issues forms the theme of this volume which brings together papers presented and discussed at the Arnoldshain VI Seminar at the Universidad Nacional de Córdoba, República Argentina in March 2005.

The papers that follow address different perspectives as influenced by the variety of their academic origin and provide a fertile area for further efforts in the way of cooperation.

The editors have the great pleasure to thank several persons and sponsors who made this Seminar a great success, scientifically as well as personally: Professor Steinberg, President of the Johann Wolfgang Goethe-University, Professor Kelm of the „Stiftung zur Foerderung der internationalen wissenschaftlichen Beziehungen der Johann Wolfgang Goethe-Universität", Prof. König, Dean of the Faculty of Economics and Business Administration of the Johann Wolfgang Goethe-University, and the Dean of the Facultad de Ciencias Económicas, Universidad Nacional de Córdoba (UNC), Prof. Ana Karl de Vega. Also, financial support for the organization of the event from the Agencia Córdoba Ciencia S.E., Gobierno de la Provincia de Córdoba, and the Secyt (Secretaría de Ciencia y Tecnología de la Universidad Nacional de Córdoba) are gratefully acknowledged. The present publication is made possible due to generous gifts from the European Central Bank (Frankfurt am Main, Germany) and the Facultad de Ciencias Económicas (UNC).

We also thank all the participants for their fruitful collaboration and the lively discussions in a wonderful surrounding in Ascochinga at the Sierras de Córdoba, and to Constanza Bessone who provided efficient assistance on the organization. Finally, the Editors give a special thank to Yasemin Ilgin, and Sybille Panholzer for their great help in preparing the publishable version of this book.

Roland Eisen

Alberto M. Díaz Cafferata

Ángel Enrique Neder

María Luisa Recalde

Frankfurt and Córdoba, July 2006

I. COMPARATIVE LATIN AMERICAN AND EUROPEAN EXPERIENCES IN A STRATEGIC PERSPECTIVE

Roland Eisen, Alberto M. Diaz Cafferata, Ángel Enrique Neder, María Luisa Recalde

This introductory chapter provides an overview of the topics discussed in the Arnoldshain Seminar VI, as well as a synthesis of the content of the papers and two round tables that provide material for a comparative approach to the challenges and responses to globalization. The chapter closes with a comprehensive vision about the topics discussed, which reflects the Editors' perception and the lively discussion that surged during the debates about the complexities of the modern international economy, and the challenges and opportunities for the construction of a better world.

The "strategic perspective" is associated to the purpose of extracting from academic research useful insights that may help improving the understanding of current economic problems, and the decision making process of economic policy, in view of international long-run phenomena. International cooperation in the design of a common strategic perspective involves, in the first place, a consensus about global influences and interactions affecting all countries of the world; about the design of national government domestic and external policies; and a common stance about international agreements for the management of economic relationships.

The two round tables, which opened the activities, were focused on practical issues with immediate policy implications. The first one on education technologies reflects the continuous interest of the cooperation programme in the improvement of university education, particularly facing the challenges of a rise in enrollment that puts pressure on the economic and human resources of the institutions. Since both the Johann Wolfgang Goethe-University and the Universidad Nacional de Córdoba have accumulated substantial experience on the application of distance learning, the experts from both universities were able to provide a rich, systematic and informed updating of the issues.

The second panel addressed an also critical topic of the contemporaneous economy that is equally relevant for economies on both shores of the Atlantic: the vertiginous growth of financial flows carry opportunities for mobilizing financial assets in benefit of savers and investors, but have at the same time also been the source of financial instability and external crises that has generated a spurt of academic research and policy discussions on related issues, such as the Basel rules.

The other contributions of participants in the Seminar are selected papers grouped in four main areas: regional economic integration, international trade and growth, institutional and methodological comparisons, and the role of information technology in the globalized world.

Two panels on comparative experiences

The first group of contributions is the result of two Panel Discussions. The first Round Table focused on „Education Technologies – Comparative Experience". The discussion was coordinated and introduced by Graziela J. de Perona, who dealt together with Gerriet Mueller and Ulrich Peter Ritter with several issues connected with today's higher education; in particular methods of distance learning and the use of ICT. Three topics were addressed: firstly, the potential benefits and limitations, especially how to cope with the expected growth in the demand for online learning; secondly, the definition of quality; thirdly, the problem of cultural diversity and the role of different actors involved in the process of online learning. Gerriet Mueller reflected on the difficulties and complexities involved in designing online courses. He pointed out several potential benefits of e-learning – including greater cooperation among institutions, a reduced need for big campuses, and an increased productivity of knowledge workers; he remarked a few potential problems, like higher technology costs, and the need for appropriate material and environment. Ulrich Peter Ritter offered a couple of examples highlighting the role of ICT on modern education since the 1970s. Numerous questions were addressed also by the audience, in particular concerning the idea that distance learning should complement rather than substitute traditional modes of teaching (and learning).

The second Round Table on „Economic and financial consequences of Basel II“ was coordinated by Roland Eisen, and contributors were Ángel Enrique Neder and Ramón Frediani. The Basel II Accord is an international agreement to enforce a global standard level for the capital adequacy ratio proposed by the Basel Committee on Banking Supervision of the Bank for International Settlements. The rules set should be fully implemented by the year 2006. The forerunner on the capital adequacy ratio was the Basel I Accord, issued in 1988 and implemented in 1992. The central point of Basel I was to demand at least 8 percent of equity for all lendings to different groups of customers. However, with this „flat rate“, the stability of the international banking system was poorly reached in the 1990s, and the number of severe banking crisis even increased. Therefore, in June 1999 the Basel Committee issued new rules taking into account credit risk, market risk and operational risk. This first pillar was „imbedded“ in new rules relating to market discipline (transparency and „publication duties“) as well as new rules and instruments for the supervision process. Neder as well as Frediani remarked on various problems and questions, taken up in the lively discussion. The most important one relates to the consequences for developing countries; and a second problem concerns the effects of Basel II on bank lending to emerging markets. And a third query relates to the credit squeeze for small enterprises! While the third problem seems to vanish, the two other problems require a differentiation between countries, in different stages of development according to GDP per capita.

Regional economic integration

In a group of four papers, the focus moves to Integration. In the first paper, Marta Podzun de Buraschi examines the feasibility of financial integration between Mercosur and the EU. There are various approaches for the analysis of integration perspectives and many studies on this subject; some of them show the heterogeneity of the countries which make up the blocs and the subsequent different effects of their specific policies. In this paper the current state of the integration process of the Mercosur and EU blocs is presented. This is done firstly in order to find out whether one can follow the other, and, secondly, to analyze the prospects of increasing their reciprocal integration, especially in relation to financial institutions and operations.

Fernando H. Sonnet examines the EU and Mercosur commercial policy's compatibility for the oilseed complex, emphasizing the effects of world protectionism on the Argentine economy. He describes the types of protection and the different instruments that have been devised to foster their application. Then an overview of the oilseed complex of the world is given and a comparative analysis of EU and Mercosur trade performance is carried out. Further, the global agreement signed in Geneva in 2004 is presented; the conclusions and perspectives are discussed. Finally, a deterministic and partial equilibrium simulation model of comparative advantages is applied, to assess the gains from trade liberalization and their welfare effects on Argentina and other competitor countries.

In a model of economic growth, Gabriele Tondl and Goran Vuksic analyze the mechanisms and possibilities of regions in Eastern Europe to catch up. They identify the role of foreign direct investment (FDI), human resources and geography. The key relationships are estimated with spatial econometric tools using data for the period 1995-2000. The authors find that FDI was paramount for growth in that period. In addition, higher level human capital and innovation were most important factors. Human capital was essential for technology transfer. Important spatial dependencies support the fact of appearing regional growth clusters. Finally, regions with good EU market access showed higher growth. These findings, so the conclusion, provide clear guidelines for economic policies.

Ensar Yilmaz and Zeynep Kaplan examine the role of Mercosur and the EU in the formation of competition policy in Argentina and Turkey. They stress the role of the regional integration process in the formation of competition policy for two reasons: Firstly, it strengthens the economic integration among member states. Secondly, it provides legal and administrative protection to the economic actors within the region. During the last decade, competition policy has emerged as a major policy issue both in Argentina and Turkey. Therefore, the authors analyze the current status of Turkey's and Argentina's competition policies, their effectiveness, institutional design and enforcement mechanisms. However, both countries' short experience with an effective enforcement system demonstrates the importance and complexity of the issue.

International trade and growth

In the next set of papers Trade and Latin America are in the forefront. Alberto M. Díaz Cafferata, Leonardo Berbotto, and David Kohn analyze the fluctuations of the current account and the causes of Argentina's long-run growth slowdown. They show that filtered Argentine GDP 1875-2002 time series display a continuously declining trend growth along the twentieth century. Searching for permanent causes of this stylized fact, short-run and long-run properties of models with international assets mobility are discussed, and the behavior of national and foreign savings – the current account (CA) – in Argentina are examined. Stylized facts show a high correlation between investment and national savings, stationarity of the CA around zero for the period 1935 - 2002 without structural breaks, high frequency of cycles, substitution of national and external savings. The evidence shows little contribution of external savings to the financing of long-run growth and the surprising recurrence of external crises despite the relatively low CA deficits and suggests elements for a pro-growth strategy.

Using a gravity equation, María Luisa Recalde and Marcelo Florensa analyze the effects of Mercosur on the Argentine agricultural international trade. They chose Per Capita Income, Population, Distance and the dummy Mercosur and Language as explicative variables. The results show that the Mercosur has impacted on the bilateral flows of agricultural products, and income and population growth explain them better than distance and language.

Ángel Enrique Neder, Carlos S. Valquez, and Carlos F. Ceballos Ferroglio examine the profitability determinants in Argentina's natural gas distribution industry. With the help of accounting data they generate a group of indices to analyze the relative profitability between 1993 and 2002 in Argentina. The authors highlight that indicators are useful for taking decisions and defining business firm strategies, as well as contributing to soften problems of asymmetric information faced by the regulator, promoting the efficiency in the regulatory actions.

In the last paper of this group Alberto J. Figueras, José L. Arrufat and Mariano Salto study provincial labor markets in Argentina. Their main interest is to explain the increasing unemployment rate either as a supply side (e. g. women labor force participation) or/and demand side (technological change, macroeconomic fluctuations, economic restructuring caused by trade) phenomenon.

Institutional and methodological comparative analysis

Institutions are often blamed for the poor performance of economies; therefore in the next group of papers this theme is examined. In the opening paper, Roland Eisen and Yasemin Ilgin analyze different types of regulations for pharmaceuticals to control for health care spending. Their point of departure is the dilemma that government should set the ceiling price of drugs low in order to reduce government's health expenditure; however, keeping in mind that this may lead to a reduction of incentives to innovate or even to an off-shoring of the production of pharmaceutical firms.

In the next paper of this group Mariana De Santis, Héctor Gertel and Verónica Herrero do a comparative analysis with respect to teachers' salaries in eight LA countries where educational reforms have been introduced in the last few years. The starting point is results on Mincer's equations to link teachers' salaries to their characteristics.

Paula Palacios, Florencia Ruiz, Héctor Gertel and Roberto Giuliodori present a review of income polarization, a concept to explain certain changes in the distribution of income. A society may be said to be polarized when it can be divided in at least two significant groups such that members of the same cluster possess similarities in terms of some attribute but still kept differentiated from members of the other cluster. They describe first results presented by several recent studies that measure income polarization in Argentina. Next the authors analyze and compare the evolution of polarization in other countries.

In the last paper of this section, Eugenia Perona discusses some methodological foundations of Comparative Analysis in Economics using Critical Realism as her yardstick. Given this background, she explains (1) how methodology can help understand reality; (2) how Critical Realism views traditional (mathematical-deductive) methods when applied to the social realm; and (3) how Critical Realism favors comparative analysis as an alternative research methodology for economics.

The role of information technology in the globalized world

The final set of papers covers the broad field of information technology (IT) and its relation to the global economy. Alexander Elsas presents a comparative study about the different stages of development of e-government in various regions of the world. First he compares regular surveys of Brown University with respect to e-government with the UNPAN surveys. In a second step he calculates the correlation between the results of the different studies as well as the correlation between EGRI (the E-Government Readiness Index) and GDP and population. These results are used for an OLS regression to test (for South Central American and for Europe) the following hypothesis: A well developed state of e-government should save costs. However, despite data problems, the results point into the other direction.

Kerstin Herhaus deals with the implementation of IT governance in global financial institutions she remarks that the establishment of an overall organizational framework fails generally because of a missing awareness and the misunderstanding of IT governance. Therefore, IT governance should be seen as a broad approach which impacts the whole financial institution, not only the IT department. To cope with these queries, objectives or metrics must be clearly defined for all bodies with respect to accountability, transparency, compliance, independence, disclosure and control.

Globalization, shorter product life cycles, new competitors and a shift from a „make-to-market" towards an „engineered-to-order" approach characterize today's environment. Peter Langner focuses his analysis on the effects of high product variety on the supply chain, in particular on the coordination and control of supplies in partner networks. He stresses the high flexibility and the dynamics which are needed in supply chains for offering highly customized products. However, distrust can be seen as one of the most cost-driving factors in B2B transactions. Therefore, the need and possibility to reduce costs because of distrust should form the basis of research.

Final remarks

The comparative experiences in a strategic perspective provide elements for the analysis and discussion, considering the process of globalization in which the economies of LA and EU are immersed. In this sense, a value added of the Seminar was the personal exchange of ideas that allowed the participants going beyond the theory and the standard sources of data from the literature. The different papers provided very attractive points of view, not only for the topics in themselves, but also because of the variety of experiences they showed. This could be lively illustrated considering the discussion of the paper presented by Yilmaz and Kaplan, who made a careful comparison of the legislation on regulatory competition policy in Argentina and Turkey. A point raised on floor intervention by participants from Argentina, is that the formal legislation in their country, in spite of being well conceived and as advanced as the European, due to less institutional efficiency in Mercosur countries, is not fully applied in practice and is therefore less useful than in the domain of the EU. So, an institutional problem was detected shedding light on the pitfalls that imply institutions working in an inadequate way and the effects that it could appear on social life.

Another aspect emerging from the papers and their discussion was the differential spatial dynamics of the effects of globalization. Widely discussed were the problems detected on labor markets, on the asymmetries of the international markets and on the downward social and economic development (particularly in emerging economies) as a consequence of the globalization process. In this way also appeared the discussion on financial markets and the consequences of globalization, highlighting the need to take into account the relationship between financial assets (including money) and contractual and regulatory institutions and their effects on developed and developing countries.

Protectionism of agricultural and industrial markets were also part of the discussion, showing the need of regulating the process of globalization, combining national policies with international regulatory frameworks, allowing the markets to operate but also controlling their negative effects.

In synthesis, the Seminar enlarged the knowledge of the comparative analysis and gave a global perspective on many topics. This could be seen, at least in part, in the next chapters of the book.

Two panels on comparative experiences

SUMMARY

OF THE PANEL I DISCUSSION ON EDUCATION TECHNOLOGIES: COMPARATIVE EXPERIENCES

Chairperson: Hada Graziela Juárez Jerez de Perona

Panelists: Ulrich Peter Ritter and Gerriet Mueller

1. Introduction

This short summary of the round table discussion represents a conclusion from three different presentations on the subject by H. G. Juárez de Perona, G. Mueller, and U.-P. Ritter, as well as a demonstration of a group learning environment by G. Mueller with summaries about class experiences, and on a diverse and rather detailed discussion with personal contributions from around twenty of the attendants. An increasing convergence of visions can generally be observed among (1) understanding the role of Information and Communication Technology (ICT) in the University Knowledge Acquisition and Learning Era, (2) in realizing, that content, structure, and organization of presence learning can substantially be improved by appropriate incorporation of electronic teaching and learning media, and (3) E-Learning has become a significant instrument in modern academic curricular conception and development.

2. Some definitional queries

Currently, regarding the multiplicity of media supported forms of knowledge transfer and acquisition; there is no final agreement on the definition of the term E-Learning. While it is controversial, whether electronic learning is already experienced with the use of downloads and PDF-documents, or with using groupware tools, or with the presentation of simulation experiences and with animation effects, some consensus on classifications of different forms of E-Learning can by now be observed. Distinctions are made between putting digital presentation and cooperation into action during face to face courses, including content presentation from special tools such as power point or from digital objects served from intra- and internet, electronic whiteboards, video conferences, or pedagogical networks via computing pools on one side, and the use of electronic learning environments from the internet or data stores (DVD, CD, etc.) on the other side. Even the latter group of learning arrangements is rather large, ranging from hyperlinked access to courseware up to virtual tutorials and seminars and even to inter university courses, to using and applying Wiki concepts, or complete lectures, open and virtual university concepts based on online service software and network support.

3. Expectations and experiences

Although substantial investments have been made in "New Media in Education" and in "E-Learning Services Facilities" in European as well as in Latin American Universities, there is relatively limited success observed, compared to previously defined ambitious expectations. Especially to get sustained projects has only shown to be of limited significance: few concepts have spread over into ongoing and regular course systems, and financial support has frequently been limited to introductory facilities only and to funding of initial resources.

Nevertheless, according to a study by HIS, a German institution to support university education, 83% of face to face learning students in Germany use electronic media material, 23% take interactive self-learning material, and almost 10% of German students undertake virtual courses and remote sessions. On average, from typical 32 hours per week students take about four hours of electronic learning sessions, and about ten percent is estimated for E-Teachers proportion. Limitations are currently observed due to acceptance and competence of teachers, early stage research orientation of projects, limited challenges to invent, restrictive infrastructures, so that now changes can be observed from content-orientation to taking extended support of structure generating actions. Generally, we may conclude that E-Learning has left the phase of multiple project and media support into a phase of being a competing and substantial regular element within the university education planning and development. Many universities have implemented so called Learning Management Systems and extended capacities for mobile access, video-conferencing, multimedia laboratories as well as integrated concepts for internet access.

A major point of the discussion has been focused on the specific challenges and the possible drawbacks of distance learning concepts. A different understanding of the role of teachers and students could be demonstrated within a virtual studio demonstration experienced during several years of project seminar sessions. Also this demonstration could show and give insight into the accessibility at any time in any place by using a peer to peer network, so that online and offline sessions might almost be combined seamlessly. With respect to quality assurance of virtual education several contributions were made as of getting alerted to existing guidelines, developing institutions' quality assurance plans and then focus for regular audits by external quality agencies.

Another major point was raised with respect to international online learning environments to bring together students and educators whose experiences of teaching and learning, respectively, belong to very different cultural traditions. While this is a very challenging aspect, in practice, most of the transnational courses currently on offer have been developed originally for local students, and usually there has been very little adaptation for globalization use. An unresolved policy issue is therefore whether support should be available for offshore educational providers delivering educational services online. While many institutions have indicated support in principle for such a development, but have risen concerns over the quality of such provision have delayed its introduction. Other jurisdictions have moved to address the issue of the quality along with automatic procedures for personalization and localization of content, technologies that have proven to successfully persist in other applications, such as portal and community software, platforms for electronic commerce, business process management and user guidance.

Related to this issue is the difference of the stage of development of countries with respect to ICT infrastructure. Along with the recommendation to avoid conforming a new pattern that would reinforce even more the distance between countries, by opening a 'digital divide', it has been argued that even more serious than that is the risk of also reinforcing the 'learning divide' (Arocena and Sutz, 2000). In this context it is less the number of telephone lines and computers available but the creativity and ability to enforce the use of new technologies. Several authors prefer to use the term Learning Economy in pointing out organizational perspectives with knowledge as the main resource and learning as the central process (Lundvall and Borrás, 1998).

4. An E-Learning Framework

Within a separate presentation given to the round table by Alexander Elsas, some advanced technologies were illustrated by an E-Learning Framework (ELF). This class of concepts is originated with a view to becoming an international E-Learning Framework and is based on a service-oriented factoring of a set of distributed core services required to support e-Learning applications, portals and other user agents. Each service defined by the Framework is envisaged as being provided as a networked service within learning organisations, typically using special style Internet or Web Services protocols, and to allow the integration of components and applications from open source, regional federations, or institutions. It is not to provide a blueprint for just another solution but to agree upon common service definitions, behaviours, data models, and interchange protocols to support managed learning environments. Since it also contains a set of the most crucial concepts in modeling business processes and the infrastructure that can support them, this could provide an integrated platform for business courses with seamless application facilities access, such as scenario design, use cases, and business process models (for more details see: http://www.elframework.org/general).

5. Concluding remarks

Some concluding remarks were made focusing state and perspectives. While pragmatic use of E-Learning concepts has made media support a daily tool to overcome typical problems with partial substitution of mass education, with integrated distance learning units, with modular composition of teaching units and examination procedures in bachelor courses, etc., there is evidence of some missing overall concepts for systematic planning and development and of efficient integration. Nevertheless, in accordance with the ongoing differentiation trend in university education, E-Learning strategies will play an important role to actively shape the scope of competitive and goal oriented setting of academic programs.

References

Arocena, R. and Sutz, J. (2000), *Knowledge, Innovation and Learning: Systems and Policies in the North and in the South, Globalisation and Localised Innovation in the MERCOSUR*, Institute of Economics of the Federal University of Rio de Janeiro – UFRJ, Rio de Janeiro.

Lundvall, B-Å. and Borrás, S. (1998), *The Globalising Learning Economy: implications for innovation policy*, Targeted Socio-Economic Research – TSER Programme, European Communities, Luxembourg.

Joint Information Services Committee (2006), *The E-Learning Framework*, http://www.elframework.org/ (last reference March 2006).

SUMMARY

OF THE PANEL II DISCUSSION ON COMPARATIVE PROBLEMS WITH BASEL II

Chairperson: Roland Eisen

Panelists A. Enrique Neder and R. Frediani

1. Introduction

The Accords of Basel I and Basel II are about banking regulation or regulation of financial intermediaries – institutions which are professionalists in coping with different **kinds of risks** (or at least they should be): credit, market, liquidity and other (operational) risks. These risks can lead to **instability** of the international banking industry and the international financial system. This is so because the financial networks are so intertwined that local bank crises can lead to international crisis and most important: bank crisis have or can have really huge **real** consequences, measured by a fall in GDP!

2. Basel I – Accord: A short history

After the break-down of the Breton-Woods-System in 1973, there were just a lot of banking crisis – but to cope with those fears of bank runs **equity** is the solution! Equity can function as a risk buffer to limit also the volume of risky business. Therefore, as put by *Frediani*, the primary function of equity in financial institutions is to cover unexpected credit and market risk losses in order to protect depositors. That is why in July 1988 the first rules were decided upon to internationally harmonize banking regulations and capital adequacy rules. Two goals are at the hearth of Basel I: First, to strengthen the stability of the international financial market system; second, to level off the differences in national banking regulation considered as impediments for international competition. This was done by unifying the notion of equity capital and by formulating rules to determine risk-weighted assets (RWA)[1].

The central point of Basel I was to demand that for all risky assets at least 8 percent of equity should be hold. Furthermore, there were instituted four weights for the different classic of risky assets, cf. Table 1.

[1] Cf. Fisher (2002), p. 4.

Table 1: Risk Weights for Type of Asset

Risk Weight	Equity	Type of Assets
0 %	0 %	Claims against OECD countries
20 %	1,6 %	Claims against Non-OECD and banks of OECD states
50%	4 %	mortgaged credits
100 %	8 %	Claims against the private non-banking sector

Source: Basle Committee on Banking Supervision (1988).

One of the critical points was that within these categories of risky assets only a very rough and raw discrimination of credit risks was made. The **quality** of debtors was only rated with respect to some groups. There was no further differentiation inside the groups.

However, the stability of the international banking system was realized only very insufficiently in the 1990s. The number of severe banking crisis even increased[2]. Furthermore, interesting developments in the financial markets[3] as well as developments of complex transactions by the banks to circumvent the supervisory rules made necessary a thoroughly revised or new accord.

3. Basel II – Accord

In June 1999 the Basel Committee on Banking Supervision published a first „consultation paper". The new **equity regulation** are formally divided into two layers: the **main documents** (i.e. the New Basel Capital Accord), and additionally an „Overview of the New Basel Capital Accord". Besides these there are **special documents** related to „The Standardised Approach to Credit Risk", „The Internal Ratings Based Approach", „The Operational Risk", „Asset Securitisation" and „Principles for the Management and Supervision of Interest Rate Risk". Overall, these new rules are imbedded in new rules for transparency and publication duties („market discipline") as well as new rules and instruments for the supervision process („Supervisory Review Process", SPP), leading to three pillars (cf. Figure 1).

---

[2] Cf. Griffith-Jones and Kimmis (1998), p. 26.

[3] E.g. the „asset backed securities" and the socalled „special purpose vehicles" can be named, cf. Litten and Cristea (2003).

Figure 1: "THREE PILLARS" of Basle II

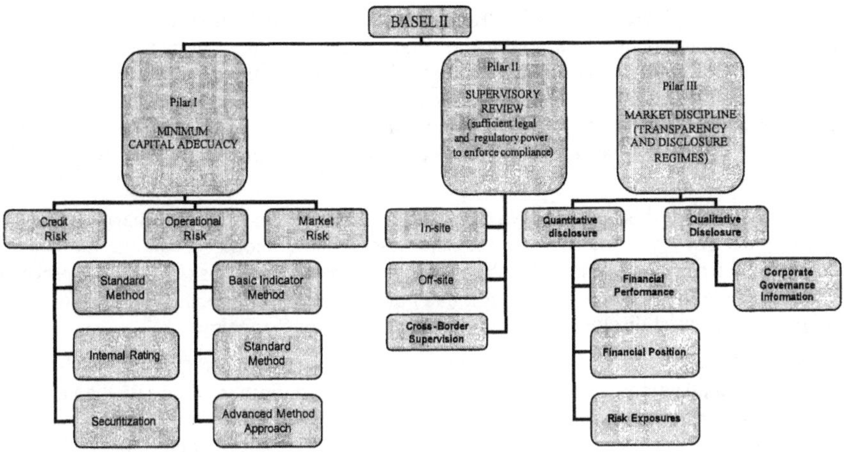

Source: Frediani (2005), p. 6.

Figure 1 shows two new things: First, besides credit risk there are market risks (introduced already in 1996 as an addition to Basle I) and operational risks. Second, there are three approaches to calculate credit and operational risks in „increasing order" with respect to risk sensitivity. While the „standard method" relates to external ratings à la S & P (where also credit default probabilities are given), and fixes risk weights (cf. Basler Committee 2003), there are two „Internal Rating - Based" (IRB) approaches, the basic or fundamental approach and the advanced IRB approach. In both approaches the following risk components are evaluated, however differently weighted: probability of default, loss given default, exposure at default and maturity.

While **market risks** relate to changes in market prices (e.g. of interest rates or asset prices), **operational risks** spring from breakdowns of new internal processes, persons or systems or even external effects (e.g. floods). With the **basic indicator approach** the operational risk of the bank is a fixed percentage (α-factor) of the average gross profitability. The standard method differentiates between various business lines and the capital requirement is calculated by multiplying these gross profitabilities with the adequate ß-factors. With the **advanced measurement approach** the banks are allowed to use their own internal loss data. There are several software packages available in the market to measure these operational risks. Nevertheless, as stressed by *Neder* and *Frediani*, Basel II still requires a definition of operational risk benchmarking; a sensitivity analysis of the final impact on capital adequacy in commercial banking; the development of special softwares and modeling for the measurement of different risk categories in banking industry; as well as an extensive fine tuning of commercial banks' internal capital estimation processes.

4. The second pillar: SRP

The „Supervising Review Process" (SRP) is an important innovation in the revision of the equity or capital adequacy accord. The **first pillar** is only one parameter, however supplemented by supervision and market discipline. Credit, market and operational risks are detailed in the first pillar. Strategic risks such as bank mergers, new business lines and new markets, risk of reputation and liquidity are not dealt with here. Therefore, the **second pillar** aims at risks of credit concentration, interest changes in the capital account as well as effects of business cycles.

The primary goal of this supervisory review process is to control the fulfillment of the capital requirements. However, additionally the supervisory board should encourage the banks to develop useful risk management function and to use them for the risk controlling processes. This continual SRP therefore has equal rights besides the capital adequacy and the control of markets via increased disclosure regimes. This was done by 4 principles[4].

Contrary to Basel I with its fixed rules, Basel II is only a „framework" which maybe subject to changes and adaptions, in particular with respect to the definition of equity, the permission of IRB's, or the risk weighting function. Although the new framework of Basle II has in principle validity only for large international banks, the scope is enlarged to the finance or holding group on a fully-consolidated base. Furthermore, the concepts are applied to all internationally active banks within a banking group (cf. Figure 2).

[4] Cf. Basel Committee (2003a), pp. 162 sqq.

Figure 2: The new scope of application of the accord

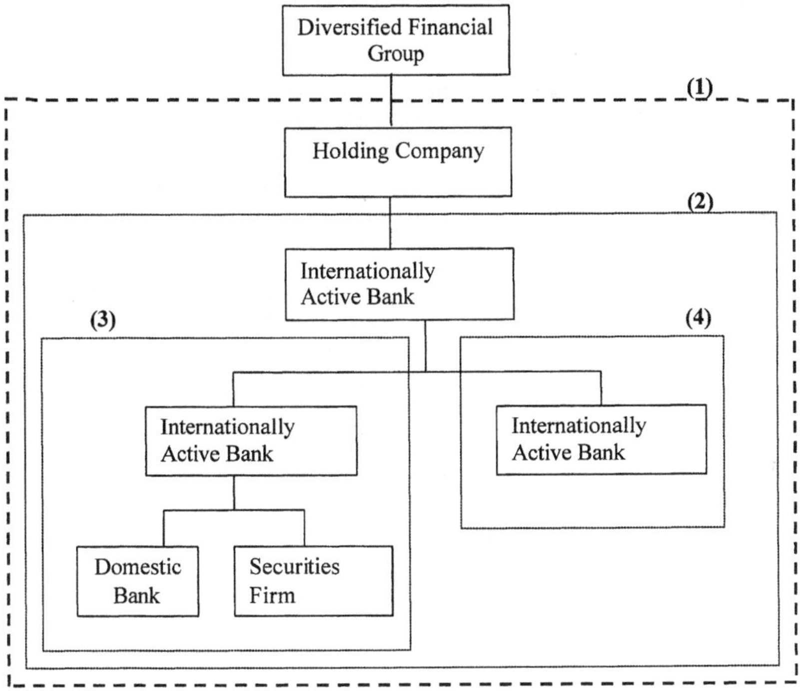

(1) Boundary of predominant banking group. The Accord is to be applied at this level on a consolidated basis, i.e. up to holding company level (paragraph 2).

(2), **(3)** and **(4)**: the Accord is also to be applied at lower levels to all internationally active banks on a consolidates basis.

Source: Basel Committee (2003a), p. 5.

However, *Neder* raised the question whether these rules should be applied to all banks, independent of their size and regional/local market (cf. also The Economist, 29.03.03, pp. 65-66).

5. Problems with and consequences of Basel II

Neder as well as *Frediani* pointed to various problems and questions related to Basel II. The most important one relates to the consequences for developing countries, e.g. with respect to the classification, to the financial flows, to external ratings and with respect to risk reduction by credit diversification. A second problem concerns the effects of Basel II on bank lending to emerging markets. A third query relates to the credit squeeze for small enterprises! This argument refers also to credit costs. Here the fear is that, not only credits are less available, but are also more expensive for small firms[5].

To avoid problems, *Neder* pleaded for the „market approach", emphasizing „Goodhart's Law" which states that public regulation will tend to collapse once pressure is placed upon it. The problem then is who can control the controller? That's why *Neder* argued for a larger role of markets in lieu of regulators. Here, different instruments (e.g. deposit insurance, issues of uninsured debt or „subordinated credits") can foster the markets' role.

For the discussion, *Frediani* put up a list of consequences: the fear of procyclical effects and the promotion of credit cycles; the danger of increasing (fixed) costs and a reduction in ROA and ROE, resulting in higher concentration of the banking industry. Other arguments raised for the discussion related to the promotion of a „secondary market" for rating services as well as the discrimination against micro-finance oriented institutions and retail banking. A last argument referred to the promotion of risk aversion in the banking industry by Basle II. Finally, it was argued that there should differentiated requirements for countries performing in different stages of development, at least three groups of countries should be distinguished according to GDP per capita (ranging up to 2000 US-$, from 2000 US-$ to 6000 US-$ and more than 6000 US-$).

---

[5] However, there is a new study carried out by (German) Postbank were according to an internal rating „90 percent of firms are equally or better off". So it seems to be the perception of more or less informed firms which is changing. Cf. FAZ (02.12.04), p. 16.

References:

Fisher, St. (2002), *Basel II: Risk Management and Implication for Banking in Emerging Market Countries* (http://www.iie.com/fisher/pdf/fisher091902.pdef).

Basle Committee on Banking Supervision (1988), *International Convergence of Capital Measurement and Capital Standards*, Basel.

Basel Committee on Banking Supervision (2003a), *The New Basel Capital Accord, Consultative Document*, Basel.

Basel Committee on Banking Supervision (2003b), *Overview of the Basel Capital Accord, Consultative Document*, Basel.

Frediani, R. (2005), Economic Consequences of Basel II, *manuscript for presentation at the Arnoldshain Seminar VI*, March 2005.

Griffith-Jones, St. and J. Kimmis (1998), *The BIS and its Role in International Financial Governance.* (http://www.eds.ac.uk/ids/global/finance/pdfs/ba2.pdf).

Litten, R. and Cristea, S. (2003), Asset Backed Securities in Zeiten von Basel II – Die geplante Eigenkapitalunterlegung nach den Basler ABS–Arbeitspapieren, in: *WM-Wertpapiermitteilungen, Zeitschrift für Wirtschafts- und Bankenrecht* 57 (Nr. 5), 213-221.

Without author, Basel II als Ursache für die Kreditklemme ist mehr Mythos als Fakt (Basel II as the reason for the credit squeeze is more a mythe than a fact), in: *Frankfurter Allgemeine Zeitung*, 02.12.2004, p. 16.

Without author, Bank Capital Rules, in: *The Economist*, 29.03.2004, 65 – 66.

Regional economic integration

IS FINANCIAL INTEGRATION FOR THE MERCOSUR – EUROPEAN UNION FEASIBLE?

Marta Podzun de Buraschi

1. Introduction

There are various ways of approaching the analysis of integration perspectives and a great many studies on the subject. Some of them show the heterogeneity of the countries which make up the blocs and the subsequent different effects of their specific policies. This paper aims at presenting briefly the current state of the integration processes of the MERCOSUR and European Union blocs, firstly in order to find out whether one can follow the other and, secondly, to analyze the prospects of increasing their reciprocal integration, especially in relation to financial institutions and operations.

The importance of political decisions is highlighted especially when these require an institutional framework which promotes and speeds up the integration process. In the case of bloc integration, other supranational institutions are required which guarantee the agreements, whose implementation is even more complicated.

Financial development contributes to economic development, mobilizing savings, allocating capital, monitoring borrowers and transforming risk.

Although macroeconomic factors are important in financial development, institutional factors such as legal and regulatory systems, as well as sector structure efficiency, are essential.

The institutional integration process in some countries in the European Union can be said to have been fully achieved in light of other experiences around the world. This claim can be made because of the gradualness of the steps followed, the tenacity or perseverance in officials' efforts, the different degrees of association tried out – liberalizing the movement of goods and people – and the macroeconomic convergence process which ended in the creation of a single currency for the region.

On the other hand, the MERCOSUR integration process, with its ups and downs, is comparatively at a standstill and it is sometimes darkened when faced with other options of regional association.

Section 1 analyzes the degree of progress in the integration of each bloc and it highlights the interrelation between economic and financial integration. Section 2 explains "cluster" methodology, or groups of homogeneous countries within Latin America, taking into consideration simple indicators to build dendograms. Section 3 revises the characteristics that MERCOSUR would lack in order to become an Optimal Currency Area. Section 4 summarizes the results by several authors on the costs and benefits of various association alternatives between blocs and it ends in some economic policy recommendations. Only some references are given out of the extensive literature on the subject.

2. Integration processes

2.1 Economic integration

Economic integration is the process by which countries eliminate certain characteristics that make them different from others, such as tariff barriers to trade, limitations on the movement of capital and people, industrial microeconomic policies, autonomous macroeconomic policies, etc. If these differences were eliminated by all countries simultaneously, a worldwide economic integration would be achieved, but only partial integration processes can be actually seen. Consequently, because of either political or economic reasons, only a world divided into big blocs can be imagined in the medium term (regionalization).

According to the barriers that are eliminated, several forms of economic integration can be found. When the agreement between countries consists in eliminating trade barriers reciprocally, there will be a Free Trade Agreement (FTA). When "rules of origin" are imposed with a view to preventing third party goods from entering a member country in order to be marketed in another member country, a Customs Union (CU) will be created. A common external tariff is established in these agreements. When a CU takes on the free circulation of capital and people, it becomes a Common Market (CM). Finally, the adoption of unifying criteria in micro and macroeconomic policies, as well as the adoption of a single currency, creates a Monetary and Economic Union (MU).

Trade liberalization is a complex diplomatic set of transformations of the trade regime.

The elimination of tariff protections has the following economic effects on: production, given producers' adjustment to the new relative prices; trade, which results in an increase of imports; fiscal income, by reducing it; and welfare, by modifying family consumption because of the changes in real income.

Progress in integration is not necessarily linear or the same as that in the EU, but it is conditioned by the economic and financial structures of the countries that make up the bloc. Countries' heterogeneity in the financial sector leads to different degrees of effectiveness in the monetary policies which can be taken.

2.2. Financial integration

The global banking system experienced some sizeable shocks in the last five years (terrorist attacks, default of the US energy corporation Enron, and so on). In spite of this, the international and European banking systems have shown remarkable robustness thanks to the diversification of their activity, consolidation and improved risk management techniques.

There is growing competition in the financial sector because of factors such as deregulation, and internationalisation. Financial firms have become increasingly active in each other business area, and in more European countries non-financial firms are offering traditional banking services.

Banks are pressured to increase income and control costs. On the income side they have to do diversification efforts, and to have scaling ambitions. To cut costs they have to streamline their organisations and concentrate more on core business. This is also reflected in a more cautious approach to risks, including the risk associated with mergers and acquisitions. A demutualization phenomenon occurred seeking more efficiency.

Developing internet banking is another way to improve the cost basis, but some European banks have been too ambitious in the past and are now scaling back their expansion plans. Most European banks continue to prefer the "multi-channel" strategy, but such a strategy also implies certain risks. The branch network remains the pivotal point. In order to put this network more efficiently to work the "open architecture" concept is gaining favour.

Financial innovation allows banks to bundle or unbundle risk more efficiently for proprietary purposes as well as customer-related business. This is reflected in the rapid development of more sophisticated approaches to risk management, such as the use of credit derivatives and securitisation.

Supervisors have to respond to this development by analysing the implications of credit derivatives and other risk transfer techniques. A major trend is the institutionalisation of the cross-sector co-operation between different authorities, which can range from memoranda of understanding to the establishment of a unified supervisor. At the European level, several initiatives have been taken in the context of the Financial Services Action Plan (FSAP), which aims to create a single EU wholesale market by 2005 and to achieve open and secure retail markets for financial services.

Related to the growing importance of consumer issues we can see that commercial banks have themselves participated in the disintermediation process, moving into areas such as investment banking and asset management. Financial innovation also permits banks to increasingly offer products where the customer takes on market risk, which is fundamentally absent in deposits repayable at par. Banks have found themselves coping with new issues relating to the sale of such products, the handling of complaints and questions of consumer redress.

a) **MERCOSUR environment**:

Within Latin America we focus the MERCOSUR Area but we identify their common phenomena.

During the nineties Latin America saw a profound process of integration into the global capital markets. The restructuring of debt through the Brady Plan (1989) marked a turn around, further impelled by the processes of capital account liberalisation. The programmes of reform and stabilisation contributed to a substantial improvement in the macroeconomic environment in most of the region with advances in price stability. In the initial phase the price stabilisation process was achieved through the pegging of exchange rates, but since the second half of the nineties all pegs have been abandoned. Despite the efforts made in fiscal policy, this was most pro-cyclical: when the economy grows, increased fiscal receipts and access to external financing stimulate government expenditure, feeding additional growth and inflation; in bad times, lower tax receipts and greater difficulties for raising financing on international markets force budgetary retrenchment, which causes additional economic contraction. This pro-cyclical bias is an additional source of volatility for macroeconomic policies, but it shows that fiscal discipline can ultimately stimulate growth potential through a reduction of the risk premium in the economy.

Financial crises have been frequent and damaging in Latin America after 1994, but economic liberalisation and his spread over effects allow greater integration with clear improvements in the financial system.

Comparing with European Union integration, Latin America shows less degree of integration, in some cases not only less than the EU today, but even less than the EU at the beginning of its regional integration process, where increasing economic integration corroborated and sustained the process of institutional integration.

3. Analysis of Methodology

3.1. Cluster Analysis

Homogeneous countries were grouped through "cluster" analysis within both blocs on the basis of various indicators which take in their integration and convergence. The stage or step of the process which they are in is highlighted. This comparative study was made for the years 1994, 1997 and 2000.

Cluster analysis classifies objects in such a way that each is very similar to those in the cluster in relation to a predetermined selection criterion. The resulting object clusters should show a high degree of internal homogeneity (within the cluster) and a high degree of external heterogeneity (among clusters). The chart results – not presented here – show extreme heterogeneity among Latin American countries and only in the year 2000 do the MERCOSUR countries fall within the same cluster.

The similarity measures taken were calculated by the Euclidean distance, which consists in the square root of the sum of square differences in the values for each variable.

$$D(i,j) = \sqrt{\sum_{k=1}^{p} (x_{ki} - x_{kj})^2}$$

Where D(i,j) measures the dissimility between country "i" and country "j" for all economic integration characteristics k form 1 to "p".

In order to select the clustering procedure, dendograms with hierarchical methods were used whose structure or hierarchy is tree-shaped. Clustering hierarchical methods begin with each object in a separate group and finish when all the objects are in the same group. The division process starts with all the objects in the same group; the objects are divided until each becomes an independent group. Non-hierarchical methods are known as K-measure clustering. In order to apply them, the number of clusters and their centers should be specified. Hierarchical clustering methods were used in this study.

3.2. Indicators of financial depth:

All variables related to the GDP have to be seen as related with the YPPP (purchasing power parity of income), which is more appropriate in cases of heterogeneous economic situations. Net interest margin measures bank efficiency when related to bank size. Bank credit to private sector evidences the degree of Bancarization and spreads are indicators of efficiency. Other variables we considered (not presented in the schedule) where Liquid and Quasi Liquid Liabilities, and Total Liquid Bank Reserves to Total Banking Assets.

In order to compare the financial systems of Latin American countries three relatively homogeneous groups where formed with the cluster method. In some cases there are large differences in terms of financial depth. Cluster 1 (Chile and Panama) is nearly four times larger than the others. The financial system is particularly small in Cluster 3 (Colombia, Dominican Republic, Ecuador, El Salvador, Guatemala, Paraguay, Peru, Venezuela plus Honduras, Bolivia and Nicaragua) in relation with their income per capita. The deeper the financial system, the more balanced the financial structure are. Again Cluster 1 has the most balanced relation between the capital markets and the banking system while all other groups have a much larger banking system. There is a high real interest rates together with the large amount of credit to the public sector in Cluster 2 (Argentina, Brazil, Mexico, Uruguay, Trinidad and Tobago and Costa Rica), that groups three of the four MERCOSUR countries. High interest rates may be consequence of an inappropriate policy mix, of fiscal policies and restrictive monetary policies over the last two decades.

The structure of bank ownership has changed substantially in the last decade in most countries. Foreign ownership has increased in all groups but Honduras, Bolivia and Nicaragua and government-ownership is extremely small except in Cluster 2 (with Mercosur countries) where it is moderate. Bank concentration has generally fallen to reach reasonable low levels by international standards but the trend changed in Cluster 1, particularly in Chile, where concentration has increased substantially from 2000 onwards.

Per capita income is an important explanatory factor of financial development but not the only one. Latin American countries have small financial systems compared to their per capita income and that they are relatively homogeneous in terms of financial depth. In fact almost all countries can be found in the worlds least financially developed group, comparing also to some regions of Asia and Eastern Europe. Latin America's financial systems are very small, financing is more bank-based and looking at efficiency and soundness the performance is mixed. It ranks last among the regions compared in terms of efficiency, measured by the net interest margin, but soundness indicators, such as asset quality and risk-weighted capital fare relatively better. Bank credit to the private sector is very low, explained by the very high real interest rates and the recurrent bank crises, the crowding-out by the public sector and the weaker institutional framework, particularly as regards creditor rights.

The domestic bond markets are relatively small, since issuance was almost exclusively external in the first half of the 1990s, but they have grown very fast in the last few years.

Stock markets are clearly larger in the most financially developed countries (Cluster 1 and 2). However, in the last few years, the markets have stagnated in nearly every country, both in terms of size and efficiency, the latter measured through the turnover. This is due partially to the general downward trend in stock market capitalization in the world but also by the large number of Latin American enterprises which have chosen to be listed in the New York Stock Exchange.

As for institutional investment, pension funds have grown relatively fast in the region, particularly in the most financially developed country, Chile, but the potential for growth in the coming years is substantial, which should contribute to the further development of the domestic bond and stock markets.

With these variables, clusters or categories for the Latin American countries were built by taking into consideration mainly financial depth and its relation with the purchasing power parity rates of income (Yppp). Out of the different years which were analyzed (1995, 1997 and 2000), 2000 shows the greatest convergence of the MERCOSUR countries – Paraguay being the only exception, which indicates that there was not always homogeneity among the countries and that they do not follow a continuous convergence process either. Financial depth shows what proportion of the purchasing power of income is used in financial assets in the different countries, drawing on the concept that the greater the development or the higher the income, the greater development of financial markets.

When economies reach commercial integration and similar macroeconomic policies are applied, these tend to converge. As the MERCOSUR agreement was signed in 1991 and tariffs among partners have been reduced ever since, a greater convergence among the countries analyzed is logical for the year 2000.

Figure 1: Financial Indicators. Latin America, Year 2000.

Countries	YPPPpercap	Credit/PBI	Financial Depth	Local Spread	Public credit	Private Credit	Libor Spread
Argentina	12377,0	33,6	91,9	2,7	10,5	23,1	4,6
Bolivia	2424,0	56,4	57,8	23,6	4,9	51,5	28,1
Brazil	7625,0	46,0	84,0	39,6	17,0	29,0	50,3
Colombia	6248,0	30,0	41,8	6,6	10,6	19,4	12,3
Costa Rica	8650,0	32,7	47,7	11,5	8,6	24,1	18,4
Chile	9417,0	74,1	159,7	5,6	6,8	67,2	8,3
Dominican Republic	6033,0	29,0	29,8	9,1	3,5	25,4	20,3
Ecuador	3203,0	0,0	5,2	8,9	0,0	0,0	9,7
El Salvador	4497,0	5,9	23,1	4,6	0,8	5,1	7,4
Guatemala	3821,0	16,1	17,3	10,7	-1,8	17,9	14,4
Honduras	2453,0	28,9	37,6	10,9	-7,5	36,4	20,3
México	9023,0	19,6	41,4	12,0	8,1	11,5	11,7
Nicaragua	2366,0	153,9	153,9	11,9	102,7	51,1	14,8
Panama	6000,0	110,8	148,3	3,1	-8,9	119,7	3,6
Paraguay	4426,0	24,5	29,9	11,1	1,7	22,7	20,3
Peru	4799,0	25,5	45,2	14,6	0,0	25,5	21,4
Trinidad and Tobago	8964,0	32,2	91,5	8,3	-1,5	33,8	10,0
Uruguay	9035,0	54,3	55,1	36,9	3,0	51,3	42,5
Venezuela, RB	5794,0	12,9	19,7	8,9	2,7	10,2	18,7

Figure 2: Latin America cluster. 2000

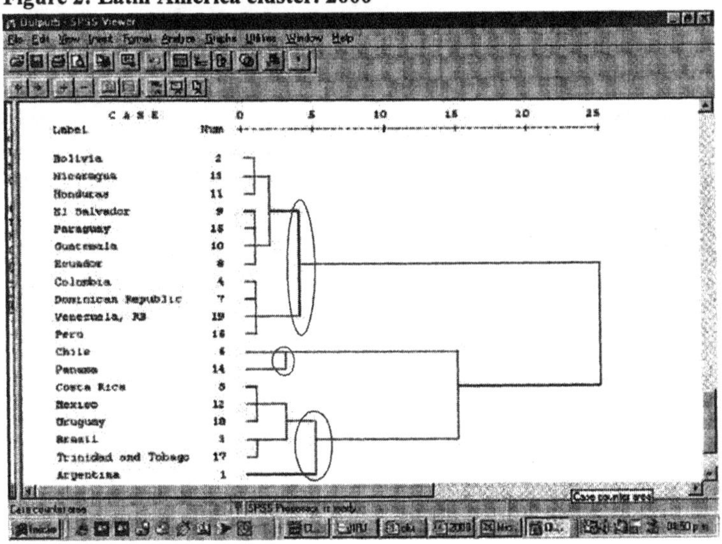

4. Does MERCOSUR comply with the requirements for an Optimal Currency Area?

Considering turnover, labor and capital markets, the banking sector, fiscal policies and the synchrony when faced with external shocks, it is possible to assess the advantages and disadvantages that the MERCOSUR as a currency area would have in comparison with the experience of the European Union.

To measure economic integration, we look at variables of economic integration suggested by the OCA theory:

a) Synchronisation of the business cycle: The higher synchronization, the lower is the cost of pursuing common policies and deepening integration.
b) Convergence of inflation rates: Deepening institutional integration is most beneficial if inflation rates are quite similar among the participants.
c) Exchange rate variability: The terms of trade should exhibit narrow fluctuations between countries pursuing inter-regional exchange rate stability.
d) Trade openness and integration: OCA theory implies that different countries can benefit more from reducing or even elimination exchange rate variability if they trade strongly with each other.
e) Financial market integration: Countries may benefit from financial market integration by allocating resources more efficiently and reducing transaction costs.
f) Convergence of interest rates: the higher the initial similarity of interest rates, the less is the cost for each country by moving to a common monetary policy.
g) Income convergence: more integration and openness should lead to more mobility of factors of production, which may result in convergence of income levels.

From the comparison of 6 EU and Mercosur countries we point out that:

European countries are more integrated since March 1957 till the European Monetary Union in January 1999 onwards. For Latin America we can look only at a shorter time period (1980-2000), where debt crises, high volatile exchange rates and high rates of inflation until 1993 characterised most of the countries. With the restructuring and stabilisation programmes the process of regional integration strengthened.

Comparing the levels of economic integration we can conclude that the degree of economic integration in Latin America is roughly close to that in Europe in the 1960s and 1970s.

Exchange rate variability in LA has been substantially higher than in Europe. Regional trade integration and openness are in Europe much larger than in LA on average. The interest and inflation rates move at the same level in Europe but not in LA. The correlation of nominal interest rates has been around 60% within the euro area during the pre-EMU period, but only around 30% for the Latin American countries. The higher degree of economic integration is also reflected in the integration of financial markets.

Business cycle correlation, inflation convergence, real interest rate correlation and financial market integration have all been persistently higher within the EU countries than among the Mercosur ones. Similarly EU Countries have substantially higher degree of real per capita GDP convergence and trade openness than Mercosur.

Mexico, Bolivia and Ecuador are among the least economically integrated countries in LA. Mexico looks more at US economy than with the rest of LA.

Economic integration among the four Mercosur countries plus two associate countries has reached a higher level then in LA as a whole. The integration process came to a temporary halt during 1987-93, explained by the difficult economic conditions present during that time due to high inflation rates, slow growth and substantial exchange rate variability.

On the whole, the finding of the cluster analysis show that both LA and Europe have become more integrated over time. In particular, the integration process of real variables (business cycle, trade and income) is generally much slower than the integration process of nominal variables (exchange rates, inflation, interest rates, and financial markets). This is a result that one would expect, given the fact that the real integration process of economies is generally much slower as it partly requires the mobility and built-up of physical factors of productions.

Economic integration in Europe occurred along geographic lines in the earlier periods, whereas it took place mainly along institutional lines since the 1980s. Countries that were most closely committed to European institutional co-operation also integrated more quickly than those joining the various stages of the institutional process only later or not all.

One of the key lessons from the European experience for LA is that intensifying institutional integration, such as for instance through the creation of a common market and the co-operation of monetary and exchange rate policies, indeed plays an important role in deepening and accelerating the process of regional economic integration.

The greater the turnover, the greater the benefits of a monetary union are. The MERCOSUR shows lower trade integration levels than Europe does.

The MERCOSUR lags behind in the process of liberalizing labor flow among countries. A greater depth in the integration of labor markets depends on legal, cultural and linguistic factors. Within the MERCOSUR cultural barriers are not very significant. The countries in the region have a common political and cultural origin and languages are similar (Portuguese and Spanish are mutually intelligible). However, legal restrictions might appear hard to change due to the great differences in regulations in the different countries.

Likewise, the countries would accept a greater depth in the integration of their labor markets only if this were not to cause large migratory flows, especially from the poorer countries into the richer countries. The great differences in income among the countries in the South American region become an obstacle. When two relatively similar labor markets are integrated, migration will remain stable and it will mainly respond to transitory regional shocks. However, when great differences are present, migration will be permanent and in only one direction.

If labor markets remain segmented, (real) salary flexibility is the only means by which convergence in the unemployment rate can be achieved. Nevertheless, if this does not occur and the labor markets are inflexible, a great divergence in unemployment rates should be expected if a single currency were to be introduced.

The liberalization of market capitals in Europe speeded the process toward a monetary union. Speculative attacks were supposed to disappear under a single currency. Does a greater integration into the international capital market imply a greater need for monetary integration? Par bond spreads in Argentina and Brazil over US Treasury bonds show that there is a strong correlation in the evolution of these instruments, suggesting that shocks tend to be caused by external factors to both countries. Spreads between Argentina and Brazil diverged only at the end of 1998 due to the Brazilian devaluation. On the other hand, intraregional capital flows are not quantitatively important when compared with capital flows from outside the region.

If capital flows are strongly correlated for the MERCOSUR economy, there would appear to be no a priori reasons to foresee an important fall in the volatility of capital flows as a result of monetary integration. A single currency in the region could eliminate speculative attacks caused by realignment expectations of the exchange rates among members' currencies. However, intraregional flows are limited and, therefore, only the realignments among partners' exchange rates in relation to currencies external to the region may cause important speculative attacks.

When the euro was launched in Europe, financial markets remained relatively segmented. The integration process has created some convergence in bank spreads and an active consolidation of the banking industry. The euro is perceived as a way of increasing competition in the banking industry. This increase was caused by a process of mergers and takeovers which led to the internationalization of the financial sector in the financial countries.

In the MERCOSUR, however, banking internationalization occurs as a consequence of the liberalization of market capitals and is associated with strong capital inflows requiring reliable financial institutions to channel them in the receiving countries.

In both cases, the increase in internal and external competition caused smaller spreads and a fall in bank's profits. Nevertheless, instead of improving efficiency, like in the United States, the European and Latin American banking industry responded by reducing the number of participants in the market with a fast consolidation and internationalization process.

However, unlike the European case, the internationalization of Latin American financial intermediaries has been characterized by integration with extraregional institutions and not with regional banks.

Monetary integration in the MERCOSUR would be a source of greater financial vulnerability if it were not implemented after laying down rules governing financial activity within the union. This would occur because in a context of unrestricted capital mobility, if regulation or tax level is lower in one of the member countries, banks will move operations toward this country in order to benefit from lower costs. This may lead to inefficient regulatory competition.

An even more serious problem is the moral risk which may be caused if regulation is not homogenized among the countries. An example might be the case in which the more fragile financial system (the one with lax prudential regulation) tries to take advantage of the lender-of-last-resort role which a single central bank would play.

To summarize, the long-term limited profits which could be earned through the consolidation of regional banks as a result of monetary integration (spread reduction) might be surpassed by the dangers associated with the possibility of regulatory competition and the existence of heterogeneous regulations.

The restriction imposed by a common monetary policy implies the need for similar fiscal policies (the same inflation tax, eventually, similar tax structures to prevent factor movement). On the other hand, once the countries form the union, there will be incentives to go into deficit beyond optimal levels because the governments consider that the monetary authority or the rest of the partners will eventually finance the deficit.

Fiscal solvency is far from guaranteed in the region. This disparity in fiscal results poses an important challenge to the implementation of a Maastricht-like treaty and, in turn, makes it an essential requirement before any kind of monetary coordination is attempted.

In a monetary union, fiscal transfers are important because they may lessen the effects generated by adverse temporary shocks affecting the union's region. If the shocks are symmetrical, there is no need to change relative prices among the economies and the monetary union becomes more attractive.

Shocks in the MERCOSUR were less symmetrical than those affecting Europe and the NAFTA. Evidence shows that although they became more symmetrical as the integration process took place, domestic shocks remain the main source of fluctuations. It can be concluded that the MERCOSUR countries may face important frictions when establishing a monetary union.

5. Costs and benefits of the Optimal Currency Area and chances of expanding it to two blocs

5.1. Costs and Benefits of a monetary union

The integration of some European countries into the European Monetary Union (EMU) brought up the discussion about the advisability of repeating this process at a level of already existing blocs in order to go deeper into the integration process.

To assess the success of a monetary union we have to contrast costs and benefits. Benefits measured as a percentage of GDP would rise with the monetary union because of the fall in the implicit transaction costs which existed when there were different currencies and because of the elimination of foreign exchange risk. Costs, in turn, would decrease as the intensity of interregional business increases, because the foreign exchange policy as a stabilization policy instrument would decline in importance as it becomes ineffective to correct asymmetrical shocks. When combining increasing benefits with decreasing costs, changes in the nominal exchange rate do not cause changes in the real exchange rate. In addition, if the commercial integration process is expanded among the potential members of a monetary union, economic cycles will be more correlated.

The greatest advantage of a monetary union lies in the trade increase between the parties and the elimination of variability in the exchange rate, whereas a higher cost would be found in the loss of monetary policy autonomy which is normally used to soften economic cycles.

Concerning to create institutional associations to support Mercosur-EU relationship, we can highlight that in December 1995 the Ministers of Foreign Affairs of Mercosur and the EU subscribed to an Interregional Framework Cooperation Agreement to strengthen relations between the two regions. In June 1999 at the Rio de Janeiro Summit, they launched the negotiations for a wide Inter-regional Association Agreement.

The EU has some specific interests in a free trade association (FTA) with Mercosur. Along with the political importance of such an agreement, the EU might expect some clear economic advantages from the liberalization of trade with the Mercosur countries. Mercosur is the most important EU´s economic partner in Latin America. EU exports to Mercosur are highly value-added, being of special importance the automobile, machinery and equipment as well as services sectors.

Mercosur´s major exporting sectors are food, beverages and tobacco, raw materials from agriculture and mining, the rest are importing sectors. The trade patterns with the EU show a similar rather more accentuated profile –food is more export oriented and manufactured products are more imported oriented. Mercosur's agricultural exports are concentrated in a few of commodities whereas the EU´s exports are more diversified including products more differentiated and highly processed products.

In the case of Brazil and Paraguay, exports of agricultural products are very concentrated. The main exporting activities are tropical agricultural products (coffee, sugar and soya). In Argentina and Uruguay exports of agricultural products are more diversified. In Argentina oleaginous products (sunflower, soya) are the most important, follo3wed by cereals (wheat, maize). In Uruguay, boneless cuts of beef (chilled and frozen), fish fillets (frozen) and citrus fruits are the activities that account for the major part of exports.

The set of agricultural and fish products imported from the EU shows more diversification than exports and it differs for every member country in spite of their generally similar profile.

5.2. Different association scenarios

Based on the Giordano-Watanuki (2000) general equilibrium model, five regions (EU, Argentina. Brazil, USA and Mexico) and 11 sectors (which can actually be regrouped in three: agribusiness, industrial and services sector) could be determined. Considering only the possibility of Mercosur-EU association, we analyzed the benefits with and without the agrarian sector.

	Giordano-Watanuki	
	MERCOSUR-EU	Idem without agrarian sector
Real GDP: EU	0,22	0,16
Argentina	0,70	0,50
Brazil	1,30	0,85
Uruguay		
Total Exports: EU	0,22	
Argentina	4,00(1)	
Brazil	4,00(1)	
Uruguay	4,00(1)	

Figure 3: Benefits of a MERCOSUR-EU Association

As a starting point, economic structure, commerce patterns and the tariffs of each country were taken in account. On the one hand Mercosur countries absorbed only 1% of European exports, but exported 26% to the zone, particularly in agribusiness, therefore we can say that the commercial structures are quite different. Tariffs from the EU to the Mercosur countries are very high, especially in the case of grains.
On the other hand Mercosur has the highest tariffs for industrial goods coming from the EU.

Figures show an increase in GDP and in Total Exports due to possible associations, both for EU and for Mercosur (its main 3 countries). Including the agrarian sector, the benefits of Mercosur countries are considerably higher than for EU. However, these benefits are also seen, even without the agrarian sector.

If we consider the possibility of a monetary union within the Mercosur, the benefits would increase considerably due to the stability, internal fiscal discipline and macroeconomic soundness.

6. Conclusion

The MERCOSUR should quickly move on to build common institutions in order to both coordinate macroeconomic policies and promote mobility of goods, capital and labour force, without overlooking educational, cultural, scientific and technological integration. In addition, in light of the increase in the concentration in large companies, the incorporation of small and medium-sized businesses to this process should be promoted. In the South Eastern Asian bloc these small and medium-sized businesses make up for 30% of exports compared with a scarce 8% in the MERCOSUR region. Progress in the consolidation of the MERCOSUR means establishing a customs union, even with a single regional currency.

The existence of different economic blocs demonstrates that the countries involved are defending their own interests and that they compete with one another in markets, transnational companies and political power. However, there is no doubt that political decisions, with the creation of supranational organizations, would speed both commercial and financial integration.

Non-tariff measures were used mainly by the United States; therefore, the effectiveness of a union among the countries in the Americas (FTAA = Free Trade Area of the Americas), made up of 34 countries, is questionable. These measures include quantitative restrictions, subsidies on some farming products, steel, textiles, apart from phytosanitary arguments of environmental defence, costumer safety, etc. The United States is the world's largest farming producer and a great exporter; therefore, it plays a prominent role in the international commodity price formation. Any distortions generated in its market affects world markets significantly. Should the FTAA project continue, this relation of forces would quickly make the MERCOSUR incompatible, thus preventing a more equitable wealth distribution.

Although integration processes within the MERCOSUR and with the European Union are almost at a standstill, unresolved issues should be taken up on the agenda set in 1994 and negotiated with the European Union and the United States in order to find the best option for each economic and political moment.

References

Behir, Mohamed H., Decreux, Y. and Guerin, Jean L. (2001), *Mercosur: Free-trade area with the EU or with the Americas?* Some lessons from the model MIRAGE, Washington: IADB.

Bouzas, R. and Svarzman, G. (2000), Estructura del comercio y de la protección arancelaria en las relaciones entre el MERCOSUR y la Unión Europea, in: *Boletín Informativo Techint*, No. 304, 53 – 68.

Carrera, J. and Levy Yeyati, E., Sturzenegger, F. (1999), Las perspectivas de la coordinación macroeconómica en el Mercosur. In: *Coordinación de políticas macroeconómicas en el Mercosur*, Carrera, J. and Sturzenegger, F. (eds.), 2000. Fondo de Cultura Económica y Fundación Gobierno y Sociedad.

Carrera, J. and Sturzenegger, F., (1999), Los resultados de la integración en el Mercosur. In: *Coordinación de políticas macroeconómicas en el Mercosur*, Carrera, J. and Sturzenegger, F. (eds.), 2000. Fondo de Cultura Económica y Fundación Gobierno y Sociedad.

Centro de Economía Internacional (2002), *Alternativas de Integración para la Argentina: Un Análisis de Equilibrio General*, Buenos Aires: Centro de Economía Internacional.

Comisión Europea (2002), *Unión Europea – MERCOSUR; Una Asociación para el Futuro*, Montevideo: Comisión Europea.

CEI (Centro de Economía Internacional). *Estadísticas*. www.cei.org

Cerro, A. M. and Pineda, J. (2002), Latin America Dilema: One or Many Monies. Empirical Evidence 1960-2000, in: *Reunión Anual AAEP*, noviembre, Tucumán.

Coiteeux, M. and Geandet, A. (2002), Does monetary union make sense for Brazil and Argentina? In: *Reunión Anual AAEP*, noviembrei, Tucumán

Diao, X., Dias-Bonilla E. and Robinson, S. (2001), *Scenarios for Trade Integration in the Americas*, International Food Policy Research Institute, http://www.cepii.fr/anglaisgraph/communications/pdf/2001/washington/diaodiazrobinson.pdf

Dorrucci, E., Frip, S., Fratzscher, M. and Mongelli, F. P. (2002): European Integration: What Lessons for Other Regions? The Case of Latin America, European Central Bank, *Working Paper* N° 185

Dusro, D. and Ochoa, H. (2002), Áreas Monetarias Óptimas; Está Latinoamérica cerca? In: *AAEP, Reunión Anual*, nov, Tucumán.

European Comission (2001), *The EU's Relations with MERCOSUR: V Ronda de negociaciones Unión Europea-Mercosur Oferta de negociación de la UE*, http://europa.eu.int/comm/external relations/mercosur /intro/ip01 963 es.htm.

European Comission (2002a), *Agriculture in the European Union - Statistical and economic information 2001.*

http://europa.eu.int/comm/agriculture/agrista/2001/ table en/en3710.pdf

European Communities (2001), Opinion of the Economic and Social Committee on the European Union negotiations with MERCOSUR and Chile: economic and social aspects, in: *Official Journal of the European Communities*, C 260 / 13, 67 – 78.

Ethier, W. J. (1998): Regionalism in a Multilateral World, in: *The Journal of Political Economy*, Volume 106, Issue 6, 1214 – 1245.

Ferrando, L., (1999). Un área monetaria para el Mercosur? In: *Coordinación de políticas macroeconómicas en el Mercosur*, Carrera, J. and Sturzenegger, F. (eds.), 2000. Fondo de Cultura Económica y Fundación Gobierno y Sociedad.

Garcia Herrero, A., Santillan, J., Cuadro, L. and Egea, C. (2002), Latin American Financial Development in Perspective, Banco de España, Servicio de Estudios, *Documento de Trabajo* N° 0216.

Giordano, P. and Watanuki, M. (2000), Economic effects of a Mercosur-European Communities Free Trade Agreement: A Computable General Equilibrium Model analysis, Experts Workshop *Briefing Notes*, Working group on European Union. http://www.sice.oas.org/geograph/south/sc-po.pdf

Martirena Mantel, A. (2003), Sobre la creación de áreas monetarias óptimas. El aporte de Robert Mundell, in: *AAEP, Reunión Anual*, nov, Mendoza.

Heyman, D. and Navajas, F. (1999), Coordinación de políticas macroeconómicas en el Mercosur: algunas reflexiones. In: Coordinación de políticas macroeconómicas en el Mercosur. Carrera, J. and Sturzenegger, F. (eds.), 2000. Fondo de Cultura Económica y Fundación Gobierno y Sociedad.

Lane, P. and Milesi-Ferretti, G. M. (2003), International Financial Integration, IMF *Working Paper* 03/086.

McKinnon, R. (1963), Optimal currency areas, in: *American economic Review*, vol. 52.

Monteagudo, J. and Watanuki, M. (2001), Regional Trade Agreements for MERCOSUR: The FTAA and the FTA with the European Union, Washington: IADB.

Mundell, R. (1961), A theory of optimum currency areas, in: *American economic Review*, vol. 51.

Ruesga, S., Carrera, J., Cunha, A., Garcia de la Crua, J.M., Nagamine, R. and Da Silva Bichara, J. (2003): Análisis del Impacto de un Acuerdo de Libre Comercio entre UE-Mercosur sobre el Mercado de Trabajo de España, Argentina and Brasil, EAWP2 <http//eawp.economistascoruna.org/archives/vol2n7/>

Schneider, G. (1994), *Perspectivas de una asociación Unión Europea-MERCOSUR, Observatorio de la Economía*, web de la FCE, UNC, Instituto de Economía y Finanzas, febrero.

Sistema Económico Latinoamericano (2001), Sexta ronda de negociaciones UE-MERCOSUR, in: *Boletin de Integración*, No. 51.

Zahler, R. and Budnevich, C. (1999), Integración financiera y coordinación macroeconómica en el Mercosur. In: Coordinación de políticas macroeconómicas en el Mercosur, Carrera, J. and Sturzenegger, F. (eds.), 2000. Fondo de Cultura Económica y Fundación Gobierno y Sociedad.

EUROPEAN UNION AND MERCOSUR COMMERCIAL POLICY COMPATIBILITY: AN ATPSM[6] MODEL FOR OILSEED COMPLEX

Fernando H. Sonnet

e-mail: fsonnet@eco.unc.edu.ar
Instituto de Economía y Finanzas
Facultad de Ciencias Económicas U.N.C.

1. Introduction

Since the creation of the GATT and the new economic world order of postwar years, the industrialized countries have shown a striking growth in their trade and financial flows. The principle of comparative advantages first, and the economies of scale and the differentiation of products in imperfect markets later, influenced intra-industrial international trade. This phenomenon took place within a context of capital mobility, innovations, technological competence and rivalry between economic groups. In this scenario, the problem of the protection of the national economies in developing countries, and the strategies and consequences of the trade policies became crucial for their growth, as a reply to the policies of industrialized countries (USA, EU, and Japan). It is evident now that these protectionist policies have affected welfare through their impact on income distribution in developing countries.

In the institutional context, the regional integration phenomenon (EU, MERCOSUR and NAFTA) was added to the postwar international institutions (IMF, WB, UN, GATT and WTO). During the second half of the 20th century a series of rounds of negotiation took place within the GATT framework. In the beginning of 2001, with the restoration of the multilateral trade negotiations within the World Trade Organization (WTO), the member states had to tackle new issues: food safety, the principle of precaution and social policy norms, besides the reduction in customs duties and tariff barriers.

In September 2003, the failure of the Cancun Ministerial Conference[7] brought to light the problems faced by international institutions with respect to the achievement of trade liberalization, trade growth, and more fairness in the economic relationships between the Great Powers and the emerging countries. The USA and other industrialized countries' refusal to discuss about agricultural subsidies and other duties led to the failure of the Conference.

The objective of this paper is to analyze the phenomenon of protectionism in the EU and in particular, to assess the effects on the Argentine oilseed industry. The emphasis is on the types of protection and the different policies usually applied.

In the first section, we analyze the trade policies implemented by the main countries that compete with Argentina in the oilseed markets (USA and EU). In the second section, Geneva Agreement on July 2004 is described. In the third section, a deterministic and partial

---

[6] Agricultural Trade Policy Simulation Model.
I am grateful to Mariano A. Somale for his collaboration in the translation of the paper. I am also acknowledged to my friend, Alberto M. Díaz Cafferata and Enrique Neder, for their comments.
[7] "Within days, six alternatives were circulated by various groups of members. While they said they were unhappy with some parts of the US-EU draft, they all followed the framework structure. Of these alternatives, the draft that received the most attention came from a new coalition of about 20 developing countries (G20). Other drafts came from four Central American countries, Japan, a European-East Asian grouping including Switzerland and Republic of Korea, Norway and Kenya.

equilibrium model[8] is applied to assess the impact of different trade policies on the argentine oilseed industry. The principal instruments of the model are tariffs, subsidies and import quotas.

1.1. The Oilseed Industry in the World Trade

In the last years, the Argentine external trade has been influenced by a series of very important events that were taking place in the world economic order. Faced with a new economic and political reality, Argentina and other MERCOSUR member countries had to re-enforce their position to equilibrate the new exchange flows that emerged from this scenario. Considering the high level of competitiveness reached by the Argentine oilseed industry[9], its extraordinary performance in the international markets has contributed to the generation of genuine foreign currency for the country.

1.2. Perspectives of external demand for oilseed products

The Expansion of the EU

The idea of expanding the European Union (EU 25) came up in December of 2000 during the Meeting of Niza. In that event, the European Council decided to foster the integrating process. The recently incorporation of the Baltic[10] countries and the Central East Europe[11] countries into the EU, will probably generate more competence to our traditional commodities. This will happen not only in the EU, but also in other markets that Argentina is currently supplying oilseeds products.

The political sensitivity that the agricultural sector has for both blocs of the Community, together with the greater supply of food will intensify the trade barriers faced by extra-community suppliers of raw materials and manufactures. In particular, the probable increase of investment in crushing industry -due to tax advantages, labor and other cheaper services in East Europe- could affect the Argentine oil exports. At the end of 2002, negotiations on 31 chapters had already been concluded; the new set of commercial preferences could have important consequences on the Argentine agricultural trade.

This phenomenon is part of the reorganization of world trade that began after World War II and the rise of economic blocs. Due to lower taxes, the absence of trade tariffs and a cheaper and more qualified labor force, the new European Union (EU 25) will throw Latin-American countries down in the ranking of investment opportunities.

G8 Group Expansion

In the recent G8 meeting there were very important declarations. We can mention the liberalization of agricultural trade in order with the objectives of the WTO Round of Doha, and the possibility in the future to incorporate China and India as members of this Group.

The growth of the Asia-Pacific area

Population and consumption growth in the Asia-Pacific Region will be one of the most important phenomena for Argentina and MERCOSUR members in the next two decades. The

[8] Agricultural trade policy simulation model (ATPSM).

[9] It represents a 20% of the total exports value of the country.

[10] Bulgaria, Slovakia, Latvia, Lithuania y Romania (The Helsinki Group).

[11] The Czech Republic, Slovenia, Estonia, Hungary and Poland (The Luxembourg Group).

estimations for this area show a population growth (2000-2020) of 67% (almost 300 millions people). Potential consumption will be intensified due to the increase in the average age from 30 to 36 years, in life expectancy from 72 to 77 years, and in the segment of population over 65 years old from 200 to 370 millions. Real per capita income would increase together with the quality of life. This would improve the diets and increase the consumption levels of food, what would have a great impact on the exports of the argentine oilseed industry.

Population aging -a consequence of mortality reduction and the greater expectancy of life-, will change consumption habits. This would require that countries like Argentina adapt their exports of food manufactures, which will have to be richer in fortifying components and contain lower levels of calories.

Another consequence of population growth will be the acceleration of the urbanization rate, what will also produce a diet diversification. Finally, some demographic investigations show migrating flows from lower per capita income countries to increasing per capita income countries.

China, with a market of 1295 millions inhabitants, is the major challenge for Argentina and the MERCOSUR bloc. Considering that the rural-urban migration will be inevitable during the developing process (industry and services), current demand of food will grow noticeably. Thus, China and India will increase their consumption of vegetable oils in 2005. Weather conditions would not be that good in India in 2004/2005, and oilseed production would diminish in 500 thousand tons. This phenomenon together with the increasing consumption will make that country import 4 million tons (Mt) of vegetable oils. In the case of soy oil, imports will raise from 0,75 to 1,14 (Mt). With respect to China, it is expected a record growth of its oilseed production, but not enough to compensate the increase in its local demand of oilseed oils. Imports would increase from 2,4 to 2,7 (Mt) in the case of soy oil and from 3,6 to 4,0 (Mt) in the case of palm oil.

The soy expansion in Brazil will be spectacular in the mid-term. This will be a threat to the USA that has traditionally dominated the soy market. In 2003/2004, the 50% of total production came from Argentina and Brazil, and this proportion will increase in the following years. The Soy American Association is worried about this phenomenon and is promoting a series of rules to mitigate the South American expansion.

MERCOSUR strengthen and consolidation

The world economic outlook forecasted for the following years points out a challenge for the MERCOSUR, particularly in the case of foods where it has natural comparative advantages and the possibility of competitiveness gains. The conquest of the great Asian market will imply strong fights against protectionist industrialized countries. It will also require a solid preparation to confront the huge firms of agricultural manufactures, which have economies of scale, make cross business and conform integrated holdings.

The MERCOSUR will have to go beyond its in-land trade frontiers. In the period 1991/2000 the intra-MERCOSUR trade grew a 246%, but the bloc experienced a negative trade balance.

1.3. The European Union and the commercial relationship with the MERCOSUR

The great complementary between the productive structures of Argentina and EU reflects the importance of the commercial relationships between them. The destinies of our exports as well as the origin of our imports reveal the necessity of a greater integration.
The Agreement of Geneva celebrated in July 2004 tried to establish the bases of consensus to overcome the obstacles for free trade and to promote greater flows of exchange. Argentina as a member of the MERCOSUR, together with the Cairns group and the countries of the Andean Community and The Caribbean, promotes free trade.
In spite of the complementary elements of the comparative advantages, Argentina and the EU have strong asymmetries that constitute a big obstacle to the commercial negotiations:

a) Due to the fact that Argentina is a small country in world trade, its negotiation capacity is limited. The exports of the EU are 33 times higher than Argentine exports and the difference between EU imports and Argentine imports is even greater. Consequently, the EU is a very important market for Argentina, but the opposite does not hold.
b) Intra sectorial trade is exiguous because the exchange specialization is the predominant fact. The agricultural and mineral items are the most significant for Argentina, while transport goods, machinery and chemical products are for the EU.

Unequal exchange in numbers

During the last decade of the 20th century the external trade of Argentina experienced strong transformations. The trade balance deficit with the EU between 1993 and 2001 explains the pronounced fall in the share of our exports in EU total imports and the constancy of the share of EU exports in Argentine imports (Table 1). Export losses were compensated with new exports to other markets, mainly within the MERCOSUR and other American countries. In the same way, there has been an increase in the shares of the imports coming from the MERCOSUR in our total imports, and this explains the fall in the rest of the world originated import shares.

Table 1: Argentine commercial exchange composition (1991-2001) (%)

	Exports by destiny		Imports by origin	
	1991	2001	1991	2001
European Union	33	17	24	23
MERCOSUR	16	28	21	29
Rest of ALCA	26	30	28	25
Rest of the world	25	25	27	23
Total	100	100	100	100

Source: CEI (Centro de Estudios Internacionales de Cancillería de Argentina).2003.

What happened to the oilseed industry?
The data of the oilseed industry (Table 2) shows that the oilseed meals and cakes for cattle feeding (mainly sunflower and soy pellets) represent the major item of argentine exports to the EU and the rest of the world. J. Galperín (2002) holds that the Common Agricultural Policy (CAP) promoted meet production protecting the forage sector (GATT Round of Dillon 1960/61), without blocking the entrance of oilseed sub-products. Oilseed meals became the

major cattle food. However, during the last decade, the fall in grain sales and the maintenance of oilseed meal sales reduced the dependency. In the case of vegetable oils the EU reduced its dependency due to the high tariff protection on raw and refined oils.

Table 2: Argentine Oilseed Complex. Export Value to EU and dependency exports ratio (1991-2001)

	Exports (U$S millions)		Dependency ratio X (EU) / X (RW)		Oilseed Complex Exports /Total Exports to EU	
	1991	2001	1991	2001	1991	2001
Oils and fats	140	79	11	5	3.5	1.7
Oilmeals and	1,200	731	44	15	30.0	15.9

X: exports; EU: European Union; RW: Rest of the World

Source: CEI (Centro de Estudios Internacionales de Cancillería de Argentina).2003.

It is interesting to analyze the role that the oilseed industry played in the growth of argentine exports between 1991 and 2001. Table 3 shows that the reduction in the exports of grains and oils to the EU started with the rise in oilseed meals-and-cakes sales.

Table 3: Contribution of argentine oilseed complex to growth exports (1991-2001).

Items	Exports Value Growth (%)		Contribution to Exports Value Growth (%)	
	EU	RW	EU	RW
Oleaginous grains	- 74	+ 415	- 106	+ 7
Oils and fats	- 44	+ 44	- 10	+ 3
Oilseed meals and cakes	+ 72	+ 185	+ 106	+ 5
Oilseed Complex Total Exports / Argentina Total Exports	-3	126	-11	+15

Source: own calculations based on CEI data.

1.4. The E.U. protectionism versus MERCOSUR liberalization.

This paragraph analyzes the trade barriers that the EU applies to reduce the access to its markets. Tariff barriers are applied mainly on agricultural products (primary goods and manufactures). As regards to the entrance of products, non-tariff barriers are more effective. Direct barriers tend to block the entrance of extra-Community products by means of a tariff structure with many of not *ad-valorem* components. These components can vary over the year and can change the level of the tariff according to the nature of the input incorporated. Therefore, *ad-valorem* equivalent average tariffs on agricultural manufactures are higher than the tariffs on the rest of the exportable items.

Non tariff barriers intensify direct tariffs and reduce even more the possibilities of entrance. The most important are: a) tariff quotas, b) Special safeguards and c) sanitary and phytosanitary norms, traciability and maximum quantities of chemical elements (standards) in grains and foods.

1.4.1. Tariff and non tariff trade barriers

a. Tariffs Barriers

A complex system[12] of different types of tariffs constitutes the actual tariff structure of the EU. Within this tariff structure, the argentine oilseed industry and the MERCOSUR are subject to a discriminatory treatment. The EU protects its agricultural sector establishing tariffs that are higher than the overall average tariffs for food, fishing, textiles and footwear. The tariff escalation[13] structure strengthens the complexity of tariffs, having a greater impact on those goods with more added values. Tariff peaks[14] are very strong barriers for certain goods.

Table 4: E.U. Basic Commercial Regime 2004

Item	Level (%)	Share (%)
1. MFN average tariff	6.5	
2. MFN average tariff		
- agriculture products	16.5	
- non-agriculture products	4.1	
3.Share of total tariffs that burden on foreign agricultural products		67
4.MFN average tariff by sectors:		
- Agriculture and fishing	10	
- Mining	0.2	
- Manufacture Industry	6.4	
5.MFN by products		
- Dairy	41.7	
- Cereals	39.6	
- Oilseeds, fats and vegetable oils	6.7	
6. ad-valorem duties		90
non-advalorem duties		10

MFN: Most Favored Nation clause.

Source: European Council. Staff Paper WT/TPR/S/136 (pp. 43 a pp.100). 2004.

[12] Ad valorem, specific and mixed tari ffs, seasonal tariffs and tariffs according to the technical ratios of the products.

[13] Tariff escalation refers to the application of higher import duties on semi -processed products and even higher on finished products compared to raw materials.

[14] Tariff peaks are relatively high tariffs amidst low tariff levels, usually levied on 'sensitive' products.

b. Non Tariff Barriers
   Non tariff instruments applied in E.U. markets reinforce the tariff barriers mentioned before:

b.1) Quantitative
   Import quotas, licenses and prohibitions.

b.2) Non tariffs duties
   Variable rights, antidumping rights and compensations.

b.3) Government policies
   Includes public purchase policies and state enterprise purchases

b.4) Custom practices
   This refers to valuation criterions and classification procedures.

b.5) Technical obstacles
   This includes sanitary and phytosanitary norms, environment norms, labeling, industrial safety and industrial standards.

As we state before, non-tariff barriers are more effective than tariff barriers. Among the most important non-tariff barriers we can mention tariff quotas, import licenses and entrance prices. A tariff quota is a two level tariff system, which applies a lower tariff for the volume of imports established in the quota and a higher tariff for the rest of the imports. Another progressive instruments are in-quota tariffs and out-of-quota tariffs.
According to the WTO, special safeguards are another type of barriers. When import volumes surpass a certain level or when import prices are lower than a reference price, these barriers allow additional custom duties.

1.4.2. Direct support, export subsidies and support prices for agricultural products

According to the data of the European Council, the agricultural sector of the EU received over 100 billions dollars in subsidies and direct payments to producers in the year 2000. This amount represented an additional income of 60% in comparison with the income of a producer of a competitive country that does not grant agricultural subsidies.
Estimates shows that the cost of the CAP (Common Agriculture Policy) for the year 2006 will be in the range of 43,9 and 41,6 billions euros (UK: thousands millions). This quantity is composed of direct support (minimum prices) and indirect support for the payment of general services. The nominal assistance coefficient shows the ratio of effective producer income to the income the producer would have earned without any kind of support. In the year 2000 this coefficient was 1,6 for all the items and 1,4 for oilseed products.

1.4.3. Preferential Trade Regimes

The EU applies different regimes according to the origin of the products. The African, Caribbean and Pacific countries (ex colonies) are the most favored, followed by the less developed countries and then the countries that have a free trade agreement.

1.5. The EU oilseeds policies

From the beginning of the EEC (European Economic Community), this has been supporting the agricultural sector through subsidies, variable exactions on imports and directs payments, which have taken different forms and intensities.

In 1966 the EEC began with the organization of an oilseed common market. This policy was similar to the one established on cereals. In this initial stage was determined an annual indicative price and an intervention price, first for the sunflowerseed and rapeseed and, then, for the soybean. The intervention price guaranteed a minimum price for the producer, which had to be respected by the storage centers. However, oilseeds, unlike cereals, could enter into the Community without paying the custom duties. To prevent the oil and oilseed meals industry from processing cheaper imported seeds, they were given a direct payment or subsidy per ton of seed originated inside the Community.

By the middle of the 70's, USA set a seizure over soybean exports. This made the Community to strengthen its oilseed policy, stimulating its production. In this regard, the indicated and intervention prices were rose, and therefore, the sown area and the production grew up to 12,2 million tons in 1987. In only 8 years the seed produced volume increased 300 per cent.

In 1986 the EEC reached high levels of expenditures in the agricultural budget, aiming to subside the farmers. In order to lessen these payments there were settled limits on production through an instrument denominated "maximum guaranteed quantities". If producers didn't respect these limits, their inputs fell down with the decrease of the indicated and intervention prices. However, the expansion of the area sown with oilseeds continued, the physical efficiency reached a top and the budgetary expenditure set aside for the help kept on growing.

Around 1990, USA presented several complaints to the GATT against the PAC for oilseeds products. In 1991 a general reform of the PAC was done, known as the "The McSharry Reform", where the oilseeds subsidies were cut down. The intervention mechanism was removed[15] since the 1992/1993 campaign and, in the same way, the indicated and intervention prices were left aside. In this way, and without import tariffs, a convergence between internal and international prices was expected; on account of which the help on oil and flour industries was also derogated. Nevertheless, to maintain the producer's incomes, an amount of direct payments per hectare was approved, according to different regions and the historic profit average; as well this help was adjustable with the international price level. In June 1992, the oilseeds crops were integrated to the herbaceous market organization[16]. The basic aims of the intervention policies haven't change (neither tariffs nor supported prices), even though the direct payments were established to be larger on oilseeds than on cereals.

For the 1994/95 campaign, after negotiating with USA, a new instrument was created, in the EU: the maximum guaranteed area for oilseeds. If a country exceeded its area quota, the direct payments decreased proportionally to the limit excess.

In the Agenda 2000, it was agreed to put on the same level, in stages, the direct payments on oilseeds crops and cereal crops. Likewise the maximum guaranteed area was removed.

---

[15] ECC Regulation n° 3766/91, 12/12/91

[16] ECC Regulation n° 1765/92

2. The Global Agreement of Geneva

In July of 2004, the representatives of the commercial blocs signed the agreement. This was the most significant event in the matter of negotiations since the beginning of the Round of Doha in Dubai (2001). This agreement constitutes a basic document without a precise content on how to manage the commercial discussions in the next Round of Hong Kong (December 2005).

The G-20 group participated in these discussions about a world system of free trade. Developing and industrialized countries that apply protectionist policies, mostly in the agricultural and agro-industrial sectors, integrate this group. Between the developed countries there is a group called Cairns that promotes free agricultural trade.

2.1. Issues discussed and the global agreement

Global agricultural negotiations are carried out within the framework of the item 13th of the Ministerial de Declaration of Doha (2001).

a) The commitments signed at Geneva aim to reach, in the long run, an agricultural agreement that contains an equitable commercial system.
b) WTO less developed countries will have to be able to apply policies that support their objectives of development, poverty mitigation and food safety.
c) The discussion about the reforms will be focused on three items: domestic support, export competence and market access. These issues should be discussed under the principle of equity.
d) The General Council recognizes the importance that cotton has for many developing countries. For this reason, cotton will be included in agricultural negotiations.

Domestic Support

Concerning to this aspect, the commitments of the Ministerial Declaration of Doha are followed to "achieve substantial reductions in domestic support that distorts trade". Consequently, longer application periods and lower reduction coefficients for all kinds of domestic support will have to be included ". Likewise, " higher levels of domestic support allowed will be subject to deeper reductions". The more developed Member States "will make a substantial reduction in their global level of domestic support".

The Agreement includes some technical specifications about the global reduction of the payments of the blue box; this reduction will be applied following a stratified formula, which implies a greater effort for the countries with actual higher payment levels. Reductions in the *minimum* level will be negotiated taken into account the principle of special and differential treatment.

The Member States of the agreement recognize the importance of the blue box in the matter of agricultural reforms. In that framework, preexisting agreements will be revised and so the member states will be able to appeal to the following measures: a) Direct payments of programs of production reduction and, b) direct payments that are not based on production. As regards to other criterions that could emerge, they will have to take into account the equilibrium between rights and obligations within the WTO framework.

In the case of the criterions of the green box, they will be examined and clarified to assure that the measures will not generate distortions on trade or production, or at least minimize the possible distortions.

Competence of Exports
In this point the Ministerial Declaration of Doha establishes "reductions in all exports subventions with the goal of reaching its progressive removal". The Geneva agreement states the elimination of the export subventions, of export credit, and of credit guaranties or insurance programs with repayment periods of over 180 days. Concerning the special and differential treatment, the developing member countries will enjoy the benefits of longer periods of application for the progressive removal of all export subventions. Public enterprises, that in these countries have special privileges to preserve the stability of consumption prices in domestic markets and guarantee food safety, will have a special consideration as regards to their monopoly condition.

Market access
The Ministerial Declaration of Doha establishes "important improvements in the matter of market access". In this way, it will be adopted the approach of the stratified formula that takes into account the different tariffs structures; reductions will be made on the base of consolidated tariffs. The progressiveness of reductions will be applied in a way that the greater reductions will affect the higher tariffs, with a flexible treatment in the case of sensitive products. Concerning the number of bands, bounds, and the reductions in each band, they will be under negotiation.

3. The ATPSM model

Effects of changes in trade policies [17]
As stated before, protectionist policies have a negative impact on the welfare of countries affected by these policies. In this section a simulation model (ATPSM) is used to evaluate the possible gains from liberalization of agricultural trade. The model was developed by the UNCTAD with the purpose of providing an additional tool of analysis in the WTO negotiations.
On the base of this model we have analyzed (F. Sonnet et al. 2004) the effects that different proposals have on the following Argentine variables: volume, value of trade and production of oilseeds, oilmeals, cakes and vegetable oils, and effects on welfare[18]. As regards to the convenience of each simulated proposal, the conclusions will depend on how each alternative affects welfare.

Characteristics of the model
The ATPSM is a deterministic partial equilibrium model of comparative advantages. A system of equations represents the demand, the supply and the agricultural trade flows of the countries included. The characteristics of the model can be summarized as follows:

- Deterministic: there are no stochastic shocks or any other source of uncertainty.
- Static: it does not take into account the dynamics to reach the equilibrium. The elasticities used in the model have been calculated for 10 years.
- Partial equilibrium

[17] UNCTAD (2002). Handbook on the UNCTAD Agricultural Trade Policy Simulation Model (ATPSM).
[18] In this paper we have only included the effects on welfare.

One of the most important and positive aspects of this model is that it includes almost all the countries of the world (176). All the important countries that affect the commercial performance of Argentina are included. Furthermore, the model includes 36 groups of countries.

The brief model

Demand and supply equations for the domestic market are:

- **Demand:** a linear function that depends on price and policy measures (all transformed to *ad-valorem equivalents*)

$$\hat{D}_{i,r} = \eta_{i,i,r}\left[\hat{P}_{wi} + \left(1 + \hat{t}_{ci,r}\right)\right] + \sum_{\substack{j=1 \\ i\neq j}}^{J} \eta_{i,j,r}\left[\hat{P}_{wj} + \left(1 + \hat{t}_{cj,r}\right)\right] \qquad (1)$$

- **Supply:** a linear function that also depends on price and policy measures.

$$\hat{S}_{i,r} = \varepsilon_{i,i,r}\left[\hat{P}_{wi} + \left(1 + \hat{t}_{pi,r}\right)\right] + \sum_{\substack{j=1 \\ i\neq j}}^{J} \varepsilon_{i,j,r}\left[\hat{P}_{wj} + \left(1 + \hat{t}_{pj,r}\right)\right] \qquad (2)$$

Current account balance shifts for a good i in a country r is described by the expression:

- Exports

$$\Delta X_{i,r} = \gamma_{i,r}\Delta S_{i,r} \qquad (3)$$

- Imports

$$\Delta M_{i,r} = D_{i,r}\hat{D}_{i,r} - S_{i,r}\hat{S}_{i,r} + \Delta X_{i,} \qquad (4)$$

and imports clears the market.

Domestic markets prices are determined by tariffs, subsidies, quotas, and incentive measures.

- Trade income changes for the country r will be:

$$?R = (P_w + ?P_w)\{(X + ?X) - (M + ?M)\} - P_w(X - M) \qquad (5)$$

- Changes in welfare in country r accounts for producer and

consumer surpluses and net government revenue.

$$\Delta W = \Delta EP + \Delta EC + \Delta RNG \qquad (6)$$

- Producer surplus takes account prices and quantities besides the change in the quota income received by the producer.

$$\Delta EP = \Delta P_p\left[S + 0.5(\Delta S_d)\right] + c\Delta U \qquad (7)$$

- Consumer surplus:

$$\Delta EC = -\Delta P_c\left[D + 0.5(\Delta D_d)\right] \qquad (8)$$

- Government income: includes income changes provided by changes in tariffs, exports subsidies, government expenditure on domestic support policies and quotas' income that producers have not received.

$$\Delta RNG = \Delta RT - \Delta SE - \Delta AD + (1-c)\Delta U \qquad (9)$$

The argentine proposal[19]

Argentina proposed the following scenarios:

Scenario 1

a) The level of intra-quota tariff is reduced in 50% for developed countries and 30% for developing countries. b) To cut down the out-of-quota tariffs by the application a coefficient of 35 in the Swiss formula[20] for developed countries and 50 for developing countries. c) To reduce the amounts of internal direct payments in 90%. d) To eliminate exports support and increase the quotas for both groups for countries.

Scenario 2

This Scenario differs from Scenario 1 only in the coefficients used in the Swiss Formula. In this case the coefficient is 25 for developing countries and 33 for developing countries.

This Scenario is also favorable for Argentina. It has a higher impact on producer and consumer prices and hence on production and consumption.

The Harbinson Proposal

This proposal consists of the following measures:

a) To reduce the out-of-quota tariffs and no reduction in the in-quota tariff. Furthermore, Harbinson propose the increase of 20 % in the quotas, for both groups of countries.

---

[19] The two scenarios simulated here were proposed by Argentina at the first Conference in Cancún.

[20] The Swiss formula, which suggests much steeper cut on higher tariffs, was proposed by Switzerland in the Tokyo Round negotiations in the 1970s, and was for negotiations on industrial tariffs. Developing countries rather favour an average tariff cut instead of steep reductions on the highest tariffs.

b) To lessen in the industrialized countries the domestic and export supports in 60% and 80 %, respectively. In the case of developing countries the levels of reductions proposed are 20% and 70%, respectively.

Simulation analysis and outcomes

Scenario 1: argentine proposal 1

In this first proposal India would receive a remarkable growth in the consumer surplus due to the fall in the vegetable oils prices. The same phenomenon would take place in the European Union. In the case of Argentina, Brazil and USA, the consumer surplus would undergo a reduction as a result of the increase of domestic prices of the oils that the liberalization of the markets would bring. Therefore, the relative prices would favor the oil producers of the mentioned countries. Finally, the net government income would reduce in China, India and Argentina in reference to the oil trade. However, in the countries of the European Union it would increase as a result of the elimination of the public cost of protection.

Scenario 2: argentine proposal 2

This proposal shows similar results compared with the proposal 1.

Harbinson proposal

The application of Harbinson proposal would generate a significant increase in consumer surplus of vegetable oils in EU and USA, whereas it would lower appreciably in India. In the case of Argentina, Brazil and China there would not be changes in the consumer surplus. The effects of this proposal would be very unfavorable for the vegetable oil industry of the European Union not thus for the one of USA. If India and Argentina consider themselves, the oil producers would receive an important increase in their surpluses. Oilseeds producer surplus would increase in USA, Argentina, Brazil and India, but liberalization would harm to farmers of China. As far as the oil producers of the EU, they would no have attractive gains.

Considering only the changes in welfare[21] due to each liberalization package, all the scenarios presented would be profitable for Argentina. In the oilseed case the Scenario 1 of the Argentine Proposal is the most convenient, while in the case of vegetable oils the Scenario 2 produces the best outcome.

It is important to note that the Harbinson[22] proposal is the only scenario in which the EU has welfare gains in the sector of vegetable oils. In the same sector, the welfare of USA is reduced in all the scenarios. In the case of China, it would have welfare losses in both sectors in the three alternatives.

---

[21] ATPSM model allows to evaluate, under each scenario, the effects on world vegetable oils and seeds, on domestic market prices received by producers and paied by consumers, on domestic consume and domestic production, on net government income and countries welfare.

[22] WTO director general's office.

Effects of changes in protectionist policies. Argentine and Harbinson proposals (2003). Changes in consumer and producer surpluses (billons of current dollars).

Scenario 1. Argentine Proposal. 1

Consumer surplus

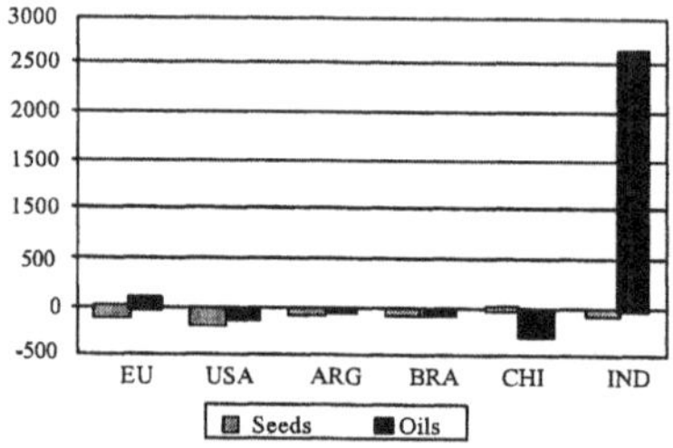

Producer surplus

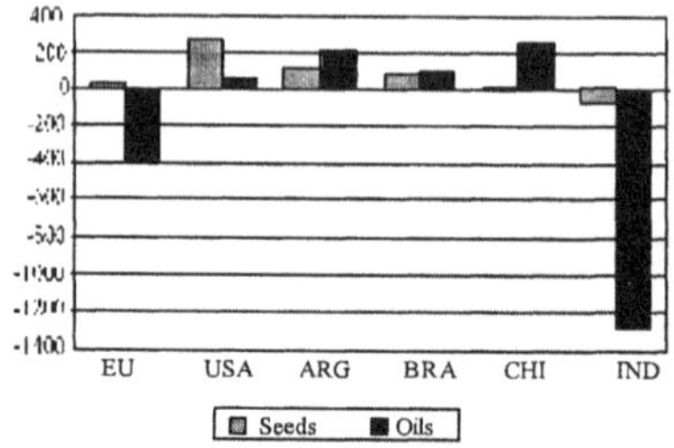

Scenario 2. Argentine Proposal. 2

Consumer surplus

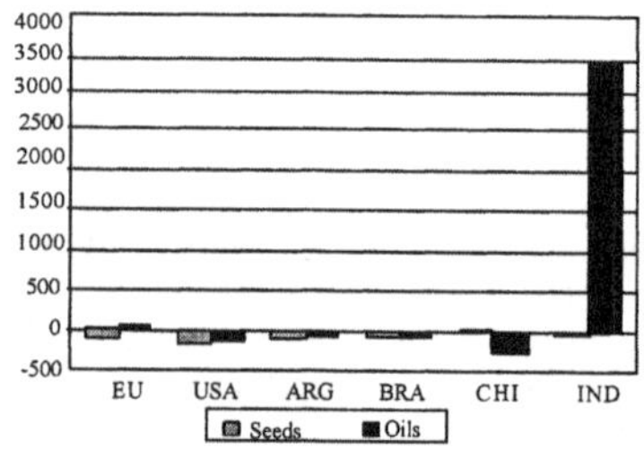

Producer surplus

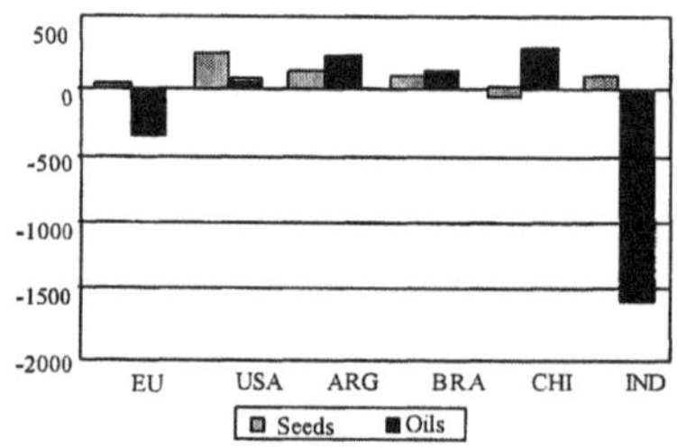

Scenario 3. Argentine Proposal. 3

Consumer surplus

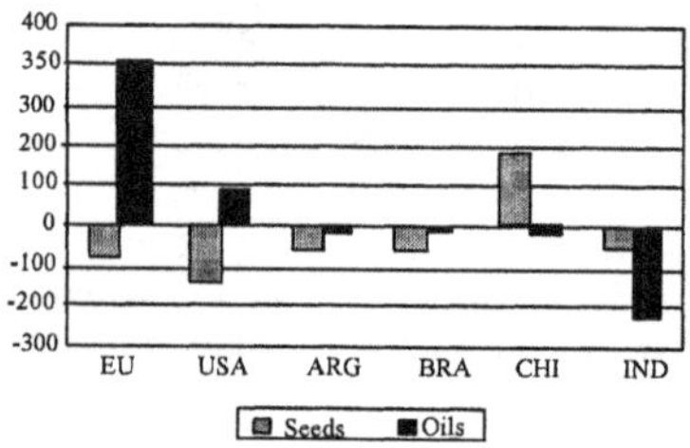

Producer surplus

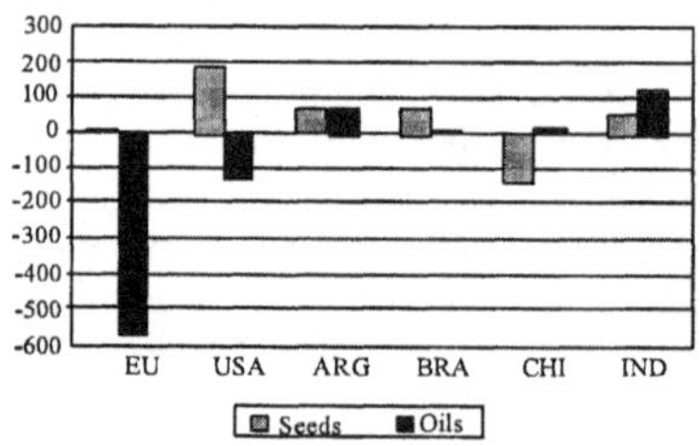

Changes in Argentine total welfare in the three alternatives presented

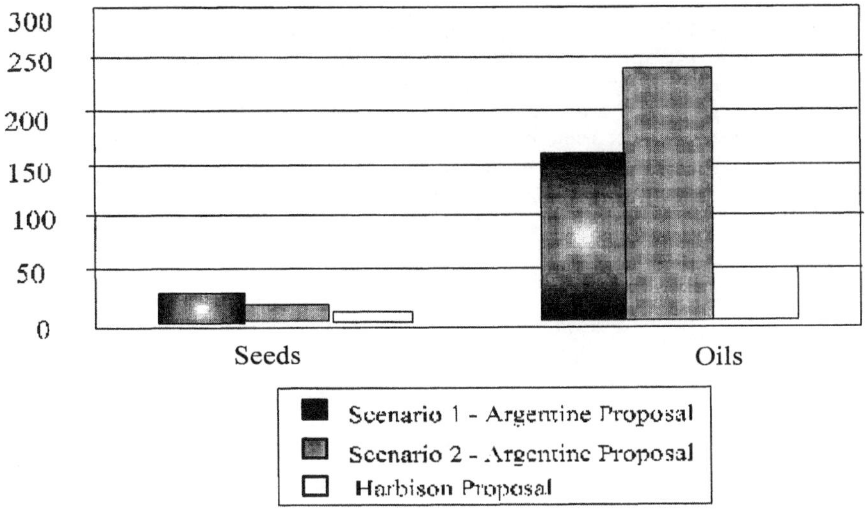

Figure 7

4. Concluding Remarks

The Geneva Agreement and trade liberalization

EU has recognized the necessity to discuss actual protection policies that gradually have been affecting the competitiveness of the agriculture activity in export developing countries. Particular issues related to tariffs, subsidies and conditions for declining exports support instruments remain without resolution; these aspects will be study henceforth.

In the future negotiation countries that trade with sensible products will have to compensate other countries by means of reducing tariffs and providing greater quotas for import licenses. Unfortunately, benefits got in Geneva Agreement could not materialize specially in those developing countries that enjoy comparative advantages such as agriculture. Furthermore, within those countries there will be both winners and losers as a consequence of trade reforms.

In the EU with high level of protection, adjustment assistance and targeted intervention could make better market failures. It is crucial to get a global agreement to delineate a world commercial system based on transparency and clear rules in order to benefit less developed countries and protect human rights of farmers. Those countries would participate in the world trade rules decisions and become on commitments about safety and nutrition. These would be priority issues in the discussion on market reforms.

European Union and MERCOSUR

Attending to EU-MERCOSUR linkages, there is no a common idea to propose a commercial policy among the MERCOSUR countries. This fact determines that each country negotiate with EU solely and sign agreements that not benefit the bloc. Although the existence of high complementary productive structure between EU and MERCOSUR the gains of a free trade area would depends on the achievement a consolidated trade policy among MERCOSUR countries. Deep and structural asymetries between blocs and strong restrictions on market access in EU are both problems without solution yet.

References

Ames, G., Gunter, L. and C. Davis (1996), Analysis of the U.S.-European Community Oilseeds Agreement, University of Georgia, *Faculty Series 96-11*.

Bouèt, A. and Dhont-Peltrault, E. (2000), How Is Trade Protectionism To Be Measure? In: *La Lettre du Cepii* N° 195.

Bouzas, R. and Svarzman, G. (2000), Estructura del Comercio y de la Protección Arancelaria en las Relaciones entre el Mercosur y la Unión Europea, *Boletín informativo Techint* N° 304: 53.

Centre for Global Agreements, Legislation and Trade (2004), The Doha Round of Negotiations and its Outlook Pos Cancun (www.teriin.org/discussion/environ/doha.pdf.).

Consejo Europeo, Comunidades Europeas (2004), Examen de las Políticas Comerciales. 44-100.

Fernández Salido, J. (2002), Análisis de Protección Arancelaria en los Mercados Agroalimentarios Mundiales, FAO, in: *Investigación Agraria* Vol 17 – N° 1: 113.

Galperin, J. (2003), En Oportunidades y amenazas para la Argentina de un Acuerdo Mercosur – Unión Europea. Un Estudio de Impacto Sectorial. Estudios del CEI N° 3 (Febrero).

Fulginity, L. and Shogren, J. (1992), Agricultural Protection in Developing Countries, American Agricultural Economics Association.

Legren, P. (2003), The Coming Collapse of Free Trade. *Britain in Europe Articles*, 1-6.

Poonyth, D. and Sharma, R (2003), The impact of the WTO negotiating modalities in the areas of domestic support, market access and export competition on developing countries: results from ATPSM. Trabajo presentado en la Conferencia "Agricultural policy reform and the WTO: where are we heading?" Capri (Italy), Jnio 23-26, 2003.

SAGPyA (2002), Impacto económico en el sector agroalimentario de la propuesta de Argentina ante la O.M.C. Ministerio de la Producción.

Sonnet F., Juárez, de Perona, G. and Lamfre, L. (2004), Integration, Protectionism and Competitiveness of the Argentinean Oilseed Industry, *Arnoldshain Seminar V. Adjusting to Globalization and Structural Change in Argentina, Brazil and Germany*. (Eds.) Díaz Cafferata. M.L. Recalde. A. E. Neder. Asociación Cooperadora Fac. de Ciencias Económicas. U.N.C.

UNCTAD (2003), *Handbook on the UNCTAD Agricultural Trade Policy Simulation Model (ATPSM)*. http://192.91.247.38/tab/ATPSMdwnlds.asp

Vanzetti, D. and Graham, B. (2002) *Simulating agricultural policy reform with ATPSM. Trade Analysis Branch.* UNCTAD. http://192.91.247.38/tab/atpsmres/Kiel.pdf

CATCHING UP OF EASTERN EUROPEAN REGIONS: THE ROLE OF FOREIGN INVESTMENT, HUMAN RESOURCES AND GEOGRAPHY*

Gabriele Tondl[a] and Goran Vuksic[b]
[a] Research Institute for European Affairs/ Wirtschaftsuniversität Wien
[b] Institute for Fiscal Studies, Zagreb

1. Introduction

This paper wishes to investigate the determinants of regional growth in the Eastern European EU candidate countries. Since their economic prospects are determined by catching-up, growth is a primary issue for these countries.

Since the mid-1990s, we observe a superior growth performance of Eastern European countries vis-à-vis Western Europe, providing evidence that a process of catching-up is underway. However, it shows that there are big internal growth differences within the Eastern European countries. Under this perspective, the question arises why growth rates differ across the regions of these countries. Why do some Eastern regions show a very dynamic growth while others only a weak?

Economic growth theory offers a number of hypotheses with respect to the determinants of growth, upon which a huge empirical literature emerged in the 1990s. Some investigated growth factors within large, worldwide country sets (e.g. Sachs and Warner 1995, Sala-i-Martin 1997, Gallup et al. 1998), others looked at growth factors within OECD economies (e.g. de la Fuente 1995, Bassanini et al. 2001). A number of studies also investigated growth factors in the EU at the regional level (e.g. Fagerberg and Verspagen 1996; Fagerberg et al. 1997; Vanhoudt et al. 2000; Paci and Pigliaru 2001; Tondl 2001; Badinger and Tondl 2003). In contrast, for Eastern Europe, there are only a few studies at the country level which investigate multiple growth factors (e.g. Campos and Kinoshita 2002) but there are practically no growth factor studies at the regional level.[23]

So far, most country studies on Eastern European growth are interested in exploring the causes of why some countries managed transition and recovery faster than others, and therefore investigated particular factors likely to influence growth in transition. Thus many growth studies focused on the role of institutional reform and market liberalization for growth in Eastern Europe (Hernández-Cáta 1997, Fischer, Sahey and Vegh 1998, Falcetti, Raiser and Sanvey 2002, Havrylyshyn 2000, Fidrmuc 2000) or of economic policies (Barlow and Radulescu 2002). Only a few studies investigate growth factors which are relevant at the post-

* Research for this paper was undertaken within the OeNB-Jubiläumsfondprojekt no. 8869 "EU integration and regional development: Prospects for Eastern Europe" financed by the Oesterreichische Nationalbank.

[a] corresponding author, Research Institute for European Affairs, Wirtschaftsuniversität Wien, Althanstrasse 39-45, A-1090 Vienna, Austria, phone: 0043 1 31336 5566, FAX: 0043 1 31336 758, e-mail: gabriele.tondl@wu-wien.ac.at

[23] There are, however, some studies which address the issue of regional specialization and employment dynamics in Eastern European countries, e.g. Resmini (2002), Traistaru and Wolff (2002) and Traistaru, Nijkamp and Longhi (2002).

transition stage such as investment, FDI and education (Fidrmuc 2000, Campos and Kinoshita 2002).
As transition was completed and regional differences in the catching-up process have become manifest in Eastern Europe, however, a general interest arises to know which are the factors important for catching up. In this view, our paper wishes to fill the gap in Eastern European regional growth analysis.
We investigate regional growth in a sample comprising 36 regions from the Czech Republic, Slovakia, Hungary and Poland, and of Slovenia for the period 1995-2000, - a time when those countries had left transition behind and had generally started to catch up (WIIW 2002). For that purpose, we created a comprehensive regional databank, EAST RegStat, compiled from national statistical data. Investigating the causes of regional growth in the post transition period we look at a variety of factors which seem to be particularly relevant in Eastern European countries, namely capital accumulation and foreign direct investment (FDI), which reached rather high levels in this period, labour force participation, which decreased due to mounting unemployment, educational attainment of secondary and higher level, where Eastern European countries partly rank fairly high, and innovation. In addition, we investigate the role of geographical factors such spatial dependencies among regions and the potential access to EU markets. An important concern of this study is also to investigate factors which may explain technological progress, manifest by a strong increase in productivity in Eastern European regions in this period. Thus we look at the role of innovation activity and technology diffusion in achieving technological progress.
The results indicate that foreign direct investment and higher level education are most important for regional growth in Eastern Europe. Regions with a better market access show superior growth. Spatial dependencies suggest a tendency of emerging growth clusters in Eastern Europe. Capital areas outperform in all factors and are at the forefront of catching up.
The rest of the paper is organized as follows: Section 2 reviews the literature and puts forward our hypotheses with respect to growth factors in Eastern European regions. Section 3 sets up the theoretical model to be tested. Section 4 describes our data set EAST RegStat and gives first insights on regional developments from the data. Section 5 explains the estimation procedure and presents the results of the estimations. Section 6 concludes.

2. Likely sources of growth in Eastern European regions in the post-transition period

Eastern European economies entered a very specific situation of economic development in 1995, where basically the downsizing of transformation was completed and rebuilding and modernization started. On average, in the period 1995-2000 regional per capita income growth amounted to 4 per cent annually, except for the Czech Republic where it was fairly weak. In particular capital areas showed higher growth, in the Czech Republic and in Poland even twice the average. (see table 1). These growth difference raise the question why some regions realized higher growth than others, meaning that they would catch up faster in income.
We start from the arguments of growth theory and the findings of empirical growth research (see e.g. Fagerberg et al. 1997, Vanhoudt et al. 2000, Badinger and Tondl 2003 for an investigation of growth factors in EU 15 regions) and propose that investment, the labour market participation rate, educational attainment, innovation activity, the stock of FDI as well

as spatial dependencies and location factors may be potential factors to explain Eastern European regional growth. Which are the arguments for these growth factors, which are the findings in the existing growth literature on Eastern Europe?
First, with respect to investment, we have to note that due to massive privatisation capital accumulation has been higher in Eastern Europe than in the EU since the mid 1990s (25 per cent versus 19 per cent on average in 1994-97; Dobrinsky 2001, Campos and Coricelli 2002), whereby foreign direct investment played an important role (13 per cent of investment in 1997/99; Campos and Coricelli 2002). On the regional level, investment activity differed importantly. In 1996-2000, regional investment rates ranged from 20 per cent in Poland to almost 40 per cent in Slovakia. In capital areas investment was two thirds higher. In Bratislava it even reached 70 per cent of GVA. (see table 2). To which extent can investment explain growth in eastern European regions? In the scarce empirical growth literature on Eastern Europe, Campos and Kinoshita (2002) propose that capital formation had a significantly positive effect on growth in Eastern European countries.

Table 1: Average growth of regional GVA p.c. in Eastern Europe 1995-2000 (in per cent)

	average	capital region	EU border regions	rest
Czech Republic	0.2	4.1	-0.7	0.0
Hungary	4.2	5.7	7.1	3.3
Poland	4.4	8.8	4.2	4.1
Slovenia*	4.6	-	-	-
Slovak Republic	4.2	5.0	5.0	3.9

Notes: * Slovenia: national level; data sources: see Appendix

Table 2: Average regional investment rate in Eastern Europe 1996-2000 (in per cent of GVA)

	average	capital region	EU border regions	rest
Czech Republic	31.7	43.7	30.8	29.3
Hungary	22.7	27.4	24.2	21.4
Poland	20.4	30.9	21.5	19.3
Slovenia*	28.4	-	-	-
Slovak Republic	39.8	74.7	74.7	28.2

Notes: * Slovenia: national level; data sources: see Appendix

Table 3: Average regional FDI stocks in Eastern Europe 1996-2000 (in per cent of GVA)

	average	capital region	EU border regions	rest
Czech Republic	26.2	59.5	21.7	21.3
Hungary	32.3	69.3	35.8	24.2
Poland	15.0	22.3	15.7	14.2
Slovenia*	15.1	-	-	-
Slovak Republic	10.7	25.3	25.3	5.8

Notes: * Slovenia: national level; data sources: see Appendix

Table 4: Human capital and innovation in Eastern Europe regions 1996-2000

attainment rate - secondary level education (in per cent of total population)				
	average	**capital region**	**EU border regions**	**rest**
Czech Republic	55.8	56.2	55.0	56.3
Hungary	37.2	38.8	39.5	36.5
Poland	43.7	44.9	44.8	43.3
Slovenia*	43.3	-	-	-
Slovak Republic	48.5	49.2	49.2	48.3
attainment rate - higher level education (in per cent of total population)				
	average	**capital region**	**EU border regions**	**rest**
Czech Republic	6.6	14.9	5.6	5.2
Hungary	7.0	12.1	6.8	6.0
Poland	6.1	9.3	6.1	5.9
Slovenia*	9.1	-	-	-
Slovak Republic	7.0	15.3	15.3	4.3
R%D expenditure (in per cent of GVA)				
	average	**capital region**	**EU border regions**	**rest**
Czech Republic	1.3	2.4	0.4	1.6
Hungary	0.5	1.4	0.2	0.4
Poland	0.5	1.8	0.3	0.5
Slovenia*	1.6	-	-	-
Slovak Republic	0.9	1.5	1.5	0.7

*Notes: * Slovenia: national level; data sources: see Appendix*

Further, we assume that in the second part of the 1990s regional growth in Eastern Europe was related to labour market developments. In the first 5 years of transformation, participation rates, i.e. the ratio of employed persons to total population, had in general significantly declined (Boeri 2000) but stabilized in the second half of the 1990s, with the exception of many Czech and Slovak regions. Demographic and labour market developments are responsible for the decline. Emigration and early retirement were important and contributed to a decline of participation rates in Eastern Europe. Skill mismatch and labour saving productivity increase lead to higher unemployment and thus to lower participation rates. Unemployment rates had steadily increased in Eastern Europe until 1994, then showed a tendency to decline until 1998 (Burda 1998), but increased again thereafter (Eurostat). After a short expansion after 1994, employment dropped again in the Czech Republic, Slovakia and Poland (WIIW 2002). Falling participation rates lead to reduced growth prospects of a region as produced output has to be shared with a larger inactive population share. The question arises to which extent participation was important for regional growth in the post-1995 period. Education, which is given a primary role in endogenous growth models, may have played an important role for regional growth in Eastern Europe because of the relatively high secondary. In the period concerned, 55 per cent of the population had finished secondary school in the Czech Republic, in the Slovak Republic 48 per cent, 43 per cent in Poland and Slovenia and 37 per cent in Hungary. Within countries, attainment rates were fairly equal. (See table 4). In the richer regions of the EU this rate stood at 41 per cent and in the less developed regions of the so called EU cohesion countries (Spain, Portugal, Greece, Ireland) the rate was only 25 per cent. Higher level education attainment rates are less striking in Eastern Europe. 6 to 9 per cent of the population had finished higher education, again with a strong concentration on capital areas, whereas the rate is 10 per cent in the cohesion countries and 16 per cent in the richer EU regions.

Given the arguments of growth theory where education provides on the one side knowledge and skills that enter into the production process (Lucas 1988; Mankiw, Romer and Weil 1992) and has on the other side a direct impact on the research capacity (Romer 1990), differences in education levels across Eastern European regions should matter for growth. The existing growth regressions for Eastern European countries provide mixed evidence. Fidrmuc (2000) found that secondary education has a positive impact on growth, whereas Campos (2002) found a negative impact.

Recent growth literature stresses that productivity growth has become the most important source of growth in advanced economies (Easterly and Levine 2001). Given the large productivity gap of Eastern countries, productivity growth should be also highly important in Eastern European regions and should play a central role to maintain the catching-up process. Dobrinsky (2001) showed in a growth accounting exercise, total factor productivity growth started to become a driving force for growth in these countries since the mid-1990s.

In principle, productivity growth can be generated either by improving knowledge and skills through education (see above), or by technological progress that either stems from own R&D or is the result of technology transfer. On average, regional R&D rates are fairly modest in the accession countries. Only in Slovenia and the Czech Republic they reach a higher value with 1.6 respectively 1.3 per cent. As higher level education, R&D activity is concentrated in capital areas, where R&D expenditures account for 1.5 to 2.4 per cent of GVA. (See table 4)

Technology transfer may play an important role for Eastern European regions: A primary source for technology transfer may be FDI, which has reached a substantial level in the Eastern European countries, not least because of lower wage costs, generous tax concessions of the recipient countries to foreign investors, and the prospect of EU integration (Sedmihradsky and Klazar 2002, Altomonte and Resmini 2001). FDI stocks in Eastern European regions had reached 32 per cent of GVA in Hungary and 26 per cent in the Czech Republic, in the other countries, the FDI stock accounted only for 10-15 per cent of GVA. Also in this context, the FDI stock was on average twice as high in capital regions. (See table 3). With FDI technology incorporated in capital goods, process knowledge and managerial skills are transferred to the host region. A number of recent studies attempted to test for technology spillovers through FDI, either on the microeconomic or on the macroeconomic level. There is a direct effect of productivity increase in the plant where FDI was received and an indirect effect on productivity of other firms in the same location or same sector (Baldwin et al. 1999). Indirect productivity spillovers may take place through labour force (Fosfuri et al. 2001) or through upstream and downstream interfirm relationships (Blomström and Kokko 1998, Markusen and Venables 1999). Technology spillovers will be conditioned on the social capability at the local level (Abramowitz 1986) in particular the education level of the local workforce (Borensztein, De Gregorio, and Lee 1998). The results of studies for Eastern countries using firm level data are mixed. Kinoshita (2000) tests for technology spillovers of FDI on local firms in the Czech Republic and finds that these depend on the extent of own R&D activity of local firms. In contrast, Djankov and Hoekman (1998), which do not account for the absorption capacity of local firms, find no clear evidence for spillovers from FDI in the Czech Republic. Macroeconomic and sectoral studies which directly assess the growth impact of FDI on the economy or sector. Those come to a positive assessment of its growth effects. Thus, Altomonte and Resmini (2001) could verify a positive growth impact of foreign owned firms on downstream and upstream firms in Poland. Similarly, Hunya (2002) and

Campos and Kinoshita (2002) found that FDI has a positive growth impact. The latter show that it depends on the level ofhuman capital in the recipient country.

As described by Resmini (2000), FDI in Eastern European countries is not targeted at labour intensive sectors, but rather on capital intensive and even science based sectors. This, and furthermore the relatively high educational level should facilitate technology transfers through FDI. Consequently, we propose the hypothesis that FDI is an excellent channel for technology transfer in Eastern European regions and thus should have lead to higher growth in regions with a high FDI stock.

Given our focus on regional economies, it is straightforward that we also check growth differences under the view of economic geography aspects and spatial effects. First, we shall check for spatial dependencies among regions in Eastern Europe. An obvious way to check for general spatial dependencies is to look at growth spillovers between regions. Such spillovers may be the outcome of a variety of interactions between regions, such as interregional trade flows, labour market interactions, productivity spillovers, etc. A number of regional growth analyses detected growth spillovers in other geographical areas, for example Rey and Montouri (1999), Fingleton (2001), Niebuhr (2001), and Kosfeld et al. (2002). There are also studies in the literature which explicitly analyse the interactions underlying such growth spillovers. For example, Cheshire and Magrini (2000) analyse interregional migration flows, Paci and Pigliaru (2001) analyse productivity spillovers across EU regions, and Paci and Usai (2001) and Funke and Niebuhr (2001) analyse regional R&D spillovers. Nevertheless, since we wish to account for the total spillover effects between regions rather than single effects, for which data is not always available, we shall focus on growth spillovers. The implication of growth spillovers is straightforward. An evidence of such spillovers indicates that a region´s growth depends on that of surrounding regions, i.e. a region ssurrounded by high growth regions will aalso show high growth, a region surrounded by low growth regions will show poor growth. This means that high growth and low growth clusters will be appearr. It is very hard for a region in a low growth cluster to move to a more dynamic growth path. This effect will be analysed by using a spatial econometric model as suggested in the spatial econometric literature (Anselin 1988, Anselin and Florax 1995, Kelejian and Prucha 1998).

Second, we shall test for the relevance of peripherality (agglomeration) effects for Eastern European regions. More precisely, we shall look at access to market demand in EU markets, whereby that access is a function of distance and quality of transport. Thus we shall test the argument that regions which are more closely located to centres in the EU with high demand and that have a better transportation link to these centres enjoy superior growth.

Of course, there are a number of other factors which may have an important influence on growth. First, as we know from country level statistics, foreign trade, above all with the EU, has become very important in the East. However, we can suppose that regions trade to a different extent. Thus it would be interesting to find out whether differences in trade intensity have led to growth differences. Intensive trade usually leads to higher growth since it unleashes pro-competitive effects and facilitates technology transfer. Furthermore, as country level studies have shown, differences in socio-political and institutional factors were responsible for early growth differences in Eastern Europe. These factors can be expected to vary even more across regions and thus could be important in explaining growth differences. Unfortunately, for both factors, there are no statistics on the regional level and therefore we cannot test for their effect.

3. The specification for estimation

To test the hypothesis proposed in the previous section, we shall use a cross section growth accounting framework, which has become standard in the empirical growth literature (see Temple 1999). We do not use a catching up model since we are not interested in the convergence dynamics within the group of Eastern European regions but in the factors of growth. Without deriving a fully specified growth mode, which is not the focus of this paper, we formulate a model following the approach of Benhabib and Spiegel (1994).
The starting point is an augmented Solow model of economic growth as specified by Mankiw, D. Romer and Weil (1992)

$$Y = AK^{\alpha}H^{\beta}L^{\gamma} \quad (1)$$

where Y is income, K is physical capital, H human capital, L labour and A total factor productivity. α, β and γ are elasticities of output with respect to physical capital, human capital and labour. We assume constant returns to scale so that $\alpha + \beta + \gamma = 1$
Equation (1) becomes

$$Y = AK^{\alpha}H^{\beta}(POP \cdot PART)^{\gamma} \quad (2)$$

if population POP is different from labour force L, and $PART$ is the participation rate L/POP.
In intensive form equation (2) becomes

$$y = Ak^{\alpha}h^{\beta}PART^{\gamma} \quad (3)$$

where per capita income $y = Y/POP$, per capita capital $k = K/POP$, and the stock of human capital per person $h = H/POP$.
Since the point of interest is to examine the causes of changes in per capita income we write the model in log differences and use this directly for estimation (Benhabib and Spiegel 1994).
All variables except for human capital (see below) will be considered in differences.

$$\Delta \ln y = \Delta \ln A + \alpha\Delta \ln k + \beta h + \gamma\Delta \ln PART \quad (4)$$

We proxy capital accumulation $\Delta \ln k$ by the investment rate INV, h is the average educational attainment rate in the population, $\Delta \ln PART$ is the change in the participation rate and $\Delta \ln A$ is technological progress measured by productivity growth.
At first, education is considered as a factor of production. It represents knowledge that determines efficiency of production. Changes in educational attainment should therefore lead to higher growth. In another sense, however, the level of education determines also the capacity to generate technological progress, i.e. productivity growth (Benhabib and Spiegel 1994; 2003; Temple 1999). Finally, education can also be a conditioning factor for technology diffusion (see below).
In the empirical growth literature, many authors (e.g. Benhabib and Spiegel 1994; Pritchett 1996) consider the level of education and not its change as the factor determining growth. The reasons for the choice of the variable are diverse and comprise also problems of data accuracy (de la Fuente and Domenech 2000). Since we watch the growth process in a fairly short time period, changes in human capital are unlikely to determine growth. Therefore the level of education of a region is considered. Two types of education will be considered. First, we look at secondary educational attainment, in which respect Eastern European countries rank fairly high in country comparisons. Second, we look at higher educational attainment which is average in these countries.

We consider several possibilities how technological progress $\Delta \ln A$ is generated. In line with endogenous growth theory, innovation activity should be the primary source of technological progress. Further, technological progress can happen by technological diffusion which clearly is more important in developing and transition economies that do not yet possess a large R&D sector. FDI may be a particularly important channel for technology diffusion.

As to the first source of technological progress, innovation, we measure R&D activity in the tradition of Romer (1990) and Aghion and Howitt (1992) by the resources devoted to R&D, R&D expenditures $R\&D_{exp}$. In line with the critique of Jones (1995), that the absolute scale of R&D resources shows little correlation with technological advance, and recent suggestions of R&D activity indicators used in empirical research (Bassanini et al. 2001, Fagerberg et al. 1997) we use a relative indicator: $R\&D_{exp} / Y$ are expenditures in per cent of GVA. Thus we can write:

$$\Delta \ln A = \delta_{11}(R\&D_{exp} / Y) \quad (5)$$

Note that according to the above arguments on education, particularly higher level education should also be a direct variable for innovation capacity.

As to the second source of technological progress, technology diffusion, we start from Nelson and Phelps (1966) and Benhabib and Spiegel (2003) and consider the potential of technology diffusion to be a positive function of the technology gap of a region. The technology gap GAP is proxied by the productivity gap of Region i with respect to the EU average:

$$GAP_i = [(Y/L)_{EU} - (Y/L)_i]/(Y/L)_i \quad (6.1)$$

so that

$$\Delta \ln A = \delta_{21} GAP \text{ and} \quad (6.2)$$

$$\Delta \ln A = \delta_{22} GAP * h \quad (6.3)$$

if we consider that the availability of human capital in the region is a precondition for technology diffusion, as suggested by Nelson and Phelps (1966) and specified by Benhabib and Spiegel (1994; 2003).

Finally, we consider that the presence of foreign direct investment enables technology transfer so that

$$\Delta \ln A = \phi_1 FDI \quad (7.1)$$

$$\Delta \ln A = \phi_2 FDI * h \quad (7.2)$$

where FDI is the stock of foreign direct investment as a share of regional GVA. Alternatively, technology transfer through FDI may be subject to the absorption capacity of the region which may be determined by its human capital as argued by Borenzstein, De Gregorio and Lee (1998) in the tradition of Nelson and Phelps (1966).

Last, we wish to include spatial aspects and new economic geography aspects in our model. We assume that there are regional growth spillovers so that a region´s growth is determined by the growth of its surrounding regions.

$$\Delta \ln y_t = \mathbf{W}\Delta \ln y_t \qquad (8)$$

where **W** is the N x N spatial weights matrix of the dimension equivalent to the number of regions N of our sample with elements w_{ij} which describes the interaction between region i and region j. We choose a contiguity spatial weights matrix where $w_{ij} = 1$ if region i and j have a common border and $w_{ij} = 0$ otherwise.[24] If growth spillovers can be verified, this indicates the existence of growth clusters.
The effect of access to market demand was tested by the following market access indicator (Schürmann and Talaat 2002):

$$ACCESS_i = \sum_{j=1}^{N} Y_j^{\psi} \cdot \exp(-\tau \cdot t_{ij}) \qquad (9)$$

Market access of region i is determined by the market size (GDP) of all other regions j located either in the EU or in Eastern Europe, Y_j. t_{ij} is the transport time from region i to region j by lorry. Regions have the higher market access the closer they are to market demand. ψ and τ are weighting parameters. Y_j thus indicates the market potential. t_{ij} is an impedance function. The weight of market potential, ψ, is usually assumed to be one, but can be larger than one if agglomerations are assumed to be more attractive. The parameter τ governs the importance of far away regions. If τ is large, far away regions are less important. If market access turns out to be important for growth, this would mean that there are tendencies of agglomeration in the sense of the New Economic Geography models (Krugman 1991). Those Eastern regions with high market access to the EU are then potential parts of the European core.
In summary, we can specify the following variants of the model which will be estimated:

$$\begin{aligned}
\Delta \ln y &= a + \Delta \ln A \quad + \quad \alpha\Delta \ln k + \beta \ln h + \gamma\Delta \ln PART + W\Delta \ln y + u_{it} \\
&= a + \delta_{11}(R\&D_{exp}/Y) \quad + \quad \ldots. \\
&= \quad \ldots. \quad + \delta_{21} GAP \quad + \quad \ldots. \\
&= \quad \ldots. \quad + \delta_{22} GAP * h \quad + \quad \ldots. \\
&= \quad \ldots. \quad + \phi_1 FDI \quad + \quad \ldots. \\
&= \quad \ldots. \quad + \phi_2 FDI * h \quad + \quad \ldots. \\
&= \quad \ldots. \quad + \quad \ldots \quad + \quad \ldots. \quad + \quad EU\text{-}ACCESS \\
&\quad + u_{it}
\end{aligned} \qquad (10)$$

[24] Alternatively to the contiguity matrix we used two weights matrix specifications where the influence of other regions' growth declined with increasing distance. One of the form $w_{ij} = d_{ij}^{-\delta}$ where d_{ij} denotes the distance between the centres of two regions and δ is the distance decay parameter which can be varied (see also Fingleton 2001; Badinger and Tondl 2003). Another took the form $w_{ij} = \exp(-\delta \cdot d_{ij})$ where again for δ various values were tried. In both cases, a high value had to be taken for δ in order to get a correctly specified spatial econometric model. This indicates that spatial dependencies diminish very fast between Eastern European regions. Therefore we selected a contiguity matrix as a spatial weights matrix.

4. Data issues and a first look at empirical developments in the regions

For this study a unique dataset, EAST RegStat, was created for which a substantial amount of data from national statistical offices was compiled and used along with data from Eurostat. The dataset covers 36 NUTS II level regions from Central and Eastern Europe, i.e. regions from the Czech Republic, Slovakia, Hungary, Poland, and Slovenia, which in the Eurostat regional system is not divided into NUTS II regions. In general, the collected data covers the period 1995-2000. For most indicators, Eurostat data was taken as the principal data source. Some missing values were taken from national statistics, if available, checking for trend consistency of time series. For several indicators, however, national statistics were the main data source. In a number of series, data for one or two missing values had to be filled by the means of extrapolation, whereby consistency was checked in various ways, e.g. by allocation of country level data to regions. The following indicators are used for our analysis:

(i) average annual real growth of GVA per capita 1995-2000
(ii) average gross fixed capital formation (all sectors) 1996-2000
(iii) average annual change in the labour participation rate 1995-2000
(iv) average secondary level and higher level educational attainment in 1996-2000 (per cent of the population with secondary/higher level education)
(v) average annual change of educational attainment rates 1995-2000
(vi) average stock of FDI in per cent of GVA, 1996-2000
(vii) market access indicator 1997[25]

Exact data definitions and sources are given in the appendix.

Note that we calculated the average growth rate by regressing annual logs of GVA on a constant and time trend, rather than computing growth from GVA from the beginning and the end of the period. This should yield growth rates which are less influenced by short term instability, as explained in Temple (1999). Growth rates of other indicators are calculated in the same fashion.

As in any empirical research on Eastern European economies, one needs to take into account that the quality of the data of this study has certain limits. The reliability of employment data is certainly not very good since there is a large shadow economy in these countries. Further, it may be difficult to compare education data across countries since quality standards differ. There are also weaknesses in the registration of citizens, so that people may live and work in different locations than registered.

5. Results of the estimation

In the following we estimated a spatial lag model assuming a contiguity matrix to model spatial dependencies.

From an econometric point of view the model can be expressed as

$$y = \rho_1 \mathbf{W}y + \mathbf{X}\beta + u_{it} \tag{11}$$

$$u_{it} = \rho_2 \mathbf{W}u + \varepsilon_{it}$$

$$\text{with } |\rho_1| < 1,\ |\rho_2| < 1$$

[25] We thank Carsten Schürmann, Ahmed Talaat and Michael Wegener for kind permission to use their access indicator statistics.

where y (N×1) is the dependent, endogenous variable and **X** (N×K) is the vector of K explanatory variables, **W** is the contiguity NxN spatial weights matrix, containing spatial weights of all regions of the sample. ρ_1 and ρ_2 are (scalar) spatial correlation parameters, and the vector β (Kx1) contains the parameters of the explanatory variables. u_{it} is a non-spherical disturbance term, while ε_{it} is assumed to be distributed NID (0, σ^2).
Since $\mathbf{W}y$ is endogenous, the OLS estimator is biased an inconsistent. Spatial econometrics offers estimation procedures that address this problem. We employ the feasible generalised spatial two stages least squares estimator (FGS2SLS) developed by Kelejian and Prucha (1998) which is computationally simpler than the ML estimator (Anselin 1988) and which is also considered as an unbiased estimator. Its asymptotoc properties are proven (Debabrata et al. 2003). Moreover, Kelejian and Prucha (1999) examined the small sample properties of the estimator in Monte Carlo simulations and found that the small sample bias is negligible.
The Kelejian/Prucha procedure involves two steps:

- In order to treat the endogeneity problem of $\mathbf{W}y$, an instrumental variable estimator (2SLS) is applied. Starting from the reduced form of equation (11)

  $$y = (I - \rho_1 W)^{-1} X\beta + (I - \rho_1 W)^{-1}(I - \rho_2 W)^{-1}\varepsilon \qquad (12)$$

  and given the conditional expectation in the reduced form

  $$E(Wy / X) = W(I - \rho_1 W)^{-1} X\beta = WX\beta + W^2 X(\rho_1\beta) + W^3 X(\rho_1^2\beta) + \ldots \qquad (13)$$

  X, WX and $W^2 X$ are used as instruments. The exogenous variable X, which is always an instrument, as well as its spatial lags are used as instruments for $\mathbf{W}y$.
- However, this IV estimation does not account for the spatial correlation in the error term $u \approx (0, \sigma^2\Omega), \Omega = (I - \rho_2 W)^{-1}(I - \rho_2 W')^{-1}$ and therefore leads to inefficient parameter estimates and biased estimates of standard errors. The solution is a feasible GLS estimation, which means running unweighted least squares on the transformed series y^* = (I-ρ_2**W**)y, **W**y^*=(I-ρ_2**W**)**W**y, and **X*** = (I-ρ_2**W**)**X**; for the estimation of ρ_2 we use the GM estimator by Kelejian/Prucha (1999), which is based on the residuals u, obtained in the first step. Again, (the same) instruments are used for **W**y^*.

Estimation is effected with an Eviews programme developed in Badinger and Tondl (2003). As a test for spatial dependence, the standardized Moran´s I statistic is use. We test for the form of spatial dependence (spatial error versus spatial lag model) with the LM_{ERR} and LM_{LAG} test statistics (see Anselin and Rey 1991, Anselin and Bera 1998, Anselin and Florax 1995).
It should be noted that the estimation constitutes a cross section analysis. Since we regard a short time period no other specification is reasonable.
After having found the correct estimator for the spatial model, it is also important to account for possible simultaneity issues and multicollinearity between regressor variables. It is likely that simultaneity is encountered between the dependent variable and investment, and to a lesser degree betwween the dependent variable and FDI stock.[26] To circumvent this problem,

[26] With FDI the likelhood of simultaneity is less severe because we use FDI stock and not flow data. In addition this potential problem may be less serious than in studies at national level. FDI inflows to countries motivated by higher growth rates are market seeking investments which are either "tariff jumping" or search for proximity to markets because of high transport costs. However, these potential trade obstacles, i.e. motives for investment, are not so strong at the regional level if regions are relatively small, which is the case in our study. It may not be necessary to invest directly into the highest growing region in order to have an easy access to its market, i.e. it

we use initial values of these regressor values instead of period averages, as frequently found in the growth literature (Temple 1999, Levine and Zervos 1998). Furthermore, the estimated models need to account for endogeneity of regressors. The table in the appendix shows the correlation matrix between regressor variables. Most importantly, we see that there is high correlation between the capital region status and investment, FDI, higher level human capital and research. Taking initial values of investment and FDI cures also the endogeneity problem between these variables and the capital dummy variable, human capital and R&D.
There is also the possibility of endogeneity between investment and output, or between the participation rate and output, which we cannot treat properly. T-Therefore the results must be interpreted with some caution.
In the following we estimate a sequence of different specifications. In all specifications, however, we estimate a spatial lag model. Table 5 contains the results of a core model (model 1) which includes as explanatory variables regional investment, changes in the participation rate and a spatial lag of growth, measuring growth spillovers from neighbouring regions. As discussed above, for investment, the initial values of the variable are taken in order to alleviate the endogeneity problem. Only the spatial lag of growth turned out to be significant in this simple specification, with positive sign and this result remain robust in all other specifications as well. The LMLAG statistic suggests that the spatial lag model is the correct form to model spatial dependencies. This indicates that regional growth rates are highly influenced by those of neighbouring regions. The coefficient remains fairly stable in all following estimations. Almost one fifth of a region´s growth is explained by growth in the neighbouring regions. This should lead to growth clusters.

Table 5: Estimation results – basic model and location factors

dependant variable: ?y								
	model 1		model 2		model 3		model 4	
intercept	-0.598	(-0.29)	0.478	(0.28)	-0.869	(-0.44)	-0.067	(-0.04)
inv	0.048	(1.06)	-0.012	(-0.29)	0.036	(0.80)	0.045	(1.10)
?part	0.246	(1.69)	0.139	(1.11)	0.283*	(1.99)	0.273**	(2.50)
capital			3.474***	(3.73)				
EU border					0.882	(1.04)		
access							0.031*	(1.81)
DCZ							-3.946***	(-4.06)
lag ?y	0.170***	(2.39)	0.165***	(2.94)	0.186***	(2.78)	0.125**	(2.10)
$?_2$	0.170		0.165		0.186		0.125	
z(I)	1.81		1.40		1.83		0.11	
LM_{ERR}	1.37		0.65		1.30		0.24	
LM_{LAG}	4.50**		5.41**		4.95**		1.10	
adj. R^2	0.33		0.51		0.46		0.76	
no. obs.	36		36		36		36	

Notes: estimated using the general spatial two stage least squares procedure given in Kelejian/Prucha 1998, t-statistics in parenthesis, z(I) is the standardised z-value of Moran's I, LM_{ERR} is the Lagrange multiplier test for residual spatial autocorrelation, LM_{LAG} is the Lagrange multiplier test for endogenous spatial lag, *** significant at the 1% level, ** significant at the 5% level, * significant at the 10% level

may be enough to produce in any region within the national borders (in case of administrative trade barriers) or if the transport costs are high, in the neighbouring region.

Given the results of the basic model, first of all we are interested to which extent location factors can explain growth differences. To test this hypothesis, we use a dummy variable for capital reegions, for regions bordering the EU, and the accessibility variable. The capital dummy variable turns out to be highly significant, confirming the impression given by the statistics in section 2 that capitals had a substantially higher growth in the concerned period than other regions. As indicated by the insignificant coefficient of the EU border dummy variable, surprisingly regions geographically close to EU regions do not show higher growth. What is important, in contrast, is the access to demand in EU markets as shown by the significantly positive coefficient of the access variable. Remember from section 3, that market access is determined by the travel time to markets.[27] This indicates that Eastern European regions with a better infrastructure link to EU markets have also better growth prospects.
Note that a dummy variable for Czech regions is used in model 4. We also tried country dummy variables for other countries to account for country specific effects, like national growth differences or national institutional characteristics. Only the Czech dummy variables turned out to be significant. We decided not to use country dummy variables in further specifications since they dominate over spatial dependencies and thus discriminate the otherwise appropriate spatial lag model.
Note that in the core model, investment is never found to be a significant growth factor. The participation rate becomes significant only in some specifications, notably in that with the Czech dummy variable, indicating that participation may be of some importance in other regions than in the Czech Republic. Lower participation rates may have been problematic under the perspective to increase welfare in terms of per capita incomes. Low participation limits income growth.

In table 6, we present the results of estimations in which endogenous growth factors are included in the core model. First, we consider a specification with human capital – secondary and higher educational attainment, in addition to investment, labour participation and a spatial lag of growth. While the coefficient of higher education is highly significant in this and later estimations, that of secondary level education is in general not. This suggests that only differences in higher level education attainment rates can explain growth differences. Since higher level education is correlated with further variables that will be tested subsequently (R&D, FDI), it will not be included in the following estimates. Further estimates (not shown here) with higher level human capital and additional non-correlated variables (EU border, Czech dummy variable) showed that the coefficient of higher level education is very stable.

---

[27] Several combinations of weighting parameters were tried for the EU ACCESS variable. The parameter ψ for the market size was permitted to take the values 0.5, 1 and 2. A value of 0.5 indicates no particular attractiveness of agglomerations, whereas with ψ =2 agglomerations are more attractive than other regions. The weighting parameter for transport time, τ , takes the values 0.01, 0.003 and 0.001, where the impact of distant regions decreases the higher is τ .

Table 6: Estimation results – model with endogenous factors human capital and innovation

	dependant variable: ?y					
	model 5		model 6		model 7	
intercept	-0.235	(-0.08)	4.615	(1.37)	3.208	(0.98)
inv	-0.013	(-0.28)	0.063	(1.45)	0.031	(0.61)
?part	0.084	(0.66)	0.100	(0.71)	0.141	(0.99)
hc_m	-0.044	(-0.80)	-0.148**	(-2.14)	-0.090	(-1.40)
hc_h	0.504***	(3.56)				
R&D_exp			1.287**	(2.44)		
R&D_ls					1.066*	(2.02)
lag ?y	0.160***	(3.28)	0.188***	(3.21)	0.159**	(2.69)
$?_2$	0.160		0.188		0.157	
z(I)	0.39		1.92		1.27	
LM_{ERR}	0.06		1.16		0.23	
LM_{LAG}	4.96**		5.22**		3.98**	
adj. R^2	0.66		0.43		0.48	
no. obs.	36		36		36	

Notes: estimated using the general spatial two stage least squares procedure given in Kelejian/Prucha 1998, t-statistics in parenthesis, z(I) is the standardised z-value of Moran's I, LM_{ERR} is the Lagrange multiplier test for residual spatial autocorrelation, LM_{LAG} is the Lagrange multiplier test for endogenous spatial lag, *** significant at the 1% level, ** significant at the 5% level, * significant at the 10% level.

The insignificance of the coefficient of medium level human capital which in one estimation even becomes significantly negative, - contrary to the expectations -, may have something to do with a skill mismatch between educational standards and labour market requirements. Similar puzzling evidence was found in the study of Campos and Kinoshita (2002) who investigated the growth impact of human capital (measured by the average number of years of schooling in the population) and found that it was negative in the period 1990-1998. They argue that human capital was artificially high in Eastern European countries, largely not coinciding with the actual qualification standards, and thus may not be such an important variable in the growth process.
Next, we wished to test to which extent innovation activity was important for growth. Two indicators are used to measure innovation activity, R&D expenditures and the share of R&D personnel in the labour force. Both variables show a significantly positive coefficient, suggesting that innovating regions do in fact have better growth prospects. In all models with endogenous growth factors, the spatial lag of growth remains significant.

In Table 7 the results of estimations with variables describing technology diffusion are given. First we tested whether the potential for technology diffusion given by the productivity gap is related with regional growth. A positive coefficient would indicate that regions with a high productivity gap benefit from technology diffusion and have higher growth rates. The results of the estimations confirm this hypothesis only if the gap is conditioned on the higher level education level of the region. The coefficient is significantly positive then. Regions with a well educated labour force are more likely to benefit from technology transfer. Alternatively, we include the regional FDI stock in our basic model, including also medium level education but not higher level to avoid endogeneity. The results suggest that FDI has been a significant variable in growth promotion over the observed period. Note that general investment includes private and public investment and of course also FDI (about 13 per cent of total investment). However, our FDI variable does not interfere with investment since the stock of FDI is regarded. While spatial growth lag turns out significant as well, none of the other variables does.

Table 7: Estimation results – model with technology diffusion (technology gap, FDI)

	dependant variable: ? y							
	model 8		model 9		model 10		model 11	
intercept	-0.376	(-0.10)	0.871	(0.25)	1.153	(0.27)	-0.724	(-0.24)
inv	0.063	(1.40)	0.054	(1.21)	0.006	(0.12)	-0.004	(-0.06)
?part	0.151	(1.07)	0.146	(1.06)	0.074	(0.56)	0.221 *	(1.74)
hc_m	-0.046	(-0.61)	-0.058	(-0.84)	-0.058	(-0.92)	-0.026	(-0.44)
hc_h					0.439**	(2.55)		
FDI	8.024**	(2.24)						
FDI*hc_h			0.666**	(2.47)				
GAP					-0.351	(-0.56)		
GAP*hc_h							0.153**	(2.07)
lag ?y	0.215***	(3.44)	0.204***	(3.47)	0.174***	(3.47)	0.161***	(3.17)
$?_2$	0.215		0.204		0.174		0.161	
z(I)	1.99		1.88		0.51		0.60	
LM_{ERR}	1.17		1.06		0.01		0.00	
LM_{LAG}	5.26**		5.35**		5.11**		3.87**	
adj. R^2	0.38		0.45		0.62		0.73	
no. obs.	36		36		36		36	

Notes: estimated using the general spatial two stage least squares procedure given in Kelejian/Prucha 1998, t-statistics in parenthesis, z(I) is the standardised z-value of Moran's I, LM_{ERR} is the Lagrange multiplier test for residual spatial autocorrelation, LM_{LAG} is the Lagrange multiplier test for endogenous spatial lag, *** significant at the 1% level, ** significant at the 5% level, * significant at the 10% level.

Further, the impact of FDI was tested if conditioned on a region's absorbtion capacity, given by the extent of higher level educational attainment. This interactive term (*FDI*hc_h*) is considered to measure the possible technology spillovers through FDI when conditioned on the educational level in the region. While we find that medium level education is no important factor to benefit from FDI, higher level education is a decisive factor. This interactive term (*FDI*hc_h*) turns out to be highly significant and positive growth determinant. The significance of other variables from the first specification remains unchanged.

In summary, we can draw the following conclusions:

(i) Our estimations suggest that the strong inflow of foreign direct investment plays a paramount role for high growth in Eastern European regions. Increased capital accumulation as such is far less important.

(ii) In addition to having a high stock of FDI, human capital, namely higher level education, and innovation activity are the most important growth factors in Eastern European regions. Higher level education is a very important factor, also because it is a conditional factor for technology transfer and technology spillovers from FDI. Surprisingly, secondary level education does not play an important role. There can even be a negative relationship between the share of secondary level education and growth if the quality of education is inadequate.

(iii) Further, there are significant spatial dependencies between closely located regions, so that a region's growth is significantly more likely to be higher if being a neighbour of other high growth regions. About a fifth of a region's growth is determined by that of surrounding regions. This indicates a tendency for growth clusters in Eastern Europe.

(iv) Capital areas have the best endowment in the essential growth factors which explains their outstanding performance in growth.

(v) There is little evidence that differences in the labour participation rate play a significant role for growth. Other factors are far more important.

(vi) Access to EU markets has become important for growth.

(vii) Regions in Eastern Europe surrounded by low growth regions, with a low stock of FDI, a low level of higher education, no R&D and poor infrastructure linkages with EU markets had no chance to catch up in income level in the period 1995-2000.

Therefore, we may guess that the exceptionally high level of secondary schooling should trigger fast growth in the Eastern European countries. However, this relationship may be less clear for a number of reasons. First, we should know that the high rate of secondary school attainment reflects the fact that vocational schools, - as opposed to general education -, have a much more important role in the accession countries than in the EU. Vocational schools account for 80 per cent of upper secondary education in the East. In the EU, only in Germany and Austria the share of vocational schools is almost equally high with 70 per cent. In contrast, vocational schools account only for 20-40 per cent in the Southern EU countries (Eurostat 2000). This explains the different size of secondary school rates across Europe. Then, as Boeri (2000) points out, qualifications in the East tend to be very narrowly specified and are often not transferable to new jobs. Therefore, high school attainment rates would not reflect the actual level of qualification.

6. Conclusions

This paper wished to shed some light on the factors that determined regional growth in Eastern Europe in the second half of the 1990s, a period when transformation was largely settled and catching-up with the EU established to a quite different degree among Eastern European regions.

We set up our hypotheses on growth factors in an economic growth model and argued that the high observed capital accumulation and high educational level in Eastern Europe might have been important for growth in dynamic regions. Further we expected that technology transfer, in particular through FDI might have played an important role. In addition, we supposed that location factors and spatial dependencies mattered for growth.

The empirical analysis was done with a sample of 36 NUTS II level regions from the Czech Republic, Slovakia, Hungary, Poland and Slovenia for the period 1995-2000. To take likely spatial dependencies into account, we set up our growth regressions in a spatial econometric framework. It turned out that a spatial lag model, where per capita income growth is also dependent on growth of surrounding regions, would be most appropriate for our context. For estimation we used the general spatial two stage least squares procedure suggested by Kelejian and Prucha (1998), a two stage instrumental variable estimator which is considered as an unbiased estimator for the spatial context with established asymptotic properties.

Our results partly prove our proposed hypotheses, partly reveal new surprising aspects.

First, we find that Eastern European capital areas clearly enjoy agglomeration advantages and have better resources in all respects (human capital, FDI, research) which makes them to growth leaders. Second, it is in particular foreign direct investment and not capital accumulation as such which was the main driving factor behind regional growth in Eastern Europe. Third, human capital, namely higher level education is the second most important growth factor in Eastern European regions after FDI. Fourth, regions with a high R&D rate are leading in growth. Fifth, we can observe regional clustering of growth, regions surrounded by high growth areas showed a high growth performance. However, as our experiments with spatial weighting matrixes have shown, spatial effects are geographically still rather limited, probably an evidence for insufficient transport infrastructures. It also shows that access to EU markets matters for growth of Eastern European regions, indicating that peripheral regions with a poor infrastructure link have worse growth prospects. Sixth, we find no clear evidence that labour market participation rates and attainment rates in secondary education play a significant role for growth. of Eastern regions. A high secondary education attainment rate may even be an impediment for growth if qualification standards do not suit the requested profiles.

Evidently, endogenous growth factors like innovation activity and human capital are important factors for regional growth. In this respect, Eastern European regions rely on similar growth factors as EU regions. However, also techno logy transfer is a main source of productivity growth in Eastern European regions. Testing the technology gap model with human capital as a conditioning factor, we find that this was a highly relevant way of technology transfer. Above all, however, FDI has to be considered as a main channel of technology spillovers, the more if combined with human capital of higher level education.

We should expect that regional disparities between Eastern European regions remain due to the outstanding basis for growth in the capital areas, the restriction of spatial interactions between regions close to each other and the peripherality of many regions. The development of transport infrastructure to overcome location disadvantages will be the task both of national and EU regional policy makers. Upgrading human capital, both medium and higher level education, and promotion of innovation activity will be a prerequisite for regions outside agglomerations to improve their growth prospects. Education will also be a key for them for attracting foreign direct investment, which will remain crucial for growth. National and EU regional policy should consider that human resources and innovation are highly important factors to establish endogenousely driven, high quality growth. Finally, policy makers must consider that FDI is the most prominent factor for catching up. Policies that would discourage FDI would endanger growth.

References

Abramowitz, M. (1986), Catching-up, forging ahead or falling behind, in: *Journal of Economic History*, 46, 385-406.

Aghion, P. and Howitt, P. (1992), A model of growth through creative destruction, *Econometrica*, 60, 323-351.

Aitken, B. J. and Harrison, A. E (1999), Do Domestic Firms Benefit from Direct Foreign Investment? Evidence from Venezuela, in: *American Economic Review*, 89(3), 605-618.

Altomonte, C. and Resmini, L. (2001), Multinational Corporations as Catalyst for Industrial Development: The Case of Poland, *William Davidson Institute Working Paper*, no. 368.

Anselin, L. (1988), *Spatial econometrics: Methods and models*, Dordrecht, Kluwer.

Anselin, L. and Florax, J. G. M. (1995), *New directions in spatial econometrics*, Berlin et al., Springer.

Badinger, H. and Tondl, G. (2003), Trade, human capital and innovation. The engines of European regional growth in the 1990s, in: *European regional growth,* Fingleton, B. (ed.). Series: Advances in Spatial Science, Heidelberg: Springer, 215-240.

Baldwin, R., Braconier, H. and Forslid, R. (1999), Multinationals, endogenous growth and technology spillovers: Theory and evidence, *CEPR Discussion Paper*, no. 2155, London: Centre for Economic Policy Research.

Barlow, D. and Radulescu, R. (2002), The Relationship between Policies and Growth in Transition Countries, in: *Economics of Transition*, 10(3), 719-745.

Barrios, S., Gorg, H. and Strobl, E. (2001), Explaining Firms' Export Behaviour: The Role of R&D and Spillovers, *GEP Research Paper*, no. 2001/27, University of Nottingham.

Bassanini, A. and Scarpetta, S. (2000), Does Human Capital Matter for Growth in OECD Countries? A Pooled Mean-Group Approach, in: *Economics Letters,* 74(3), 399-405.

Bassanini, A., Scarpetta, S. and Hemmings, P. (2001), Economic Growth: The role of policies and institutions. Panel data evidence from OECD countries, *OECD Economics Department Working Paper*, no. 283, Paris: OECD.

Benhabib, J. and Spiegel, M. (1994), The role of human capital in economic development: Evidence from aggregate cross-country data, in: *Journal of Monetary Economics*, 34(2), 143-173.

Benhabib, M. and Spiegel, J. (2003), Human capital and technology diffusion, *Working Paper*, no. 2003/02, Federal Reserve Bank of San Francisco.

Blomstrom, M. and Kokko, A. (1998), Foreign Investment as a Vehicle for International Technology Transfer, in: *Creation and transfer of knowledge: Institutions and incentives*, Navaretti, G.B. et al, (eds.). Heidelberg and New York: Springer, 279-311.

Boeri, T. (2000), *Structural change, welfare systems, and labour reallocation: Lessons from the transition of formerly planned economies*, New York and Oxford: Oxford University Press.

Borensztein, E, De Gregorio, J. and Lee, J.W. (1998), How Does Foreign Direct Investment Affect Economic Growth? In: *Journal of International Economics*, 45(1), 115-135.

Braconier, H., Ekholm, K. and Midelfart Knarvik, K.H. (2001), In Search of FDI-Transmitted R&D Spillovers: A Study Based on Swedish Data, in: *Weltwirtschaftliches Archiv/Review of World Economics*, 137(4), 644-665.

Burda, M.C. (1998), The Consequences of EU Enlargement for Central and Eastern European Labor Markets, *CEPR Discussion Paper*, no. 1881, London: Centre for Economic Policy Research.

Campos, N.F. and Coricelli, F. (2002), Growth in Transition: What We Know, What We Don't and What We Should, in: *Journal of Economic Literature*, 40(3), 793-836.

Campos, N.F. and Kinoshita, Y. (2002), Foreign Direct Investment as Technology Transferred: Some Panel Evidence from the Transition Economies, *William Davidson Institute Working Paper*, no. 438.

Carkovic, M. and Levine, R. (2002), Does Foreign Direct Investment Accelerate Economic Growth? *Working Paper*, University of Minnesota.

Carmeci, G. and Mauro, L. (2002), The Convergence of the Italian Regions and Unemployment: Theory and Evidence, in: *Journal of Regional Science*, 42(3), 509-532.

Cheshire, P. and Magrini, S. (2000), Endogenous Processes in European Regional Growth: Convergence and Policy, in: *Growth and Change*, 31(4), 455-79.

Debabrata, D., Kelejian, H. and Prucha, I. (2003), Finite sample properties of estimators of spatial autoregressive models with autoregressive disturbances, in: *Papers in Regional Science* 82 (1), 1-26.

De Gregorio, J. (1992), Economic growth in Latin America, in: *Journal of Development Economics*, 39(1), 59-84.

de la Fuente, A. (1995), Catch-up, Growth and Convergence in the OECD, *CEPR Discussion Paper*, no. 1274, London: Centre for Economic Policy Research.

de la Fuente, A. and Domenech, R. (2000), Human capital in growth regressions: How much difference does data quality make? *CEPR Discussion Paper*, no. 2466, London: Centre for Economic Policy Research.

de-la-Fuente, A. (1996), On the Sources of Convergence: A Close Look at the Spanish Regions, *CEPR Discussion Paper*, no. 1543, London: Centre for Economic Policy Research.

Djankov, S. and Hoekman, B. M (2000), Foreign Investment and Productivity Growth in Czech Enterprises, *World Bank Economic Review*, 14(1), 49-64.

Dobrinsky, R. (2001), Convergence in per capita income levels, productivity dynamics and real exchange rates in the candidate countries on the way to EU accession, *Interim Report*, no. IR-01-038, IIASA – International Institute for Applied Systems Analysis, Luxenburg.

Easterly, W. and Levine, R. (2001), It's Not Factor Accumulation: Stylized Facts and Growth Models, *World Bank Economic Review*, 15(2), 177-219.

Eurostat (2000), Educating young Europeans. Similarities and differences between the EU member states and the Phare countries, in: *Statistics in focus*, theme 3 – 14/2000.

Fagerberg, J. and Verspagen, B. (1996), Heading for Divergence? Regional Growth in Europe Reconsidered, in: *Journal of Common Market Studies*, 34(3), 431-448.

Fagerberg, J., Verspagen, B. and Caniels, M. (1997), Technology, Growth and Unemployment across European Regions, in: *Regional Studies*, 31(5), 457-466.

Falcetti, E., Raiser, M. and Sanfey, P. (2002), Defying the Odds: Initial Conditions, Reforms, and Growth in the First Decade of Transition, in: Journal of Comparative Economics, 30(2), 229-250.

Fidrmuc, J. (2000), Liberalization, Democracy and Economic Performance during Transition, ZEI Economic Policy Papers, no. B05-2000, Bonn: Centre for European Integration Studies.

Fingleton, B. (2001), Theoretical economic geography and spatial econometrics: dynamic perspectives, in: Journal of Economic Geography, 1, 201-225

Fischer, S., Sahay, R. and Vegh, C.A. (1998), How Far is Eastern Europe from Brussels? IMF Working Paper, no. 98/53, Washington: International Monetary Fund.

Fosfuri, A., Motta, M. and Ronde, T. (2001), Foreign Direct Investment and Spillovers through Workers' Mobility, in: Journal of International Economics, 53(1), 205-222.

Funke, M. and Niebuhr, A. (2000), Spatial R&D spillovers and economic growth – Evidence from West Germany, HWWA Discussion Paper, no. 98, Hamburg, Hamburgisches Weltwirtschafts-Archiv.

Gallup, J.L., Sachs, J.D. and Mellinger, A.D. (1998), Geography and Economic Development, NBER Working Paper, no. 6849, Cambridge, MA: National Bureau of Economic Research.

Havrylyshyn, O. and van Rooden, R. (2000), Institutions Matter in Transition, but so do Policies, IMF Policy Working Paper, no. 00/70, Washington: International Monetary Fund.

Hernandez Cata, E (1997), Liberalization and the Behavior of Output During the Transition From Plan to Market, *IMF Working Paper*, no. 97/53, Washington: International Monetary Fund.

Hunya, G. (2002), Recent Impacts of Foreign Direct Investment on Growth and Restructuring in Central European Transition Countries, *WIIW Research Report*, no. 284, Vienna: WIIW.

Jones, C.I. (1995), R&D-Based Models of Economic Growth, in: *Journal of Political Economy*, 103(4), 759-784.

Kelejian, H. and Prucha, I. (1998), A generalized two-stage least squares procedure for estimating a spatial autoregressive model with autoregressive disturbances, in: *Journal of Real State Finance and Economics*, 17, 99-121.

Keune, M. (2000), Employment problems and regional differences in Central and Eastern Europe: the need for local development initiatives, in: *Integration and Transition in Europe*, Petrakos, G., Maier, G. and Gorzelak, G. (eds.). Routledge.

Kinoshita, Y. (2000), R&D and Technology Spillovers via FDI: Innovation and Absorptive Capacity, *William Davidson Institute Working Paper*, no. 349.

Klazar, S., Sedmihradsky, M. and Vancurova, A. (2001), Returns of Education in the Czech Republic, in: *International Tax and Public Finance*, 8(4), 609-620.

Kosfeld, R., Eckey, H.F. and Creger, C. (2002), Regional Convergence in Unified Germany: A Spatial Econometric Perspective, *Volkswirtschaftliche Diskussionsbeiträge*, no. 41/02, Universität Kassel.

Krugman, P. (1991), Increasing Returns and Economic Geography, in: *Journal of Political Economy*, 99(3), 483-99.

Levine, R. and Zervos, S. (1998), Stock Markets, Banks and Economic Growth, in: *American Economic Review*, 88(3), 537-558.

Lodde, S. (2000), Education and Growth: Some Disaggregate Evidence from the Italian Regions, in: *International Review of Economics and Business*, 47(2), 267-293.

Lucas, R.E. (1988), On the mechanics of economic development, in: *Journal of Monetary Economics*, 22(1), 3-42.

Mankiw, G., Romer, D. and Weil, D. (1992), A contribution to the empirics of economic growth, in: *Quarterly Journal of Economics*, 107, 407-437.

Markusen, J. R and Venables, A. J. (1999), Foreign Direct Investment as a Catalyst for Industrial Development, in: *European Economic Review*, 43(2), 335-356.

Nelson, R. and Phelps, E. (1966), Investment in humans, technological diffusion, and economic growth, in: *American Economic Review*, Papers and Proceedings, 61: 69-75

Niebuhr, A. (2001), Convergence and the effects of spatial interaction, *Jahrbuch für Regionalwissenschaft*, 21, 113-133.

Paci, R. and Pigliaru, F. (2001), Technological diffusion, spatial spillovers and regional convergence in Europe, *CRENoS Working Paper*, no. 01/01, University of Cagliari.

Paci, R. and Usai, S. (2000), Externalities, knowledge spillovers and the spatial distribution of innovation, in: *GeoJournal*, 49(4), 381-390.

Paci, R., Pigliaru, F. and Pugno, M. (2001), Disparities In Economic Growth And Unemployment Across The European Regions: A Sectoral Perspective, *CRENoS Working Paper*, no. 01/3, University of Cagliari.

Piazolo, D. (1999), Growth Effects of Institutional Change and European Integration, in: *Economic Systems*, 23(4), 305-330.

Pritchett, L. (1996), Where has all the education gone? *World Bank Working Papers*, no. 1581.

Resmini, L. (2000), The Determinants of Foreign Direct Investment in the CEECs: New Evidence from Sectoral Patterns. In: Economics of Transition, 8(3), 665-689.

Resmini, L. (2002), Specialization and Growth Patterns in Border Regions of Accession Countries, *ZEI Working Paper*, no. B17-2002, Bonn: Centre for European Integration studies.

Rey, S. and Montouri, B. (1999), US regional income convergence: A spatial econometric perspective. In: *Regional Studies*, 33(2), 145-156.

Romer, P. (1990), Endogenous technological change, in: *Journal of Political Economy*, 98(5), 71-102.

Sachs, J.D. and Warner, A. (1995), Economic convergence and economic policies, *NBER Working Paper*, no. 5039, Cambridge, MA: National Bureau of Economic Research.

Sala-i-Martin, X. (1997), I Just Ran Two Million Regressions, in: *American Economic Review*, 87(2), 178-183.

Schürmann, C. and Talaat, A. (2000), *Towards a European Peripherality Index. Final Report*, Report for General Directorate XVI Regional Policy of the European Commission, Dortmund: IRPUD.

Temple, J. (1999), The New Growth Evidence, in: *Journal of Economic Literature*, 37(1), 112-156.

Tondl, G. (2001), *Convergence after divergence? Regional growth in Europe*, Springer, Wien, Heidelberg, New York: Springer.

Traistaru, I. and Wolff, G.B. (2002), Regional Specialization and Employment Dynamics in Transition Countries, *ZEI Working Paper*, no. B18-2002, Bonn: Centre for European Integration Studies.

Traistaru, I., Nijkamp, P. and Longhi, S. (2002), Regional Specialization and Concentration of Industrial Activity in Accession Countries, *ZEI Working Paper*, no. B16-2002, Bonn: Centre for European Integration Studies.

van Pottelsberghe de la Potterie, B. and Lichtenberg, F. (2001), Does Foreign Direct Investment Transfer Technology across Borders? In: *Review of Economics and Statistics*, 83(3), 490-497.

Vanhoudt, P., Matha, T. and Smid, B. (2000), How Productive Are Capital Investments in Europe? EIB Papers, 5(2), 81-106.

WIIW (2002), Countries in Transition 2002, *WIIW Handbook of Statistics*, Vienna: WIIW.

APPENDIX

EAST RegStat
Data and definitions

36 NUTS II level regions from
Czech Republic, Slovakia, Hungary, Poland, Slovenia, time period 1995-2000

	DEFINITION	SOURCE
Gross Value Added	nominal and real GVA in Euro, at 1995 prices and 1995 exchange rates.	1995-1999 EUROSTAT. 2000 GUS, SURS, CSU, KSH and INFOSTAT.
Population	Total population.	CZ, HU, SI: 1995-1999 EUROSTAT, 2000 extrapolation. PL: 1995, 1998-1999 EUROSTAT, 1996 and 2000 GUS. SK: 1996-1999 EUROSTAT, 1995, 2000 INFOSTAT.
Employment	Total employment. Number of persons employed.	CZ and HU: EUROSTAT. PL: GUS. SI: SURS. SK: 1997-2000 INFOSTAT, 1995-1996 extrapolation based on GDP trend.
R&D expenditures	Total expenditures for research and development in business sector, government sector and higher education sector.	CZ: 1995-1997 EUROSTAT, 1998-2000 extrapolation. HU: KSH. PL: GUS. SI: EUROSTAT. SK: 1995-1997 EUROSTAT, 1998-2000 INFOSTAT.
R&D employment	Total employment in research and development in business sector, government sector and higher education sector.	CZ: 1995-1997 EUROSTAT, 1998-2000 extrapolation. HU: KSH. PL: GUS. SI: EUROSTAT. SK: 1995-1997 EUROSTAT, 1998-2000 INFOSTAT.
Gross Fixed Capital Formation	Gross fixed capital formation in Euro, at 1995 prices and 1995 exchange rates.	CZ: 1995-1999 EUROSTAT, 2000 allocation of country investment. HU: KSH. PL: 1998-1999 EUROSTAT, 1995-1997 and 2000 extrapolation, allocation of country investment. SI: SURS. SK: 1995-1999 EUROSTAT, 2000 from country data.

Foreign Direct Investment	Stock of foreign direct investment in Euro, at 1995 prices and 1995 exchange rates.	CZ: 1998-2000 CNB, 1995-1997 extrapolation based on allocation of country FDI stock. HU: calculated using regional data from KSH and allocation of country FDI stock. PL: calculated, based on regional FDI flows and allocation of country FDI stock. SI: WIIW. SK: 1996-2000 NBS, 1995 calculated from country FDI stock.
Education	Educational attainment. Number of persons who have completed secondary and higher level education. Secondary level education includes ISCED-97 sectors 3 and 4. Entrance is at age 15-16 after compulsory school. It comprises general education preparing for university entrance, vocational schools and also upper secondary level apprenticeship programmes of the dual system in Germany. Higher level education corresponds to ISCED-97 sectors 5 and 6. Sector 5 includes short degrees like bachelor (UK), Fachhochschule (D) and laurea breve (I), but also longer higher education programmes like Diplom (D) and master (UK). Education in section 6 awards an advanced research qualification, like PhD programmes and doctoral studies. (See OECD, education at a glance 2002, Paris, OECD)	EUROSTAT Labour Force Survey for CZ: 1998-2000, HU: 1997-2000, PL: 1998-2000, SI: 1996-2000, SK: 1999-2000. Other years extrapolation.
Market access	Market access indicator: The *market size* and the *distance* of the region of destination are taken into account. Market size is represented by regional population or GDP. Distance corresponds to travel time between two regions by different modes of transport.	Institute for Spatial Planning (IRPUD), University of Dortmund. For details see: Schürmann, C., Talaat, A. (2000): *Towards a European Peripherality Index. Final Report*. Report for Directorate General XVI Regional Policy of the European Commission. Dortmund, IRPUD.

NOTES: CZ - Czech Republic, HU - Hungary, PL - Poland, SI - Slovenia, SK - Slovak Republic;

Data sources: CNB - Czech National Bank, CSU - Czech Statistical Office, EUROSTAT – Statistical Office of the EC, GUS - Polish Official Statistics, INFOSTAT Institute of Informatics and Statistics Slovakia, KSH - Hungarian Central Statistical Office, NBS - National Bank of Slovakia, SURS - Statistical Office of the Republic of Slovenia, WIIW - Vienna Institute for International Economic Studies.

List of variables used in the estimations

Δy	average growth of real GVA per capita, 1995-2000, in per cent
Δpart	average growth of participation rate (employment / population), 1995-2000, in per cent
inv	average investment rate (investment / GVA), 1996-2000, in per cent
RD_e	R&D expenditures in per cent of GVA, average 1996-2000
hc_m	per cent of population (all ages) with secondary educational attainment in total population, average 1996-2000
hc_h	per cent of population (all ages) with higher educational attainment in total population, average 1996-2000
GAP	productivity gap to EU average in 1995. GAP_i=($productivity_{EU}$ - $productivity_i$)/$productivity_i$, whereby *i* indicates the region
*GAP*hc_h*	interaction term GAP and higher level educational attainment
*GAP*hc_m*	interaction term GAP and secondary level educaitonal attainment
FDI_s	stock of FDI in per cent of GVA, average 1996-2000
*FDI_s*hc_m*	interaction term FDI and secondary educational attainment rate
*FDI_s*hc_h*	interaction term FDI and higher level education
ACCESS	market access indicator to EU regions, using GDP as measure for market size, ranges from 0-100, 100 = best access.
EU border	Dummy variable for regions located at the border with the EU.
DCZ	Dummy variable for Czech regions.

Cross correlations between variables

	dt_y	*i*	*dt_PART*	*hc_m*	*hc_h*	*RD_e*	*RD_ls*	*FDI_s*	*FDI_s*hc_h*
dt_y	1.00	0.00	0.41	-0.47	0.38	0.06	0.23	0.15	0.24
i	0.00	1.00	-0.27	0.45	0.66	0.54	0.70	0.36	0.47
dt_PART	0.41	-0.27	1.00	-0.51	0.12	-0.14	0.00	0.01	0.01
hc_m	-0.47	0.45	-0.51	1.00	0.04	0.45	0.17	0.01	0.05
hc_h	0.38	0.66	0.12	0.04	1.00	0.49	0.88	0.61	0.82
RD_e	0.06	0.54	-0.14	0.45	0.49	1.00	0.68	0.44	0.49
RD_ls	0.23	0.70	0.00	0.17	0.88	0.68	1.00	0.47	0.71
FDI_s	0.15	0.36	0.01	0.01	0.61	0.44	0.47	1.00	0.91
*FDI_s*hc_h*	0.24	0.47	0.01	0.05	0.82	0.49	0.71	0.91	1.00
GAP	-0.14	-0.04	0.03	-0.25	-0.35	-0.39	-0.39	-0.20	-0.31
ln_GAP	-0.25	-0.04	0.01	-0.14	-0.39	-0.39	-0.42	-0.24	-0.35
*ln_GAP*hc_h*	0.20	0.71	0.13	-0.03	0.75	0.20	0.62	0.36	0.51
*ln_GAP*hc_m*	-0.51	0.26	-0.32	0.51	-0.32	-0.04	-0.26	-0.20	-0.28
EU_Border	-0.10	0.33	-0.16	0.20	0.18	-0.13	0.02	0.02	0.00
capital_area	0.32	0.65	-0.03	0.19	0.76	0.81	0.75	0.61	0.70
EU_access	-0.40	0.58	-0.48	0.67	0.26	0.41	0.23	0.39	0.33

Continuation: Cross correlations between variables.

	GAP	*ln_GAP*	*ln_GAP*hc_h*	*ln_GAP*hc_m*	*EU_Border*	*capital_area*	*EU_access*
dt_y	-0.14	-0.25	0.20	-0.51	-0.10	0.32	-0.40
i	-0.04	-0.04	0.71	0.26	0.33	0.65	0.58
dt_PART	0.03	0.01	0.13	-0.32	-0.16	-0.03	-0.48
hc_m	-0.25	-0.14	-0.03	0.51	0.20	0.19	0.67
hc_h	-0.35	-0.39	0.75	-0.32	0.18	0.76	0.26
RD_e	-0.39	-0.39	0.20	-0.04	-0.13	0.81	0.41
RD_ls	-0.39	-0.42	0.62	-0.26	0.02	0.75	0.23
FDI_s	-0.20	-0.24	0.36	-0.20	0.02	0.61	0.39
*FDI_s*hc_h*	-0.31	-0.35	0.51	-0.28	0.00	0.70	0.33
GAP	1.00	0.96	0.27	0.67	-0.04	-0.37	-0.16
ln_GAP	0.96	1.00	0.28	0.78	-0.02	-0.47	-0.10
*ln_GAP*hc_h*	0.27	0.28	1.00	0.21	0.22	0.39	0.19
*ln_GAP*hc_m*	0.67	0.78	0.21	1.00	0.12	-0.27	0.34
EU_Border	-0.04	-0.02	0.22	0.12	1.00	0.09	0.54
capital_area	-0.37	-0.47	0.39	-0.27	0.09	1.00	0.39
EU_access	-0.16	-0.10	0.19	0.34	0.54	0.39	1.00

THE ROLE OF MERCOSUR AND THE EUROPEAN UNION IN THE FORMATION OF COMPETITION POLICY IN ARGENTINA AND TURKEY

Ensar Yilmaz
Zeynep Kaplan

Faculty of Economics and Business Administration
Yildiz Technical University

1. Introduction

The role of regional integration process in the forming of competition policy has a crucial importance for two major reasons; first it strengthens the economic integration among the member states; second it provides legal and administrative protection to the economic actors within the region.

Both Argentina and Turkey are at the early stage of developing an effective competition policy. During the last decade, competition policy has emerged as a major policy issue in both countries. This paper examines the current status of Turkey's and Argentina's competition policies, their efficiency, institutional design and enforcement mechanisms. However, both countries' short experience in the shaping of an efficient enforcement system demonstrates the importance and the complexity of the issue.

The purpose of this paper is to analyse the experiences of Turkey and Argentina in designing competition policy. The paper consists of three sections. In the first section of the paper, scope, objectives and instruments of competition policy have been identified. In the second section, the development and implementation of the competition policy within the Mercosur and Argentina has been evaluated. In the last section, the evaluation of Turkish competition framework and the impact of the Customs Union Agreement on Turkish competition policy has been examined.

2. Competition Policy: Conceptual Framework

2.1. A Definition

Competition policy is not a new issue and it has been on the agenda of many developing countries. In the international context, major developments that have taken place such as; globalisation of the world economy, reduction or elimination of trade barriers and the rapid technological progress. And all these developments have led the attention drawn towards the enforcement of competition rules for the efficient use of resources in the international level. "Competition policy, also known as "antitrust policy," is defined as the body of laws and regulations governing business practices (horizontal or vertical agreements between enterprises, abuses of dominant positions, monopolization, mergers and acquisitions). Broader definitions of competition policy exist in some countries, which include all government policies which affect competition such as aids and subsidies to enterprises, regulation of prices and output of monopolies, and demonopolization" (OECD, 1994:8).

Governments intervene in the operation of a market based economy for various reasons. The primary rationale for government intervention through competition policy is a) to respond to market failures, b) to limit abuses of market power, and c) to improve economic efficiency. Competition policy is seen as an important policy instrument for governments to regulate the private sector. Both at the national and international level countries are being asked to reform their competition policy and build effective institutions. Many developed countries, especially OECD countries, were very quick to implement competition policy and enforce competition laws to maintain and ensure competition in their markets. Diverging competition policies and enforcement methods result in enforcement and administrative costs for private sector as well as governments. Greater convergence in the field of competition contributes primarily to international economic efficiency particularly by paving the way for international flows of goods, services, capital and technology.

2.2. The Objectives of Competition Policy

There is a general consensus that the primary purpose of competition policy is to protect and preserve competition as the most appropriate means of ensuring the efficient allocation of resources in free market economies by lower consumer prices, higher quality products and better product choice.

The objectives of competition policy have been subject to various controversies. Within this concept, there are four objectives of competition policy that may be identified as (Neumann, 2001:1);

a) establishing a competitive order as an end in itself to safeguard economic freedom, b) maintaining a competitive order to foster economic efficiency and technological and economic progress, c) providing for a level playing field of fair competition, which implies prohibition of deceptive and fraudulent practices, threat, exortion and blackmail as well as unfair advantages through government subsidies, d) maintaining a decentralized structure of supply because small and medium-sized enterprises are considered as the backcone of a democratic society.

The basic objective of competition is the achievement of economic efficiency. There are a number of other broader objectives such as: a) prevention of abuse of economic power, b) freedom of trade, freedom of choice and access to markets, c) reducing the adverse effects of government intervention in the marketplace, d) facilitating economic liberalisation, including privatisation, deregulation, and e) promoting trade and integration within the regional economic groups. All these objectives have vital importance for the establishment of modern competition policies, laws and institutions. In order to achieve these objectives competition policies and regulations need to be applied uniformly and internationally throughout the economy with a minimum of exemptions.

There are several instruments of competion policy. The instruments of competition policy prohibit, penalize and deter anti-competitive practices and help to remove obstacles to competition. Competition policy embodies various kinds of instruments that are conventionally classified as: the control of mergers, the restrictive agreements, state aids and abuse of dominance.

Control of mergers: A merger arises when two or more firms join to become single entity. Most countries with competition policies have some form of merger control. The rationale for merger control is to enable competition authorities to regulate changes in market structure and to prevent firms from gaining market power than to attempt to control market power once it exists. Although most mergers pose little or no threat to competition within a marketplace, some mergers would seriously harm competition by significantly increasing the probability of exercising market power.

Restrictive agreements: Restrictive agreements relate to agreements, between firms, which prevent competition, or restrict competition, or in some way distort competition within a market. There are two types of agreements that may raise concerns of anti-competitive conduct; horizontal and vertical agreements. A horizontal merger involves the acquisition of merger with an actual or possible competitor. A vertical merger, however, involves the acquisition of merger with a supplier of an input or a customer. Horizontal agreements should be distinguished from the vertical agreements that it govern the interface between supplier and customers. These agreements may distort resource allocation, encourage inefficiency and restrict the competitors' ability to compete independently within a market.

State aids: A crucial element of consideration in any competition framework relates to state aids. State aid is a sort of state intervention used to promote a certain economic activity. State aids imply that specific economic sectors, practices or regions are treated more favourably than the others. State aid measures can be a serious barrier to competition since government restraints on competition damages economic growth and industrial competitiveness.

Abuse of Dominance: Dominance is a position of considerable economic power held for a period of time by a firm over customers and suppliers in a market. More specifically, it is the ability of a firm to restrict output and thus raise prices above the level that would prevail in a competitive market, without existing rivals or new entrants in due time taking away its customers (Faul and Nikpay, 2000:122). “Two cases of abusing market power are to be distinguished according to German law, namely the exploitation of buyers or sellers and interference with the freedom of competitiors. Exploitation is assumend to exist if a dominant firm or a cartel charges prices in excess of those which under effective competition are likely to obtain. On the other hand, interference with the freedom of competitors occurs if a dominat firm or a cartel prejudices the opportunities of competitors substantially and without sufficient justification.” (Neumann, 2001:134).

2.3. Regional Integration and Competition Policy

At the regional level, many regional integration arrangements such as European Union (EU) and Mercosur[28] have included provisions or protocols concerning competition policy in their founding agreements to improve regional economic efficiency and to introduce some degree

[28] “Mercosur” is the Spanish abbreviation for “Mercado Común del Sur” (Southern Common Market).

of fairness in trade between member countries.[29] Harmonisation of competition policies within the region has proven to be a crucial element of integration. At the regional level, harmonization of competition policies is a necessary step for integration to boost the efficiency gains associated with market enlargement. Initiatives taken in competition issues not only strengthen economic integration among the member states, but also provide legal and administrative protection to the economic actors within the region. The importance of applying the rules and regulations related to competition makes it possible to integrate the regional group effectively, to reinforce the competitive environment and to restrain the anti-competitive practices that affect the trade between member states.

According to de Araujo (2001b) initiatives in the field of competition policy play an important role in regional trade agreements for three main reasons. First, such provisions stimulate the coherence of domestic policies, as the goals of promoting efficiency and consumer welfare become priority topics on the negotiating agenda. Second, they provide the conditions for a balanced treatment of foreign direct investment, whereby the discussion about market access and other investor's rights is complemented by a set of mechanisms for controlling competitive business practices. Third, they establish the institutional background for regulatory reform of monopolistic industries, particularly in the area of public services, thus facilitating trade liberalization in this area.

3. Mercosur and the Development of Competition Policy in Argentina

3.1. The Development of a Competition Policy in Mercosur

Regional integration in Latin America began with a series of bilateral economic arrangements that had been taking place between Argentina and Brazil in the late 1980s and 1990s with the end of military dictatorships. The main goal was to seek for a new level of integration among the countries to secure their fragile democratic regimes where it was not able to take fundamental regulatory reforms. As a consequence, Argentina and Brazil recognized the importance of forming a regional economic cooperation as a crucial element of the process of domestic economic reforms and signed the Program for Integration and Economic Cooperation in 1986. Later, in 1988, Brazil and Argentina signed the Treaty for Integration, Cooperation and Development that based on the formation of a common market within ten years, with the gradual elimination of tariff and non-tariff barriers and coordination of the macroeconomic policies of both states. To supplement former agreements, in 1990, with the Act of Buenos Aires signed by Brazil and Argentina, it was decided to creating a common market that came into effect in 1995.

Mercosur, which is the result of an effective and strategic restructuring of the Brazilian-Argentina relations, was established with the Treaty of Asuncion on March, 26 1991 among Argentina, Brazil, Uruguay, and Paraguay. Chile (1996), Bolivia (1997) and Peru (2003) also signed association agreements with Mercosur. Mercosur was firstly established as a free trade area, implementing a process of trade liberalization among the member states. The Treaty of

[29] Some other regional integration arrangements such as North American Free Trade Agreement (NAFTA), Common Market for the Eastern and Southern Africa (COMESA) and Andean Pact have also included provisions concerning competition policy in their agreements.

Ouro Preto[30] (1994) marked the start of attempts to realize a common market and added several important events contributed to strengthen Mercosur. Treaty also established an institutional framework for Mercosur, which was inspired by the EU model[31]. The free movement of goods, persons, services and capital, the elimination of customs tariffs and non-tariff barriers, the creation of a common external tariff against third countries and the adoption of a common trade policy was amended by the Treaty establishing the "common market" to go into force in January 1995.

Harmonisation of competition policies within the region is a crucial instrument for eliminating barriers to the development of the common market. The Treaty of Asuncion also underlined the importance of competition as a fundamental feature to ensure the equitable distribution of the benefits of regional integration to the member states and to protect the competition process in the region. In fact, in a customs union, harmonization of competition policies is a main concern for reinforcement of the integration process. In December 1994, during its meeting, the Mercosur Trade Council approved a document titled "Basic Elements of the Defense of Competition in Mercosur" which was designed to coordinate national legislation in the field of competition and to prevent anticompetitive actions within the region. At its second meeting, Mercosur Trade Council approved a draft "Protocol for the Defense of Competition within Mercosur" which has similar characteristics with the Brazilian law. An important development took place in December 1996, when Mercosur countries signed the final Protocol for the Defense of Competition –the so-called Fortaleza Protocol- that established an ambitious set of guidelines toward a common competition policy in the region. The purpose of the Protocol for the Defense of Competition is the defense of competition in the framework of the Mercosur. The vital elements of Fortaleza Protocol are (Oliveria, 2000:37);

a) Adoption of anti-competitive practices,

b) The creation of specific procedures to investigate, adjudicate and sanction anticompetitive practices,

c) Incorporation of a timetable on the implementation of merger control,

d) Promotion of cooperation among national competition authorities.

The Fortaleza Protocol implies that a) all member countries must have an autonomous competition agency, b) the national law will cover the whole economy, c) the competition authority will be strong enough to challenge other public policies whenever necessary, and d) the member countries will share a common view about the interplay between competition policy and other governmental actions (de Araujo, 2001b:234). "Moreover, the goals of the Fortaleza Protocol are threefold. First, it provides mechanisms to control firms' anticompetitive practices with Mercosur competition policy dimension. Second, it calls for convergent domestic laws to ensure similar conditions of competition and independence among firms regarding the formation of prices and other market variables. Third, it provides

---

[30] Six different inter-governmental institutions have been established with the Treaty of Asuncion and The Treaty Ouro Preto namely; the Council, the Commerce Commission, the Common Market Group, the Joint Parliamentary Commission, the Forum and the Secretariat.

[31] One of the major characteristics of Mercosur is that it functions on the basis of a 100% intergovernmental structure and rejects any notion of supranationality.

an agenda for surveying public policies that distort competition conditions and affect trade among the member countries" (de Araujo, 2001b:234-235).

Mercosur countries took another step in the field of competition in December 2002 with the signing of the Regulation on Application of the Competition Protocol in Mercosur. This regulation established the Mercosur Competition Committee (CDC), which is responsible for enforcing the Fortaleza Protocol, to allocate the competences and to examine anticompetitive actions within the region. It also established to promote cooperation and coordination between the national competition authorities of the member states. During 2003, Mercosur countries stepped forward in building a competition policy framework for the region, by approving the Protocol for the Defense of Competition. In July 2004 Mercosur countries approved the Joint Antitrust Cooperation Agreement to encourage cooperation between member countries regarding the enforcement of antitrust laws and regulations, as well as technical cooperation among the antitrust authorities. Joint Antitrust Cooperation Agreement points out the increasing importance of competition issues in the member states.

Over the last years, Mercosur countries have created or reformed their competition policy frameworks. Indeed, Fortaleza Protocol and the following developments initiated a new phase in the field of competition policy within the Mercosur. "Within Mercosur competition policy is viewed in a broader context which include the whole range of government policies that effect competition at both local and national level, including trade liberalization instruments (anti-dumping and countervailing duty measures), foreign investment regulation, property rights protection both with respect to licensing restrictions and levels of foreign and domestic investment and bankruptcy of public and private enterprises" (Nogueira, 1998:30). However, Mercosur countries faced a few challenges and the effectiveness has been hampered because of the limiting degree of heterogeneity in national legislations within the region. Firstly, there had been a lack of competition culture in these countries. Paraguay and Uruguay have no competition law regimes, while in Argentina and Brazil, although such legislation do exist, their concept, structure and purposes differ from each other. In other words, among the member states only Brazil and Argentina have adequate competition laws and regulations and experience in enforcing legal decisions. Continuing the process of development in competition issues triggers interest towards the formation of an effective competition policy also in Paraguay and Uruguay. Furthermore, a major difficulty arises from the lack of both the transparency of the decision-making process and the supranational authority where the competition institutions have an intergovernmental nature. In this context, formation of an efficient and independent supranational competition authority has a vital importance. "Apart from these problems, the lack of rules on merger control, minimum requirements for notification of mergers and state aids also exists. Moreover, some problems of an institutional nature persists, preventing effective implementation of the existing rules and regulations" (Andrade, 2003:12).

3.2. Argentina's Competition Policy

The Argentina economy has undergone a remarkable change since the late 1980s. Prior to late 1980s, Argentina had a long history of protection, administrative control regulations and intervention of public sector where government owned or controlled many different enterprises. These companies represented a large portion of the Argentine economy that made competition policies useless. This situation has changed drastically when Menem government came into power in 1989 and made significant structural reforms. As a result of structural reforms that begun in the late 1980s a new approach towards competition policies have aroused. Indeed, the primary objective behind these structural reforms was to introduce competitive forces in the marketplace.

Although competition policy has been on the agenda at the national level since 1919, the initiatives for forming a modern competition policy started in 1980s with the enforcement of Competition Act 22.262 and the creation of National Commission for Competition Defense (CNDC). During this period, the effectiveness of Argentinian competition policy has been hampered for a number of reasons (Rowat et al.,1997):

a) lack of 'per se' prohibitions against price-fixing, bid-rigging, etc.;

b) lack of provisisons for mergers and acquisitions including as part of the privatisation process; c) a shortage of staff and budgetary resources in the Competition Commission;

d) the lack of indepence of the Competitition Commission;

e) and the lack of understanding and support by the public as well as the business community on the merits of competition policy all of which should be rectified.

The Defense of Competition Act (law 25,156), came into force on September 29th, 1999 and abolished the existing Competition Law in force since August 1980 (law 22,262). The new law regulates, using an approach similar to that used in the law it superseded, the agreements and practices restricting competition and market access, as well as the abuse of a position of dominance and created a new independent enforcement body known as the National Tribunal for the Defense of Competition (TNDC)[32], with more comprehensive competences than its predecessor, the CNDC to enforce the prohibitions of the law. The Law has clearly defined two different objectives (http://www.bomchil.com):

a) the prosecution of prohibited practices, virtually following in the footsteps of Law 22,262, and

b) the prior notification of certain economic concentrations, very much similar to the EU merger control regime.

The objective of Argentinean competition policy is to ensure the proper functioning of the markets, guarantee free competition, and punish behaviour that lowers, restricts, or distorts competition or takes improper advantage of a market position to the detriment of the public interest. Argentinean competition policy applies to any individuals or legal entities performing economic activities in Argentina.

Merger control regime was introduced in late 1999 for the first time in Argentina. "Since then, especially during the 2000 and 2001 the Argentinean competition authoroties were almost completely devoted to merger control issues. Some 232 transactions were reported during that period, of which the great majority were foreign-to-foreign mergers" (Toom, 2004:3). "During 2003 CNDC investigated possible anticompetitive effects of 32 mergers and aquisitions notiffied on that year and on the second semester of the previous one. With regards to most of them CNDC did not expressed any concern and so were cleared. It also

[32] The formation of the TNDC is long overdue. Until then, issues regarding competition policy and law are currently under the control of CNDC.

should be noticed that during 2003, CNDC has imposed four fines due to out-of term notification of mergers and acquisitions, two in the passenger air-transport industry, one in health insurance sector and the last one in gasoline station sector" (OECD, 2004:2-3).

Table 1: Resulting Operations of Concentration during the Period September 1999-March 2001 and April-December 2001

Sector	Number of Cases	Decision of the Commission			Nature			
		Authorized	Conditional	Non-authorized	H	V	H-V	C
Sept.1999-March 2001	180	173	6	1	154	16	10	
April-Dec. 2001	43	40	3		22	3	11	7

Source: http://www.mecon.gov.ar/cndc/memoria00/cap3.pdf p.48, 73

(H: Horizontal, V: Vertical, H-V: Horizontal-Vertical, C: Conglomerate)

3.3. The Regulatory Body in Argentina: National Commission for Competition Defense

Since 1980's the Argentinian Competition Law has been enforced by the CNDC. CNDC is created under the Secretariat of State for Commerce and International Economic Negotiations. It consists of one president, and four members, appointed by the Minister of the Economy. CNDC has the powers to (www.sice.oas.org): a) carry out studies relative to competition, structure and size of markets, b) require from National, Provincial or Municipal authorities the information deemed necessary, c) summon the presumed liable subjects and witnesses, take testimonies and perform confrontations, d) perform the necessary expert inspection to analyze books, documents, trade papers, and other elements relevant to the survey, control inventories, verify sources and costs of raw materials and other goods, e) request opinions and reports from persons or private entities about the investigated behaviors, existing practices in these matters, and other issues of interest related to the investigation, f) hold hearings with the involvement of plaintiffs, complainants, presumed liable subjects, witnesses, and experts, g) request the freezing of goods from the corresponding Judge, h) decide, at any stage of the proceedings, as a preventive measure, that physical persons involved, be it directly or because of their involvement or cooperation in other acts committed by persons of an ideal existence, may not leave the country without the judge's prior authorization. The decision might be appealed before the courts indicated in Article 27, giving the authorization relative to and only with a restitution effect.

Decisions taken by the CNDC are sent to the Secretariat of Technical Coordination of the Ministry of Economy and Production. Recently, the CNDC does not have budgetary autonomy due to lack of its ability to generate its own financial resources. The financial resources assigned to CNDC annually come from the budget of the Ministry of Economy and Production.

4. European Union and the Development of Competition Policy in Turkey

4.1. The Treaty of Rome

Competition policy has been a crucial element of the European integration process and regulations concerning competition dating back to the establishment of the Community. The main objective of the EU has been laid down in the Treaty of Rome as "the creation of a common market between the member states" and "the establishment of a system that would ensure that competition is not distorted in the internal market". Within this framework, the Treaty of Rome included a separate section entitled "Competition Policy" and basic provisions related to competition policy of the EU have been provided between the Articles 85-94 of the Treaty of Rome. These articles define the rules of competition with the aim of maintaining the free movement of goods and services and forming an effective competitive environment. Indeed, the main goal of the provisions regarding competition issues was the creation of a common market among the member states. Briefly, there are two fundamental objectives that lie at the heart of EU competition policy: a) the promotion of European integration and b) the promotion and maintenance of competitive markets within the Union. With the establishment of the Community in 1958, member countries started to amend their own national competition laws parallel to the provisions provided in the Treaty. Principally, the member countries must cooperate fully with the EU competition *acquis* that covers control of mergers and state aid policies. Moreover, all recent bilateral free trade agreements concluded by the EU have included provisions on competition law and policy, although they vary in scope depending on the contexts of signatory countries; one of them being Turkey.

4.2. Customs Union Agreement and Steps toward a Competition Policy in Turkey

Relations between Turkey and the EU goes back to a long history. Turkey applied for an association agreement with the Community in 1959, only one year after its establishment. An association established between the European Economic Community and Turkey with the signing of the Ankara Agreement in 1963. Ankara Agreement paved the way for Turkey's full membership in the EC through the establishment of a customs union in three phases (preparatory stage-transitional stage-final stage) and promoted the strengthening of trade and economic relations between the parties. Turkey officially applied for membership in 12 April 1987, but the EC stated that although Turkey was eligible for full membership, she had not yet fulfilled the necessary conditions. On 1.th January 1996, the Customs Union (CU) between the EU and Turkey came into effect, which has proved a critical stage in preparing Turkey for full EU membership. The Helsinki European Council of December 1999 declared that Turkey was accepted as a candidate for membership of the EU and it marked the beginning of a new era for both parties. As a consequence of the Helsinki European Council, the EU Commission prepared an Accession Partnership for Turkey and the Turkish Government adopted its National Program for the Adoption of the EU *acquis* in March 2001. Finally, the decision of the European Council meeting in December 2004 to start accession negotiations with Turkey in 3 October 2005 will give impetus to political and economic reform efforts to enable the adoption of the *acquis* in different areas.

Prior to 1980, Turkey was following an economic policy based on import substitution and strict foreign exchange rate controls. In the beginning of 1980s, Turkey has taken important steps in order to create an open and competitive macroeconomic structure by adopting the principles of free market economy. Trade liberalisation has been an important aspect of Turkey's economic policy and in this context capital movements were liberalised, trade barriers were eliminated, and economic reform started in order to decrease government intervention in the economy. Consequently, crucial steps were started in order to benefit of a fully functioning market economy. However, the 1980s' trade liberalisation was not followed by an extensive regulatory reform. Indeed, 'the dominance of the state in the economy continued in many aspects of economy' (OECD 2002c: 23). Moreover, 'the reforms also paid little attention to the fact that the governance of a well functioning market economy required well functioning institutions and an efficient and accountable system of government' (OECD 2002c: 23).

Trade liberalisation has intensified economic integration of Turkey with the rest of the world and led to the formation of CU agreement between Turkey and the EU, which has been in force since January 1, 1996. Turkey is the only country, which has established a customs union before becoming a full member of the EU. At this point, it should be stated that Turkey is a non-member country and so that it is not represented in the EU institutions and decision-making process. The CU agreement covers only trade in industrial and processed agricultural goods. Agricultural goods will be included in the CU following Turkey's adaptation to the EU's Common Agricultural Policy.

CU agreement has worked as a catalyst for Turkish institutional reforms in different areas. Indeed, with the entry into force of the CU agreement in 1996, Turkey abolished all duties and equivalent charges on imports of industrial goods and processed agricultural goods from the EU, started to implement the EU's Common External Tariff on imports of industrial goods from third countries. Turkey also harmonised its laws with EU legislation on trade, adopted competition law and intellectual property rights, established the Competition Board and the Patent Office.

4.3. Turkish Competition Policy

The development of an effective Turkish competition policy has been both supported by internal (the shift toward a more liberalised market economy) and external (the expansion of relations with the EU) forces. The CU agreement was essential in designing the Turkish competition law. Indeed, Turkish competition policy was designed on the basis of the EU model and the enactment of the Competition Law and the establishment of an independent Competition Authority have been mainly due to Turkey's obligation under the Ankara Agreement (1963) which required the harmonization of their laws and policies concerning competition. In fact, the Turkish Competition Law largely originates from the Rome Treaty Articles 85-94. 'Article 16 of the Ankara Agreement envisaged that principles referred to in the provisions of the Rome Treaty concerning competition, tax and the alignment of legislation be applicable within the association relationship' (TCA 2002:2-3). "The EU model was regarded as appropriate, partially because Turkey's relationship with the EU was regarded as an important vehicle for integration into the world economy" (OECD 2002a:9). Besides, the CU Agreement which entered into force between the EU and Turkey on January

1, 1996 has also played an important role for the design and enactment of Turkish Competition Law and the enactment of competition law was an obligation that Turkey had to develop during the CU negotiations.

The competition law (Law No.4054)[33] which entered into force on December 1994 established a Competition Authority that began its operations in November 1997, three years after the adoption of the law. Thus, although the first attempts to establish a national competition law started in the 1970s, competition policy became a priority in the mid 1990s with the singing of CU agreement. "The lag between enactment of Competition Law and its enforcement is to a large extent a reflection of the ambivalence on the part of both Turkey and EU regarding Turkey's accession to EU and the stop and go nature of the progress that has been made in that regard" (Mumcu and Zenginobuz, 2001:1).

Turkish Competition Policy mainly focuses on a wide range of activities that are listed under three headings (Mumcu and Zenginobuz 2001: 3):

a) Prevention of agreements and concerted practices that restrict competition,

b) Abuse of dominant position and monopolization,

c) Control of mergers and acquisitions.

The development of an effective and explicit competition policy has been an important and early achievement in Turkey's regulatory reform process and the process of reducing the government involvement in the economy was accompanied by the establishment of an adequate competition policy. Although competition policy and institutions are active, competition policy is not yet fully integrated into the general policy framework since many areas of the economy still remain under government control or ownership. The Competition Act's prohibition against anti-competitive agreements is slightly broader than the EU model (OECD, 2002b: 9). "Turkey's law adds an interesting innovation to deal with tacit collusion, a "concerted practice presumption" that is designed for oligopolistic markets in which proving over, subjective agreement is often difficult" (OECD, 2002c:70). Concepts about the abuse of dominance are also parallel with the EU regulations.

Turkey now has a comprehensive competition law and a credible institution (OECD 2002b: 29). "Generally, Turkey's anti-trust legislation appears to be largely modeled on the main principles of EU *acquis*. As regards secondary legislation, Turkey has introduced many of the block exemption regulations. Further alignment is necessary, in particular in view of the Community's evolving policies on vertical restraints and horizontal cooperation agreements" (European Commission, 2004:92). However, the 2004 Regular Report on Turkey's Progress Towards Accession assesses that 'major efforts concerning alignment in the adjustment of state monopolies and companies having exclusive and special rights are needed'. Moreover, 'promotion of competition should be taken into account during the privatisation process' (European Commission, 2003: 73). Further efforts concerning alignment in block exemptions, adjustment of state monopolies and companies having exclusive and special

[33] As stated in the Act on the Protection of Competition (The Act No. 4054) the purpose of the Competition Act is to prevent agreements, decisions and practices preventing, distorting or restricting competition in markets for goods and services, and the abuse of dominance by the undertakings dominant in the market, and to ensure the protection of competition by performing the necessary regulations and supervisions to this end. For further details about the act, see; http://www.rekabet.gov.tr/word/ekanun.doc

rights is needed (European Commission, 2003: 74). One of the most problematic areas remains in the monitoring of state aids. Currently, there is no supervisory authority deal with monitoring anti-competitive state aids. "The benefits of reducing direct state involvement in the economy could be compromised by a proliferation of indirect distortions and preferences that also distort competition. As a consequence, the need for a centralised control of anti-competitive state aids and setting up an independent authority in charge of monitoring state aid is widely recognized (European Commission, 2004:92, OECD, 2002c:78).

Table 2: Applications and Decisions 5.11.1997 - 31.12.2002

		1997	1998	1999	2000	2001	2002	Total
Violations of Competition	Applications	22	177	220	255	213	265	1152
	Decisions	9	44	306	262	211	217	1049
Mergers and Acquisitions	Applications	8	59	80	103	82	115	447
	Decisions	5	52	76	101	88	102	424
Exemptions & Negative Clearance	Applications	–	245	44	41	42	35	407
	Decisions	–	12	64	23	52	35	186
Total	Applications	30	481	344	399	337	415	2006
	Decisions	14	108	446	386	351	354	1659

Source: OECD Annual Report on Competition Policy in Turkey, 2002

4.4. The Regulatory Body in Turkey: The Competition Authority

The Competition Authority is mainly responsible for competition investigations, assessment of mergers and acquisitions, exemptions and negative clearance. The Competition Authority is politically and financially independent and can act against abuses of a dominant position and practices that lower or restrain competition. Indeed, according to Article 20 (Law No.4054), the Competition Authority has a public legal personality, and full administrative and financial autonomy and it is not subject to instructions and directives of any governmental body. The Competition Board which is the decision-making body of the Competition Authority is responsible for implementing the Act. Competition Board has been given extensive investigative powers. The Board is also empowered to determine and publish the categories of mergers and acquisitions that require prior notification to the board.

5. Conclusion

The core objective of competition policy is to preserve and protect the process of competition, not competing with a view to maximizing economic efficiency (both allocative and dynamic) by achieving efficient market outcomes in the form of lower consumer prices and better quality products. The purpose of the integration block is to establish a common market and the fundamental elements for it. The efficiency of competition will increase the efficiency of the common market. This paper has discussed the role of regional integration efforts on the formation of competition policy and institutions in Turkey and Argentina.

Mercosur is a customs union in formation. As in any customs union, harmonization of competition policies is a priority area for consolidation of the integration process. The Argentinean competition authority (CNDC), in this process, has successfully managed to gradually allocate more resources to prosecution of anticompetitive practices.

In accordance with the international practice and with the Argentine and Brazilian laws, the Mercosur Protocol adopts the effects doctrine claiming extraterritorial jurisdiction over anticompetitive conducts taking place abroad but producing effects inside the Mercosur. Overlapping jurisdiction may therefore occur not only between common and national laws inside the Mercosur, but also in relation to competition rules around the world and especially of the EC Treaty considering the close inter-regional trade relations.

In Turkey, the independent Competition Authority so far (since its establishment in 1997) has granted block exemptions for certain categories of agreements and published communiqués on mergers and acquisitions. Actions were taken recently against restrictive business practices.

State economic enterprises, despite all the efforts of privatization, still play a significant role in the economy and that Turkey's state aid system is generous. All of these aspects will change with effective implementation of competition policies. Over time, concentration ratios will decrease with privatization, the share of state economic enterprises in the Turkish economy will decline and Turkey's state aid system will become compatible with EU rules.

One consequence of the impact of EU on Turkish Competition Law is that it is largely compatible with the competition policies and rules of EU. There are, however, some exceptions, such as the silence of Turkish Competition on the extremely important issue of public undertakings. The evidence regarding application of the Law on public undertakings can be described at best as mixed. Moreover, liberalization, privatization, and regulation in a number of very important sectors are yet to be accomplished. The impact of Competition Law on the evolution of this process has certainly been less than satisfactory, and the role of Competition Authority less than clearly defined.

Obviously, Turkey's obligation under the Customs Union Agreement with EU concerns not only the adoption of a competition law that is compatible with that of EU, but also its effective enforcement.

The role and importance of competition law and policy in the both Argentina and Turkey is still evolving and it is too early to judge the overall effectiveness of the competition laws.

References

Andrade, M.C. (2003), Competition Law in Mercosur: Recent Developments, in: *Boletin Latinoamericano de Competencia*, No. 17, July.
URL: http://europa.eu.int/comm/competition/international/others/

Argentinean Competition Authority (2003), *Report on Competition Policy and Competition Law Enforcement 2003.*
URL: http://www.mecon.go v.ar/cndc/memoria03/memoria03_english.pdf

CNDC (2002), Argentinian Report on Competition Policy.
URL: http://www.mecon.gov.ar/cndc/memoria02/memoria02_english.pdf

De Araujo Jr., J. T. (2001a), Toward a Common Competition Policy in Mercosur, paper prepared for the conference on "Competition Policy in Infrastructure Services: Second Generation Issues in the Reform of Public Services" organized by the Infrastructure and Financial Markets Division and the Multilateral Investment Fund of the Inter-American Development Bank, Washington, D.C., April 23-24.
http://www.sice.oas.org/tunit/staff_article/tav01_merc_e.asp

De Araujo Jr., J. T. (2001b), Competition Policy, in: *Toward Free Trade in the Americas*, Salazar, J. M. and Robert, M. (eds.), Washington, DC. Brookings Institution - Secretary Economic Monitoring, URL: http://www.fazenda.gov.br/seae/artigos/Chap11.pdf

De Araujo Jr., J. T. and Tineo, L. (2000), *Competition Policy and the EU-Mercosur Trade Negotiations*, URL: http://www.sice.oas.org/compol/Articles/cpeumerc.doc

De Araujo Jr., J.T. and Tineo, L. (1997), *The Harmonization of Competition Policies Among Mercosur Countries*, Organization of American States Trade Unit, July.
URL: www.fazenda.gov.br/

European Commission (2003), 2003 *Regular Report on Turkey's Progress Towards Accession.* URL: http://europa.eu.int/comm/enlargement/report_2003/pdf/rr_tk_final.pdf

European Commission (2004), *2004 Regular Report on Turkey's Progress Towards Accession*, SEC(2004) 1201, Brussels.
URL: http://europa.eu.int/comm/enlargement/report_2003/pdf/rr_tk_final.pdf

Faul, J. and Nikpay, A. (2000), *The EC Law of Competition*, Oxford University Press, Oxford. URL: http://www.oup.co.uk/pdf/0-19-876538-X.pdf

Inan, M. and Öz, G. (2001), Turkish Competition Law and the Impact of the Customs Union Decision', in: *Turkey and Central and Eastern European Countries in Transition*, Togan, S. and Balasubramanyam, V. N. (eds.), Basingstoke, Palgrave.

Inter-American Deve lopment Bank (2004), Argentina: Institutional Challenges in Promoting Competition, Second Annual Meeting of the Latin American Competition Forum, June 14-15. URL: http://www.iadb.org/res/publications/pubfiles/pubS-193.pdf

International Competition Network (ICN) (2002), *Merger Notification and Procedures Template: Argentina*, Version 1.1 July 12.
URL: http://www.mecon.gov.ar/cndc/argentina_icn_merger_template.pdf

Martin, S. (2001), Competition Policy. In: *The Economics of the European Union: Policy and analysis*, Artis, M. and Nixson, F. (eds.), third edition, Oxford University Press, Great Britain.

Mumcu, A. and Zenginobuz Ü. (2001), *Competition Policy in Turkey*, paper prepared for the ERF 8th Annual Meeting in Cairo, 15-17 January, 2002.
URL: http://www.econ.boun.edu.tr/papers/pdf/wp-01-17.pdf

Neumann, M. (2001), *Competition Policy: History, Theory and Practice*, Edward Elgar, Great Britain.

Noguiera, U.B. (1998), Brief Review of Competition Policy in the Southern Common Market (Mercosur), in: *Boletin Latinoamericano de Competencia*, No. 4, Part 1, August.
URL: http://europa.eu.int/comm/competition/international/others/

OECD (1994), Interim Report on Convergence of Competition Policies, in: *General Distribution* OCDE/GD(94)64, June. URL:
http://www.olis.oecd.org/olis/1994doc.nsf/0/203b9411ca29e796c12562eb000d64f8?OpenDocument>

OECD (1996), Competition Policy and Efficiency Claims in Horizontal Agreements, in: *General Distribution* OCDE/GD(96)65,
URL: http://www.oecd.org/dataoecd/1/4/2379526.pdf

OECD (2002a), *Annual Report on Competition Policy in Turkey 2002.*
http://www.oecd.org/dataoecd/22/10/2509455.pdf

OECD (2002b), The Role of Competition Policy in Regulatory Reform, in: *OECD Reviews of Regulatory Reform, Regulatory Reform in Turkey.*
URL: http://www.oecd.org/ dataoecd/3/0/27068413.pdf>

OECD (2002c), Turkey: Crucial Support for Economic Recovery, in: *OECD Reviews of Regulatory Reform*, Paris.

OECD (2002d), Enhancing Market Openness Though Regulatory Reform, in: *OECD Reviews of Regulatory Reform, Regulatory Reform in Turkey.*
URL: http://www.oecd.org/ dataoecd/40/9/1840760.pdf

OECD (2004), *Annual Report on Competition Policy Developments in Argentina 2003*, DAFFE/COMP(2004)26.
URL: http://www.oecd.org/dataoecd/12/4/34427781.pdf

Oliveira, G. (2000), Aspects of Competition Policy in Mercosur, Boletin Latinoamericano de Competencia, No.11, December.
URL: http://europa.eu.int/comm/competition /international/others/

Republic of Turkey (2003), *National Programme for the Adoption of the Acquis.*
URL: http://www.abgs.gov.tr/NPAA/up.htm

Rowat, M., Lubrano, M. and Porrata Jr., R. (1997), Competition Policy and Mercosur, in: *World Bank Technical Paper* No. 385, Washington D.C.

SICE, *Functions of Enforcement Bodies: Argentina.*
URL: http://www.sice.oas.org/cp_comp/english/dlr2/ebfunc_e.asp#ARG

Toom, M. A. den (2004), The Application of ICN's Recommended Practices for Merger Notification Procedures in Argentina: What Should be Changed to Achieve Full Consistency? In: *Boletin Latinoamericano de Competencia*, No.18, Februray, paper prepared for the IBA Conference held in Mexico City on 26 June 2003 "Competition Law and Policy in a Global Context".
URL: http://europa.eu.int/comm/competition/international/others/

Turkish Competition Authority (TCA) (2001), *Annual Report*.
URL: http://www.rekabet. gov.tr/word/rapor2001/bir.doc

Turkish Competition Authority (TCA) (2002), *Annual Report*.
URL: http://www.rekabet. gov.tr/word/rapor2002/bir.doc

International trade and growth

FLUCTUATIONS OF THE CURRENT ACCOUNT AND THE CAUSES OF THE ARGENTINE LONG-RUN GROWTH SLOWDOWN

Alberto M. Díaz Cafferata*, Leonardo Berbotto, David Kohn

1. Introduction

The issue

After a brief spurt of rapid economic expansion at the end of the XIXth Century, the Argentine trend rate of economic growth decelerated continuously, along a historical span of more than a century, since about the time of the Baring Panic in 1891 until today. The long-run evolution of trend GDP at constant prices is best described analytically by a continuous growth slowdown as shown in Figure 2.1 (Díaz Cafferata, 2004). The paper tackles this issue of the secular decline of Argentine long-run trend growth looking for permanent causes. Since the problem is the trajectory of aggregated economic activity along more than a century, it is convenient to disentangle trends from cycles. In this perspective, a presumption is that a given sustained long-run growth rate would be related to the magnitude of long-run investment flows, which shall in turn be financed by national and external savings.

Low and declining Argentine national savings in the last quarter century, can finance only low investment rates. Can a higher investment and further growth be financed with foreign savings? What does the theory and empirical studies suggest? The discussion here is developed in three parts. Firstly, GDP series are filtered and selected characteristics of the long-run trend growth showing a secular slowdown are portrayed. Secondly, the theoretical relationship between the current account (CA) and growth, as well as international empirical studies, are summarily reviewed. Thirdly, estimations useful to formulate stylized facts of the CA and of the participation of national savings in the financing of investment flows are performed.

Long-run economic growth and growth slowdown in the economy open to financial flows

The process of modern economic growth eludes simple explanations, as a long history of unsolved polemics in the literature demonstrate. Further, since a long-run growth decline as a secular problem is certainly not a general occurrence in modern times, the particular phenomenon of *growth slowdown* has received less attention. Authors that have discussed the Argentine economic history neither have concluded with a precise identification of causal mechanisms, nor have even agreed on an appropriate systematic characterization of the process.

---

* Corresponding author. Instituto de Economía y Finanzas, Facultad de Ciencias Económicas. Universidad Nacional de Córdoba. Av. Valparaíso s.n. Ciudad Universitaria. 5000, Córdoba. República Argentina. Mail: diazcaf@eco.unc.edu.ar. A previous version was presented at the XXXVII Jornadas Internacionales de Finanzas Públicas, U.N.Córdoba, September 2004. Comments by M. Cecilia Gáname, Elena Resk and Jorge Fornero are gratefully acknowledged.

As preliminary steps to a more comprehensive understanding of the Argentine growth decline, examination of different partial influences and channels of transmission are useful to provide insights on pieces of the complex mechanism. We address here the Argentine case as a problem of growth in the open economy when there is borrowing and lending, as different from the mechanisms related to resource allocation and trade policy distortions that are stressed when the - implicit or explicit- model assumes trade in commodities only.

The issue of external savings and its international mobility can be addressed in a model of an open economy with assets trade in two different ways. The first, restricting the assets price, is the interest rate arbitrage condition. The argument is that when the economy faces a lower international rate of interest (when issuing foreign debt) than the expected return of home projects, they will be financed with external savings. The presence of distortions result in negative effects on country risk, shrinking investment possibilities, as stressed by Avila, 2000. Note however that an arbitrage restriction is specifically related to the price of financial assets, but actual flows may not appear in the model. The second is related to the economy budget constraint. It highlights the intertemporal character of the income-expenditure relationship and specifies a CA. The issue is the possibility to run external deficits to finance investment and the risk and effects of external crisis. The short-run behavior of the CA in smoothing consumption (Lanteri, 1996) or financing a macroeconomic recovery *à la* Harrod-Domar (Easterly, 1997) shall be distinguished from the possible contribution to long-run growth.

National and external savings

We are interested in the behavior of external savings along extended periods of time in Argentina and whether there is a regular flow of external financing of investment or rather it presents discontinuities related to the pattern of external crises.

A paper by Schmidt-Hebbel and Serven, 1999, provides an international perspective on the evolution of savings and growth. Since the mid sixties, there has been a steady decline in the world overall saving rate, but regional patterns are widely dissimilar: in the period 1965-1973 national saving ratios in East Asia and the Pacific -excluding China- were 18.3% of GNP, climbing to 27.6% in the decade from 1984 to 1993. In China the savings to GDP ratio went from 25.3% to 36.8%. In acute contrast, during the same years saving rates in sub-Saharan Africa went down from 10.5% to 6.4%. Savings rate in Latin America show a declining trend.

In a time horizon of almost seven decades, starting in 1935, Argentine savings at constant 1993 prices show a peak in 1977 (Figure 1.1), then went gradually down until the mid nineties and had a short recovery until 1998. In percentage of GDP, far from the rising savings trend ratio in East Asia, the savings/GDP ratio in Argentina in the period 1935 to 2002 fluctuated around an average of 19.5% percent. Values are equal or above to 22% in only 12 years out of 68 observations, grouped into 3 temporal clusters: i) 1936, 1937, 1938; ii) 1943, 1946, 1947, 1948; and iii) in the 1970s: 1973, 1976, 1977, 1978, 1980. After a 23% value in 1980, the saving rate has remained below 20% during almost a quarter century. This process will be documented further in section 4[34].

---

[34] Chisari *et al*, 1992, disaggregate public and private savings in Argentina.

Figure 1.1
National savings in Argentina, 1935-2002

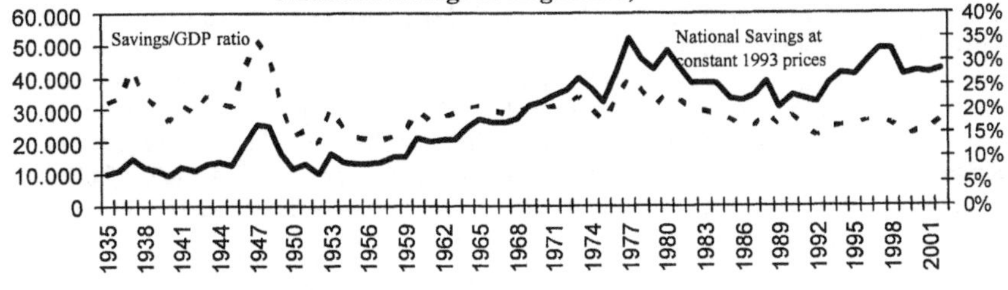

Source: authors' calculations. Joined series: 1993-2002, MECON (pesos 1993); 1980-1993, Ministerio de Economía (pesos 1986); 1970-1980, CEPAL with BCRA data (pesos 1970); 1950-1970, BCRA (pesos 1960); 1935-1950, Secretaría de Asuntos Económicos (pesos 1950).

CA deficits persistence and the interruption of external savings flows

Schmidt-Hebbel and Serven formulate six stylized facts on savings and related variables. **i.** The world saving rate has been declining and the world real interest rate has been increasing since the 1970s; **ii.** Saving rates show diverging patterns across regions during the past three decades; **iii.** Long-term saving rates and income levels are positively correlated across countries; **iv.** Long-term saving rates and growth rates are positively correlated across countries; **v.** Long-term saving rates and investment ratios are strongly positively correlated across countries; and **vi.** Long-term saving and foreign aid flows are negatively correlated across aid-receiving countries.

The global perspective we obtain from empirical studies is, on the one hand, that there appears not to be a clear positive effect of external savings on growth. On the other hand, investment and growth are strongly related to national savings, and the substitution of national and external savings as well as the external vulnerability created by a net debtor position must be weighted for a balance of benefits and cost of external savings flows.

Schmidt-Hebbel and Serven consider that the positive correlation of national savings to investment and growth performance suggests that there may exist virtuous cycles of saving and prosperity. But also, that there may exist poverty traps of undersaving and stagnation. Two questions appear: firstly, whether an increase in savings may contribute to long-run growth; secondly, whether higher national savings ratio would help achieve higher levels of investment without the weaknesses of external vulnerability that comes together with the use of external savings.

A preliminary working hypothesis may now be stated. The observed declining trend growth trajectory and recurrent external crises of the Argentine economy are related to the low national savings generating, in turn, low long-run investment below the requirements of accumulation and adoption of rapid technological advance and structural change. A low national savings rate in Argentina allows only for a low trend growth along time; consequently higher investment and growth shall be financed with external savings flows. But as shown below, the historic contribution of external savings has not been substantial on average, and highly irregular. These features are presumably related to the presence of imperfect financial markets and controls in capital movements, together with the vulnerability that results both from a low structural exports/GDP ratio and reputation.

The reminder of the paper is organized as follows. Section 2 examines the statistical properties of Argentine long-run growth, and builds stylized facts using filtering procedures to disentangle long-run features from cycles. Section 3 surveys the role of national and foreign savings in theoretical long-run growth models in the open dependent economy; the exposition is organized starting from the empirical problem of the low long-run growth. Section 4 examines national and external savings series as represented by the CA balance and interprets the empirical results from the theoretical point of view. Section 5 concludes.

2. Stylized facts of Argentine GDP; secular growth slowdown and a long-run perspective of the 2001 external crisis

In this section the long-run behavior of Argentine Gross Domestic Product (GDP) between 1875 and 2002 is portrayed by means of different filtering procedures. The results are consistent with the suggestion in Díaz Cafferata, 2004, that there is a continuous trend growth slowdown along the whole XXth Century. Consequently, permanent causes have been probably operating earlier than the usually suggested break in growth with the Great Depression.

The trend growth slowdown, a long-run vision: is there a structural long-run process?

Argentina's dismal long-run economic performance, in acute contrast with optimistic prospects at the middle of the XXth Century that the country was likely to become one of the leading economies of the world, have puzzled analysts. The critical magnitude of the social problem generated by the fall in investment in the eighties, climbing unemployment that continued in the nineties despite the GDP growth and the effect of the recent crisis, asks for an adequate diagnostic and a policy response. But one noted defect of economic policy in Argentina has been historically the absence of a stable growth strategy. A much needed basic consensus regarding the political basis for the organization of society will be stimulated by a more precise understanding of the problem. A starting point is the apparent long-run process of decline, when it started, which are the relevant characteristics and which are the causes. Is there a structural long-run process? Are there permanent structural causes? As explained in Section 1, to help us understand these issues we focus on the role of the CA.

Cortés Conde, 1996, distinguishes four periods of Argentine growth: i. 1875-1912 with a yearly GDP per capita growth rate of 3.9%; ii. 1912-1927, with negative growth of -0.3%; iii. a new change of tendency to 3% in 1927-1947; iv. 1947-1975 depicts a 1.6% growth. The author concludes that the main characteristic of the economy in the long run is the discontinuity of growth, with years of acceleration and recurrent interruptions always caused by external crisis (p 20).

This paper purports to provide elements to help understand the intriguing Argentine long-run performance failure. It is worth exploring the presence of a long-run statistical process generating the data and seeking to identify structural economic causes that explain the trajectory of the economy in the whole period.[35] Figure 2.1, that depicts a declining growth along the trend path of GDP, provides such a perspective.

Figure 2.1a:
Argentina, 1875-2002. A declining rate of trend GDP growth. Polynomial adjustment.

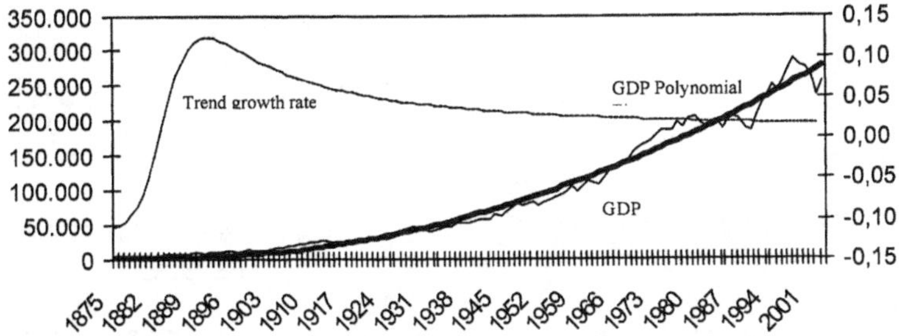

The GDP series at constant 1993 prices was built using data from the following sources: 1993-2002, MECON (pesos 1993); 1980-1993, Ministerio de Economía (pesos 1986); 1970-1980, CEPAL with BCRA data (pesos 1970); 1950-1970, BCRA (pesos 1960); 1935-1950, Secretaría de Asuntos Económicos (pesos, prices 1950); 1900-1935, CEPAL (pesos, prices 1950), 1875-1900, Cortés Conde (pesos, prices 1895)[36].

Figure 2.1 (a), (b), (c), provides the results of three alternative methods of filtering the Argentine GDP trajectory between 1875 and 2002. Figure 2.1a, displays the GDP series and a second degree polynomial adjustment. Reading the polynomial regression as a first approximation to the trend behavior of GDP, the growth rate of this line can be interpreted as the long-run trend growth rate of the economy.

The more striking feature of this trajectory is the rising trend growth in the first years until the last decade of the XIXth Century and the change of sign at that time followed by a continuous trend growth slowdown to our days, along the whole XXth Century, as noted in Díaz Cafferata, 2004, and Díaz Cafferata and Fornero, 2003.

To provide additional evidence on this issue, two further filtering procedures have been performed. Figure 2.1b results from the application of the Hodrick-Prescott filter. The boxes display the alternative trend growth when lambdas equal to 17, 100 and 500 are used.

[35] Though the Cortés Conde data is GDP *per capita* and we use GDP, we are stressing the possible existence of a continuous, compared to a discontinuous, process. Further filtering with GDP per capita would be useful for a stricter comparison with Cortés Conde.

[36] The series may be downloaded from the web page of the Instituto de economía y Finanzas, Facultad de Ciencias Económicas, Universidad Nacional de Córdoba: www.eco.unc.edu.ar/ief/

Figure 2.1 b:
GDP growth. Hodrick-Prescott filtering. Argentina: 1875-2002.

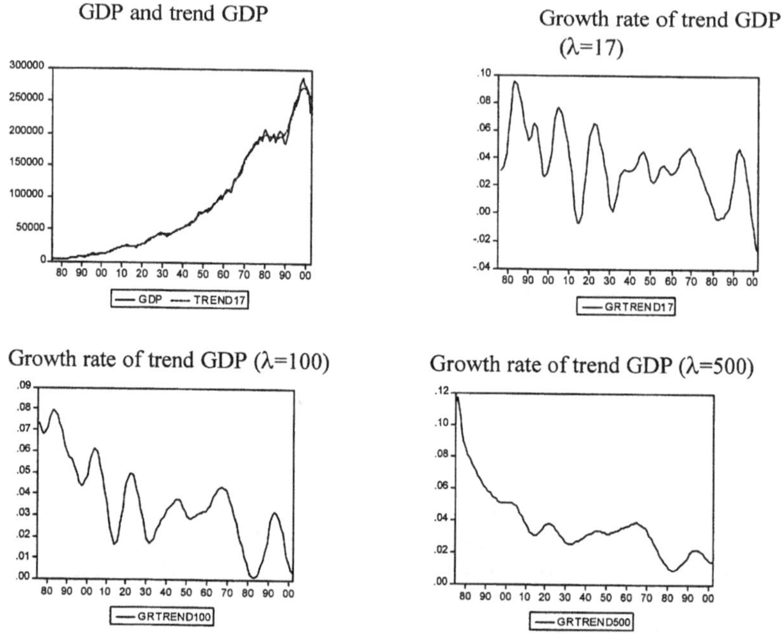

Lastly, Figure 2.1c, corresponds to the use of the State Space model. It is obtained when a "trend + 1 cycle + irregular" model is used, with stochastic trend and slope, and with several interventions (level breakpoints and irregulars) following the "auxiliary residuals" methodology.

Figure 2.1c, GDP Growth. State-Space model.

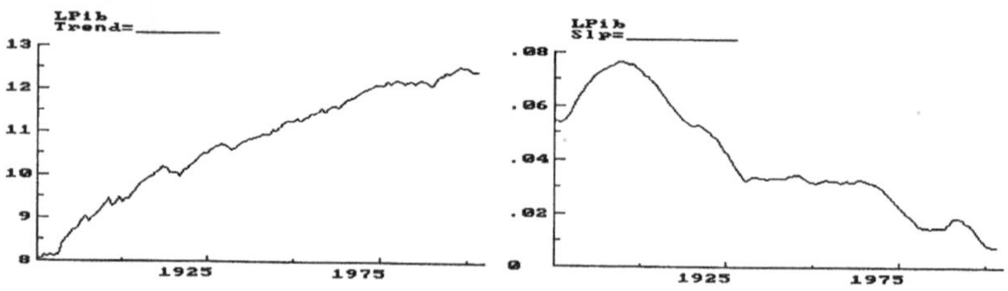

The results from both filtering procedures are not identical -and there is not a generally accepted procedure to select one. In particular, the point in time when the trend growth ceases to increase and starts its declining growth path differs in the chosen alternatives. But all of them provide the same disquieting picture of a declining long-run trend growth slowdown, that differs from the Cortés Conde description in the emphasis put here on the search for a long-run process and for permanent structural causes of the secular trend growth slowdown. We deem both perspectives are not competitive: taken together and harmonizing them will provide a better understanding of the Argentine economy.

Casual examination of the different parts of Figure 2.1 suggests indeed two explanations; on the one hand the existence of several negative shocks along time, on the other hand the operation of permanent causes. The exploration here is driven by the hypothesis that there is in fact a long run process. That there is a continuity of structural characteristics of the economy, such as distance from large markets, the type of sectoral specialization, policy induced distortions, culture and institutions, that help explain the observed path of GDP. In this vein Mundlak, Cavallo and Domenech, 1989, p 9, argue that the "phenomenon hast lasted too long simply to be a response to exogenous random shocks".

The reason for this inertia must lay in the domain of policies that were pursued when such shocks occurred and when they did not. Gerchunoff and Llach, 2003, agree with the vision of a long run stagnation, but consider an error to base the explanation on the introduction of distortions by the state in the post-war period. They point out that the growth slowdown had already started to manifest in the decade of the 30s[37]. Díaz Cafferata, 2004, notes that there was possibly an even earlier relevant break in growth, suggesting that the transition years from accelerating to declining growth occurred at some point around the end of the XIXth Century. If this is the case, at least some of the permanent causes of the growth problem might have been present in the economy before the forcible transformations caused by the two Great Wars.

Growth policy implications: structural problems or policy failures

The theoretical discussion, together with the stylized facts will provide suggestions for the interpretation of the evolution of the Argentine economy. We are interested in policy strategy implications specifically relevant for long-run growth, as methodologically different -though in general not independent- from the management of medium-run cycles or macroeconomic instability. The focus in this paper is placed in the characteristics of national and external savings flows as expressed by the CA, its role in the operation of the economy and growth under the assumed small open economy structure, and the implications in the framework of a growth strategy.

Understanding the long-run trajectory of growth to influence it

More than a half century ago, Tinbergen, 1942, addressed the problem of the dynamics of trend movements, namely, economic movements along decades or even centuries; the economic analysis of the phenomenon of long-run growth focuses on the determinants of long-run economic growth and the possible ways to influence it. He warns that it is necessary to discuss if it is correct the implicit dissociation from the dynamics of real short-run movements.

Tinbergen points out that a study of tendencies makes sense when the "periodic" movements deviate only temporarily from the trend movement. With this perspective we try here to find

---

[37] Gerchunoff and Llach, 2003, p 422.

evidence of the existence of such a path that possesses the statistical properties to be considered a "gravity" trajectory that we might call a "structural gravity centre growth path". An advantage of having a theory of tendency is the possibility to discriminate the influence of policies in the short and long-run; a theory of long-run movements is a step in this direction.

In the spirit of Tinbergen, the observed growth path of a national economy may be interpreted as the outcome of permanent structural features. The implication being for the Argentine case is that if the historical long-run path has been governed by a certain rule, to break the inertial structural slowdown key features of the organization of the economy must be transformed. Olivera, 1975, concludes with the aid of a model that changing structural social features is difficult due to the "resistance" of the existing structure to change. Practical problems of this kind were experienced during decades by central planning economies trying to implement "reform" plans.

Even if a formal testable model is not reached, the results may still be useful from a policy perspective because "the familiarity with the phenomenon will provide hints about the possibility of control". Consequently, filtering procedures applied clearly suggest such a statistical declining long-run trend of the rate of GDP growth.

3. Open economy short-run and long-run growth processes, and the CA

Having stated the issue as a long-run problem of growth, in this section the relationship between the CA and growth is explored. To start, we comment on models that address the causality from trade in commodities to economic growth. Consequently, the influence of factors mobility will be ignored here. The next step is to recognize assets mobility, opening the discussion of the role of national and external savings to finance investment; a discussion of the Feldstein-Horioka puzzle and empirical results for Argentina follows. Note that it is important to define the relevant time horizon of the analysis otherwise conclusions would not maintain[38].

An intertemporal dynamic model of an open economy with production and international asset mobility will contain the minimal elements to address theoretically the issue of Argentine long-run growth. We refer briefly to its characteristics and its implications to inquire about possible causes of the growth slowdown.

Commodities trade and growth

Concerning the relation between openness and growth the case focusing on trade will be discussed first briefly as a reference point. The phenomenal difference between the growth rates of East Asian economies and the Latin American economies, says Leamer, 1995, raised

---

[38] Two other features of interest can be mentioned: identification of long-run processes along real time as compared with formal steady state equilibrium growth; and the difference between regular deterministic processes -as in the traditional models-, and the presence of uncertainty and stochastic shocks. On turn the expectations concerning shocks affect the perceptions of agents and the demand for national assets, influencing the sustainability of a current account balance.

the hypothesis that the reason was the degree of openness to international trade[39]. He discusses a regression reported by Ram, 1985:

$$\dot{Y}_t = -1.034 + 1.072\dot{L}_t + 0.130(I/Y)_t + 0.124\dot{X}_t + e_t$$

with the usual interpretation of variables. It is assumed that technology is a function of the level of exports. Leamer notes that the estimation is based on the hypothesis that the differences in growth rates are caused by differences in the openness to international trade. The equation **relates exports to growth through goods markets**, under the assumption that aggregate output is a function of capital, labor and technology, the latter being itself a function of exports. Several questions emerge, such as whether the effect of openness is in the level or in the growth rate of GDP; or in any case how to properly measure openness[40]. Leamer concludes that despite a gain in general understanding of the determinants of growth, and the impression that growth is enhanced by openness, much of the great variation in cross-country growth remains unexplained.

Attention to commodities markets point out as key variables the operation and possible distortions of internal terms of trade and the real exchange rate, and the growth problem is focused in the inefficient allocation impairing exports performance and export-led growth. Consequently, the policy implication is that the potential gain from opening the economy eliminating tariffs cause the anti-exports bias. However, as long as arguments based on the real side do not consider trade in debt, they are not able to address explicitly the presence and the role of assets markets. The integrated world market does not incorporate the problem of the amount and sources of savings to account for the financing of gross capital formation and the possible role of external savings: such savings must equal investment in each economy separately.[41]

Let us review what further insights are provided when allowing for capital mobility, i.e. external savings flows. The change in focus does not mean exports become irrelevant. Rather, exports performance may again be important for growth in this new framework, but now in a different role, not specific of the dynamics of commodities production but mainly as a condition for the sustainability of the intertemporal CA equilibrium. The issue arises due to the fact that when there is external financing the dependent economy's debt payments requires, not just an adequate flow of savings, but also foreign currency must be generated for the economy with a negative services account via a trade balance surplus. Let us consider the characteristics of intertemporal models.

The time horizon: short-run adjustments versus long-run processes

In the next three subsections we will discuss the short-run movements in the CA, the long-run growth and finally, some models with short-run payment problems, incentives to repudiate and crisis of confidence.

---

[39] Detailed discussions on this proposition show that there is still a lack of consensus (Rodrik and Rodríguez, 2000; Wälde and Wood, 2004).

[40] Cfr. Pritchett, 1996; Leamer, 1995. The growth of exports or the initial ratio of exports to GDP are two possibilities, but these measures may be explained by government intervention or comparative advantage, or the variation in exports growth may not be exogenous to the determinants of GDP growth.

[41] Findlay, 1984, p.219.

a- Short-run: the intertemporal approach to trade in assets, for consumption smoothing or shock absorber.

The interpretation of CA imbalances: the intertemporal approach vs the Mundell-Fleming model

New insights have appeared on the interpretation of CA equilibrium that enable us to compare the intertemporal approach with the traditional Mundell-Fleming model. In Obstfeld and Rogoff, 1995, they emphasize that the intertemporal approach to the CA, incorporating a flexible budget constraint, provides insights to understand CA patterns in the process of growth. They note however empirical puzzles. In a simple model with infinitely lived agents, optimal ratios of foreign debt to output five or ten times the observed values would be admissible. Models with finite-lived dynasties would tend to correct this contradiction, but they present other problems, like the prediction that government deficits lead to CA deficits. The task of building and empirically applying richer and more realistic intertemporal models will not be, they warn, an easy task. The reason is the complexity of handling relevant cases that are far from the frictionless, full information, complete markets ideal, both in domestic and international capital markets, including in the latter the sovereign default risk. Despite these difficulties, they deem the intertemporal model is superior to the Mundell-Fleming in providing a rationale for an unbalanced CA as a possible outcome of efficient trade across time.

Consequently, in the perspective of the intertemporal approach, the important lesson to be learned, is to be aware of the empirical observation that **CA deficits and surplus may be the outcome of efficient behavior**. But the effects of CA deficits on growth shall be carefully analyzed to extract correct implications of the intertemporal approach principle. What else can be said about the CA in the growth process?

b- The long-run trajectory of a growing economy

In contrast with the transitory movements in the CA that are related to short-run adjustment, the problem we are interested in is that of long-run growth. In this regard: is it theoretically possible to generate, and sustain, long-run growth financed by flows of foreign savings? What does the international experience teach on this regard?

To start, let us review the Stages of the Balance of Payments Hypothesis.

International borrowing and the hypothesis of stages of the balance of payments

If there is investment and international assets mobility new possibilities for growth appear. A stagnant poor country with low levels of capital deepening and productivity may escape the 'poverty trap' by its ability to finance accumulation and modernization of capital beyond national savings possibilities. The intertemporal budget constraint allows borrowing in the early stages of development, and repaying the debt when the economy moves to higher levels of income along its growth path. Despite the plausibility of the argument, Halevi, 1971, p. 104, synthesizes and examines empirically different versions of the hypothesis of the existence of stages of growth without finding convincing evidence consistent with it.

The *Stages of the balance of payments hypothesis* suggests that there is an evolution of the CA in the growth process. A country follows a sequence from a borrowing to a lending economy along a sequence of periods in the development process from a poor to a high income economy. The path may be described in a four phases cycle[42]: in the early stages of growth the economies are net borrowers using foreign savings to finance investment, reverting gradually to become net lenders in the mature stages. I. In the first stage an underdeveloped economy is a net borrower. A country rich in natural resources and low national savings attracts foreign capitals; exports are concentrated in a few primary products. II. The flow of capital helps to develop activities in which the developing country possess comparative advantage, allowing the country to have a surplus trade balance, with national savings still below investment and the CA in deficit. III. In the next stage the increased savings allows the country to pay back the debt, and may be able to become a new lender, with a surplus in its balance of trade. IV. Lastly, the economy becomes an evolved lender, investing abroad.

The intertemporal models with assets mobility provide the rationale for equilibrium superavits or deficits of the CA either to smooth consumption or to finance growth. Taken together, the developments of the intertemporal equilibrium approach and the stages hypothesis, provide a mechanism for CA imbalances financing growth, and indicate that the existence of CA imbalances is theoretically compatible with intertemporal equilibrium.

The observational counterpart of this argument would be that a country that is in its first stage, growing with the use of external savings, would exhibit persistent CA deficits during all the temporal length of the stage, and that the deficit would evolve gradually into a balanced CA and later into a superavit, as the economy moves to more advanced stages of development.

The implication of intertemporal models is that deficits or superavits are not essentially good or bad. However, at this point it is natural to ask, on the one hand, under what circumstances the CA deficits of a country are sustainable, i.e. external savings constitute an effective source for financing a long-run growth process. On the other hand, to identify events under which a CA crisis may develop like policy inconsistency, vulnerability to external shocks or ´animal spirits´.

c- Models with short-run payments problems, incentives to repudiate and crisis of confidence. Sudden stops and reversals of the CA

The globalization of financial markets and the events in the nineties have triggered a revival of the discussion on the area of savings and financial flows. The recent literature on the external vulnerability of an economy, the sustainability of CA deficits and the determinants and effects of sudden stops in external savings flows and reversals of the CA, such as Edwards, 2004; Calvo, Izquierdo y Mejía, 2003; Milesi-Ferretti and Razin, 1996, suggest new insights to our discussion.

The discussion of optimal decisions in international borrowing has been brought to the center of the scene. If the problem is long-run growth, the consequences of the accumulation of debt by the borrowing country should be evaluated.

Along time, consumption, capital accumulation and interest payments are paid either from current income or accumulation of debt. When the debt increases so do the interest payments, and at a certain point benefits to repudiate the debt (the present discounted value of interests) may be higher than costs (given by the difficulty to access international financial markets and

[42] Different descriptions and number of stages have been suggested. Cfr. Razgallah, 2004, and its references.

to finance international transactions). But note that lenders can calculate which is the level of indebtness for which it would be optimal for the borrower to decide to repudiate, and would not lend to this point. If lenders would not lend more than the maximum amount of repayments that the country is able, or willing, to make, the solution to the planning problem incorporates a constraint in credit. A shock may change the probabilities of different states of the world. Circumstances that generate a ′panic′ and a ′crisis of confidence′ may create a self-fulfilling prophecy affecting a country with temporary problems that is however able and willing to pay its debt in the long-run. Part of the problem arises when a large fraction of the total debt has to be paid in the short-run. In this case there is also a problem with the possible conflict between individual and collective lenders' behavior in estimating benefits and costs of rescheduling.

Unsustainability caused by inconsistency or vulnerability to exogenous shocks. The recent debate on CA reversals and sudden stops. Deterministic or stochastic paths.

The path of long-run Argentine growth, besides the feature of declining growth along the trend, has not been regular. Rather, it has been once and again broken at different times, and usually due to external crises as was mentioned above quoting Cortés Conde, 1996. This feature requires attention because the causes may be on the one hand purely exogenous and unexpected; on the other hand, the breaks may be the outcome of built-in problems of the country′s economic structure. We have learned that there may be equilibrium superavits and deficits generating CA cycles. But even when deficits or superavits are not good or bad *per se*, they may not be sustainable. In fact, countries suffer external crises. The empirical observation of high frequency cycles suggests that they may be inconsistent with the realization of optimal plans, due to temporal inconsistency or lack of information. Consequently, a question arises on how a smooth equilibrium growth path is generated and which modelling features are adequate to the understanding of the presence and effects of crisis considering savings behavior. What kind of shock and responses generate growth cycles or slowdown? (such as in natural resources growth booms or neoclassical decreasing marginal productivity case?). What does the empirical evidence suggests?

The distinction between *a priori* **sustainable and unsustainable** strategies is best understood in a deterministic modelling framework. In the presence of stochastic shocks appears as a relevant feature the degree of **vulnerability** of the economy. A particular strategy may not be sustainable or unsustainable a priori; but the choice of strategy incorporates an element of risk.

Following this line of reasoning we should ask which are the characteristics of the economy or policy choices that determine the degree of vulnerability; e.g. an economy that is a natural resources based exporter may be subject to terms of trade shocks; an economy with a weak exports performance may have difficulties to maintain external financing due to deterioration of external solvency ratios.

In this perspective, there is an important role for forecasting key variables. In the document of the Ministry of Economics "Argentina en Crecimiento", the path of growth during the nineties was consistent with an exports dynamics that would reach 50 billion dollars in the year 2000. Contrary to this expectation exports stagnated after 1997, contributing to the rise in the perceived risk of default as perceived by foreigners (see Mussa, 2002). Romer, 2001 (p 574-576) points out that when a fiscal policy involves an ever-rising ratio of debt to GDP with a government trying to violate his budget constraint the forced change is likely to take the form of a crisis rather than a smooth transition. If there is a default it involves a transfer from foreigners to domestic residents, providing an incentive to default. Some of the most important costs of the crisis arise when the foreigners that were buying large quantities of the country's assets cease to do so and the trade balance must swing sharply towards surplus; for this to happen there must be a large depreciation of the real exchange.

4. Stylized facts: statistical properties of investment, national saving and the CA Empirical estimation: trends of investment, national savings and foreign savings

At this point let us comment briefly about the empirical estimations. Leamer, 1995, argues that in international trade no theory has been tested in the sense of placing it genuinely at risk; as a result all models that were ever contemplated survive empirical testing, and it is also usually extraordinarily difficult to translate a theoretical model into an empirical application. But if a model is taken as an organizing devise there is no reason to test it. Instead, empirical work shall help identify empirical circumstances in which the model is useful and other circumstances in which it is misleading. Following the alternative "estimate, don´t test", that asks for a balance between issues, theory and data, in previous sections the conceptual framework has been laid. In this section investment, national savings and external savings in Argentina will be examined.

Investment

To start, Figure 4.1 describes eloquently the serious problem in investment. The average I/GDP ratio for the whole period is 19.7% -similar to the 19.5% of national savings, as reported in Section 1. A growing trend was interrupted in 1977 almost four decades ago. In 2002 the gross investment in Argentina is at the level of the sixties.

For a perspective on the long-run behavior of investment along the 68 years examined, trend and cycles were disaggregated using the HP filter with a standard lambda equal to 100. The dotted line in Figure 4.2 is the trend, and the continuous line the rate of change in the trend, i.e. the trend rate of growth of total investment: it increases shortly at the beginning of the series until 1946. Then it decelerates to zero and again with a stable growth of about 3% until 1970. After this point a striking behavior is the interruption of the increasing trend during almost two decades in the 1970s and 1980s, and the -only transitory- recovery until the last part of the 1990s.

Figure 4.1:
Argentina. Gross Investment, 1935-2002 at Billion 1993 prices, and share of Gross National Investment in GDP

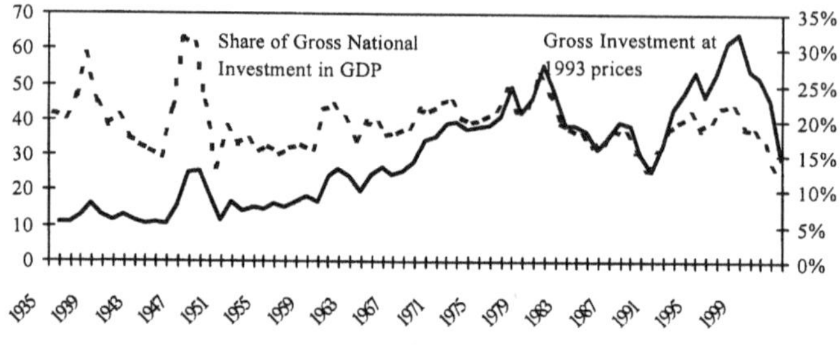

Figure 4.2:
Argentina. Gross investment 1935- 2002. Constant 1993 prices. H-P filtering. ? =100.

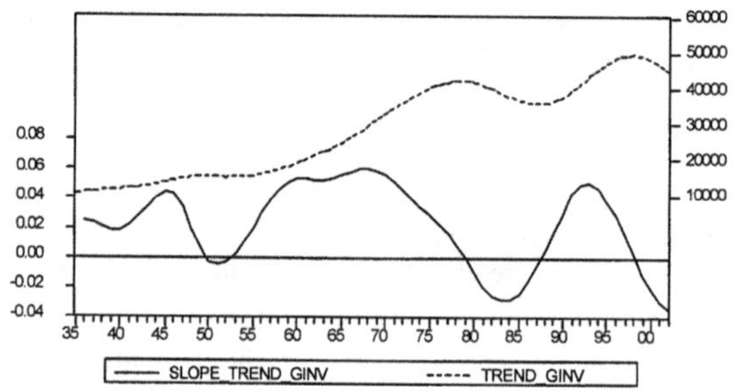

Savings and investment

The next step is to determine the relationship between the gross investment rate and savings. Figure 4.3 provides a graphical synthesis of contemporaneous behavior of investment rates and national savings rates: dotted lines were drawn at the 20% level, to highlight orders of magnitude. Out of 68 annual data, in 32 observations both investment and savings rates are lower than 20%. In 39 years the rate of investment is below 20%.

Figure 4.3
Argentina. Shares of Gross Domestic Investment and National Savings in GDP 1935- 2002.

Again, the HP filtering is useful to provide a description of the long-run evolution of the series. In the left panel of Figure 4.4 the trends of total investment and savings are depicted. Two main periods are apparent: until the beginning of the 1990s the trend of total investment follows closely the trend of national savings, with the external financing at the beginning of the decade followed by the rapid change of behavior of the CA is visible.

The right panel of Figure 4.4 shows the phenomenon in terms of rates. The CA presents a surplus -negative foreign savings- between the mid 1930s and the first years of the 1950s. After this point, until 1965, even when the CA presents occasional superavits, the trend of the CA share is negative -positive foreign savings- during these fifteen years. A quarter century with trend foreign savings continuously close to zero follows: compare this evolution with the path of trend growth of investment, and an hypothesis of causality worth further attention emerges. The link is again suggested by the recovery of investment in the 1990s contemporaneously with the presence of CA deficits. To explore the statistical properties of this suggested relationship, a simple correlation between the trends of the series as a share of GDP was estimated, and the results are shown in Table 4.1. The interesting feature is the high correlation of investment rate and national savings rate. The correlation between external savings rate and investment is negative, and also is the relation between external savings rate and national savings rate.

Figure 4.4:
Argentina. Trends of Gross Domestic Investment, National Savings and Foreign Savings 1935- 2002. Constant 1993 prices. H-P filtering, lambda = 100.

Trend of Gross Domestic Investment, national savings and foreign savings (the CA)

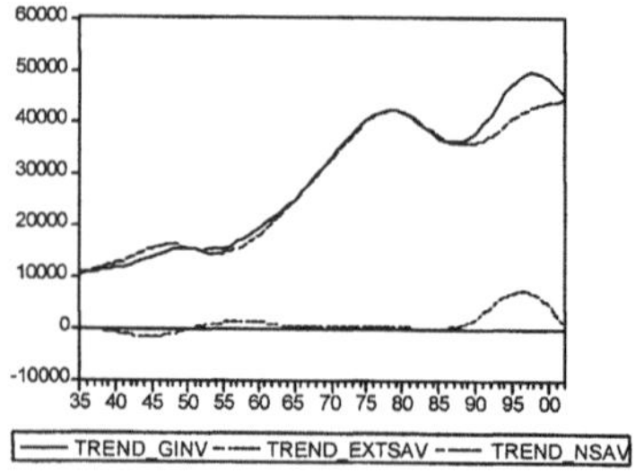

Trend of shares of investment, national and foreign savings in GDP.

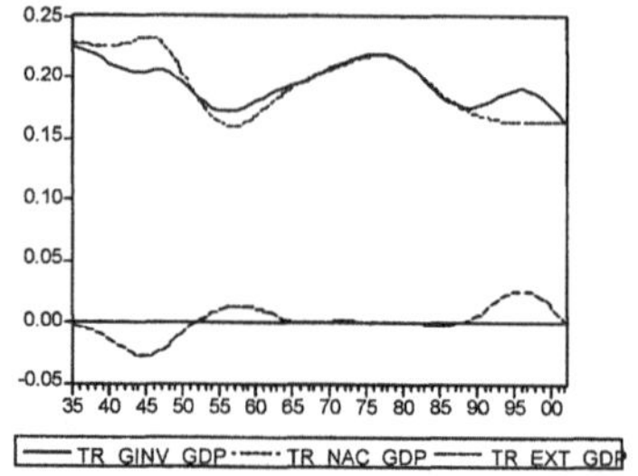

Table 4.1: Long-run correlation matrix 1935-2002

	GInv/GDP	Sext/GDP	Snat/GDP
GInv/GDP	1	-0.5	0.899
Sext/GDP		1	-0.828
Snat/GDP			1

Cycles of investment and savings

The cycles that result from the filtering can be interpreted as a reflection of short-run phenomena. For the characterization of the cycles, as in Sturzenegger and Moya, 2002, two different criteria were used. One defines the cycles as absolute variations in the time series; the other considers the cycles *à la* Lucas as deviations from the trend. The cycles of the first type have an average of around 2 years for the three series, somewhat longer for the expansive than for the contractive cycles. As regards the cycles as deviations, the results are shown in Figure 4.5 (a), (b), (c).

The changes in sign of the cyclical component is frequent. In 68 years, only as an exception the series of investment exhibits five continuous years below the trend in 1940-1945, and five continuous years above the trend during 1996-2000. We are interested in foreign savings: CA surpluses or deficits around the trend also move frequently, with the longest cyclical negative foreign savings -CA surplus- in 1963-1968; and the longest continuous CA cyclical deficits between 1997 and 2001. A general conclusion can be drawn comparing those frequent fluctuations with the hypothetical regular behavior of an economy along the path consistent with the "stages" hypothesis: a stable rising trend of total investment would be observed; at early stages a period of continuous trend CA deficits corresponding to the contribution of external savings would be found, with occasional deviations that do not alter the trend; national savings in this transition period would be constant or rising slowly as a fraction of GDP.

Are foreign and national savings substitutes in the short run?

Reinhart and Talvi, 1997, use the cyclical correlations to determine the behavior of national and foreign savings in Latin American and Asian countries for 1970-1995. They find that in all cases national and foreign savings are substitutes, reducing the increase in investment resulting from a rise in the CA deficit.

Our estimation of this relationship in Argentina is 0.01 for the whole period 1935-2002, as shown in table 4.2a. This relationship is not constant along time. The correlation is -0.12 for 1935-1990, and 0.26 during the "globalized" decade of the 1990s.

Additionally, we estimate the cyclical correlations between the series taken as a share of GDP and the values appear to be higher and negative. The results are shown in table 4.2 b. The relationship between external and national savings is –0.33 for the whole period. Similar results are obtained for the subperiods: -0.32 for the first one, and –0.53 for the period that goes from 1991 to 2002.

Figure 4.5: Time series cycles as deviations – HP filtering (lambda 100) 1935-2002.

Gross internal investment

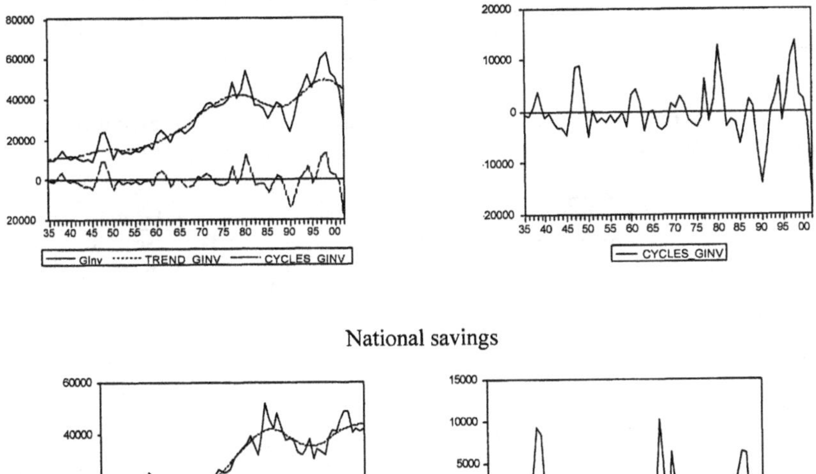

National savings

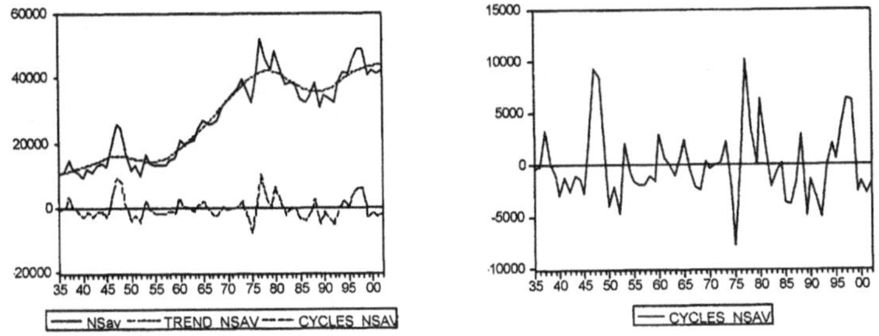

Foreign savings

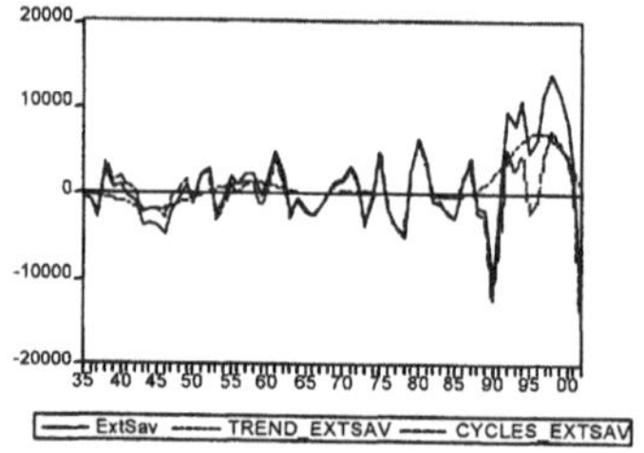

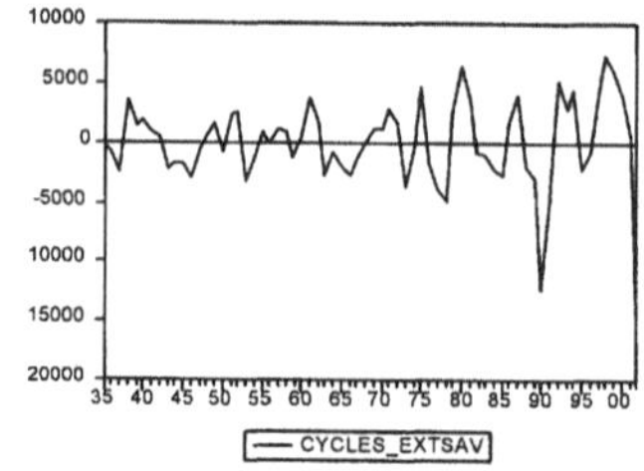

Table 4.2 a: Short run cyclical correlations between the series: Gross Domestic Investment (GDI), National Savings (Sn) and External Savings (Se).

	1935-2002		
Cycle	GDI	Se	Sn
GDI	1	0.75	0.67
Se		1	0.01
Sn			1

1935-1990		
GDI	Se	Sn
1	0.61	0.71
	1	-0.12
		1

1991-2002		
GDI	Se	Sn
1	0.90	0.66
	1	0.26
		1

Table 4.2 b: Short run cyclical correlations between the series: Gross Domestic Investment (GDI), National Savings (Sn) and External Savings (Se) as shares of GDP (Y)

	1935-2002		
Cycle	GDI/Y	Se/Y	Sn/Y
GDI/Y	1	0.49	0.66
Se/Y		1	-0.33
Sn/Y			1

1935-1990		
GDI/Y	Se/Y	Sn/Y
1	0.44	0.71
	1	-0.32
		1

1991-2002		
GDI/Y	Se/Y	Sn/Y
1	0.88	-0.07
	1	-0.53
		1

Reversals and growth in Argentina

A "reversal" is defined by Edwards, 2004a, as a reduction in the CA deficit of at least a 4% of GDP. Since in the case of Argentina the size of the deficits make this definition useless, the average for the deficits in the whole period -CA surpluses were not included- was used as the norm: we consider there is a reversal when there is a change in the CA deficit of at least 2.48% of GDP (which is the simple average of CA deficits during the whole period).

Table 4.3 shows the years when reversals of the CA occurred in Argentina. The first row shows the magnitude of the reversal; the second and third row are the changes in GDP before and after the episode, showing that a reversal is likely to be the consequence of a crisis which is followed by a positive short run cyclical upturn. A second point is of interest for our purposes:

CA deficits do not seem to survive difficulties in aggregate activity.

Table 4.3: Argentina. Reversals of the CA (changes of at least 2.48%)

Year of reversal	1939	1950	1953	1963	1973	1976	1988	1995	2002
? CA%	-4.51	-2.67	-6.64	-4.07	-3.02	-3.61	-2.82	-2.51	-7.67
? GDP	2.05	-0.05	0.00	-1.98	2.91	-0.30	0.32	1.40	-7.71
%*	3.41	-0.67	5.59	9.73	2.36	1.47	-4.42	6.81	

*** Simple average percentage change in GDP: year of the reversal and two years before and after the reversal**

There is on average a reversal every 7.6 years (in the first 34 years 1935-1968, reversals are found every 8.5 years, in contrast to 6.8 years in 1969-2002). There are five reversals, every six years, between 1973 and 2002).

Long-run relationship of national saving and investment and the Feldstein-Horioka puzzle.

The CA debate over the relation between savings and investment basically stems from the so called "puzzle" resulting from the Feldstein and Horioka (1980) observation. In regressions of average investment rates on average saving rates for the OECD countries using various periods from 1960-1974, R2 values between 0.83 and 0.91 were found, an apparently unexpected result if capital is internationally highly mobile.

In a regression for Argentina we found also a positive relationship between saving and investment rates both as a share of GDP, but the R2 takes a value of 0.50 in the whole period, possibly as a consequence of the instability of the data. These are contemporaneous correlations. In an alternative experiment, Van Rensselaer and Copeland, 2000, used an error correction model developed by Jansen and Schulze (1996) and Jansen (1996) to determine if a long-run relationship exists between savings and investment rates. The Jansen model is:

$$\Delta I_t = \alpha + \beta \Delta S_t + \gamma (S_{t-1} - I_{t-1}) + \delta S_{t-1} + \varepsilon_t$$

where the steady state solution is :

$$\alpha + \gamma (S^*_{t-1} - I^*_{t-1}) = 0$$

If in the long run the intertemporal budget constraint is fulfilled, the saving rates and investment rates exhibit a long-run relationship. The CA would is stationary around *-alpha/ gamma* (if *gamma* is different from zero; and if *alpha*=0, the CA is stationary around zero). *If delta* is significantly different from zero, the CA does not converge to a constant in the long run; *beta* measures the short run correlation. We performed similar estimations for Argentina with the following results:

gamma =0.54 (significant), suggesting that there exists a long-run relationship between the savings and investment time series, and that the CA is stationary, the unit-root test (augmented DF) rejects the null at 1% significance.

alpha and *delta* are not significant: the CA fluctuate around zero. The short run relationship is significantly different to zero (*beta=0.557*). These results are similar to the findings of Van Rensselaer and Copeland.

A new calculation following the two subperiods used in Lanteri, 1996, before and after 1977, reached the same conclusion as above for the first subperiod; but for the second one we found that the CA is not stationary (there is no evidence to reject the DF null of u-root). If long-run national savings and investment tend to move together, the CA unbalances are transitory, and the CA would eventually operate only as a shock absorber, principally on the 1935-1977. Closer examination of the statistical properties of the individual series, appear as a potentially useful step for further understanding of the process.

5. Concluding remarks

Financing long-run growth may be associated to persistent CA deficits, during the time that external savings fill the gap between the investment requirements of accumulation and structural change. The gradual accumulation of such deficits increases the negative net assets position of the country as well as the required interest payments in the outstanding debt. For the CA deficits to be persistent (and be able to finance long-run investment) there must be consistence of economic policies.

In the case of Argentina we find that the behavior of external savings is irregular, and not consistent with a possible contribution to long-run growth as, for example, under the stages of growth hypothesis. Finding the reasons for that behavior would be a contribution to understand important features of growth financing and for the explanation of the long-run growth slowdown: foreign savings did not compensate the low and declining national savings rate. But the international experience tells that the general case is that persistent CA deficits as required by the external financing of growth are an exception. Growth tends to be correlated with national savings, and national and external savings appear as substitutes.

The suggestion provided by simple models of an open economy with assets mobility that as long as a country has profitable opportunities will be a recipient of financial flows shall be examined in each case, as discussed in the recent literature, in terms of the effects of accumulated debt on the perception of foreign agents of the capacity or the willingness to pay of the debtor. Complex interactions determine a projection of a profile of borrowing-repaying sequence of the aggregate economy subject to exogenous shocks. Payment of the debt requires both building savings capacity and dynamic exports to generate foreign currency. Attention shall be devoted to the possibilities to increase national savings, and the benefits and costs of policies providing incentives for national savings, such as fiscal mechanisms and the stability and efficiency of the financial system.

References

Ávila, J. (2000), Riesgo argentino y performance macroeconómica. Universidad del Cema. Buenos Aires.

Burmeister, E. and Rodney Dobell, A. (1970), Mathematical theories of economic growth. McMillan Publishing Co. New York.

Calvo, G., Izquierdo, A. and Mejía, L. (2003), On the empirics of sudden stops. Working Paper, Interamerican Development Bank.

Chisari, O., Rozenwurzel, G., Fanelli, J. M. and Frenkel, R. (1992), Ahorro público y recuperación del crecimiento en la Argentina. 25as Jornadas de Finanzas Públicas. UN de Córdoba.

Cortés Conde, R. (1998), Progreso y declinación de la economía argentina. Fondo de Cultura Económica. Buenos Aires.

Cortés Conde, R. (1996), La Economía Argentina en el Largo Plazo. Editorial Sudamericana/Universidad de San Andrés, Buenos Aires.

Díaz Cafferata, Alberto M., 2004. Inercia estructural del crecimiento económico argentino: el ahorro doméstico, el ahorro externo y la salida exportadora. In: *Perspectivas de Crecimiento.* Academia Nacional de Ciencias Económicas.

Díaz Cafferata, A. M. (1994), Cambio tecnológico, obsolescencia del capital y desocupación, en la transición de la apertura comercial. Anales de la Asociación Argentina de Economía Política. XXIX Reunión Anual, Universidad Nacional de la Plata, Octubre.

Díaz Cafferata, A. and Fornero, J. (2003), Tendencias y quiebres del grado de apertura exportadora de Argentina, y el marco internacional, 1884-2002. *XXXVIII Reunión Anual de la Asociación Argentina de Economía Política.* Universidad Nacional de Cuyo. Mendoza.

Easterly, W. (1997), The ghost of financing gap, *Mimeo.* World Bank. July.

Edwards, S. (2004), Financial openness, sudden stops and CA reversals. National Bureau of Economic Research *Working Paper* N° 10277. January. http://www.nber.org/papers/w10277

Edwards, S. (2004a.), Thirty years of current account imbalances, current account reversals and sudden stops. *NBER Working Paper* N° 10276 January, http://www.nber.org/papers/w10276

Feldstein, M. and Horioka, C. (1980), Domestic savings and international capital flows, in: *Economic Journal*, Vol 90 (June); 314-329.

Findlay, R. (1984), Growth and development in trade models. In Jones and Kenen, 1984.

Gerchunoff, P. and Llach, L. (2003), *El ciclo de la ilusión y el desencanto. Un siglo de políticas económicas argentinas.* Editorial Ariel. Buenos Aires.

Grossman, G. and Rogoff, K. (eds), (1995), *Handbook of international economics.* Vol 3. Elsevier Science B.V.

Halevi, N. (1971), An empirical test of the Balance of Payments stages hypothesis, in: *Journal of International Economics*, Vol. 1, N1 (February);103-117.

Hodrick, R. and Prescott, E. (1997), Post-war business cycles: an empirical investigation, in: *Journal of Money, Credit and Banking*. Vol. 29, N.1; 1-16.

Jansen, W. J. (1996), Estimating saving-investment correlations: evidence for OECD countries based on an error correction model. In: Journal of International Money and Finance. Vol. 15; 749-781.

Jansen, W. J. and Schultze, G. G. (1996), Theory-based measurement of the savings-investment correlations with an application to Norway. In: *Economic Inquiry*, Vol. 34; 116-132.

Jones, R.W. and Kenen, P. B. (1984), *Handbook of International Economics*. North Holland.

Lanteri, L. (1996), Consumo smoothing y la cuenta corriente, AAEP.

Leamer, E. E. (1994), Testing trade theory. In: *Survey in international trade*. Greenaway and Winters, 1995.

Milesi-Ferretti, G. and Razin, A. (1996), Current account sustainability. Princenton Studies in International Finance. N81. October.

Mundlak, Y., Cavallo, D. and Domenech, R. (1989), Agriculture and Economic Growth in Argentina, 1913-84. International Food Policy Research Institute. *Research Report* 76.

Mussa, M. (2002), Argentina and the Fund. From triumph to tragedy. Institute for International Economics. *Mimeo*.

Obstfeld, M. (1999), Foreign resource inflows, savings and growth. In Schmidt-Hebbel, Klaus and Luis Serven (eds), 1999a.

Obstfeld, M. and Rogoff, K. (1996), *Foundations of international macroeconomics*. The MIT Press, Cambridge, Massachusetts.

Obstfeld, M. and Rogoff, K. (1995), The intertemporal approach to the current account. In Grossman and Rogoff (eds), 1995.

Olivera Julio H. G. (1975), El gradualismo y las políticas de ajustes, in: *AAEP X Reunión Anual*.

Pritchett, L. (1996), Measuring outward orientation in LDCs: can it be done? In: *Journal of Development Economics*. Vol. 49; 307- 335.

Ram, R. (1985), Exports and economic growth: some additional evidence, in: *Economic Development and Cultural Change* 33, 2; 415-425.

Razgallah, B. (2004), *The balance of payments stages 'hypothesis': a reappraisal*. CERSEI 3. Université Pantheón-Assas (Paris II)

Reinhart, C. M. and Ernesto T. (1997), Capital flows and saving in Latin America and Asia: a reinterpretation. *Mimeo*, University of Maryland.

Rodriguez, F. and Rodrik, D. (2000), Trade policy and economic growth: a skeptics guide to the international literature, Working Paper.

Romer, D. (2001), *Advanced Macroeconomics*. McGraw-Hill. Boston.

Schmidt-Hebbel, K. and Serven, L. (1999), Saving in the world: the stylized facts, In Schmidt-Hebbel and Serven (1999a) (eds.).

Schmidt-Hebbel, K. and Serven, L. (eds), (1999a), *The economics of savings and growth. Theory, evidence and implications for policy*. Cambridge U.P. USA.

Sheffrin, S. and Woo, W. (1990), Present value tests of an intertemporal model of the current account. In: *Journal of International Economics*. Vol. 29; 237-253

Sturzennegger, A. and Moya, R. (2002), Ciclos económicos en Argentina: 1884-1990. Versión preliminar. *Mimeo*.

Tinbergen, J. (1942), Zur theorie der langfristigen Wirtschaftsentwicklung. *Weltwirtschaftilches Archiv*, Band 55, Heft I; 511-549. Also in: Ensayos de teoría económica, ed Tecnos, Colección de Ciencias sociales 42, Madrid, 1965, 249-283.

Rensselaer, V., Copeland, K. and Copeland, J. B. (2000), Savings and investment rates in Latin America: en error correction analysis. In: *Journal of Economics and Finance*. Vol.24, N2 (Summer); 195-205.

Wälde, K. and Wood, C. (2004), The empirics of trade and growth: where are the policy recommendations? *European Commision Economic Papers*. N204 (May)

EFFECTS OF MERCOSUR ON THE ARGENTINE AGRICULTURAL INTERNATIONAL TRADE: AN APPLICATION OF A GRAVITY EQUATION[43]

María Luisa Recalde and Marcelo Florensa
Instituto de Economía y Finanzas - UNC

1. Introduction

The effects of the economic integration are mainly two (Bela Balassa, 1967): trade creation which manifests as the appearance of new trade currents among the member countries and domestic production is replaced. This effect is possible when the member countries of an agreement reduce their rates to the imports of third countries as part of the commitment of arriving at a common external rate. Trade deviation, on the other hand, consists in the substitution of the imports of the countries that are not members of the agreement (products of lower cost) for imports of the member countries (products of higher cost). Trade creation minus trade deviation yields the net effect of a trading block on the rest of the world[44].

Mayes (1978) points out that if the barriers to trade, the rates and the quotas are eliminated, trade creation should be expected to increase; if the trade rates related to a certai country are eliminated, not modifying those in use with the rest of the countries, it could be expected that the imports of the first country would be increased at the expense of the imports of the other countries (trade deviation).

The discussion of only these effects, which are short term effects, leaves aside the consideration of other important changes occurring in international trade as a consequence of integration and are originated in the specialization in the production that stems from the comparative advantages, the economies of scale, the changes in the terms of trade, changes in the levels of efficiency of the companies as a consequence of the larger external competition, changes in the rate of growth, etc. Lipsey (1975).

The measurement of such effects has led numerous authors to the construction and application of the so called models of trade impact, which measure ex-post effects of integration on the trade flows of the member countries. Although some of these models have been developed using a general or partial equilibrium model, most such models have used the so-called "gravity equation".

The process of integration of the MERCOSUR begins with the subscription by Argentina and Brazil, of the Argentinean-Brazilian Cooperation and Integration Treaty in 1986, within the ALADI . The signature of the Treaty of Asunción (1991), which is the start of MERCOSUR,

[43] The collaboration of Ivan Iturralde, Iván Julio and Belen Gonzalo, members of the work team, is highly appreciated.

[44] Aitken(1973) considers a third alternative, defining the increments in the trade between the member and non member countries of an agreement as external creation of trade.

constitutes a free trade zone among Argentina, Brazil, Paraguay and Uruguay. It establishes the objective of reaching a common market that would begin to work in the year 1995. The Treaty establishes an initial reduction of 40% to the tariffs for the countries of the block and to be applied as from June of 1991 with biannual reductions in order to eliminate them by the year 1995, the same year when a common external tariff would be reached.

The aim of this work is to develop an econometric framework to determine whether the MERCOSUR has had an impact on the international trade of agricultural products of Argentina. This framework is based on the specification and estimation of a gravity equation. It has proved a very useful tool in modelling bilateral currents of trade. In this model, the hypothetically currents of trade that may have occurred if the integration had not been implemented would be estimated. The structure that data generates in the period after the integration, known as "the world" *(monde* in French) while the *antimonde* refers to the scenario that has existed, over the same period, but without such an agreement. Obviously, the biggest difficulty in this type of models is the estimation of the *antimonde*. The impact of the integration process is defined as the difference between the predictions of both structures assuming that this difference is statistically significant. It is generally assumed that the trade in the *antimonde* remains constant, beginning in a period close to the signature of the agreement. Nevertheless, the effects of the integration are essentially dynamic.

The way to introduce the dynamic aspects consists in upgrading the estimated parameters of the gravity equation, taking the first year in wich the impact of the commercial integration is evidenced, as the starting point. To dynamize the estimated parameters, the Kalman Filter is used. This is a recursive algorythm which is generally used in the linear models. The Kalman Filter allows to compute a new vector of coefficients when we have new information However, as the forecast horizon lengthens, the explanatory power of these regressions decreases because the forecast for the next period is based on a previous forecast and not on observable data. Nevertheless, this approach is more realistic than assuming that nothing has occurred over the post-integration period.

Results demonstrate that since the signature of the Argentinean-Brazilian Cooperation and Integration Treaty of 1986, the process of integration of the Mercosur started to impact on the international trade of the agricultural products of Argentina. From the application of this model, it may be inferred that income and population are, on average, the variables that better explain the bilateral flows of the agricultural trade of Argentina. The distance and the language, on the other hand, are of little significance.

This paper has been divided into five main sections. In the next section a description of the evolution of the international trade of the agricultural sector of Argentina is introduced. Section III deals with the econometric framework used in this paper. In section IV, the main results are elaborated and finally the concluding remarks are made.

2. Argentine Agricultural Trade

The Argentinean agricultural international trade has been increased around 10 times in the period 1966-2001. The total trade of these products can be explained almost exclusively by the export performance. In fact, the imports have only represented between 4% and 6% of the annual exports. This is the reason for the important structural surplus over the whole period (Figure 1). Nevertheless, the exports have been losing relative importance especially since the mid 1980s, when it represented about 40% and later reached little over 20% (Figure 2). The agricultural products exports have been unstable but show a strong correlation with a small volume of imports.

Figure 1: Evolution of Argentine agricultural trade in u$s millions

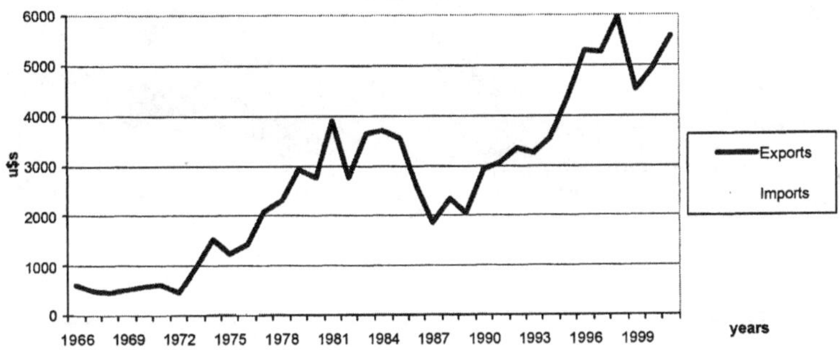

Figure 2: Agricultural Imports and Exports share in Argentinean International Trade

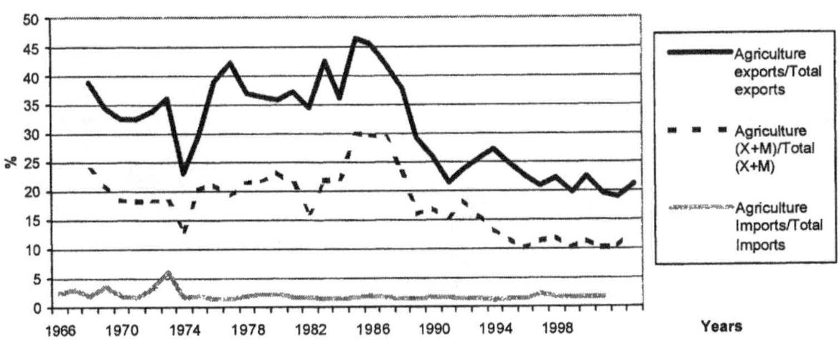

A fact that should be pointed out is the diversification that took place in the exports of agricultural products. At the beginning of the period, exports were mainly constituted by grains (chapter 10) and at the present time this item represents near 50%, the rest being concentrated on only three items: fish and seafood, fruits, seeds and oilseeds (chapters 3, 8 and 12) (Figure 3).

As concerns imports, until 1990 fruits have represented the bulk (chapter 8); as from that year, imports have been diversified, and the seeds and oilseeds grew more significant (chapter 12) in the second half of the 90's when the import of transgenic seeds was incresead (Figure 4).

Figure 3: Agricultural Exports by Chapter in u$s millions

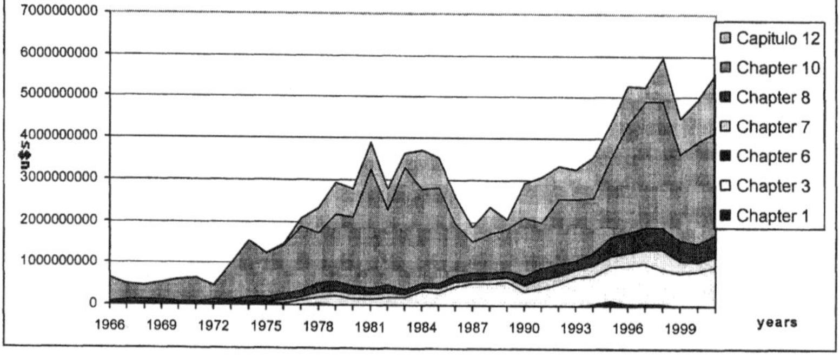

Figure 4: Agricultural Imports by Chapter in u$s millions

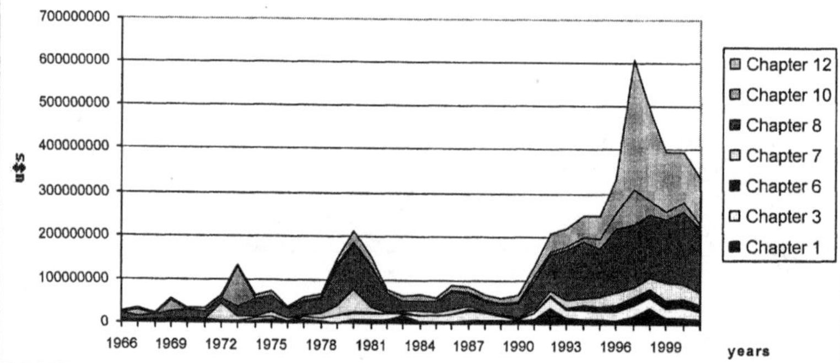

With regard to the geographical trade distribution, Table 1 and 2 show the main origins and destinations of the Argentinean agricultural trade. Three facts can be pointed out concerning exports: the high participation of Russia (former U.S.S.R.) between 1977 and 1984, the increase since 1982 of the importance of the Arab countries and, since 1987 the relative growth of the countries of the Mercosur (especially Brazil), to the detriment of the European

Union members. For example, until the year 1971, Italy was a very important destination (almost 30%) and later it diminished to less than 5%. These changes in the destination of the exports have improved the diversification of the trade of agricultural products.

Table 1: Geographical Distribution of the Argentine Agriculture Exports (%)

EXPORTS	1966	1971	1976	1981	1986	1991	1996	2001
Germany	3.36	2.94	2.24	1.22	4.08	5.26	1.58	0.38
Belgium	2.39	2.61	2.08	0.69	2.99	1.05	1.39	1.96
Spain	5.47	17.31	6.82	3.28	3.97	8.43	8.00	10.09
France	1.02	1.10	0.69	0.48	1.25	2.31	1.62	1.02
Italy	27.64	30.64	17.44	4.24	5.53	7.80	2.73	3.67
United Kingdom	3.17	1.78	0.73	0.09	0.16	1.55	1.74	0.90
Netherlands	4.84	4.56	7.46	4.44	8.25	16.76	10.00	3.51
EUROPEAN UNION	47.88	60.93	37.45	14.43	26.23	43.16	27.06	21.53
Russia (Former U.S.S.R.)	11.08	1.98	10.23	63.19	1.32	0.02	0.32	0.89
China	13.45	1.01	0.00	0.56	2.29	1.17	1.86	15.24
Japan	1.52	11.20	8.46	0.91	9.43	5.94	4.26	2.59
United States and Canada	0.24	1.06	0.67	0.96	1.60	2.29	3.06	4.28
Brazil	12.44	8.08	16.21	5.55	12.21	20.49	25.74	20.93
Paraguay and Uruguay	0.91	0.31	1.07	1.74	0.71	0.95	1.88	1.12
MERCOSUR	13.35	8.38	17.28	7.29	12.93	21.44	27.62	22.04
Chile	3.09	6.30	4.33	0.53	0.27	0.50	1.25	2.75
REST OF LATIN AMERICA	3.97	1.91	5.16	4.94	7.72	5.68	6.53	3.16
ARAB COUNTRIES	0.20	0.46	3.23	0.28	7.81	3.91	7.63	8.70
REST OF THE WORLD	0.41	0.06	0.08	0.04	0.64	1.89	2.64	4.21
Total	100	100	100	100	100	100	100	100

Source: "Comercio Exterior" Bulletin - INDEC.

The image is different when the imports are analyzed (Table 2). Except for the year 1973, the participations are relatively stable and concentrated on three origins, Mercosur, United States and Canada and European Union.

Trade with the Mercosur has shown a similar behavior to that of the rest of the world, but with some particular characteristics. In the exports, since 1988, there has been an increase in almost all the items, but chapter 10 shows a bigger increase. Different from the overall exports, this chapter clearly prevails as export item.

Table 2: Geographical Distribution of Argentine Agriculture Imports (%)

IMPORTS	1966	1971	1976	1981	1986	1991	1996	2001
IMPORTS	1966	1971	1976	1981	1986	1991	1996	2001
Germany	0.50	1.25	1.62	1.05	1.05	1.53	0.76	0.44
Belgium	0.27	0.26	0.05	0.14	0.01	0.03	0.01	0.07
Spain	2.09	2.99	1.47	2.32	1.29	1.69	1.61	2.00
France	4.26	0.94	0.75	0.99	1.13	0.82	1.39	1.52
Italy	0.59	1.35	1.18	1.53	0.62	1.08	2.01	1.63
United Kingdom	2.22	0.28	0.10	0.20	0.00	0.06	0.20	0.48
Netherlands	2.65	3.98	3.97	1.23	0.90	2.43	0.96	0.93
EUROPEAN UNION	12.58	11.06	9.15	7.47	5.00	7.64	6.94	7.07
Russia (Former U.S.S.R.)	0.00	0.00	0.03	0.00	0.00	0.83	0.00	0.00
China	0.06	0.00	0.00	0.10	0.00	0.06	0.66	0.46
Japan	0.00	0.03	0.03	0.17	0.12	0.11	0.16	0.12
United States and Canada	17.79	15.73	17.14	13.50	11.97	17.56	27.28	10.52
Brazil	50.36	43.71	55.40	20.25	25.27	24.86	9.93	11.12
Paraguay and Uruguay	4.81	8.31	5.51	6.62	6.51	7.63	3.29	19.78
MERCOSUR	17.79	15.76	17.17	13.67	12.09	17.67	27.44	10.64
Chile	6.72	3.96	3.84	7.75	17.84	19.21	18.53	15.86
REST OF LATIN AMERICA	3.13	3.64	4.48	11.77	2.51	0.66	2.05	1.51
ARAB COUNTRIES	0.01	0.04	0.00	0.11	0.01	0.14	0.20	0.09
REST OF THE WORLD	4.54	13.51	4.42	32.28	30.78	21.29	30.95	33.46
Total	100.00	100.00	100.00	100.00	100.00	100.00	100.00	100.00

3. The Model: The Gravity Equation

The first attempt to use the gravity model to measure the effects of the integration was carried out by Aitken(1973) who used a cross-section analysis based on the developments of Linnemann and Tinbergen. By means of the use of dummy variables, the effect that the integration in the European Economic Community (EEC) and the European Association of

Free Trade (EFTA) had on the member countries in the period 1959-67 was considered. An equation for each year of this period with the purpose of testing the existence and magnitude of the integration effects was used. This equation was also calculated for several years previous to the period of the integration in order to have a vision of the forces that were acting before the creation of the EEC (1951-67).

In this first method, Aitken (1973) used the dummy variables, called preference variables. The estimation of the gravity equation allowed him to determine the first year in which the effects of the integration took place, by means of the observation of the levels of significance of the preference variables. Then he obtained the gross trade creation for each one of the blocks. This procedure fails to distinguish between trade creation and trade deviation.

In a second method, Aitken (1973) eliminated the estimated coefficients corresponding to the preference dummy variables of the last year in which the integration had not caused effects (cross section of the year 1958). This structure was then projected for the post-integration period. This procedure allowed him to evaluate external creation and trade deviation. A method similar to the first one that Aitken used was also used in later works by Aitken and Obutelewicz (1976), Sapir (1981) and Brada and Méndez (1985) for other commercial agreements.

Pelzman (1977) developed a more sophisticated method than those used by other authors (level of significance of the preference dummy variable) to detect the structural breaks. This method consisted in selecting a period of pre-integration in which the gravitational equation was estimated. The estimated parameters were then used to project the trade flows among the member countries over the post-integration period. The difference between the current trade volume among the member countries and the prospective volume would be a consequence of the integration. The pattern was applied for a group of countries belonging to the CMEA (Council of Mutual Economic Assistance) for the period 1954-70.

In spite of the advances introduced by Pelzman (1977), it is necessary to highlight that the structure of the gravity equation is basically static, because it doesn't take into account the evolution of the trade flows over the time. This means that if there were no integration, factors like the penetration of exports in external markets, the levels of efficiency of the firms, the appearance of economies of scale in production, the evolution of non-tariff barriers, the economic cycles, etc. would remain constant or their effects on the international trade would be exactly compensated (Mayes, 1978).

Among the papers that have applied the gravity equation to measure the trade flows, that by Martínez-Zarzoso and Nowak-Lehmann (2002) is worth mentioning. They use a variant of the gravity equation to classify the products according to the sensitivity to geographical and economic distance. They argue that the products that are highly sensitive to the economic distance (using as proxy the absolute differences in the per-capita income) and to the geographical one, they are the best candidates for future exchanges between the European Union and the Mercosur. They considered the empiric pattern applying the methodology of panel data to see the effects on the trade flows between pairs of countries. In the estimation, they used two explanatory variables, infrastructure and exchange rate. The results show that the different products have different sensitivity to distances.

On the other hand, Groot, H.L. et.al (2003) applied the gravity model to study the effect of the institutions on trade flows. They considered whether the quality of the governments, especially the aspects related to homogeneity and institutional quality, have an impact on trade flows.

Finally, Sanz (2000) and Sanz and Gil (2001) have been able to solve the problems associated to the static outline derived from the use of the gravity equation, with the application of the so-called space-state model and the Kalman Filter. The methodology used in this paer is based on the estimation of a gravity equation with the following specification:

$$X_{ij} = AY_i^{\beta 1} Y_j^{\beta 2} L_i^{\beta 3} L_j^{\beta 4} D_{ij}^{\beta 5} e^{u_{ij}} \qquad (1)$$

where

X_{ij} = the current value of sales from country i to country j
A = a constant term
Y = income
L = population
D_{ij} = distance between countries i and j
u_{ij} = the error term

The structure of the gravity equation is static. The measurement of the integration effects on international trade demands that the gravity model coefficients, the β_i, change over time. As it has been mentioned before, factors such as the penetration of exports in foreign markets, the firms efficiency, the exploitation of economies of scale, the evolution of nontariff barriers, the economic cycles, etc. are dynamic. It is well known that there are many alternatives to modelling the dynamics, but it has been considered particularly convenient to express the gravity equation in State-Space Form (SSF).

The SSF has, in general, two equations. One of them called measurement equation, relates the vector of observable variables, Y_t, to a vector of non-observable variables, α_t, called state vector, in the following way [45]:

$$Y_t = Z_t \alpha_t + d_t + \varepsilon_t \qquad (2)$$

where

t = 1, ...,T
Y_t is a vector of n elements
α_t is a vector of m elements
Z_t is an n x m matrix
d_t is a vector of n elements
ε_t is an n x 1 vector of serially uncorrelated disturbances with mean zero and covariance matrix H

[45] The symbols used are those adopted by Harvey (1989)

In general, the elements of α_t are not observable; however, they are known to be generated by a first-order Markov process, which has the following structure:

$$\alpha_t = T_t \alpha_{t-1} + c_t + R_t \eta_t \tag{3}$$

where

$t = 1,...,T$
α_t y α_{t-1} are m x 1 vectors
T_t is an m x m matrix
c_t is an n x 1 vector
R_t is an m x j matrix
η_t is an j x 1 vector of serially uncorrelated disturbances with mean zero and covariance matriz Q.

Equation 3 is the transition equation.
Once the model has been expressed in SSF, a group of algorythms, known as Kalman Filter, can be applied. The advantage of using the Kalman Filter is that it provides a statistically optimum estimator, in the sense that it minimizes the mean square error of the state vector at the moment t, t = 1,... T; providing a solution to the dynamic regression model.
The Kalman Filter is used to estimate the *antimonde* essentially, in an dynamic way, applying it on the gravity equation.
Following the previous notation, the model in matrix terms would be:

$$\begin{aligned} M_t &= X_t \beta_t + \mu_t \qquad t = 1,\ldots,T \\ \beta_t &= C\beta_{t-1} + \upsilon_t \end{aligned} \tag{4}$$

where

M_t = an N x 1 vector of trade flows during period t
X_t = the N x k matriz of exogenous variables of the gravity equation
β_t = the so-called $k \times 1$ state vector that defines the structure during period t
μ_t = an N x 1 vector of random errors wich is distributed as $N \;\square\; (0, H_t)$

The model that independently generates each β_t is given by:

$$\beta_{i_t} = c_i \beta_{i_{t-1}} + \upsilon_{i_t} \qquad i = 1,2,\ldots,k \qquad t = 1,\ldots,T \tag{5}$$

which is to say that C is diagonal in equation 4. The errors vector υ_t has a normal distribution with a vector of mean zero and variance and covariance matrix Q, with Q being $k \times k$ diagonal matrix. Furthermore, the initial state vector β_0 is assumed to be uncorrelated to any of the random errors μ_t and υ_t, which are also uncorrelated to each other.
Therefore the Kalman Filter, for the present model, is the following:

a) Prediction Equations:

$$\begin{aligned} b_{t/t-1} &= C b_{t-1} \\ P_{t/t-1} &= C P_{t-1} C' \end{aligned} \qquad (6)$$

b) Updating Equations:

$$\begin{aligned} b_{t/t} &= b_{t/t-1} + P_{t/t-1} X_t' F_t^{-1} (M_t - X_t b_{t/t-1}) \\ P_{t/t} &= P_{t/t-1} - P_{t/t-1} X_t' F_t^{-1} X_t P_{t/t-1} \end{aligned} \qquad (7)$$

where

$$F_t = X_t P_{t/t-1} X_t' + H_t$$

c) Smoothing Equations:

$$\begin{aligned} b_{t/T} &= b_t + P_t C' P_{t+1/t}^{-1} (b_{t+1/T} - b_{t+1/t}) \\ P_{t/T} &= P_t - P_t C' P_{t+1/t}^{-1} (P_{t+1/T} - P_{t+1/t}) P_{t+1/t}^{-1}{}' C P_t' \end{aligned} \qquad (8)$$

This algorythm uses all the available data on the previous integration trade flows and none of the post-integration period data, defining a different *antimonde* for each year of the post-integration period.

4. Results

Data

The information used in this paper is composed of by 35 annual cross-sections that cover the period 1967-2001. The bilateral flows between Argentina and 23 countries have been taken into account: Germany, Belgium, Bolivia, Brazil, Canada, Chile, China, Colombia, Spain, United States, France, Italy, Japan, Mexico, the Netherlands, Paraguay, Peru, Portugal, United Kingdom, Russia (ex USSR), South Africa, Uruguay and Venezuela. In this way, there would be 46 observations per year which represented between 85% and 95% of the Argentinean agricultural international trade.

The trade flows data were obtained from the publications" Comercio Exterior Argentino" of the INDEC[46]. The exports and imports corresponding to the chapters of the Common Nomenclature of the Mercosur (CNM)have been used:

1: livestock
3: fish and seafood
6: plants and flowers
7: vegetables, plants and roots and nutritious tubers
8: edible fruits; citrus, melons and watermelons
10: grains
12: seeds and oilseeds; herbal plants, straw and forage

[46] The data corresponding to the period 1984-1989 were obtained from *Departmento deTrabajos Especiales*, INDEC because, in this period, the publication "Comercio Exterior" was not in circulation.

The data of per-capita incomes and populations were obtained from of International Financial Statistics, version 11.54 in CD-ROM, year 2001, published by the International Monetary Fund.
The data corresponding to the distances were obtained from the database of available international trade on the Jon Haveman web page.

Estimation Results

The first empiric papers that used the gravity pattern to model the bilateral flows of trade, among which is Aitken's (1973), made use of a log-linear specification of the gravity equation. Later, Sanso, Cuairan and Sanz (1993) showed that the specification of the gravity equation in logarythm terms does not necessarily constitute the best functional form. As the pattern in logarythm represents a special case of the Box-Cox transformation, an appropriate analysis in the best functional way would consist in estimating the optimum parameters of such transformation.
Therefore, for each year the following model has been specified[47]

$$M_{ij}^{\lambda_0} = \beta_0 + \beta_1 y_i^{\lambda_1} + \beta_2 y_j^{\lambda_2} + \beta_3 L_i^{\lambda_3} + \beta_4 L_j^{\lambda_4} + \\ + \beta_5 D_{ij}^{\lambda_5} + \beta_6 \text{Merco} + \beta_7 \text{Lenguaje} + \mu_{ij} \qquad (9)$$

where

M, L y D = as previously defined

y = per capita income [48] (i is for the exporter country and j for the importer)

Merco = a dummy variable that takes the value 1 if the Argentine trade flow is held with a Mercosur member

Lenguaje= a dummy variable that takes the value 1 if the trade flow is with a Spanish speaking country.

λ_i = is the Box-Cox parameter associated with each variable

As the objective of this paper is to quantify the effects of the Mercosur on the Argentinean agricultural trade, the MERCO dummy variable is intended to determine the first year when the impact of the agreement takes place.
The Language dummy variable controls the importance of the language on the bilateral trade. The results of the estimation of the equation 9 are shown in Table 3.

---

[47] The procedure to estimate the parameters of the Box-Cox transformation is dealt with in detail in the appendix.

[48] Sanso, Cuairan and Sanz (1993) show that the gravity equation is better when per capita income instead of the GDP or GNP is used.

Table 3. Maximum Likelihood Estimation of the Box-Cox Parameters (lambdas)

Year	λ_0	λ_1	λ_2	λ_3	λ_4	λ_5
1967	0.12	-2.17	1.31	-0.90	-0.64	-0.78
1968	0.10	-2.17	-2.05	-0.71	0.56	0.76
1969	0.11	-0.76	-1.47	-0.69	0.35	0.58
1970	0.05	-2.17	0.91	-0.72	-0.44	-0.50
1971	0.09	-2.19	0.25	-0.72	0.35	-0.58
1972	0.13	-2.05	0.02	-0.71	0.08	0.08
1973	0.12	-2.22	-1.78	-0.65	0.69	0.61
1974	0.12	-0.95	-1.90	-0.76	0.62	-0.61
1975	0.05	-1.97	0.72	-0.79	0.26	0.01
1976	0.08	-1.87	0.32	-0.82	-0.56	0.76
1977	0.10	-0.82	0.96	-0.73	0.36	-0.96
1978	0.13	0.99	0.73	-0.68	0.35	0.83
1979	0.14	-1.21	0.93	-0.65	0.38	0.39
1980	0.09	-1.82	1.32	3.11	0.48	-0.83
1981	-0.01	-2.09	0	-0.82	0.53	-0.12
1982	0.01	-1.42	0.60	2.93	0.44	-0.86
1983	0.08	-1.73	2.05	-0.66	0.54	-0.18
1984	0.06	-1.70	0.38	-0.69	0.30	-0.03
1985	0.08	-0.99	1.16	-0.81	0.41	0.40
1986	0.09	-1.87	1.30	2.45	0.60	-0.89
1987	0.15	-1.69	1.15	-0.76	0.40	-0.85
1988	0	-1.09	1.29	-0.74	0.61	0.46
1989	0.03	-1.67	0.36	2.12	0.73	-0.96
1990	0.05	-1.01	1.16	-0.77	0.52	-0.75
1991	0.03	-0.61	1.61	-0.78	0.92	0.69
1992	0.05	-0.35	2.12	-0.64	-0.71	0.12
1993	0.07	-1.06	1.76	-0.75	-0.70	-0.89
1994	0.07	-0.39	1.46	-0.68	0.38	-0.76
1995	0.07	-0.57	1.30	-0.64	1.09	-0.86
1996	0.13	-0.54	1.57	-0.62	0.49	-0.73
1997	0.15	0.03	1.75	-0.70	0.27	0.57
1998	0.13	-0.88	1.79	1.84	0.65	-0.86
1999	0.14	-1.68	1.52	-0.81	0.77	-0.95
2000	0.08	-1.01	1.66	-0.69	-0.70	-0.85
2001	0.06	-1.16	1.16	-0.67	0.52	-0.57

Once the optimum functional form has been determined, the variables are properly trasformed and used to estimate the β_i by ordinary least squares. Table 4 shows the results.

The sign of the coefficients that accompany the per-capita income and population variables is positive, as the gravity equation predicts. On the other hand, the coefficient of the distance variable has unexpected sign, for the years 1967,1970-1972, 1974-1975,1977, 1980-1982, 1986-1987, 1989-1990, 1995-1996, 1998-1999 and 2001. The correct sign should be negative.

With respect to the statistical significance of the coefficients, the 0.05 level is taken and the following is verified:

a) $y_i^{\lambda_1}$ is statistically significant except for the years 1973, 1978-1984, 1988, 1996-1997 and 1999
b) $y_j^{\lambda_2}$ is not statistically significant for the years 1967-1968, 1970, 1972-1975, 1980 and 1983
c) $L_i^{\lambda_3}$ is not statistically significant for the years 1967-1968, 1970-1976, 1980-1983, 1990, 1995, 1998-1999 and 2001.
d) $L_j^{\lambda_4}$ is not statistically significant for the years 1967-1970, 1972-1973, 1976, 1984, 1992-1994, 1998 and 2000.
e) D_{ij} is statistically significant only in 1992 and 1997

Concerning the dummy variables, the language variable is only significant in 1977, 1986, 1988-1989, 1994, 1996; therefore, it can be stated that Argentina doesn't enjoy more trade, on average, with the Spanish speaking countries.
What is outstanding is that the Merco dichotomic variable begins to be statistically significant as from 1986. For the period 1986-2001, this variable is not significant except for the years 1991-1992 and 1997. Therefore, there is evidence in favor of 1986 as the first year in which the integration produces effects on the bilateral trade flows. The year 1986 coincides with the signing of the Argentinean-Brazilian Cooperation and Integration Treaty within the framework of ALADI. This way, the period 1967-1985 is held to be that of pre-integration. To define the *antimonde*, the Kalman Filter should be applied to the betas estimated in this period.

Table 4 – OLS Estimation of the Position Parameters (β)

Year (D.S)	β_0 (C)	β_1 (gdppc$_i$)	β_2 (gdppc$_j$)	β_3 (population$_i$)	β_4 (population$_j$)	β_5 (distance)	β_6 (Merco)	β_7 (language)	$R2$
1967	-935165.15*	1487139.40*	0.000195	1438.76	22780.09	164164.46	16.953857	2.689609	0.148
	(462942.38)	(725734.10)	(0.00033)	(2430.32)	(131757.06)	(218723)	(10.4773)	(6.6542)	
1968	-1398806.6*	1014972 *	551589.63	476336.93	0.000201	-0.000032	6.5602714	-0.01147	0.274
	(530746.3)	(486539.97)	(443959)	(284878.33)	(0.000119)	(0.000028)	(6.988733)	(5.49062)	
1969	-745134.82*	688.6578 *	49480.75*	493706.80 *	0.007589	-0.000255	11.6445	1.732715	0.273
	(347199.72)	(340.1705)	(22034.0)	(238690.46)	(0.005)	(0.00049)	(8.28501)	(6.39418)	
1970	-652799.95*	573136.62 *	0.002577	274644.02	1061.1113	940.6784	7.44644	1.913508	0.214
	(291165.24)	(269510.11)	(0.00192)	(192652.52)	(1924.42)	(2134.70)	(4.0078)	(2.4599)	
1971	-1349757.9*	2151273.6 *	0.810883*	261174.41	0.00656 *	5706.3546	10.0501	5.1131	0.332
	(523566.21)	(716929.40)	(0.39920)	(302972)	(0.002895)	(9730.748)	(6.4312)	(4.0167)	
1972	-1405648 *	1463039.3 *	4.5458	496352.47	0.56089	0.042824	17.2325	-0.94750	0.238
	(669081.51)	(694852.23)	(3.10531)	(428337.96)	(0.602951)	(1.48080)	(11.4063)	(7.55007)	
1973	-2507670.2*	4303121.3	506250.64	191606.26	0.0000217	-0.000261	8.40735	-4.66570	0.242
	(1192499.2)	(2601815.9)	(351461)	(143750.13)	(0.0000123)	(0.000372)	(9.44484)	(7.31007)	
1974	-1997664.9	3638.9485 *	1005796.7	1102493.3	0.000108 *	18831.04	18.6368	8.02308	0.298
	(1427375.8)	(1756.6354)	(773801)	(1003254.2)	(0.000044)	(24334.83)	(10.3718)	(6.28136)	
1975	-1577543.6*	677541.81 *	0.008135	986576.33	0.017771 *	0.69031	6.87185	3.4555	0.341
	(722554.68)	(281970.69)	(0.00468)	(579003.79)	(0.007947)	(1.40933)	(4.03095)	(2.62233)	
1976	-4250613.3*	670635.76 *	0.653705*	3201948.8	5798.2374	-0.000018	8.43043	3.65976	0.386
	(2052991.5)	(286140.93)	(0.19151)	(1681901.3)	(25922.21)	(0.000022)	(6.41964)	(5.01552)	
1977	-2717610.9	1830.7167 *	0.003426*	1007650 *	0.008380 *	1302121.9	17.8114 *	10.71395 *	0.465
	(1643148)	(676.8737)	(0.00011)	(447124.12)	(0.002733)	(1621067)	(6.85513)	(4.38547)	
1978	-865801.6 *	3836.57	0.038246*	590026.61 *	0.014324 *	-0.0000051	16.795778	12.9784	0.413
	(425416.76)	(2757.209)	(0.00991)	(291330.26)	(0.00536)	(1.373271)	(10.27469)	(8.303146)	
1979	-725501.57*	24448.544	0.007232*	477593.82 *	0.0126432 *	-0.009969	25.34989	14.76329	0.452
	(343354.6)	(15508.73)	(0.00205)	(223967.53)	(0.003818)	(0.017512)	(14.9148)	(10.8961)	
1980	-1273410.8	1920070.2	0.000041	1.55e-026	0.000462 *	185080.21	10.0003	0.86768	0.321
	(828995.4)	(1416951)	(0.00002)	(1.42e-026)	(0.000199)	(202728.2)	(5.0053)	(3.20190)	
1981	-909863.07*	375987.77	1.25928 *	600822.79	0.000536 *	0.243868	2.2258	1.32942	0.360
	(393840.16)	(256180.86)	(0.42259)	(306296.41)	(0.000017)	(3.58421)	(1.38221)	(0.85272)	
1982	-146564.1	50475.194	0.00890 *	2.011e-026	0.000384 *	96355.311	3.09394	2.17086	0.315
	(127040.85)	(29248.97)	(0.00440)	(1.33e-025)	(0.00013)	(107563.4)	(1.611)	(1.066)	
1983	-465921.52*	246652.22	0.000510	215731.51	0.000199 *	-39.7886	4.91981	-0.65865	0.312
	(218681.35)	(195434.79)	(0.00032)	(123880.74)	(0.0000687)	(39.8374)	(6.81821)	(4.18709)	
1984	-668706.35*	217148.26	0.204113*	377316.46 *	0.006162	-2.1323133	6.0876316	2.070178	0.287
	(267204.69)	(159464.55)	(0.07239)	(177098.92)	(0.00529)	(3.73624)	(5.76414)	(3.66160)	
1985	-3543266.8*	3996.9786 *	0.000248*	2879716.2 *	0.0019686 *	-0036207	8.30403	4.69297	0.404
	(1363957.9)	(1878.2142)	(0.00006)	(1109989.3)	(0.0007336)	(0.005371)	(5.05708)	(3.72109)	
1986	-5122852.8*	8189724.9 *	0.000082*	1.6670e-020 *	0.0000561 *	685851.2	12.76396 *	8.50769 *	0.453
	(1816095.7)	(3097864.6)	(0.00002)	(7.419e-021)	(0.0000221)	(517988.2)	(5.51709)	(3.74279)	
1987	-4718883.5*	1061436.8 *	0.000672*	2998246.3	0.006969 *	153173.2	28.8440 *	10.9320	0.488
	(2060199.2)	(443261.45)	(0.00018)	(1629109.8)	(0.0023407)	(770183.6)	(14.1406)	(8.73474)	
1988	-324523.65*	1518.102	0.000017*	242123.03 *	0.0000145 *	-1.73e-046	2.162999 *	1.535626 *	0.533
	(137093.08)	(1188.4863)	(0.00004)	(102827.01)	(0.0000465)	(9.76e-047)	(0.96494)	(0.72638)	
1989	-1508008.9*	1402901.9 *	0.156853*	6.81e-018 *	0.00000334 *	642979.28	5.074128 *	4.744155 *	0.580
	(593787.36)	(367906.36)	(0.03044)	(2.09e-018)	(7.8681e-07)	(494198.4)	(2.23083)	(1.634851)	
1990	-835265.12	3847.1906 *	0.000110*	634023.71	0.0001638 *	11893.961	6.497344 *	3.608525	0.488
	(559222.05)	(1746.46)	(2.57e-05)	(449254.59)	(5.50e-05)	(49666.18)	(3.2144)	(1.9590)	

Table 4 (continuation) – OLS Estimation of the Position Parameters (β)

Year (D.S)	β_0 (C)	β_1 (gdppc$_i$)	β_2 (gdppc$_j$)	β_3 (population$_i$)	β_4 (population$_j$)	β_5 (distance)	β_6 (Merco)	β_7 (language)	$R2$
1991	-773247.8 *	148.4428 *	1.14e-06 *	604353.83 *	3.68e-08 *	-0.0000442	2.07680	0.166729	0.524
	(377704.49)	(68.9740)	(2.20e-07)	(295297.08)	(1.56e-08)	(0.0000235)	(1.9855)	(1.55512)	
1992	-570415.55*	40.62757 *	9.17e-09 *	124496.58 *	267428.25	-0.563514 *	-0.563514	2.16957	0.498
	(245472.07)	(13.4165)	(1.99e-09)	(47145.64)	(145352.6)	(0.23582)	(3.15267)	(2.15606)	
1993	1758985.7 *	8500.4396 *	3.35e-07 *	1190999.5 *	221738.97	-118811.91	8.83858 *	3.952127	0.402
	(726264.67)	(3691.06)	(9.57e-08)	(524565.63)	(205371.8)	(441587.49)	(4.13575)	(2.54111)	
1994	-429610.20*	72.26291 *	5.63e-06 *	297055.88 *	0.001436	-2594.9462	8.34648 *	5.82831 *	0.430
	(185979.78)	(31.01128)	(1.44e-06)	(135205.05)	(0.00093)	(73920.658)	(4.0629)	(2.5180)	
1995	-328095.56	290.48085 *	2.60e-05 *	149373.5	1.86e-09 *	84167.68	9.0713 *	4.29048	0.506
	(302354.69)	(142.1222)	(6.65e-06)	(76419.135)	(9.04e-10)	(276787.44)	(4.18188)	(2.61254)	
1996	-558809.28	624.96051	5.63e-06 *	325044.18 *	0.00079 *	25706.61	25.02492*	18.0737 *	0.460
	(234256.07)	(323.0208)	(1.33e-06)	(134816.31)	(0.000348)	(141558.44)	(11.65853)	(7.26305)	
1997	-1960988.3	3.429070	1.33e-06 *	1381348 *	0.066917 *	-0.002325 *	14.778276	0.527694	0.435
	(908822.68)	(3.620802)	(3.45e-07)	(640175.92)	(0.025705)	(0.001035)	(14.55771)	(11.42584)	
1998	-1075162.3	14353.797 *	6.27e-07 *	1.032e-15	22.54e-05	911274.48	29.9121 *	17.1767	0.392
	(775919.60)	(6962.3423)	(1.73e-07)	(8.48e-16)	(1.32e-05)	(666468.17)	(11.26728)	(7.389908)	
1999	-11243717 *	2859640.2	1.110993 *	5971641.9	3.75e-06 *	2128931.6	37.73842*	14.147474	0.445
	(4880390.4)	(2368396.6)	(2.77e-06)	(4065588.6)	(1.56e-06)	(2927142.9)	(13.22751)	(8.0795818)	
2000	-1354418*	6802.96*	5.57e-07*	857519.64*	221730.97	-100572.92	7.384823*	3.21727	0.459
	(566486.44)	(3165.02)	(6.5872e-08)	(393424.22)	(197205.7)	(320445.79)	(2.877513)	(3.151164)	
2001	-751738.6	3462.47*	0.00012*	507218.96	0.0002047*	10803.16	6.9437*	3.06852	0.472
	(447377.6)	(1519.42)	(2.50e-05)	(359403.67)	(6.6029e-1)	(16496.15)	(3.091258)	(1.993506)	

Note: the * means that the variable is significant at the 5 percent level.

5. Concluding Remarks

The international trade of Argentinean agricultural products has shown an unstable performance in the period under consideration, and it can be explained almost exclusively by the exports performance. The imports have represented between 4% and 6% of the annual export, which explains the important commercial surplus of the sector over the whole period.

As for the composition of the exports by product type, it is necessary to highlight the diversification that took place over the recent years. At the beginning of the period, the grains constituted almost the whole exports while, at present, they represent near 50%.

Concerning the destination of the exports, the increase of Mercosur participation must be mentioned as well as the decreasing participation of the European Union.

The gravity framework provides better explains the bilateral trade flows of agricultural products better for the period 1985-2001. The same can not be said for the period 1967-1984. From the application of the model, it is possible to conclude that the income and the population are, on average, the variables that better explain the bilateral flows of the agricultural trade of Argentina. The distance and the language, on the other hand, have little significance. However, Martínez-Zarzoso and Nowak-Lehmann (2002), when they analyze the manufactured goods and use the panel data, they find that the distance is statistically significant for the explanation of the bilateral flows.

The results show that the Mercosur has impacted on the bilateral flows of agricultural products, especially since the signature of the Argentinean-Brazilian Cooperation and Integration Treaty in 1986, within the framework of ALADI. This makes the year 1986 the first year of the post-integration period, not 1991, the year in which the treaty of Asunción was signed and the Mercosur was started off.

In order to feed the Kalman Filter, the pre integration period should span the years from 1986 to 1991. However, for that particular period in history, it so happens that the gravity equation showed a very poor fit to the data. For this reason, it would be necessary to look for additional explanatory variables that could improve the fit of this framework. Although the specification used has been successful to analyze the trade flows of the agricultural sector in other countries, it doesn't seem to be the most appropriate for the Argentinean case.

References

Aitken, N. D. (1973), The Effect of the EEC and EFTA on European Trade: A Temporal Cross-Section Analysis, in: *American Economic Review* 63 (5): 881-92.

Aitken, N. D. and Lowry, W. R. (1973), A Cross-Sectional Study of the Effects of LAFTA and CACM on Latin American Trade. In: *Journal of Common Markets Studies*, (June), 11(4), 326 - 36.

Aitken, N. D. and Obutelewicz, R.S. (1976), A Cross-Sectional Study of EEC Trade with the Association of African Countries. In: *Review of Economics and Statistics* 58 (4): 425-33.

Balassa, B. (1967), Trade Creation and Trade Diversion in the European Common Market, in: *Economic Journal*, March, 77, 1-21.

Balassa, B. (1974) Trade Creation and Trade Diversion in the European Common Market: An Appraisal of the Evidence. In: *Manchester Sch. Econ. Soc. Stud.*, (June),42 (2) 99-135.

Brada, J. and Méndez, J.A. (1985), Economic Integration among Developed, Developing and Centrally Planned Economies: A Comparative Analysis. In: *Review of Economics and Statistics* 67 (4): 549-56.

Deardoff, Alan (1995), Determinants of Bilateral Trade: Does Gravity work in a neoclassical world? *NBER Working Paper Series* 5377.

Evenett, S. Y. and Keller, W. (1998), On Theories Explaining the Success of the Gravity Equation. *NBER Working Paper Series* 6529.

Feenstra, R., Markusen, J. and Rose, A. (2001), Using The Gravity Equation To Differentiate Among Alternative Theories Of Trade. In: *Canadian Journal of Economics*, Vol. 34, Issue 2, 430-447.

Feenstra, R., Markusen J. and Rose, A. (1998), Understanding the home market and the Gravity Equation: the role of differentiating goods. *NBER Working Paper* 6804.

IMF, (2001), International Financial Statistics, version 11.54 en CD-ROM.

Groot, H.L., Linders, G, Rietveld, P. and Subramanian, U. (2003), The Institutional Determinants of Bilateral Trade Patterns. *Tinbergen Institute Discussion Paper*. IT 2003-044/3.

Harvey, A. C. (1989), Forecasting, Structural Time Series Models and the Kalman Filter.

Cambridge, Cambridge University Press.

Haveman, J., Distances Database http://www.eiit.org/Trade.Resources/TradeData.html

Kreinin, M. E. (1972), Effects of the EEC on Imports of manufacturers, in: *Economic Journal* (Sept) Vol. 82, 897-920.

Lipsey, R.G. (1957), The Theory of Customs Unions: Trade Diversion and Welfare. In: *Económica*, Vol.24, (93): 40-46.

Martinez-Zarzoso, I. and Nowak-Lehman, F. (2002), Explaining MERCOSUR sectoral exports to the EU: The role of economic and geographical distance. Instituto Ibero-Americano de Investigaciones Económicas, *Working paper* No. 85.

Martinez-Zarzoso, I. and Nowak-Lehman, F. (2003), Augmented Gravity Model: An Empirical Aplication to Mercosur-European Union Trade Flows. In: *Journal of Applied Economics*, Vol. VI, No. 2, 291-316.

Mayes, D. G. (1978), The Effects of Economic Integration on Trade, in: *Journal of Common Market Studies* 17 (1): 97-121.

Meinhold, R. and Singpurwalla, N.(1983), Understanding the Kalman Filter, in: *American Statistician* 37(2): 123-127.

Nogués, J., Sanguinetti, P. and Sturzenegger, F. (2001), Argentina y la agenda de negociaciones comerciales internacionales: el MERCOSUR, el NAFTA y la Unión Europea. ABA, Buenos Aires.

Pelzman, J. (1977), Trade Creation and Trade Diversion: in the Council of Mutual Economic Assistance: 1954-70. In: *American Economic Review* 67 (4).

Sanso, M. B., Cuarán, R. and Sanz, F. (1993), Bilateral Trade Flows, the Gravity Equation, and Functional Form. In: *Review of Economics and Statistics* 75 (2): 266-275.

Sanz, F. and Gil, J. M. (2001), An Assessment of the Agricultural Trade Impact of Spain´s Integration into the EU. In: *Canadian Journal of Agricultural Economics* 49(1), 53-69.

Sanz, F. (2000), A Kalman Filter-Gravity Equation Approach to Assess the Trade Impact of Economic Integration: the Case of Spain, 1986-1992. In: *Weltwirtschaftliches Archiv* 136 (1): 84-109.

Sapir, A. (1981), Trade Benefits under the EEC Generalized System of Preferences. In: *European Economic Review* 15 (3): 339-55.

Truman, E. M. (1969), The European Economic Community: Trade Creation and Trade Diversion. *Yale Economic Essays* 9: 201-257.

Verdoorn, P. J. and Schwatrz, A. N. R. (1972), Two Alternative Estimates of the Effects of EEC an EFTA on the Pattern of Trade. In: *European Economic Review*, 3 (1): 291-335.

Yeats, A. (1997), Does Mercosur's Trade Performance Raise Concerns about the Effects of Regional Trade Arrangements? *Policy Research Working Paper* 1729. World Bank.

Winters, L. A. (1987), Britain in Europe: A Survey of Quantitative Trade Studies. In: *Journal of Common Market Studies* 25 (4): 122-141.

APPENDIX:

The Box-Cox transformation for a variable X (in our case $M_{ij}, y_i, y_j, L_i, L_j, D_{ij}$) is defined as

$$X^{(\lambda r)} = \begin{cases} (X^{\lambda r} - 1)/\lambda r & \text{si } \lambda r \neq 0 \\ \log X & \text{si } \lambda r = 0 \end{cases} \qquad r = 0,1\cdots,5 \qquad \text{(A1)}$$

Different values of λr will define different functional forms.
In equation 9, not only the πn ($n = 0,1,\cdots,7$) should be estimated, but also the λr. They are, in fact, the values of the latter which define the optimum functional form. The estimation of the parameters of the gravity equation as well as those of the functional form should be solved simultaneously. This can be carried out by applying the maximum likelihood method.
Let us assume, in general terms, that we have a cross section constituted by N observations for each one of the T available years, and that the observations of the different years are independent. In this case, each year can be estimated separately. The proceeding is the following (where the subscript $t = 1,\cdots,T$ has been omitted in order to simplify the notation).
Let $y^{(\lambda)}$ be an $Nx1$ observations vector of the dependent variable, for a certain year, and $X^{(\lambda)}$ an Nxk observations matrix of the exogenous variables for the same yea (in this case $k = 8$). If the $Nx1$ error terms vector is represented with U, we can write:

$$y^{(\lambda)} = X^{(\lambda)}\pi + \mu \qquad \mu \sim N(0,\sigma^2 I) \qquad \text{(A2)}$$

where π is a πn vector of parameters.
The likelihood function for the sample is, under the specified assumptions

$$L(\pi,\lambda; y, X) = \text{constant} - (\text{N}/2)\ln\sigma^2 - \left(\frac{(y^{(\lambda)} - X^{(\lambda)}\pi)^T (y^{(\lambda)} - X^{(\lambda)}\pi)}{2\sigma^2}\right) + (\lambda 0 - 1)\sum_{i=1}^{N}\log y_i$$

If the λ vector is known, the usual methods of estimation work (with the variables appropriately transformed) . If it is unknown but all of its elements are equal to λ_C, it would be necessary to choose λ_C in order to maximize the support function.
The search for the optimum value of λ_C can be done, because the logarithm of the concentrated likelihood function depends only on λ_C and it is enough to go through the search algorythm to estimate such value.
For the case in which each λr is different, the logarithm of the generalized likelihood function for each value of λ turns out to be:

$$\tilde{L}(\lambda) = \text{constant} \; - (N/2)\ln\tilde{\sigma}^2(\lambda) + (\lambda 0 - 1)\sum_{i=1}^{N} \ln y_i \qquad \text{(A3)}$$

where $\tilde{\sigma}^2(\lambda)$ is the maximum likelihood estimator of σ^2.
In this case, the application of a search procedure is not possible. Nevertheless it is possible to apply the non-linear least squares . The algorithm consists in taking $\lambda 0$ as a guide parameter in the optimization process. Once $\lambda 0$ is determined, the other parameters are estimated using non-linear least squares.
In this way, for each value of $\lambda 0$, the estimators of the parameters are obtained with the purpose of giving the support function its maximum value, since the likelihood finally depends on this parameter. Thus, it is enough to select the value of $\lambda 0$ (symbolized with $\tilde{\lambda} 0$) that maximizes

$$\tilde{L}(\lambda 0) = \text{constant} \; - (N/2)\ln\tilde{\sigma}^2(\lambda 0) + (\lambda 0 - 1)\sum_{i=1}^{N} \ln y_i \qquad \text{(A4)}$$

with

$$\tilde{\sigma}^2(\lambda 0) = \left[\left(y^{(\lambda 0)} - X^{(\tilde{\lambda}(\lambda 0))}\tilde{\pi}(\lambda 0)\right)^T \left(y^{(\lambda 0)} - X^{(\tilde{\lambda}(\lambda 0))}\tilde{\pi}(\lambda 0)\right)\right] \Big/ N \qquad \text{(A5)}$$

where $\tilde{\lambda}(\lambda 0)$ and $\pi(\lambda 0)$ are the vector that maximizes the support function for each value of $\lambda 0$. Once $\tilde{\lambda} 0$ is found, the remaining maximum-likelihood estimators, $\tilde{\lambda}(\tilde{\lambda} 0)$, $\pi(\tilde{\lambda} 0)$ and $\tilde{\sigma}^2(\tilde{\lambda} 0)$ are obtained in a straight forward way.

DETERMINANTS OF PROFITABILITY IN THE DISTRIBUTION OF NATURAL GAS IN ARGENTINA

A STUDY BASED ON PERFORMANCE INDICATORS

Ángel Enrique Neder* (FCE-UNC[a])
Carlos Santiago Valquez (FCE-UNC)
Carlos Fernando Ceballos Ferroglio (Aguas Cordobesas)

1. Introduction

The objective of this paper is to make a comparative analysis of the relative profitability of the gas distribution companies (Distcos) in Argentina, in the period 1993-2002. The aim is to identify the main determinant factors of the evolution of relative firm profitability and the general industry behavior, using performance indicators. These indicators allow measuring the relative technical and economic performance of the Distcos. Since an important proportion of the information needed for this analysis is of wide availability, the application of the methodology constitutes an additional advantage, particularly taking into account the well-known problems of getting information to carry out empirical studies in Latin America. The period selected was that because 1993 was the first year of operation after the privatization of the service and 2002 was the year when tariffs were frozen (besides, 2002 was the last year with disposable information).

In synthesis, the methodology is very efficient because it permits to obtain outstanding results with a minimum of information, adding value to the accounting information.

The paper is organized as follows: First, a description of the natural gas industry in Argentina is presented. Section II contains the analysis of the methodology, describing the applied indicators. In section III data used in the calculation of the indicators and the assumptions are described. In Section IV the results are analyzed, and Section V contains the main conclusions. In appendixes, tables with the obtained indicators and basic data are presented.

1.1. The natural gas industry in Argentina

After the privatization of *Gas del Estado* (the state-owned Distco) at the end of 1992, the industry was divested horizontally and vertically, as well. The market was vertically split into producers, transportation companies (Transcos) and Distcos. The national regulator (Enargas) controls Transcos and Distcos, both natural monopolies, while the producers (Repsol-YPF, Petrobras, Total, among others) operate under no regulation. Considering the horizontal break-up, two transportation licenses and nine distribution licenses were awarded to private firms.

The final-consumer tariffs are composed by three elements: the wellhead gas price, the transportation charge, and the distribution charge. The first one is set after a negotiation between producers, on the one hand, and distributors and big consumers, on the other hand;

* Correspondence author: Facultad de Ciencias Económicas. Universidad Nacional de Córdoba. Av. Valparaíso sin número, Ciudad Universitaria, C.P. 5000. Córdoba, Argentina. E-mail: eneder@eco.unc.edu.ar
[a] Facultad de Ciencias Económicas - Universidad Nacional de Córdoba, Argentina.

meanwhile transportation and distribution charges are fixed by Enargas. The wellhead gas price passthroughs to final users, being modified in May and October in order to reflect changes in seasonal natural gas demand. The tariff rates or margins of transportation and distribution activities are set by price-cap, which is not applied to a basket of services but to each individual service. So, distribution companies are able to offer discounts to different types of costumers. Tariffs are modified at different time of the year to update their components. So, transportation and distribution tariffs are modified in July and January according to a PPI-X+K formula, where PPI is the Producer Price index of the United States, X is an efficiency factor and K is a factor that remunerates the required investments to expand the network and improve the quality[49]. In May and October, tariffs are modified in order to reflect changes in the wellhead gas price.

Final consumers are distinguished between consumers under tariffs (residential, commercial, and government consumers) and those who are able to select if they continue paying for it to the distributor (interrupted distribution services -ID-, interrupted transportation services -IT-, firm distribution services -FD- and firm transportation services -FT-) or if they contract the wellhead gas to a producer. In the last case, end consumers by-pass the Distcos only paying the respective charges to the Distco and to the Transco.

However, in spite of regulation, from 2002, and as consequence of the end of the convertibility regime and of the law of economic emergency n° 25.561, tariffs have been *pesified*[50] and they have remained unchanged up to date[51], showing a break in the regulatory regime set in December of 1992. This situation is even worse when we consider the macroeconomic impacts of the devaluation occurred at the beginning of 2002. In effect, during that year the inflation rate was 77%[52] and the fall in the GDP was about 11%, generating two negative effects: the first one on the cost of inputs and the second one on the industrial gas demand.[53]

2. Methodology

The methodology follows the proposed one by Banker *et al* (1993 and 1996). Applications of this methodology can be found in Fraquelli and Vannoni (2000) for the case of the telecommunications in Europe and in Colomé *et al* (2002 and 2003) for the case of the telecommunications in Argentina and for the case of the distribution of drinking water in Cordoba (Argentina), respectively. Using accounting and technical information, it is possible to assess the evolution of profitability of the natural gas distributors and to explain such evolution as a consequence of changes in prices and quantities (outputs and inputs).

[49] X and K factors are set every five years in tariff reviews. These factors can be applied biannually. However, in the 1997 tariff review they were implemented once and for all the five years period. The backgrounds of this type of regulation can be reviewed in Armstrong *et al* (1995), Green and Rodríguez Pardina (1999), and Laffont and Tirole (2000).

[50] Until 2002, tariffs were set in dollars but collected in pesos taking into account the convertibility exchange rate ($1=US$1). After the devaluation, they were kept in their values in pesos despite the great devaluation.

[51] February 2005.

[52] Taking into account wholesales internal prices (IPIM).

[53] For a more detailed analysis of the natural gas industry in Argentina see FIEL (1999), International Energy Agency (1999) and Valquez (2002).

2.1. How to obtain the performance indicators?

To measure the economic and financial performance of the firms, it is possible to use a revenues-expenses indicator, π. This indicator is computed as the ratio between revenues and expenses, representing the revenue generated by each monetary unit spent by the firm. *A priori*, some conclusions (some of them obvious) on profitability can be extracted; for instance, the difference between the indicator and the unity represents the obtained margin by the firm.

Additionally, this indicator permits to carry out comparisons for a firm at different moments of the time, or for different firms at the same time, being possible two type of analysis: the time series one and the cross-section one.

However, the usefulness of this indicator is limited, inasmuch as the observed variations in it can appear by two causes (or a combination of them): changes in prices, and/or modifications in the quantities.

The methodology permits to analyze, separately, the effects of the variations in quantities and prices on profitability. Then, by breaking up the revenues-expenses indicator into four technical indicators we can identify, individually, the effects that changes in productivity, alterations in the input and output prices, changes in the product mix[54], and changes in the capacity utilization, have on profitability.

In this way, the possible universe of analysis is enlarged since we have more detailed information about the causes of the variations in the profitability. At the same time, the number of policy instruments for the firm is increased, as well as for the regulator.

In calculating the indicators we will use the following symbols:

Y_{jt}^{k}: Quantity produced of the good[55] k by each firm j during year t. Being $k = c,m$; c is the number of connections and m is the quantity of cubic meters delivered. Factors c and m vary between 1 and L, which are the categories of consumers. Therefore, it would have (depending on the information) $2L$ products.

P_{jt}^{k}: Price of the good k produced by each firm j during year t.

X_{jt}^{i}: Quantity of the input i demanded by the firm j during year t, being $i = f,v$ and $f = 1,\ldots,F$ and $v = 1,\ldots,V$, where f and v are fixed and variable factors, respectively.

W_{jt}^{i}: Price that the firm j pays for the input i during year t.

Q_{jt}^{i}: Optimal quantity[56] of the input i demanded by the firm j during year t, at actual capacity level used by the firm.

G_{jt}^{i}: Optimal quantity of the input i used by the firm j during year t, but under the assumption of a standard use (the average of the industry) of the capacity.

2.1.1. Revenues-expenses indicator

General assumptions:

- The firms under study produce and sell two kinds of goods: access or connection to the network and natural gas to L client categories. Alternatively, taking into account the degree of detail in the available information, it could be considered that firms produce two kinds of goods for each client category: one of them is the potential availability of natural gas (whose price is related to the fixed charges). The other is the quantity of cubic meters of

---

[54] Product mix is the share of each product or service in total sales.

[55] "Goods" are also referred to services and/or products.

[56] This is the quantity that the firm would be demanding if it were operating on the efficiency frontier.

natural gas effectively distributed (in this case, prices are related to the variable charges included in the tariff). Therefore, each firm provides $2L$ goods, remembering that L is the number of client categories.

- Two kinds of inputs are considered: the fixed and the variable production factors.

With these assumptions we can operate with a reduced number of mathematical expressions, which are easily applicable to specific analyses. In this way, the revenues-expenses indicator of a firm, for a definite period, can be specified as follows:

$$\pi_{jt} = \frac{\sum_{k=1}^{2L} P_{jt}^{k} Y_{jt}^{k}}{\sum_{f=1}^{F} X_{jt}^{f} W_{jt}^{f} + \sum_{v=1}^{V} X_{jt}^{v} W_{jt}^{v}} . \tag{1}$$

This indicator would show the firm profitability in the corresponding period, t.[57]

Making the ratio between the indicators for the period t and a base level (π_{jt}/π_0) and subtracting the unit, it is obtained the variation value in the firm profitability between the year t and the base level (0). The base level must not necessarily refer to a definite period. Also, we can take as a comparison base the values registered by a specific firm -considered efficient-. Or we can take some firms that can be compared, or else to suppose the existence of a hypothetical firm -where the values of the relevant variables can be obtained from the average of the values for all the firms under study-. In this manner, the ratio π_{jt}/π_0 will represent the *relative profitability* (*RPROF*) of the firm j in year t with respect to the efficient firm, to the firm to compare, or with respect to the hypothetical firm. In this paper, we determined the base level values as the average of all the firms and for all the periods, that is to say, considering the existence of an average hypothetical firm.

2.1.1.1. Breaking-up the index of relative profitability into four technical indicators

As it was previously mentioned, the objective is to separate the ratio of relative profitability (π_{jt}/π_0) into four technical indicators which deliver more information to evaluate the relative performance of the firms. The four technical indicators are productive efficiency; price recovery; input-output mix; and variation in capacity utilization.

2.1.1.1.1. Productive efficiency (PE)

The indicator that represents the productive efficiency of the firms will be calculated as the ratio between total expenses in productive factors (fixed and variables) when optimal quantities (Q) are used, over total expenses in productive factors (also fixed and variables) for the quantities effectively used by the firms (X).

The mathematical specification of this ratio is the following:

$$EP = \frac{\sum_{f=1}^{F} W_{jt}^{f} Q_{jt}^{f} + \sum_{v=1}^{V} W_{jt}^{v} Q_{jt}^{v}}{\sum_{f=1}^{F} W_{jt}^{f} X_{jt}^{f} + \sum_{v=1}^{V} W_{jt}^{v} X_{jt}^{v}} . \tag{2}$$

[57] Actually, in order to obtain the profitability, we should subtract 1 from the ratio.

Input prices (W) are those of year t. Therefore, the only source of variation in the total expense is given by the used quantities. The greater the EP value, the greater the productivity of the firm in year t. This means that the use of inputs by each firm and for each period is closer to the required optimal level.

The optimal quantities are defined as follows:

- **Optimal quantity of the variable inputs in year** t **(** Q^v_{jt} **):** these quantities are estimated from an efficiency frontier of input requirements. Inputs are manpower, third party services, production aggregate factor, capital, and wellhead gas. In the case of the inputs related to manpower, third party services, and production aggregate factor, the estimated models are based on Battese and Coelli (1992) [see also Coelli (1996), and Coelli, Rao, and Battese (1998)]. They consist in panel data models where it is supposed that the technical inefficiency varies along time. The estimated functions have the following general specification:

$$X^v_{jt} = z_{jt} \cdot \alpha + \varepsilon_{jt} + \omega_{jt} , \tag{3}$$

where z_{jt} is a vector of explanatory variables[58]; α is the vector of the coefficients to be estimated; ε_{jt} is the stochastic error term which is considered independent and identically distributed as a normal-distribution function with mean zero and a constant variance, and ω_{jt} is a non-negative random variable which captures the technical inefficiency of the firm. The term ω_{jt} is defined as follows:

$$\omega_{jt} = \{\exp[-\eta(t-T)]\}\omega_j \tag{4}$$

where T is the total number of years of the period, η is a parameter to be estimated, and ω_j is considered independent and identically distributed as a truncated normal distribution function with mean μ and a constant variance.

The optimal quantity of the wellhead gas input for each distributor is obtained from the percentage of minimum gas losses observed during the analyzed period. It is important to remember that the farther distributors are from the gas wells, the greater their percentage of losses. Therefore, to calculate the efficient quantity of gas purchased by a distributor it is not possible to apply the loss percentage of other firms located closer to the gas wells.

- **Optimal quantity of the fixed inputs in year** t **(** Q^f_{jt} **):** In the same way as the variable inputs, the optimal quantity of fixed input is estimated from an efficiency frontier of capital factor requirement (measured by the network size). The explanatory variables, including the constant, have been cubic meters delivered, number of cities with the service, number of residential costumers, and a time trend.

2.1.1.1.2. Price Recovery (PR)

This indicator permits capturing the effect of changes in prices -not only from outputs but also from inputs- on firms' profitability. It is calculated as the ratio between two profitability indicators. The numerator is the profitability indicator (revenues/expenses) valued at prices of the firm, and for the year under discussion, while the denominator is the

---

[58] Explanatory variables were the constant, and the following list: for manpower and production aggregate factor the variables were cubic meters delivered, network size (in kilometers), number of residential costumers; for third party services variables were cubic meters delivered, network size (in kilometers), number of cities where the service is provided, and a time trend.

same index but valued at base level prices.[59] In that ratio, the input quantities are expressed at their efficient levels (to isolate only the effect of prices and eliminate that of quantities), meanwhile the output quantities are those of the current year.

Mathematical specification is:

$$PR = \frac{\dfrac{\sum_{k=1}^{2L} P_{jt}^{k} Y_{jt}^{k}}{\sum_{f=1}^{F} W_{jt}^{f} Q_{jt}^{f} + \sum_{v=1}^{V} W_{jt}^{v} Q_{jt}^{v}}}{\dfrac{\sum_{k=1}^{2L} P_{0}^{k} Y_{jt}^{k}}{\sum_{f=1}^{F} W_{0}^{f} Q_{jt}^{f} + \sum_{v=1}^{V} W_{0}^{v} Q_{jt}^{v}}}. \tag{5}$$

Rearranging this ratio we can get the following expression:

$$PR = \left[\frac{\sum_{k=1}^{2L} P_{jt}^{k} Y_{jt}^{k}}{\sum_{k=1}^{2L} P_{0}^{k} Y_{jt}^{k}}\right] \cdot \left[\frac{\sum_{f=1}^{F} W_{0}^{f} Q_{jt}^{f} + \sum_{v=1}^{V} W_{0}^{v} Q_{jt}^{v}}{\sum_{f=1}^{F} W_{jt}^{f} Q_{jt}^{f} + \sum_{v=1}^{V} W_{jt}^{v} Q_{jt}^{v}}\right] \tag{6}$$

In this way, the indicator PR could be seen as the product of a Paasche index for the sales, and the inverse of a Paasche index for the expenses in productive factors. So, an increase in the price of final goods respect to the base level ($P_{jt}^{k} > P_{0}^{k}$), for all j and k generates an increase in profitability. At the same time, an increase in the input prices - captured by the second factor of the right hand side of (6)- produces a decrease in profitability. This is the reason why the inverse of the Paasche index is taken.

2.1.1.1.3. Input-output mix (IOM)

With this ratio is possible to observe the impact of changes in the relative participation of different products or services on total sales -despite the fact, for example, we had the same volume of sales-. Not only changes in output quantities, but also a variation in the use intensity of the productive factors could be observed.

This indicator is defined as follows:

$$IOM = \frac{\dfrac{\sum_{k=1}^{2L} P_{0}^{k} Y_{jt}^{k}}{\sum_{v=1}^{V} W_{0}^{v} Q_{jt}^{v} + \sum_{f=1}^{F} W_{0}^{f} G_{jt}^{f}}}{\dfrac{\sum_{k=1}^{2L} P_{0}^{k} Y_{0}^{k}}{\sum_{v=1}^{V} W_{0}^{v} Q_{0}^{v} + \sum_{f=1}^{F} W_{0}^{f} G_{0}^{f}}}. \tag{7}$$

[59] Base level prices could be that of the *Hypothetical* firm, calculated as the average of all firms and for all the periods, or, alternatively, that of the firm chosen as the representative one.

The only source of variation in the indicator is given by the differences in quantities of goods and factors used each year respect to the base level quantities.

This ratio can be rearranged in the following way:

$$IOM = \left[\frac{\sum_{k=1}^{2L} P_0^k Y_{jt}^k}{\sum_{k=1}^{2L} P_0^k Y_0^k}\right] \cdot \left[\frac{\sum_{v=1}^{V} W_0^v Q_0^v + \sum_{f=1}^{F} W_0^f G_0^f}{\sum_{v=1}^{V} W_0^v Q_{jt}^v + \sum_{f=1}^{F} W_0^f G_{jt}^f}\right]. \tag{8}$$

In this way, the indicator becomes the product of two ratios: the first one (a quantity Laspeyres index) shows the changes in profitability due to modifications in the sold quantities, being constant the prices in the base level. The second one shows the variation in profitability due to changes in optimal quantities of the inputs maintaining input prices constant, also in their base levels. In this ratio the input quantities of year t are included as denominator, because an increase of them -being prices constant- generates an increase in total expenses and a decrease in the relative profitability.

The fixed factors are evaluated at their optimal levels and considering a standard use of capacity, while the variable factors are assessed at their optimal levels but considering actual capacity levels.

Analytically, Q_{jt}^v supposes optimal requirements of the variable input v by the firm j in period t and permits the used capacity to vary; meanwhile G_{jt}^f supposes a standard level of capacity.

The way of calculating G_{jt}^f is the following:

$$G_{jt}^f = L_0 \cdot \sum_{m=1}^{L} Y_{jt}^m \tag{9}$$

where L_0 is equal to

$$L_0 = \frac{\sum_{t=1}^{T} \sum_{j=1}^{N} Q_{jt}^f}{\sum_{t=1}^{T} \sum_{j=1}^{N} \sum_{m=1}^{L} Y_{jt}^m} \tag{10}$$

and it indicates the average optimal quantity of fixed input that the whole industry needs to produce one unit of product. Therefore, G_{jt}^f shows the optimal quantity of fixed input that should be employed by the firm, given its current production level, if the average optimal requirements of the industry were respected.

2.1.1.1.4. Variation in capacity utilization (CU)

If the optimal requirements of the fixed input, valued at standard capacity, were compared with the same requirements but at current capacity, an index of the variation in capacity utilization could be obtained.

The mathematical expression for this indicator is:

$$CU = \frac{\sum_{v=1}^{V} W_0^v Q_{jt}^v + \sum_{f=1}^{F} W_0^f G_{jt}^f}{\sum_{v=1}^{V} W_0^v Q_{jt}^v + \sum_{f=1}^{F} W_0^f Q_{jt}^f}. \tag{11}$$

For any factor, Q_{jt}^i $(i = v, f)$ assumes optimal input requirements and permits a variation in capacity, meanwhile G_{jt}^f assumes optimal fixed input requirements and a standard level of capacity. In this way, if $G_{jt}^f > Q_{jt}^f$, this means that more fixed input is used to produce the same quantity at standard capacity compared with the current capacity used by the firm. This implies that this firm is more efficient than that of the base of comparison.

2.1.2. Verification

A way of verifying that the breaking up of profitability index into four indicators has been done properly consists in multiplying them so as to obtain the original value of the profitability index.

The index of relative profitability is the following:

$$\frac{\pi_{jt}}{\pi_0} = \left[\frac{\sum_{k=1}^{2L} P_{jt}^k Y_{jt}^k}{\sum_{k=1}^{2L} P_0^k Y_0^k}\right] \times \left[\frac{\sum_{f=1}^{F} W_0^f X_0^f + \sum_{v=1}^{V} W_0^v X_0^v}{\sum_{f=1}^{F} W_{jt}^f X_{jt}^f + \sum_{v=1}^{V} W_{jt}^v X_{jt}^v}\right]. \tag{12}$$

Equation (12) must be equal to:

$$\frac{\pi_{jt}}{\pi_0} = \frac{\sum_{f=1}^{F} W_{jt}^f Q_{jt}^f + \sum_{v=1}^{V} W_{jt}^v Q_{jt}^v}{\sum_{f=1}^{F} W_{jt}^f X_{jt}^f + \sum_{v=1}^{V} W_{jt}^v X_{jt}^v} \cdot \frac{\sum_{k=1}^{2L} P_{jt}^k Y_{jt}^k}{\sum_{k=1}^{2L} P_0^k Y_{jt}^k} \cdot \frac{\sum_{f=1}^{F} W_0^f Q_{jt}^f + \sum_{v=1}^{V} W_0^v Q_{jt}^v}{\sum_{f=1}^{F} W_{jt}^f Q_{jt}^f + \sum_{f=1}^{V} W_{jt}^v Q_{jt}^v} \cdot$$
$$\cdot \frac{\sum_{k=1}^{2L} P_0^K Y_{jt}^k}{\sum_{k=1}^{2L} P_0^K Y_0^k} \cdot \frac{\sum_{v=1}^{V} W_0^v Q_0^v + \sum_{f=1}^{F} W_0^f G_0^f}{\sum_{v=1}^{V} W_0^v Q_{jt}^v + \sum_{f=1}^{F} W_0^f G_{jt}^f} \cdot \frac{\sum_{v=1}^{V} W_0^v Q_{jt}^v + \sum_{f=1}^{F} W_0^f G_{jt}^f}{\sum_{f=1}^{F} W_0^f Q_{jt}^f + \sum_{v=1}^{V} W_0^v Q_{jt}^v} \tag{12a}$$

Simplifying terms it is possible to obtain:

$$\frac{\pi_{jt}}{\pi_0} = \left[\frac{\sum_{k=1}^{2L} P_{jt}^k Y_{jt}^k}{\sum_{k=1}^{2L} P_0^k Y_0^k}\right] \cdot \left[\frac{\sum_{v=1}^{V} W_0^v Q_0^v + \sum_{f=1}^{F} W_0^f G_0^f}{\sum_{f=1}^{F} W_{jt}^f X_{jt}^f + \sum_{v=1}^{V} W_{jt}^v X_{jt}^v}\right]. \tag{12b}$$

Considering that for the base level quantities $X_0^i = Q_0^i = G_0^i$, then it is verified that equations (12) and (12b) are identical.

3. Data and assumptions

3.1. Outputs

The outputs were the number of residential connections and the cubic meters delivered of natural gas, divided between residential costumers [R], compressed natural gas [GNC], and the rest of categories gathered in one group.[60] The number of connections is included to show access service to the network given by distributors, meanwhile cubic meters reflect consumption.

Prices were obtained from the ratio between gross sales of each output and its corresponding quantities.

3.2. Production factors

To work with a reasonable number of productive factors, these can be aggregated in five large categories:

Personnel: The total labor expense takes into account remuneration and social security charges. The number of employees gives the quantity of this factor. The price of this factor is the average wage paid by the firm.

Capital: The second production factor considered is capital. The book value of the depreciations is the proxy for total expense in this factor. [61] As a proxy of capital, the extension of the distribution network, in kilometers, was used. The price of capital for each firm was obtained from the ratio between depreciations and the network size.[62]

Third party services: The total expense in this input was obtained from the items related to third party services showed in the firm balance sheets. Quantities of this input were calculated as the ratio between the total expense in this input and its price. The price of this service is calculated as a weighted average of averages wages and the IPIM (industrial wholesale price index).

Aggregate production factor: This production factor considers all those costs that cannot be attributable to personnel, capital, third party services, and wellhead gas. Therefore, the total expenditure in this factor is obtained from the "total operating costs" net of the costs of wellhead gas, personnel, third party services, and capital depreciation. The prices of this aggregate factor were approximated by means of the IPIM price index. The quantities of the aggregate factor were calculated as the ratio between the total expense in this factor and the representative price index.

---

[60] It was necessary to make a group of categories due to the fact that Distcos do not give detailed information on those consumers who can make a commercial by pass. This is so because the firms consider that this information is strategic. The impossibility of distinguishing the revenues of industrial clients under tariff of those that make commercial by pass, would not be a problem if perfect arbitrage is assumed.

[61] Despite the fact the capital-good-depreciation criterion (showed in the Financial Statements) is only accountable and does not reflect the true economic cost of using capital, the difficulty in calculating economic depreciation for a heterogeneous set of goods obliged us to adopt this criterion.

[62] Alternatives for calculating this price could be the following:

- Considering the yield of own capital and that of third parties, known as WACC (Weighted Average Cost of Capital).
- Approximating the cost of using the capital as the sum of nominal interest rate and the depreciation rate.

Wellhead gas: The total expense of the wellhead gas bought by distributors to producers to be delivered to their clients under tariff is obtained from the respective balance sheets, taking into account the proper cost of the wellhead gas and the charges of the contracted transport capacity. Quantities are obtained adding the average gas losses to the gas delivered to own costumers. The price is obtained from the ratio between total expense and quantities of this input. Industry and firms average values of prices and quantities are showed in Annex 2 not only for inputs, but also for outputs.

4. Results

With the data presented in section III two types of studies were carried out. In the first, the methodology was applied to the analysis of the evolution of the whole industry profitability, and in the second comparisons by firms were carried out. In both cases, the principal determinants of profitability, and the commercial policies that originated the relative differences in firm profitability, were tried to identify.

4.1. Analysis of the industry profitability

For computing the industry indicators it was considered that the quantities of goods and factors are given by the sum of quantities of goods and factors for each one of the following six firms: Centro, Metrogas, Cuyana, Pampeana, Sur, and Ban. Then, this is equivalent to consider an "aggregate" firm. Nowadays, there are nine Distcos, which provide the natural gas distribution service in Argentina. Despite discarding three firms (Gasnor, Litoral, and Gasnea), it does not generate distortions in the results since the market share of this three firms is about less than 8% of residential clients and less than 19% of total gas consumption. Besides, since Gasnea was incorporated to the market in 1999, its inclusion is not correct to determine the industry evolution during the first years after privatizations.[63]

The industry prices of services and factors were determined using a weighted average of the prices of each firm. The results are shown in Figure 1.[64]

Figure 1. Performance indicators of the Industry

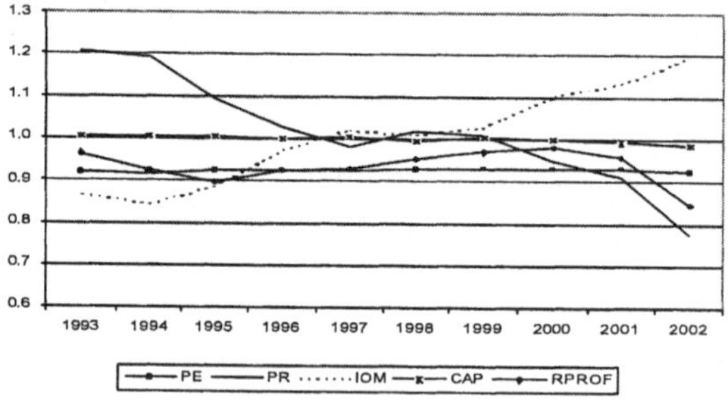

[63] Gasnor and Litoral were not included since they didn't provide enough information.
[64] The numbers of the indicators are shown in Annex 1.

<u>Relative Profitability index</u> (*RPROF*): This indicator, which reflects the profitability of the industry, showed a growing trend, particularly from the moment when network expansions and investments began to bear fruit, especially from a technical point of view. However, in the extremes of the analyzed period, important decreases were observed in the indicator. During the first years of the period (1993 to 1995) it was due to the lack of revenues (despite the fact that a big level of investment had been made) and also as a consequence of the Tequila Crisis. And on the other extreme of the period as a consequence of the crisis of 2001 and the devaluation of 2002, both impacting through the increase in operating costs and the freezing of tariffs.

<u>Variation in capacity utilization</u>: This indicator was relatively stable in the whole period under analysis. Therefore, it was not a relevant explanatory element of the variations in the industry profitability.

<u>Productive efficiency</u>: This indicator showed a similar conduct to that of capacity utilization and, consequently, it did not influence significantly in the evolution of the industry profitability. However, their values were smaller than those of the *CU* index were.

<u>Price recovery</u>: It was observed a diminishing tendency in the whole period. It could be due to a reduction in output prices, or due to an increase in input prices, or else due to an increase in both prices, being larger the increment of input prices, or else due to a decrease in both prices, being larger the decrease in output prices. To identify which of these reasons was the determinant of the tendency, this index was split into their components: output and input prices.

Considering the period 1993-2001, the decrease in the index of price recovery is a consequence of the combination of an increase in input prices with a lightly diminishing tendency in output prices (see Figure 2). The net decrease in this indicator between 1993 and 1996 obeys, among other reasons, to a relative stability in the Price Recovery index via output and a sharp increase in the indicator via inputs. Between 1997 and 1999 both indicators showed a similar evolution (reflected in the stability of the Price Recovery index) and between 2000 and 2002 it was observed an important decrease in the index because input prices raised faster than output prices. The steep slope of the input prices line in 2002 (see Figure 2) is due to the great impact that devaluation and inflation had on the Distcos' operating costs.

Figure 2. Industry Price Recovery

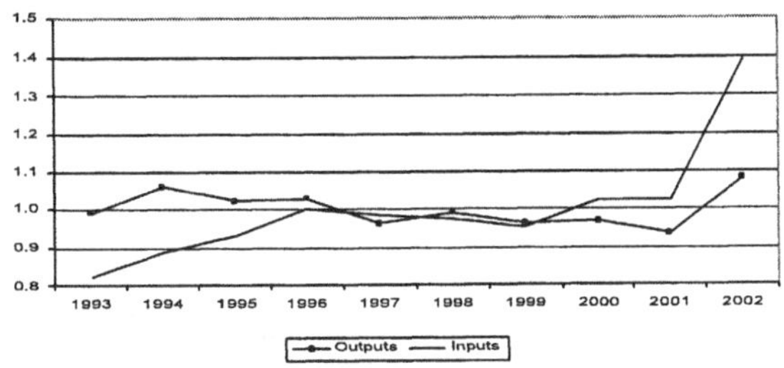

Input-output mix indicator: This indicator showed a growing tendency in the whole period and it is particularly noteworthy the inverse symmetry of its evolution compared with that of the Price Recovery index. To identify the reasons of the evolution of the index this could be broken up taking into account the behavior of input and output quantities.

As we can appreciate in Figure 3, between 1993 and 1995 the spread between the indicator for input and output quantities was stable in relative terms, manifestly diminishing in 1996 (what made raise the value of the Input-output mix indicator). Between 1997 and 2002 the evolution of the indicator for output quantities is above that of input quantities. So, the general indicator continued to grow.

Figure 3. Industry Input-Output Mix

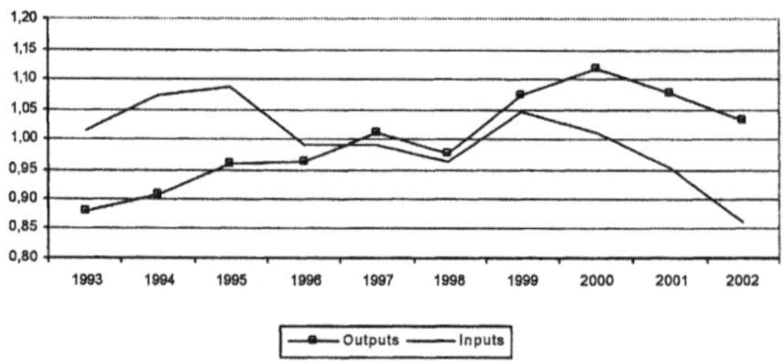

In synthesis, the natural gas distribution industry in Argentina showed a growing profitability between 1995 and 2000, moment from which a decrease is observed as a consequence of the institutional crisis and economic depression. This became more notorious after the devaluation in 2002, which dwindled profitability to smaller values than those observed in 1995.

Regarding the factors that determined the evolution of profitability, it can be observed that productive efficiency and variations in capacity utilization did not result significant in its determination. On the other hand, we can observe how the share of the Price Recovery index was decreasing in importance as a profitability determinant. It was compensated by an increase in the relative participation of the Input-output mix indicator. That is to say, to avoid profitability deterioration, firms would have adapted themselves to the cut in their margins (due to the cost increase) modifying the use intensity of the factors and increasing the participation in the sales of those services that contribute more to the revenues.

4.2. Relative profitability by firm

Along the period, this indicator showed, for all the firms[65], a stable or increasing trend until 2000 (see Figure 4). As a consequence of the 2001 crisis, the relative profitability of all the firms suffered a marked deterioration that is more notorious with the crisis of the devaluation and the freezing imposed on tariffs in 2002. During the period, Cuyana was the

[65] With the exception of Metrogas.

only firm that had values for the indicator above one (with the exception of 2002), while Metrogas, Pampeana and Sur maintained it in a value smaller than one. Centro showed a constant growth in the indicator until the crisis and Ban, after an initial decrease in the first two years of the license, showed a growing tendency in the indicator.

Figure 4. Relative Profitability by firm

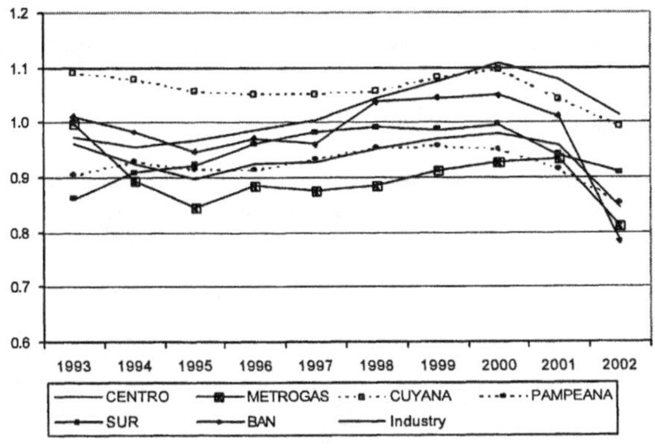

Since the indicator for each firm is the ratio between the relative revenues (to the expenditures) of the current year respect to the base level year (that are the same for all the firms and for all the years), if some firm shows a value greater than one, it implies that the revenue for each expended peso is greater than that for the base level. This represents a relative greater position of profitability.

4.2.1. Productive efficiency

The calculation of this indicator was made using efficiency frontiers. So, the maximum value that it could reach is one. Consequently, those Distcos that have an indicator value closer to the unit, will be reflecting a more efficient use of their inputs. That is to say, they will be closer to the efficient requirements of inputs in order to supply the service (see Figure 5).

Figure 5. Productive Efficiency by firm

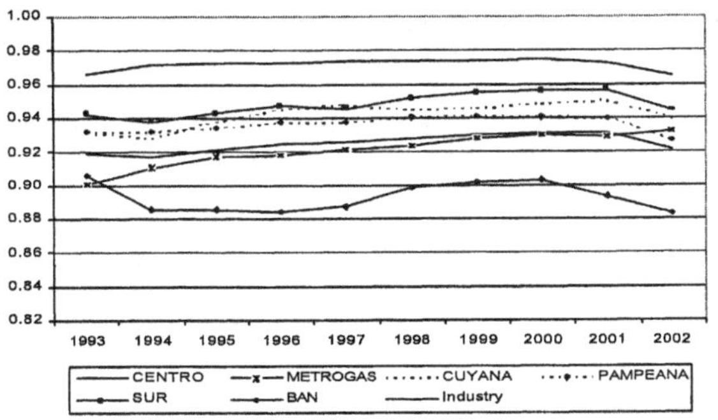

The firm that showed the highest value for the Productive Efficiency indicator (and, at the same time, very stable as a consequence of being very close to the efficiency values) was Centro with a rank for the indicator between 0.96 and 0.98. The rest of the firms, with the exception of Ban, showed an improvement in the indicator along the period. In 2002 a decrease in the indicator was observed for all the firms, with the exception of Metrogas. This was particularly due to the smaller efficiency in the use of the aggregate input, which also has a greater participation in the indicator owing to the observed increase in its relative price (with respect to the other inputs). Ban appears as the firm with the smallest productive efficiency and with the least defined tendency.

4.2.2. Price recovery

It is observed, for the whole period, a diminishing trend in the indicator for all Distcos. It could have been as a consequence of an increase (decrease) of input prices to a greater (smaller) rhythm than output prices (see Figure 6).

Figure 6. Price Recovery by firm

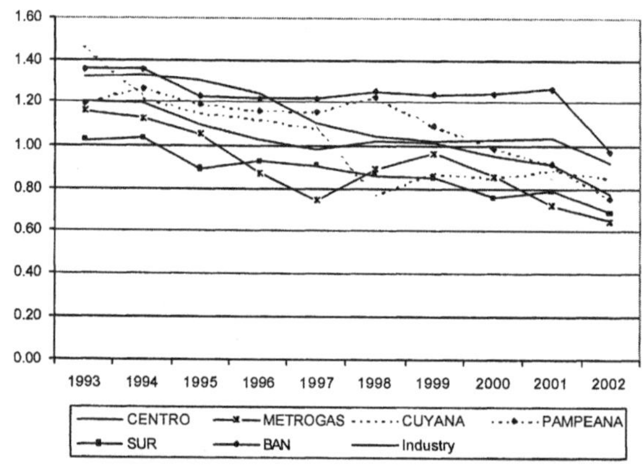

For a better interpretation of the incidence of this indicator on Distcos' relative profitability, the Price Recovery indicator was broken up into its two components: the evolution of output prices and the evolution of input prices.

Considering output prices (see Figure 7), it could be observed a certain stability until 2002, year in which this indicator increases. On the one hand, as a result of the economic crisis, the sales to large costumers fell down, which meant a greater participation of the residential consumption and, since the average tariffs of this client category is larger, the Price recovery indicator (taking into account output prices exclusively) increased. That is to say, a higher price (implicitly) appeared. On the other hand, the discounts distributors used to give to their big (industrial) costumers were eliminated. This determined in 2002 the positive effect (greater relative profitability) observed.

Ban and Sur showed, systematically, smaller values for this indicator. In the case of Sur it would have been a consequence of a smaller transport and distribution charge than the industry average (because they are closer to the gas basins). In the case of Ban, the smaller relative price could be due to the greater participation of industrial consumption (with smaller transport and distribution charges) related to the rest of distributors.

Figure 7. Price Recovery by firm (Outputs)

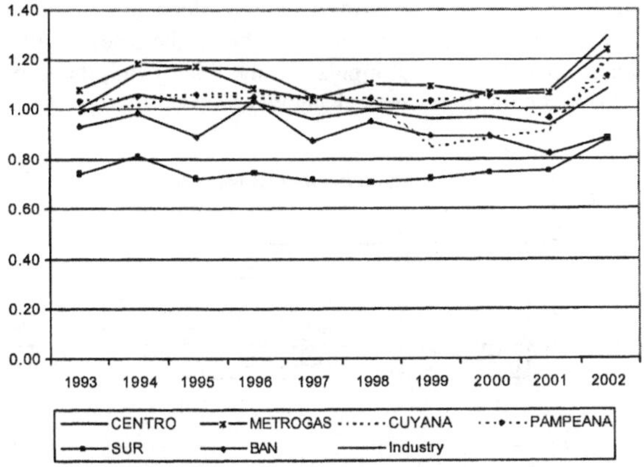

Regarding input prices (see Figure 8), a growing tendency is observed along the period, which is the result of a raise in the labor cost (per worker) and also of increases in the cost of the aggregate input (measured by the IPIM). This situation was more notorious in 2002, compensating the positive effect on output prices.

Figure 8. Price Recovery by firm (Inputs)

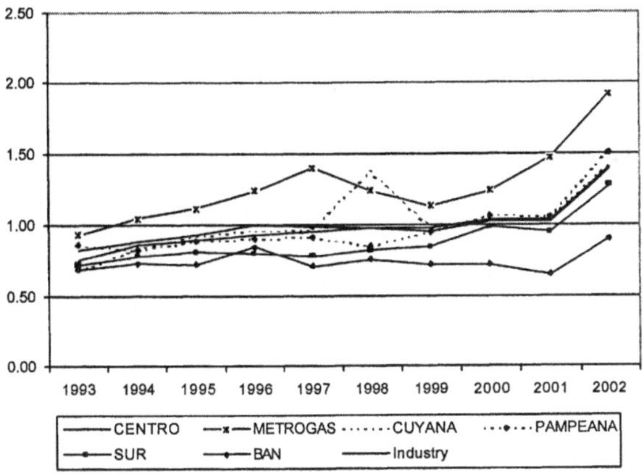

Generally speaking, Ban, Centro, Sur, and Pampeana had smaller labor costs and a smaller cost of the capital input as well. The observed peak in 1998 for Cuyana obeyed to an increase in the wellhead gas price what was a consequence of a decrease in the sales to their own clients.[66]

4.2.3. Input-output mix

This indicator shows a soft growing tendency along the period (see Figure 9). Some reasons could explain that tendency. On the one hand, the sales of all outputs increase to a greater path than the purchases of all inputs. On the other hand, the sales privilege outputs of greater relative price, or the purchases of inputs are oriented to those that are low-priced in relative terms.

Figure 9. Input-Output Mix by firm

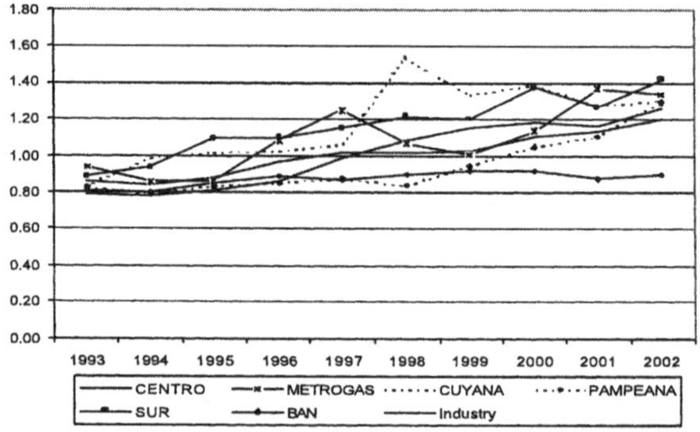

It is also feasible to break up the indicator into the evolution of output quantities and input quantities in order to determine which of those explanations results the most suitable.

Regarding the outputs, all Distcos show a growing tendency with the only exception of Metrogas (see Figure 10).

Figure 10. Input-Output Mix by firm (outputs)

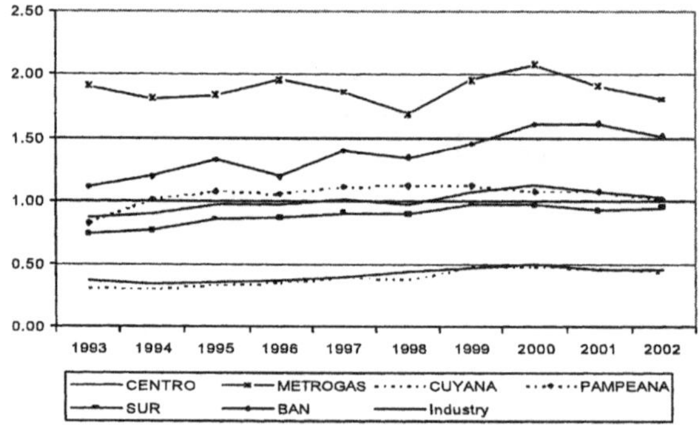

66 It should be remembered that the input wellhead gas price is the ratio between the amount paid for the purchased gas (mainly take-or-pay contracts) and the sales to their own clients.

The observed tendency would be mainly explained by sales growth and not for a better output mix, since this is a developing market. In developed markets the improvement of this indicator only is able to appear if a better output mix were present. The difference in levels observed among Distcos is a consequence of their relative size. So, Metrogas, Ban, and Pampeana are above the average. The less stable evolution showed by Metrogas would be a consequence of a greater development of its market where the output mix is very important.[67]

Regarding the input mix (see Figure 11), a marked stability can be observed along the period, especially for Cuyana[68], Centro, and Sur, and to a lesser extent in Pampeana. This could indicate that there is a substitution between inputs. The difference in levels appears again and it would be representing differences of relative sizes among Distcos.

Therefore, the growth in the Input-output indicator is determined, mainly, by an increase in its numerator, that is to say, a better output mix.

Figure 11. Input-Output Mix by firm (inputs)

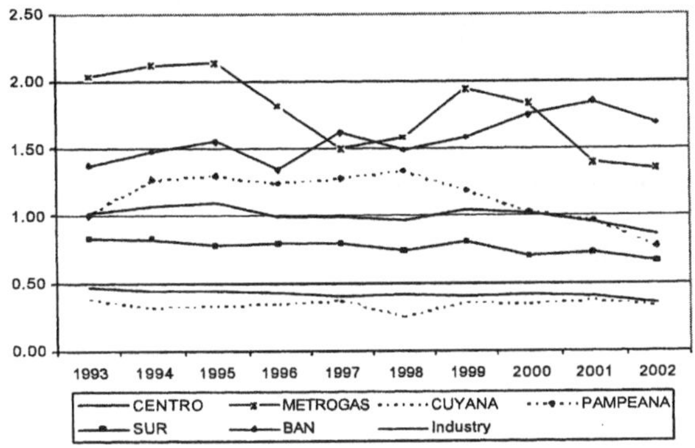

4.2.4. Variation in capacity utilization

A value greater than one in this indicator shows that the optimal quantity of capital needed to distribute a cubic meter of natural gas, given the averages of the industry, is greater than that the firm needs to produce efficiently. Therefore, this firm results more efficient in using their capacity. However, observing values smaller than one would be showing that the network expansion was greater than that of the average of the industry. This could be reflected in the cases of Cuyana, Pampeana, and, specially, Centro, firm for which the indicator fell down along the period (see Figure 12).

---

[67] This was possible to say because detailed information of revenues by type of costumer was obtained.

[68] The fall observed in 1998 could be explained by the decrease in purchases of wellhead gas, which was a consequence of commercial by pass.

Figure 12. Variation in Capacity Utilization by firm

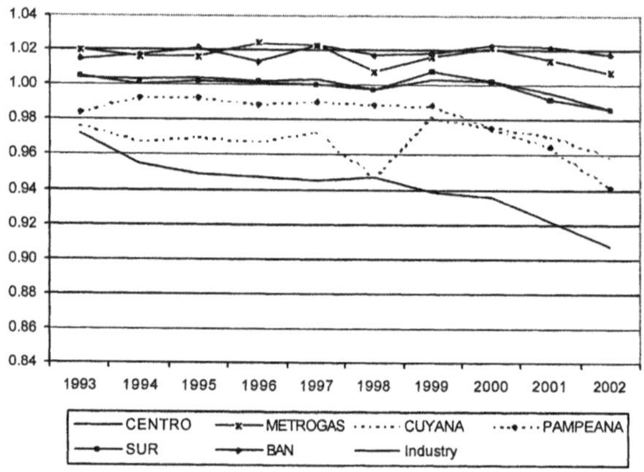

5. Conclusions

The proposed methodology constitutes a simple way of determining the origin of a firm profitability that is providing a public service (in this case, the natural gas distribution) related to other firms of the sector and along the time. That is to say, the methodology allows determining the effects that some situations (e.g. changes in productivity, in input or output prices, in output mix and in variation in capacity utilization) have on profitability. So, for example, it is possible to determine if the increase in profitability is a consequence of an increase in the tariffs or a consequence of a better allocation of productive resources. An additional advantage is based on the use of accounting information (of public character). In this way, it results feasible to elaborate performance indicators for the firms, particularly considering costs, prices, and productivity.

On the other hand, besides explaining some stylized facts for the firms, which are very important at the time of defining business strategies, the methodology also results in an important instrument for the regulatory authority. For example, it allows to soften the problems of asymmetric information, meanwhile it facilitates the regulator a better information for the calculation of the tariffs; at the same time it would offer some elements for the calculation of the efficiency factor.

From the analysis of the results, we can conclude that the industry presented a growing tendency in profitability until the devaluation of 2002. Notwithstanding, the majority of Distcos finished in 2002 with values of relative profitability lower than those of 1993.

After breaking up the indicator of relative profitability, the following tendencies can be appreciated: productive efficiency and the use of capacity are relatively stable in the whole period, price recovery shows a decreasing tendency (particularly influenced by the increase in input prices) and input-output mix had a growing tendency.

References

Armstrong, M., Cowan, S., Vickers, J. (1995), *Regulatory Reform. Economic Analysis and British Experience*. The Press MIT. Cambridge, Massachusetts, London, England.

Banker, R. D., Chang, H. H. and Majumdar, S. K. (1993), Analyzing Underlying Dimensions of Firm Profitability. In: *Managerial and Decision Economics,* Vol 14, N° 1, January-February, 25-36.

______ (1996), A Framework for Analyzing Changes in Strategic Performance, in: *Strategic Management Journal,* Vol 17, N° 9, November, 693-712.

Battese, G.E., and T. J. Coelli (1992), Frontier Production Functions, Technical Efficiency and Panel Data: With Application to Paddy Farmers in India. In: *Journal of Productivity Analysis,* Vol 3, 153-169.

Coelli, T. (1996), A Guide to FRONTIER Version 4.1: A Computer Program for Stochastic Frontier Production and Cost Function Estimation. *CEPA Working paper 96/07.*

Coelli, T., Prasada Rao, D. S. and Battese, G. (1998), *An Introduction to Efficiency and Productivity Analysis.* Kluwer Academic Publishers. Norwell Massachusetts.

Colomé, R. A., Neder, A. E. and Ceballos Ferroglio, C. F. (2000), Indicadores de Eficiencia y Rentabilidad en la Prestación de Servicios Públicos: El Caso del Agua Potable en Córdoba. In: *Anales de la Asociación Argentina de Economía Política,* XXXVIII Annual Meeting, November, Mendoza, Argentina.

Colomé, R. A., Neder, A. E. and Ceballos Ferroglio, C. F. (2004), Relative efficiency in Argentina's telecommunications industry. In: *Adjusting to globalization and structural change*, Díaz Cafferata, A. M., Neder, A. E. and Recalde, M. L. (eds.). Universidad Nacional de Córdoba, Argentina.

ENARGAS (several issues). *Informe Enargas.* Buenos Aires, Argentina.

Fraquelli, G. and Vannoni, D. (2000), Multidimensional performance in telecommunications, regulation, and competition: analyzing the European major players, in: *Information Economic and Policy,* Vol. 12, 27-46.

FIEL (1999), *La Regulación de la Competencia y de los Servicios Públicos. Teoría y experiencia argentina reciente.* Fundación de Investigaciones Económicas Latinoamericanas. Buenos Aires, Argentina.

Green, R. and Rodríguez Pardina, M. (1999), *Resetting Price controls for Privatized Utilities. A Manual for Regulators.* EDI Development Studies. Economic Development Institute of The World Bank. Washington D.C. USA.

International Energy Agency (1999), *Regulatory Reform in Argentina's Natural Gas Sector.* USA.

Laffont, J. J. and Tirole, J. (2000), *Competition in Telecommunications.* The MIT Press. Cambridge, Massachusetts, London, England.

Valquez, C. S. (2002). Un modelo empírico de oligopolio para el mercado mayorista de gas natural en Argentina. *Anales de la Asociación Argentina de Economía Política,* XXXVII Annual Meeting, November, Tucumán, Argentina.

Appendix 1

Performance Indicators

Table 1. REVENUES -EXPENSES

Firm	1993	1994	1995	1996	1997	1998	1999	2000	2001	2002
CENTRO	0.9734	0.9570	0.9665	0.9865	1.0025	1.0441	1.0736	1.1072	1.0789	1.0147
METROGAS	0.9992	0.8929	0.8429	0.8851	0.8763	0.8835	0.9125	0.9258	0.9335	0.8099
CUYANA	1.0933	1.0781	1.0568	1.0526	1.0523	1.0562	1.0816	1.0972	1.0435	0.9947
PAMPEANA	0.9052	0.9295	0.9156	0.9135	0.9334	0.9537	0.9583	0.9511	0.9150	0.8522
SUR	0.8617	0.9081	0.9220	0.9610	0.9830	0.9907	0.9863	0.9970	0.9404	0.9083
BAN	1.0126	0.9820	0.9478	0.9710	0.9599	1.0357	1.0453	1.0504	1.0116	0.7842
INDUSTRY	0.9637	0.9241	0.8967	0.9242	0.9279	0.9546	0.9686	0.9792	0.9573	0.8435

Table 2. PRODUCTIVE EFFICIENCY

Firm	1993	1994	1995	1996	1997	1998	1999	2000	2001	2002
CENTRO	0.9657	0.9719	0.9720	0.9730	0.9734	0.9735	0.9734	0.9746	0.9726	0.9644
METROGAS	0.9008	0.9110	0.9175	0.9183	0.9210	0.9236	0.9275	0.9303	0.9293	0.9321
CUYANA	0.9315	0.9286	0.9379	0.9448	0.9480	0.9452	0.9459	0.9484	0.9501	0.9402
PAMPEANA	0.9320	0.9325	0.9342	0.9372	0.9376	0.9404	0.9410	0.9408	0.9399	0.9272
SUR	0.9429	0.9382	0.9430	0.9472	0.9455	0.9516	0.9549	0.9560	0.9570	0.9445
BAN	0.9058	0.8855	0.8856	0.8844	0.8870	0.8987	0.9013	0.9033	0.8939	0.8831
INDUSTRY	0.9196	0.9169	0.9215	0.9243	0.9256	0.9275	0.9303	0.9315	0.9312	0.9221

Table 3. PRICE RECOVERY

Firm	1993	1994	1995	1996	1997	1998	1999	2000	2001	2002
CENTRO	1.3214	1.3313	1.3029	1.2394	1.1059	1.0465	1.0244	1.0254	1.0361	0.9210
METROGAS	1.1587	1.1252	1.0486	0.8731	0.7458	0.8893	0.9630	0.8565	0.7233	0.6447
CUYANA	1.4590	1.2185	1.1506	1.1227	1.0760	0.7659	0.8733	0.8518	0.8847	0.8466
PAMPEANA	1.1973	1.2656	1.1922	1.1600	1.1529	1.2239	1.0917	0.9891	0.9144	0.7513
SUR	1.0249	1.0335	0.8915	0.9237	0.9056	0.8584	0.8514	0.7561	0.7846	0.6865
BAN	1.3596	1.3586	1.2289	1.2188	1.2187	1.2559	1.2386	1.2391	1.2623	0.9687
INDUSTRY	1.2067	1.1929	1.0968	1.0278	0.9791	1.0197	1.0118	0.9496	0.9131	0.7759

Table 4. INPUTS-OUTPUTS MIX

Firm	1993	1994	1995	1996	1997	1998	1999	2000	2001	2002
CENTRO	0.7853	0.7751	0.8046	0.8641	0.9851	1.0825	1.1472	1.1840	1.1614	1.2596
METROGAS	0.9387	0.8575	0.8624	1.0786	1.2476	1.0672	1.0057	1.1385	1.3699	1.3390
CUYANA	0.8240	0.9851	1.0100	1.0258	1.0604	1.5416	1.3351	1.3922	1.2792	1.3030
PAMPEANA	0.8248	0.7941	0.8288	0.8502	0.8725	0.8385	0.9443	1.0480	1.1042	1.2997
SUR	0.8876	0.9357	1.0946	1.0974	1.1484	1.2168	1.2041	1.3769	1.2638	1.4216
BAN	0.8102	0.8030	0.8528	0.8893	0.8688	0.9024	0.9194	0.9183	0.8775	0.9010
INDUSTRY	0.8649	0.8427	0.8839	0.9713	1.0203	1.0127	1.0261	1.1047	1.1321	1.1962

Table 5. VARIATION IN CAPACITY UTILIZATION

Firm	1993	1994	1995	1996	1997	1998	1999	2000	2001	2002
CENTRO	0.9714	0.9543	0.9486	0.9466	0.9454	0.9467	0.9384	0.9357	0.9219	0.9070
METROGAS	1.0199	1.0157	1.0161	1.0235	1.0226	1.0078	1.0158	1.0207	1.0138	1.0067
CUYANA	0.9764	0.9672	0.9696	0.9673	0.9729	0.9464	0.9807	0.9756	0.9704	0.9590
PAMPEANA	0.9835	0.9919	0.9920	0.9883	0.9896	0.9882	0.9879	0.9753	0.9641	0.9413
SUR	1.0047	1.0007	1.0019	1.0009	0.9996	0.9968	1.0075	1.0018	0.9910	0.9854
BAN	1.0149	1.0165	1.0212	1.0129	1.0221	1.0169	1.0184	1.0220	1.0218	1.0173
INDUSTRY	1.0042	1.0025	1.0037	1.0016	1.0036	0.9966	1.0028	1.0022	0.9946	0.9855

The breaking up of the performance indicators

Table 3.a. PRICE RECOVERY (OUTPUTS)

Firm	1993	1994	1995	1996	1997	1998	1999	2000	2001	2002
CENTRO	1.0061	1.1453	1.1662	1.1582	1.0560	1.0184	1.0020	1.0674	1.0749	1.2929
METROGAS	1.0815	1.1830	1.1735	1.0865	1.0416	1.1055	1.0962	1.0650	1.0647	1.2356
CUYANA	0.9929	1.0223	1.0628	1.0753	1.0380	1.0494	0.8502	0.8834	0.9183	1.1933
PAMPEANA	1.0351	1.0528	1.0586	1.0482	1.0557	1.0444	1.0338	1.0571	0.9640	1.1320
SUR	0.7414	0.8076	0.7201	0.7432	0.7127	0.7069	0.7198	0.7454	0.7470	0.8755
BAN	0.9327	0.9868	0.8851	1.0344	0.8732	0.9499	0.8944	0.8905	0.8170	0.8823
INDUSTRY	0.9932	1.0602	1.0217	1.0303	0.9653	0.9940	0.9649	0.9697	0.9358	1.0817

Table 3.b. PRICE RECOVERY (INPUTS)

Firm	1993	1994	1995	1996	1997	1998	1999	2000	2001	2002
CENTRO	0.7614	0.8603	0.8951	0.9345	0.9548	0.9731	0.9781	1.0410	1.0374	1.4038
METROGAS	0.9333	1.0514	1.1191	1.2444	1.3966	1.2431	1.1383	1.2435	1.4720	1.9168
CUYANA	0.6805	0.8390	0.9236	0.9577	0.9647	1.3702	0.9736	1.0372	1.0380	1.4094
PAMPEANA	0.8645	0.8319	0.8880	0.9036	0.9157	0.8533	0.9470	1.0688	1.0543	1.5067
SUR	0.7234	0.7814	0.8077	0.8045	0.7869	0.8235	0.8455	0.9859	0.9521	1.2753
BAN	0.6860	0.7263	0.7202	0.8487	0.7165	0.7564	0.7221	0.7187	0.6472	0.9107
INDUSTRY	0.8231	0.8888	0.9315	1.0025	0.9860	0.9748	0.9537	1.0211	1.0249	1.3941

Table 4.a. INPUTS-OUTPUTS MIX (OUTPUTS)

Firm	1993	1994	1995	1996	1997	1998	1999	2000	2001	2002
CENTRO	0.3691	0.3420	0.3552	0.3716	0.4034	0.4465	0.4686	0.4970	0.4645	0.4489
METROGAS	1.9131	1.8148	1.8428	1.9572	1.8646	1.6854	1.9546	2.0868	1.9110	1.8008
CUYANA	0.3133	0.3111	0.3363	0.3519	0.3913	0.3782	0.4777	0.4822	0.4716	0.4443
PAMPEANA	0.8256	1.0085	1.0710	1.0533	1.1106	1.1179	1.1197	1.0775	1.0708	1.0073
SUR	0.7388	0.7703	0.8536	0.8629	0.9064	0.8971	0.9747	0.9632	0.9205	0.9473
BAN	1.1111	1.1908	1.3238	1.1900	1.4018	1.3414	1.4513	1.6031	1.6194	1.5147
INDUSTRY	0.8774	0.9051	0.9620	0.9632	1.0116	0.9780	1.0745	1.1191	1.0782	1.0309

Table 4.b. INPUTS-OUTPUTS MIX (INPUTS)

Firm	1993	1994	1995	1996	1997	1998	1999	2000	2001	2002
CENTRO	0.4700	0.4413	0.4415	0.4300	0.4095	0.4125	0.4084	0.4198	0.4000	0.3564
METROGAS	2.0382	2.1163	2.1369	1.8146	1.4945	1.5793	1.9436	1.8330	1.3949	1.3448
CUYANA	0.3803	0.3158	0.3330	0.3430	0.3690	0.2453	0.3578	0.3463	0.3687	0.3410
PAMPEANA	1.0011	1.2700	1.2922	1.2388	1.2728	1.3332	1.1857	1.0281	0.9698	0.7751
SUR	0.8324	0.8232	0.7799	0.7863	0.7892	0.7373	0.8095	0.6996	0.7284	0.6664
BAN	1.3714	1.4829	1.5523	1.3381	1.6134	1.4865	1.5785	1.7458	1.8455	1.6811
INDUSTRY	1.0144	1.0740	1.0883	0.9917	0.9915	0.9657	1.0471	1.0131	0.9524	0.8618

Appendix 2
Mean, maximum and minimum values of the industry and by firm

	Average	Max.	Min.	Firm Averages					
				Centro	Metrogas	Cuyana	Pampeana	Sur	Ban
Input quantities									
Personnel (n° employees)	641	1329	263	326	1112	299	807	547	752
Capital (km of distribution network)	13347	22786	6207	10174	13840	7669	18912	11064	18426
Aggregate production factor[a]	173114	483927	60223	78963	382520	80256	161962	98151	236833
Third party services[a]	83917	237673	9414	38519	121135	23614	100908	60987	158340
Purchased wellhead gas (millions of cubic meters)	3009	6829	534	1148	5430	914	3391	2254	4920
Input prices									
Personnel ($)	33348	57842	20850	27781	40141	33599	29952	31518	37097
Capital ($)	1522	5251	681	829	2968	1237	1289	1112	1696
Aggregate production factor (IPIM)	112	184	98	112	112	112	112	112	112
Third party services (index)[b]	144	236	100	144	144	144	144	144	144
Purchased wellhead gas ($)	0.0672	0.1249	0.0378	0.0728	0.0865	0.0724	0.0678	0.0587	0.0451
Output quantities									
Residential (millions of cubic meters)	956	2012	246	316	1762	331	909	1257	1159
GNC (millions of cubic meters)	197	527	9	157	441	108	139	14	320
Rest of Services (millions of cubic meters)	2306	4769	756	1017	4062	986	2750	1566	3456
Residential connections (thousand)	768	1865	240	357	1784	296	770	340	1062
Output prices ($)									
Residential	0.1397	0.2021	0.0828	0.1406	0.1599	0.1450	0.1423	0.0911	0.1593
GNC	0.0868	0.1241	0.0596	0.0866	0.0971	0.0792	0.0849	0.0662	0.1070
Rest of Services	0.0593	0.0842	0.0282	0.0715	0.0667	0.0598	0.0641	0.0535	0.0404
Fixed charge for residentials	46.68	48.93	45.16	47.45	46.47	46.87	46.66	46.45	46.15

[a] Ratio between the corresponding input expense (from balance sheet) and the corresponding price.

[b] Average weighted index of the IPIM and the average wages of the industry.

Econometric Results

SFA Estimations of input requirements

Personnel

Variable	Coefficient	Standard error	Statistical t
Constant	-82.6669	66.5113	-1.2429
Sold gas	0.0516	0.0128	4.0258
Capital	0.0292	0.0047	6.2273
Residential clients	0.0000	0.0001	0.5702
sigma-squared	9778.3013	822.6240	11.8867
Gamma	0.7635	0.0591	12.9227
Mu	18.9759	74.6610	0.2542
Eta	0.1107	0.0190	5.8309
Maximum Likelihood function	-313.9314		
LR test of the one-sided error	43.5303		

K2.out

Variable	coefficient	standard error	statistical t
Constant	-1516.3681	1.0000	-1516.3681
Sold gas	0.7856	0.9961	0.7887
Cities	40.7909	1.0000	40.7909
Residential clients	0.0038	0.0034	1.1111
Time	488.1380	1.0000	488.1380
sigma-squared	17188784.0000	1.0000	17188784.0000
Gamma	0.9702	0.6068	1.5990
Mu	0.0000	1.0000	0.0000
Eta	0.0159	0.8001	0.0198
Maximum Likelihood function	-478.9697		
LR test of the one-sided error	127.7430		

I1a1.out

Variable	coefficient	standard error	statistical t
Constant	26.6845	15.7118	1.6984
Sold gas	0.0257	0.0068	3.7826
Capital	-0.0040	0.0011	-3.7559
Residential clients	0.0001	0.0000	6.5357
Sigma-squared	1386.3934	1.3785	1005.7552
Gamma	0.0139	0.0996	0.1391
Mu	8.7657	17.8918	0.4899
Eta	-0.3629	0.4296	-0.8445
Maximum Likelihood function	-291.0049		
LR test of the one-sided error	0.2831		

32a1.out

Variable	**coefficient**	**standard error**	**statistical t**
Constant	2.5153	7.6786	0.3276
Sold gas	0.0028	0.0022	1.2693
Capital	0.0071	0.0011	6.2094
Cities	-0.1358	0.0831	-1.6350
Time	-5.3979	1.2112	-4.4565
Sigma-squared	603.4586	51.3793	11.7452
Gamma	0.7362	0.0298	24.6761
Mu	-42.1546	39.7289	-1.0611
Eta	0.1801	0.0533	3.3777
Maximum Likelihood function	-238.9790		
LR test of the one-sided error	2.4595		

PROVINCIAL LABOR MARKETS IN ARGENTINE: A STUDY OF THEIR BEHAVIOUR USING EPH DATA

A. J. Figueras, Mariano Salto and Jose Luis Arrufat
(Are also part of the investigation team: Dolores de la Mata and María Laura García)

1. Introduction

Argentinean structural labor markets rigidities were tried to be solved, during the 90's, with a reduction in the tax burden, without any positive result (at least in appearance). Nevertheless, it is important to point out that the empirical evidence shows that reductions in tax burdens have positive effects only in countries with more flexible labor markets (such as the United States, even though with minimal results but maybe because they partly offset by the current "Job Destroying" technical revolution). This means that tax burden reductions in economies with structural labor markets rigidities (as is the case in Argentina) could be potentially beneficial only in the long run, while having no significant impact in the short run.

We must remember that the total effect of a variation in the market conditions, arises as a result of adding the income effect (changes in the level of income affect the level of employment) and the substitution effect (assuming a constant level of income and changes in the labor's relative price) and we should keep also in mind the effects caused by the evolution of Labor Supply. During the 1990's, these three effects contributed to change previous equilibrium levels of the labor market variables. Such changes had differential impacts across geographic space, largely because areas differ with regard to the structural features, such as specialization and location, among others. Account must also be taken of idiosyncratic behavior on the part of provincial supply of labor. At the theoretical level, four possible situations may arise:

a. Employment rises but Unemployment also increases.
b. Employment rises but Unemployment falls.
c. Employment falls and Unemployment increases.
d. Employment falls and Unemployment also falls.

	Employment Rises	**Employment Falls**
Unemployment Increases	Case A	Case C
Unemployment Decreases	Case B	Case D

Was the fall on Labor Demand the main problem during the 90's?

It is unnecessary to demonstrate that in recent years labor market has suffered several shocks from the demand side as well as the supply side, specially due to rapidly insertion of women in the labor market (particularly in highly populated which also have complex productive structure agglomerates). As an explanation for the increase in unemployment in Argentine, several authors have put forward the prevalence of some key demand side aspects (such as technological change, macroeconomic fluctuations or economic restructuring caused by opening of the economy to foreign trade), but some studies also point to increases in labour supply[69].

Up to this point, some of questions arise: How much of the unemployment rate is explained by an expansion in labor supply? And how much can be attributed to weaknesses in labor demand? Now, in order to answer these questions, the following analysis is presented, we should make clear that it is not our intension here to model the labor market, but just to generate a method to classify different agglomerates according to its behavior *"inside the evolution"* of their own labor markets.

2. New calculation procedure

As an essay to isolate the impacts of changes in labor demand and the variation of labor supply on regional unemployment levels, we have devised a simple process that, we consider, allow us to distinguish *different circumstances* respect a referential patron.

We won't be using here determinate labor demand and supply functions, instead, we will just consider spots observations from EPH. The Referential Patron refers to a hypothetical position of *"maximum" labor demand* and *"minimum" labor supply*. This entails a situation with minimum supply excess (or unemployment).

Taking advice of remarks made to a previous paper (Figueras, Arrufat and Diaz, 2002) we will dismiss the rate transformation into population values and we will use only rates.

Let us begin with a simple diagram that permits us state the mechanism of the new calculus procedure (Figure I). Suppose that wages are fixed[70] at W_0 (this assumption is presented only for didactical reasons because it does not affect the calculus procedure). At this salary, the "maximum" referential labor demand

Figura 1 - Mercado Laboral

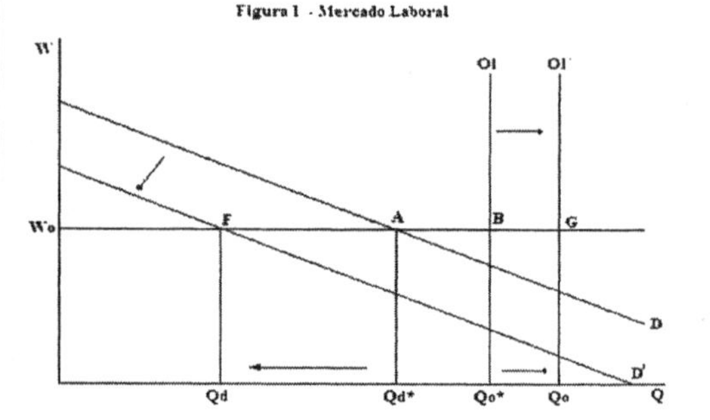

[69] Commercial opening-up, government structure rationalization (including privatization) and prices determinate by market forces prompted resources reallocations from less efficient sectors to more efficient ones. But reallocation requires a long period of time causing unemployment. Gerchunoff & Kacef (1996) proposed different ideas to reduce the unemployment cost: To deepen the reforms; Markets even more flexible; Train human capital in order to make it more competitive and improve mo bility.

[70] We shall also point out that the expression "expansion" in labor supply does not necessarily means a displacement in labor supply function but it may also be a movement inside the function. Then, an expansion in labor supply can be attributed to a displacement of the labor supply function to the right, to the movement from one point to another inside the same function; or may be both factors can happen at the same time, a displacement and a movement. This paper does not attempt to distinguish these factors, only pretends to advance in what we have called "expansion" (or factors) in labor supply (or labor demand) (for further details see, cfr. A.Figueras,A.Díaz Cafferata y J.Arrufat, "Evolución del desempleo regional: análisis a través de casos", Anales AAEP, 2002)

("A" point) and "minimum" referential labor supply ("B" point), determines a theoretical unemployment level of "A-B".

If labor demand falls to D' and labor supply increases to O', then we obtain a new level of unemployment ("F-G" gap), larger than its predecessor, as a result of a "double" contribution: "FA" (a fall in labor demand) and "BG" (an increase in labor supply). Our objective is to estimate these two gaps.

The first problem that arose was the determination of the two "referential" levels. With some degree of subjectivity, and analyzing INDEC's national data, we have decided to adopt for comparison: Labor Supply: the arithmetic mean for the years 1980/1983. Because we understood that during this historical period labor supply had a small participation. Labor Demand: the arithmetic mean for the years 1986/1987. We assume this period as a "maximum" labor demand because inflation pushed down real wages.

Points F and G correspond to real data while points A and B are subjective references, calculated as the average of certain periods of time that we suppose correspond to high labor demand, in one side, and low labor supply, on the other.

It is true that this level of unemployment it is not representative of any year in particular, it is only a theoretical level that we will use as a guideline and it is denominated as "Optimum Feasible Level" (NOP by its abbreviation of the Spanish language).

Let us begin with the calculation procedure. We begin by considering that[71]: $E = PEA - U$ in the expression above we divide by total population (PT) and obtain: $\frac{E}{PT} = \frac{PEA}{PT} - \frac{U}{PT}$ in the second term of the right hand side of this equation, we divide and multiply by PEA, which after reorganizing becomes: $\frac{E}{PT} = \frac{PEA}{PT} - \frac{U}{PEA}\left(\frac{PEA}{PT}\right)$

we finally obtain the following expression: $TE = TA - u * TA = TA(1-u)$

In order to understand what we have done, suppose the selected guideline levels include: employment rate qd* = 0.373 and activity rate qo* = 0.383; the observed data in a single semester of the year (in a province) are: activity rate qo = 0.418 and employment rate qd = 0.328, calculated as: $TE = 0.418(1-0.215) = 0.3281$

As a digression let's say that, using the same methodology, we have calculated employment rates for the periods whose average will provide us with reference point A (qd*). Reference TA comes from average of the EPH rates, which provides us with reference point B (qo*).

Starting from these references, our intention is to calculate, as we said before FA and BG, which will give us total unemployment variation (VDT), therefore: FA + BG = VDT

The contribution attributable to a "fall" in labor demand plus the contribution ascribable to a "rise" in labor supply, results in an increasing of unemployment rate compared to Optimum Feasible Level.

$$(qd^* - qd) + (qo - qo^*) = VD + VO = VDT$$

[71] Where E correspond to the number of people employed, PEA to labor supply, U the number of unemployed, PT total population, TE the employment rate, TA the activity rate and u the unemployment rate.

suppose now that for a single wave of EPH, the employment rate is 0.328 and the PEA rate 0.418, according to the last expression: $(0.373-0.328)+(0.418-0.383)=4.49\%+3.5\%$

But these percentages of change in labor unemployment refer to percentages with regard to total population. In order to improve our understanding, we should transform them into percentages relating to PEA (Corresponding to INDEC's measures), interpreting PEA as the "participation rate" (not in number of people), therefore:

$$\frac{VD}{PEA_{observed}}+\frac{VO}{PEA_{observed}}=\frac{VDT}{PEA_{observed}}$$

returning to our numerical example: $\frac{4.49\%}{41.8\%}+\frac{3.5\%}{41.8\%}=10.74\%+8.37\%=19.11\%$

Summing up, we start from an unemployment rate of 21.5% and PEA rate of 41.8%, which together bring about an employment rate of 32.8% and consider the theoretical reference point (NOP) (benchmark) of 2.39%. The observed unemployment rate of 21.5% can be attributed to a fall in labor demand of 10.74% and an increase in labor supply of 8.37%, which will give us the total unemployment variation of 19.11% regarding NOP. (VD + VO + NOP = 10.74% + 8.37% + 2.39% = 21.5%).

3. Empirical Evidence

NOP had been calculated for every Urban Agglomerate (Chart 1) as well as VD and VO.

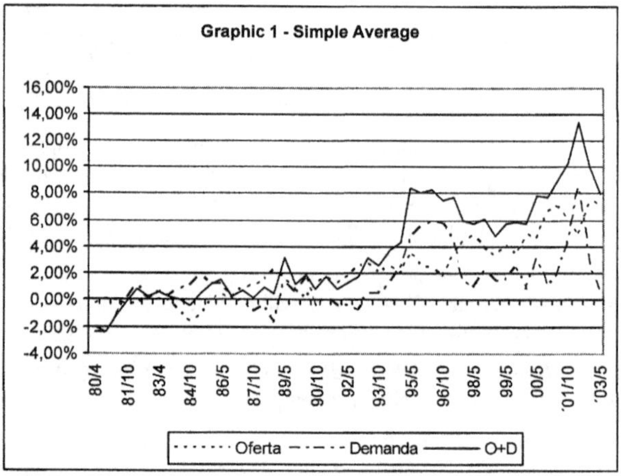

In order to systematize the procedure, firstly it is defined the main factor preponderant (using the methodology presented in Annex 1) trying to develop, according some certain criteria, an explanation for the increasing in the unemployment rate. Secondly, it is presented taxonomy of problems, using Difficulty Levels (of supply, demand and market) (according the methodology presented in Annex 2). Lastly, these qualitative levels are easily "quantified" for statistical analysis in order to distinguish Urban Agglomerates with greater problems.

It is interesting to observe the evolution of the "aggregated behavioral" of all Urban Agglomerates, but instead of using INDEC's national unemployment index (Total "national vision": a weighted average, mostly explained by Capital Federal, Buenos Aires, Cordoba and Rosario) we have worked with the arithmetic mean considering that all Urban Agglomerates have the "same weight" in the national unemployment level (Total "regional vision"). Results are presented in Graphic 1, it is useful to point out that "demand's downward pressure" [excepting the period of the Mexican Crisis (October 1994 to May 1997) and 2002] since 1987 has been clearly underneath than the "supply's increasing pressure". This aloud us to state that, in the "national aggregated", the main difficulty through the last 15 years (to 2002) seem to be not a 'great contraction' in labor demand (as people tend to think in Argentine) but a very weak evolution that could not reach the huge development of labor supply (in rates terms).

Besides, if we consider the variability level (relative to the national unemployment arithmetic mean) of every factor (Demand, Supply and its addition) seems to be a very fast convergence from high Coefficient of Variation in the beginning of the 80's to very small values in the mid 90's (Graphic 2). This could be a sign that "problems" or difficulties in every Urban Agglomerate labor markets have been put all in the same level.

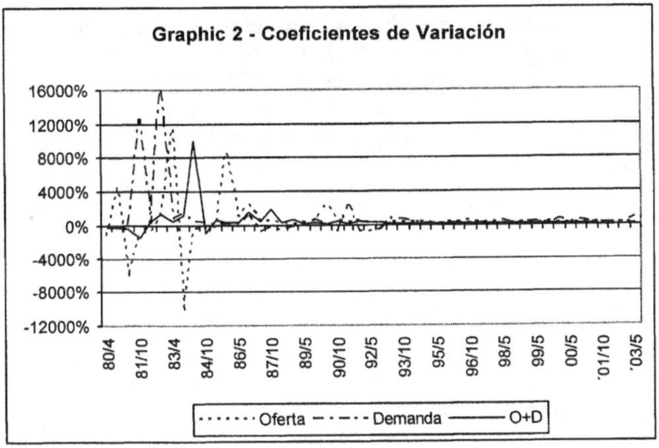

In order to produce a global vision of the situation, and trying to systematize the procedure, we have developed Charts II.a and II.b, were we present a main determinant factor for each Urban Agglomerate in every measure point, following the procedure presented in Annex I.

From Chart II.a, it is clear the great weight of Labor Supply as the main explanation for higher unemployment in the Urban Agglomerates and in aggregated values, at least from 1991.

Analyzing the results for the "weighted" national aggregated (INDEC's index), we found that only one measure can be attributed to mainly Demands problems (May 2002), and in 24 other measures the main problem correspond to Supply pressures (with 20 "blanks", that means, unemployment was not above 3% of NOP values).

In Capital Federal, since 1980 to 1985 main problems can be ascribed to Labor Demand and from 1986 until May 2002 all the measures shows Supply problems. Similar considerations apply for: La Plata, Catamarca, Comodoro Rivadavia, Neuquén, Salta, San Juan, San Luis and Greater Buenos Aires (Conurbano Bonaerense).

The Urban Agglomerates with main problems attributed to insufficient Labor Demand are: Resistencia, Jujuy, Tucumán and especially Rosario and Santa Fe. Some Urban Agglomerates stands out because of their excellent performance: Posadas, Santiago del Estero (!!) and especially Rio Gallegos, Formosa (!!) and Mendoza.

In Chart II.b, for simplicity reasons, we have choosen sub periods that can be easily related to different macro national policies: 1980/83 (opening-up attempt), 1985/90 (economy with a significant degree of State intervention), 1991/94 (successful period of Convertibility Law), 1995/2001 (decadent period of Convertibility Law), 2001/2002 (devaluation) and 2002/2003 (recovery).

In our attempt to distinguish between different situations, we have subjectively defined some taxonomy of problems, referring to difficulty levels (ND). In this way, we have worked with categories inside labor supply, demand and market, according the classifications stated in Annex II. For statistical evaluation, ND levels have been transformed to numbers, i.e.: "No Difficulty" assumes zero value, ND1 equal to 1, ND2 to 2 and so on. We have worked in a similar way for *"supply difficulties"* and for *"demand difficulties"*. Following this procedure we obtain averages values for every Urban Agglomerate and for every measure point.

Applying this procedure we have observed that difficulties in each market have been increasing through the years. While in 1985/90 ND1 is the predominating level, in 1991/94 changes to ND2, in 1995/2001 goes up to ND3 and finally in 2001/2002 reaches the top of the list (ND4 and ND5). During 2002/03 a recovery period starts, and the number of agglomerates with ND5 reduces substantially (only one agglomerate, Conurbano, remains at ND5).

Similar situation is reproduced in labor supply difficult levels (Chart IV). During 1985/90, neither S4 nor S5 cases have come out, in 1991/94 one S5 case shows up, in 1995/2001 six cases appeared, in 2001/02 eight, and in 2002/03, eleven agglomerates turn to high difficult levels. This, maybe, could be attributed to the "additional worker hypothesis", that has arisen since the last years of the previous century.

The increasing "difficulties" due weaknesses in Labor Demand had also happened (Chart V). The numbers of D1 cases had reduced and, on the other hand, D3 and D4 cases had steadily grown up. In this way, we start from zero D3 cases in 1985/90 to one case in 1991/94, three cases in 1995/2001, six cases in 2001/02 and goes back again to three cases in 2002/03. Meanwhile, D4 showed a similar performance: from zero cases in 1985/90 and 1991/94, to two cases in 1995/2001, and eight in 2001/02, showing (clearly) the preponderant situation during the lasts years of the convertibility period. Recovery starts in 2002/03, with the predominance of D1 and No Difficult cases.

The trend is very clear if we observe the arithmetic mean: Supply pressures are steadily increasing (and Urban Agglomerates tend to have similar behavior, if we compare Coefficients of Variation (CV). Demand weaknesses are growing since the late 80's until the Devaluation period, returning to a bearable situation in "October 2002 - May 2003". Market difficulties have risen (from 0.57 to 3.7) until Devaluation period, and then they descend in the last recorded measures (to 3.04). Trend between agglomerates is remarkable (from 1.49 to 0.4 and then drops to 0.51).

If we apply cross correlation to market ND with its components (supply and demand) and using the six sub periods (for the entire group of Urban Agglomerates), seems that greater values during the 80's are tied to Demand's ND (0.9; 0.51). But, in the 90's they change to Supply's ND (0.84; 0.76; 0.64; 0.66) and, at the same time, Demand's ND turns to very small or even negatives values (0.08 and 0.15) (Chart VI).

Lastly, considering the values of Total "regional vision", the arithmetic mean of all Urban Agglomerates (every agglomerate has the same "weight") and inspecting charts III, IV and V; we compare this values against the six larger labor supply cities (Capital Federal, Greater Buenos Aires "Conurbano", La Pata, Rosario, Cordoba and Mendoza) and we obtain that above Total are: With Supply Difficulties: Capital Federal, La Plata and Conurbano. With Demand Difficulties: Rosario, Cordoba and Conurbano. With Market Difficulties: Capital Federal, La Plata, Conurbano and Rosario.

And below this "regional" average are: With Supply Difficulties: Cordoba, Rosario and Mendoza. With Demand Difficulties: Capital, La Plata and Mendoza. With Market Difficulties: Cordoba and Mendoza.

4. Concluding Remarks

Starting from a very simple set up and using assumptions which are not very restrictive, we have developed a statistical for the evolution of Argentine labor market. The main empirical findings have already been reported and the will not be repeated here. Instead, we will just point out that considering the values of Total "regional vision" we obtain that above Total are: With Supply Difficulties: Capital Federal, La Plata and Conurbano. With Demand Difficulties: Rosario, Cordoba and Conurbano. With Market Difficulties: Capital Federal, La Plata, Conurbano and Rosario.

And below this "regional" average are: With Supply Difficulties: Cordoba, Rosario and Mendoza. With Demand Difficulties: Capital, La Plata and Mendoza. With Market Difficulties: Cordoba and Mendoza.

It is important to remark that, even though "little surprising" but in accordance with previous works (using less sophisticated diagrams, like in Díaz C. & Figueras 1999; Figueras, Arrufat & Díaz C., 2002; y Figueras & Salto, 2003), values shows that labor difficulty's main axis is found, during the 90's, in labor supply factors; *standing out with labor demand's problems* Corrientes, Resistencia, Jujuy, Rosario, Santa Fe and Tucumán.

Labor supply factors refer to workers exhibiting a pro-cyclical behavior during the first five years of the 1990's , but also to a *long-term* behavior, grounded on culture, which has led to a significant increase in women's tendency to enter the labor market (especially, in greater Urban Agglomerates, like Capital Federal and the Conurbano).

References

Arrufat, J. L., Díaz Cafferata, A. M. and Figueras, A. J. (1998), Regional Unemployment time series. Argentina & Germany in the 1980's and 1990's. IIIrd Arnoldshain Seminar. U. Sao Paulo. October.

Arrufat, J. L., Díaz Cafferata, A. M. and Figueras, A. J. (1999a), Apertura, integración y tendencias regionales de la desocupación en Argentina. In: *Mancha Navarro*, Tomás and Daniel Sotelsek (Eds.), 2001.

Cuadrado Roura, J. R. (1998), Divergencia vs. convergencia de las disparidades regionales en España. In: *Eure*, Nro. 72, S. de Chile.

Díaz Cafferata, A. M. and Figueras, A. J. (1999), *La desocupación en Argentina. Una Visión regional.* Edición Centro de Estudios Científicos y Técnicos (Cecyt). FACPCE. Buenos Aires.

Figueras, A. J., Díaz Cafferata, A. M. and Arrufat, J. L. (2002), Evolución del desempleo regional: análisis a través de casos, *Reunión AAEP*, Tucumán.

Figueras, A. J. and Díaz Cafferata, A. M. (2001), *Nuevas Lecturas de Política Económica* (Argentina en la Globalización), Eudecor, Córdoba.

Figueras, A. J. and Salto, M. (2003), Mercado Laboral Regional, in: *Jornadas Inter. de Finanzas Públicas*, Córdoba.

Gerchunoff, P. and Kacef, O. (1996), *Un análisis de la evolución reciente del mercado de trabajo,* IDI de la UIA.

Mancha Navarro, T. and Sotelsek, D. (Eds.) (2001), Convergencia Económica e Integración, *España.*

Ponce, C. (1999), Cambio Estructural y Desempleo. In: *El futuro del Empleo*. Fund. de Emp., Córdoba.

Jimeno Serrano, J. F. (1996), *La persistencia del para*, FEDEA, Madrid.

Mondino, G. and Montoya, S. (1994), *Anatomía del desempleo*, Novedades Económicas, IEERAL, Córdoba.

Montoya, S. (1997), *Desempleo en Argentina*, Nov. Económicas 193, IEERAL, Córdoba.

Neffa, J.C. (1983), Enfoques alternativos para el análisis del empleo, in: *Económica*, Universidad Nacional de La Plata, Vol. XXX, N° 1.

Sánchez, C. (1979), Fuerza laboral y desempleo oculto en Argentina, Estudios 9, IEERAL, Córdoba.

Annex I - Methodology for Chart III definition:

The logical procedure is:

- Are Supply and Demand negatives? If answer is Yes, then "OK"
- If NO; ask: is S+D above 3%? If answer is NO leave "Blank"
- If YES then ask: Is D>3? If answer is YES, then ask: Is (D/S+D)>0.50? If answer is YES then "D"; if answer is NO, then "S" (supply pressure).
- If answer to D>3 is NO, then ask: Is S>3? If answer is YES, then "S"
- If answer to S>3 is NO; then ask: Is (S/S+D)>0.50? If answer is YES, then (.)
- If answer is NO, then (**)

Annex II – Classifications

In our attempt to distinguish between different situations, we have subjectively defined **some taxonomy of problems**, referring to difficulty levels (ND). In this way, we have worked with categories inside labor supply, demand and market, according the next classification:

Difficulty Level:

- 5: If VDT/PEA is above 15%
- 4: If VDT/PEA is above 10% but below 15%
- 3: If VDT/PEA is above 7% but below 10%
- 2: If VDT/PEA is above 3% but below 7%
- 1: If VDT/PEA is above or equals 0% but below 3%
- No Dif: If VDT/PEA is negative

Chart I – Optimum Feasible Level (NOP)

	Qo*	**Qd***	**NOP**
Capital Federal	38.90%	40.18%	-1.28%
Catamarca	32.51%	30.74%	1.77%
Comodoro Rivadavia	36.73%	33.57%	3.15%
Conurbano	38.90%	37.30%	1.60%
Córdoba	38.08%	35.68%	2.39%
Corrientes	34.15%	32.55%	1.60%
Formosa	35.01%	31.30%	3.72%
Jujuy	34.78%	32.24%	2.54%
La Plata	36.24%	35.76%	0.49%
La Rioja	34.51%	33.96%	0.56%
Mendoza	39.48%	35.19%	4.29%
Neuquén	38.01%	35.83%	2.18%
Paraná	35.03%	33.70%	1.32%
Posadas	36.10%	33.64%	2.46%
Resistencia	34.94%	33.31%	1.63%
Río Gallegos	39.38%	37.27%	2.11%
Rosario	39.69%	36.55%	3.13%
Salta	34.08%	32.70%	1.38%
San Juan	33.34%	31.64%	1.70%
San Luis	35.19%	35.37%	-0.18%
Santa Fe	37.87%	34.08%	3.79%
Santiago del Estero	36.15%	32.28%	3.87%
Tucumán	36.69%	33.88%	2.80%
Total *“national vision”*	38.13%	36.71%	1.42%
Total *“regional vision”*	36.34%	34.29%	2.04%

Source: Own calculations based on INDEC data.

Chart II. a: Market Situation: Preponderant Factor

Urban Agglomerate/Period	1980-83	1984-90	1991-94	1995-2001 (m)	1991-2001 (m)	2001(o) - 2002 (m)	02 (o) - 2003 (m)
Cap. Federal	D	S	S	S	S	S	S
Catamarca			S	S	S	S	S
Com. Rivadavia			S	S	S	S	S
Conurbano			S	S	S	D	S
Córdoba	OK			D	(**)	D	S
Corrientes				D	D	S	S
Formosa		OK					
Jujuy				D	D	D	S
La Plata		S	S	S	S	S	S
La Rioja	D	(.)	D	S	S	D	S
Mendoza		OK	OK	OK	OK		
Neuquén			S	S	S	S	S
Paraná		(**)	D	S	S	S	S
Posadas	OK					D	
Resistencia				D	D	D	D
Río Gallegos	OK	OK					OK
Rosario	OK			D	D	D	S
Salta		(.)	S	S	S	S	S
San Juan		(.)	S	S	S	S	S
San Luis	D	(.)	S	S	S	D	S
Santa Fe	OK		S	D	D	D	D
Sgo del Est.	OK	OK	OK			D	
Tucumán		S	D	D	D	D	D
Total "national vision"			S	S	S	S	S
Total "regional vision"	OK			S	S	D	D

(m): Mayo ; (o): Octubre

Ok	7	4	2	1	1	0	1
B	15	13	9	4	4	3	4
(.)	0	4	0	0	0	0	0
(**)	0	5	0	0	1	0	0
S	0	3	11	13	13	10	16
D	3	0	3	7	6	12	4

Source: Own calculations based on INDEC data.

Chart II. b: Market Situation: Preponderant Factor (Total)

Urban Agglom	*La Plata*	Cat-am	*Cba*	Corr	Resist.	Com. Riv	Par	For	Ju-juy	La Rioja	*Mza*	Pos	Neuq
abr 1980			OK					OK		D			OK
oct 1980		OK				OK		OK		D	OK	OK	
abr 1981		D						OK		D	OK		
oct 1981									OK	D	OK	OK	OK
abr 1982								OK		D			OK
oct 1982						OK		OK		D		OK	
abr 1983	D		OK			OK	(.)			D	OK		OK
oct 1983	(.)					OK		OK		S	OK		
abr 1984	(.)					OK		OK		D	OK		
oct 1984	D					OK				D		OK	
may 1985	S			S		OK				D			
nov 1985	D			D		OK	(.)		S	D	OK		
may 1986	D	S		D		OK	(.)		OK	D			
nov 1986	S				(**)			OK	OK		OK		OK
abr 1987	S		OK		S		(.)	OK					
oct 1987	S				S	OK			OK	S	OK		
may 1988	(**)		OK		S					S	OK		
oct 1988	S				S		S				OK		
may 1989	S	S		D	S	(.)	D			S	OK		S
oct 1989	S						D	OK			OK		

may	1990	D	S				S	D			(**)			
oct	1990		S					D			S	OK		S
jun	1991	S		OK			S	D			S			
oct	1991	S	S	OK							S	OK		
may	1992	S	S	OK			S				D	OK		
oct	1992	S					S	S			D			S
may	1993	S	S				S	S			S	OK		S
oct	1993	D	S			D	S	D			D	OK		S
may	1994	S	S		D			D			D		S	S
oct	1994	S		(.)	D	D	S	D			D	OK		S
may	1995	S	S	D	D	D	S	D		D	D			D
oct	1995	S	S	D	D	D	S	D		D	D			D
may	1996	S	S	D	D	D	S	S		D	D	OK		S
oct	1996	S	S	D	D	D	S	D		D	D	OK		S
may	1997	S	S	D	D	D	S	D		D	D			S
oct	1997	S	S	S	S	D	S	D	OK	D	S	OK	OK	S
may	1998	S	S	D	S	D		S	OK	D	S	OK	OK	S
ago	1998	S	S	S	D	D		S	OK	D	S	OK		S
oct	1998	S	S	S	S	D	S	S	OK	D	S	OK	OK	S
may	1999	S	S	S	S	D	S	S		D	S			S
ago	1999	S	S	S	D	D	D	S		D	S			S

Continuation Chart II. b: Market Situation: Preponderant Factor (Total)														
Urban Agglom		***La Plata***	**Cat-am**	***Cba***	**Corr**	Resist.	Com. Riv	**Par**	**For**	**Ju-juy**	**La Rioja**	***Mza***	**Pos**	**Neuq**
oct	1999	S	S	S	D	D	S	S		D	S	OK		S
may	2000	S	S	S	D	D	S	S		D	S			S
oct	2000	S	S	S	D	D	S	S		D	S	OK		S
may	2001	S	S	S	D	D	S	S		D	S			S
oct	2001	S	S	D	S	D	S	S		D	D			S
may	2002	S	S	D	S	D	S	S		D	D		D	S
oct	2002	S	S	D	S	D	S	S		S	S			S
may	2003	S	S	S	S	D	S	S		S	S			S
	S	33	28	10	9	5	23	17	0	3	20	0	1	24
	D	6	1	9	16	21	1	13	0	17	24	0	1	2
	(.)	2	0	1	0	0	1	4	0	0	0	0	0	0
	Ok	0	1	7	0	0	10	0	14	4	0	27	7	5
	Blanco	7	19	22	24	22	14	15	35	25	4	22	40	18
	(**)	1	0	0	0	1	0	0	0	0	1	0	0	0

Continuation Chart II. b: Market Situation: Preponderant Factor (Total)													
Urban Agglom		Salta	SJ	SL	Rio Gall	*Ros*	S Fe	Sgo	Tuc	*Cap. Fed*	*Con-urb*	Total	TPS
abr	1980	OK		S	OK		OK			D			OK
oct	1980					OK	OK	OK		D			
abr	1981				OK			OK		D			
oct	1981					OK		OK	(.)	D			OK
abr	1982	(**)		D	OK				(**)	D			
oct	1982		D	D	OK					D			
abr	1983	D		D			OK			D			
oct	1983	D		D						D			
abr	1984	D	(.)	D		OK				D			
oct	1984	S		D		OK		OK	S	D			
may	1985	D		D				OK	D	S			
nov	1985	S	S	D	OK				D	S			
may	1986	S	(.)	S					D	D			
nov	1986	(**)	S	S				OK	S	S			
abr	1987		S	(**)	OK			OK	S	S			
oct	1987		S	S	OK		OK			S			
may	1988			S	OK				S	S	(**)		
oct	1988		S	S						S			
may	1989	D	D	S		D	S		S	S	S	S	(.)
oct	1989			S				OK	D	S	D	(.)	
may	1990	D	S	S				OK	D	S	D	(.)	
oct	1990	S	S	S				OK		S			
jun	1991		S	S		(**)	S	OK	S	S		S	
oct	1991			S				OK	(.)	S			
may	1992	S		S				OK	S	S	(.)	S	
oct	1992	S	S	S				OK	D	S	(.)	S	
may	1993	S		S			S	OK	D	S	S	S	S
oct	1993	S		S		D	S	OK	(**)	S	S	S	
may	1994	S	S	S		D	S	OK	D	S	S	S	S
oct	1994	S	S	S		D	S	OK	D	S	S	S	(.)
may	1995	S	S	S		D	D		D	S	S	S	D
oct	1995	S	S	S		D	D		D	S	S	S	D
may	1996	S	S	S		D	D		D	S	D	S	D
oct	1996	S	S	S		D	D		D	S	S	S	D
may	1997	S	S	S		D	D		D	S	S	S	S
oct	1997	S	S	S		D	D		D	S	S	S	S
may	1998	S	S	S		D	D		D	S	S	S	S
ago	1998	S	S	S		D	D		D	S	S	S	S

Continuation Chart II. b: Market Situation: Preponderant Factor (Total)

Urban Agglom		Salta	SJ	SL	Rio Gall	*Ros*	S Fe	Sgo	Tuc	*Cap. Fed*	*Con-urb*	Total	TPS
oct	1998	S		S		D	D		D	S	S	S	S
may	1999	S	S	D		D	D			S	S	S	S
ago	1999	S	S	S		D	D		(.)	S	S	S	S
oct	1999	S	S	S		D				S	S	S	S
may	2000	S	S	D	OK	D	D		D	S	S	S	S
oct	2000	S	S	S		D	S		S	S	S	S	S
may	2001	S	S	S		S	D		S	S	S	S	S
oct	2001	S	S	D		S	D		D	S	D	S	S
may	2002	D	S	D		D	D	D	D	S	D	D	D
oct	2002	S	S	S	OK	S	D		D	S	S	S	D
may	2003	S	S	S	OK	S	D		D	S	S	S	D
		28	29	33	0	4	7	0	9	38	21	26	14
		7	2	12	0	19	17	1	23	11	5	1	7
		0	2	0	0	0	0	0	3	0	2	2	2
		1	0	0	11	4	4	18	0	0	0	0	2
		11	16	3	38	21	21	30	12	0	20	20	24
		2	0	1	0	1	0	0	2	0	1	0	0

Source: Own calculations based on INDEC data.

Chart III – Labor Market Difficulty Level							
Urban Agglom./ Period	**80-83**	**84-90**	**91-94**	**95-2001 (m)**	**2001 (o) - 02 (m)**	**2002 (o) - 2003 (m)**	**Weighted Average**
Río Gallegos	0	0	0	0	0	0	0.00
Formosa	0	0	0	0	1	0	0.04
Mendoza	0	0	0	0	1	0	0.04
Sgo del Est.	0	0	0	0	2	1	0.09
Posadas	0	1	1	0	2	1	0.55
Jujuy	0	0	0	3	4	4	1.00
Com. Rivadavia	0	0	2	2	3	2	1.02
Córdoba	0	0	1	3	4	4	1.17
Resistencia	0	1	1	2	4	3	1.19
Neuquén	0	0	2	3	4	4	1.34
Santa Fe	0	1	2	2	4	4	1.36
Total "regional vision"	0	1	1	3	4	4	1.47
Corrientes	0	1	1	3	5	4	1.51
Rosario	0	1	1	3	5	4	1.51
San Juan	1	2	2	2	4	3	1.83
Conurbano	0	1	2	4	5	5	1.96
Tucumán	1	2	2	3	4	3	2.11
Catamarca	1	1	2	4	5	4	2.13
Total "national vision"	1	1	2	4	5	4	2.13
Paraná	1	2	2	3	5	4	2.15
La Rioja	2	2	2	3	4	4	2.28
La Plata	1	2	2	4	5	4	2.43
Salta	1	2	2	4	5	4	2.43
San Luis	2	2	3	3	4	4	2.45
Cap. Federal	3	2	3	5	5	4	3.21
Average	0.57	1.00	1.43	2.43	3.70	3.04	-
Standard deviation	0.84	0.85	0.95	1.50	1.49	1.55	-
Coefficient of variation.	1.49	0.85	0.66	0.62	0.40	0.51	-
No Dif	15	8	5	5	1	3	-
ND1	7	9	6	0	2	2	-
ND2	2	8	12	4	2	1	-
ND3	1	0	2	10	1	3	-
ND4	0	0	0	5	10	15	-
ND5	0	0	0	1	9	1	-

Source: Own calculations.

Chart IV – Labor Supply Difficulty Level							
Urban Agglomerate/ Period	**1980 - 1983**	**1984 - 1990**	**1991 - 1994**	**1995-2001 (m)**	**2001(o) – 2002 (m)**	**2002 (o) - 2003 (m)**	**Weighted Average**
Santiago del Estero.	0	0	0	0	0	0	0.00
Río Gallegos	0	0	0	0	1	0	0.04
Formosa	1	0	0	0	0	0	0.17
Mendoza	1	0	0	0	1	0	0.21
Resistencia	0	1	0	0	0	1	0.34
Jujuy	1	0	0	0	1	4	0.38
Rosario	0	0	1	0	2	3	0.38
Posadas	0	1	2	0	0	0	0.64
Santa Fe	0	1	2	0	1	2	0.77
Córdoba	0	0	1	2	1	2	0.85
Corrientes	0	0	0	2	4	4	0.89
Tucumán	0	2	1	1	1	2	1.17
La Rioja	0	1	1	2	2	4	1.28
Total "regional vision"	0	1	1	2	2	4	1.28
Paraná	1	1	1	2	4	3	1.49
Com. Rivadavia	1	1	2	2	2	3	1.57
San Luis	1	1	3	2	1	3	1.70
Total "national vision"	1	1	2	3	3	0	1.77
Neuquén	1	1	2	3	4	4	1.98
Conurbano	1	1	2	4	3	4	2.21
Salta	1	1	2	4	4	4	2.26
San Juan	1	1	2	4	4	4	2.26
Catamarca	0	2	3	4	5	5	2.64
La Plata	0	2	2	5	5	5	2.74
Cap. Federal	1	3	5	5	5	5	3.72
Average	0.48	0.87	1.39	1.83	2.22	2.70	-
Standard Deviation	0.51	0.81	1.27	1.80	1.78	1.77	-
Coefficient of Variation.	1.07	0.94	0.91	0.99	0.80	0.66	-
No Dif	13	8	7	9	4	6	-
S1	12	13	6	1	7	1	-
S2	0	3	9	7	4	3	-
S3	0	1	2	2	2	4	-
S4	0	0	0	4	5	8	-
S5	0	0	1	2	3	3	-

Source: Own calculations

Chart V – Labor Demand Difficulty Level							
Urban Agglomerate / Period	**1980 - 1983**	**1984 - 1990**	**1991 - 1994**	**1995-2001 (m)**	**2001 (o) - 02 (m)**	**2002 (o) - 2003 (m)**	**Weighted Average**
Com. Rivadavia	0	0	0	0	1	0	0.04
Mendoza	0	0	0	0	1	1	0.09
Catamarca	1	0	0	0	0	0	0.17
Neuquén	0	0	0	1	1	0	0.32
Cap. Federal	2	0	0	0	0	0	0.34
San Juan	1	1	0	0	0	0	0.47
Posadas	0	0	0	1	3	2	0.49
Río Gallegos	0	0	2	1	0	0	0.62
La Plata	1	1	1	0	1	0	0.68
Salta	1	1	0	1	2	1	0.87
Total "regional vision"	0	1	1	1	2	1	0.87
Formosa	0	0	1	2	4	1	0.94
Santiago del Estero	0	0	0	3	3	1	1.00
Conurbano	0	1	1	1	4	2	1.00
Total "national vision"	1	1	0	1	3	4	1.04
Córdoba	0	1	0	2	4	2	1.11
Santa Fe	0	0	0	3	4	3	1.13
San Luis	2	1	0	1	4	2	1.17
Paraná	1	1	2	1	2	1	1.21
La Rioja	2	1	2	1	3	0	1.38
Rosario	0	1	1	3	3	2	1.51
Tucumán	1	1	2	2	4	3	1.66
Corrientes	1	1	3	2	3	1	1.70
Jujuy	0	1	2	4	4	1	1.96
Resistencia	1	1	2	4	4	3	2.21
Average	0.61	0.57	0.83	1.43	2.39	1.13	-
Standard Deviation	0.72	0.51	0.98	1.27	1.56	1.06	-
Coefficient of variation	1.19	0.90	1.19	0.89	0.65	0.94	-
No Dif	13	10	13	6	4	8	-
D1	9	15	5	10	4	8	-
D2	3	0	6	4	3	5	-
D3	0	0	1	3	6	3	-
D4	0	0	0	2	8	1	-
D5	0	0	0	0	0	0	-

Source: Own calculations

Chart VI: Cross Correlation Coefficients							
Sector	1980 – 1983	1984 – 1990	1991 – 1994	1995 - 2001 (m)	2001(o) - 2002 (m)	2002 (o) – 03 (m)	Average
Market ND vs Demand ND	0.90	0.51	-0.28	-0.19	0.08	0.15	0.08
Market ND vs Supply ND	0.23	0.59	0.84	0.76	0.64	0.66	0.82
Multipe correlation coefficient	-	-	-	-	-	-	0.45

Source: Own calculations

Chart VII: Cross Correlation per Urban Agglomerate		
Urban Agglomerate	**Market ND vs Demand ND**	**Market ND vs. Supply ND**
Capital. Federal	-0.25	0.58
Catamarca	-0.49	0.90
Comodoro Rivadavia	0.67	0.95
Conurbano	0.81	0.89
Córdoba	0.89	0.95
Corrientes	0.63	0.60
Formosa	0.87	-0.25
Jujuy	0.90	0.28
La Plata	-0.41	0.97
La Rioja	0.53	0.80
Mendoza	1.00	-0.25
Neuquén	0.87	0.99
Paraná	0.54	0.96
Posadas	0.64	0.20
Resistencia	0.85	0.77
Río Gallegos	Not computable	Not computable
Rosario	0.93	0.23
Salta	0.65	0.94
San Juan	-0.58	0.69
San Luis	0.51	0.20
Santa Fe	0.81	0.36
Sgo del Est.	0.61	Not computable
Tucumán	0.68	0.96
Total "Visión Nacional"	0.86	0.95
Total "Visión Regional"	0.90	0.31

Source: Own calculations

Institutional and methodological comparisons

PRICE REGULATIONS IN THE PHARMACEUTICAL MARKET - A COMPARATIVE PERSPECTIVE

Prof. Roland Eisen[α]
Johann Wolfgang Goethe - University, Frankfurt

Yasemin Ilgin[β]
Johann Wolfgang Goethe - University, Frankfurt

1. Introduction

Why should government intervene in pricing of pharmaceutical firms? Or should they intervene at all? To answer these questions one could start with the classical distinction between supply and demand sides of pharmaceutical market. According to the different interest groups the answers will be different. Fact is that most governments face rising health care expenditures, especially expenditures on drugs (Figure 1). In attempts to contain the expenditures for drugs or other health care services, different countries took various regulation strategies.

The modern medical science has particularly been progressive with biotechnological medical acquisitions on one side, but the very same acquisition is quoted in literature to be one of the reasons for cost explosion in health care systems. Technical progress itself creates needs, which exist at the most concealed, i.e. technical progress is the greatest cost driver itself (Krämer (1996)). Besides new technologies, demographic patterns, market imperfections, the method and length of regulatory approval, inadequate product differentiation for the same medical indication category, and brand loyalty can be identified as crucial factors for rising pharmaceutical expenditures. Market failures are caused by supply side entry barriers, e.g. patents, by agency relationships, and by moral hazard. Moral hazard occurs because of the specific demand structure comprised of four segments: the physicians, who prescribe the pharmaceuticals, the pharmacists who dispense them, the patients who consume, and governments or insurers who pay. Due to the occurring moral hazard in this prescribing process, it is not secured that competition alone could guarantee efficient prices (Mrazek (2002)).

[α] Roland Eisen is Professor of Economic and Labor Market Policies, Economic Department of Economics and Business Administration at the J. W. Goethe University of Frankfurt, Mertonstr. 17, 60054 Frankfurt, Germany, e-mail: eisen@wiwi.uni-frankfurt.de.

[β] Yasemin Ilgin is Research Assistant at the Institute of European Health Policy and Social Law (INEGES), J. W. Goethe-University of Frankfurt, e-mail: ilgin@wiwi.uni-frankfurt.de.

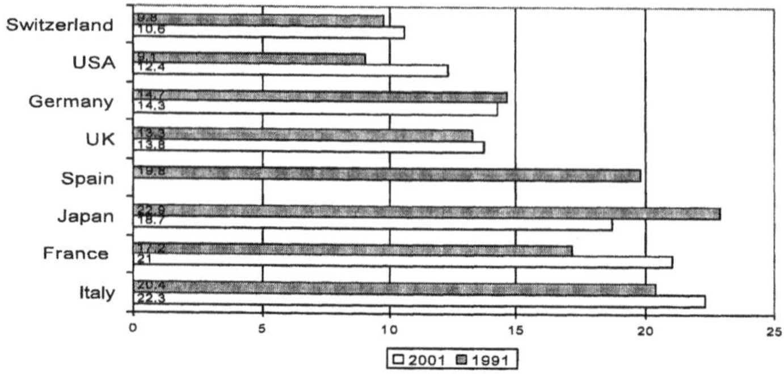

Source: OECD

* Germany 1992 (for 1991), Spain 1990 (only available value) und UK 2002 (for 2001).

Figure 1: Share of Drug Spending of the total Health Care Spending in Europe, Japan, and USA (1991 and 2001*)

On account of the international expansion of the pharmaceutical market and the globalization of the drug industry, multinational economic evaluation is an important aspect in public policy and corporate decisions. Nevertheless, only few multinational economic evaluations have been made due to the fact of missing comparable data. Therefore, in order to draw a qualitative multinational comparison a review of the different existing national price regulation schemes is necessary.

The paper is organized as follows. In the first section an overview of the current situation in the health care market and several developments in the pharmaceutical market will be given. In the second section important aspect for the pharmaceutical pricing are touched on as for example the free-rider problem, moral hazard, and also the cost structure of drugs in general. The objective is to illustrate current problems of the production of pharmaceuticals. The main and third section of this paper contributes to the price regulation, in particular the aims of price regulation and the various types of national price regulations. At the end an evaluation is given. The different implications and conclusions will be discussed in the last section.

2. Crucial Factors in Pharmaceutical Pricing

2.1. Free-rider Problem and Moral Hazard

In the recent literature opinions do not differ in the point that first nations have incentives to free ride on the enormous sunk costs of pharmaceutical firms (PHs), and try to apply the marginal cost pricing in order to maximize the welfare. For the social insurance systems this means that governments, as a monopsony buyer for pharmaceuticals, has strong vested interest to concentrate on the short-run interests of containing the own pharmaceutical budget implying that the own measures are negligible on the manufactures' incentives for R&D that result out of their global earnings. Hence, each country has an intencive to successively reduce the prices up to the marginal costs while ignoring global joint costs (Danzon (1997b)).

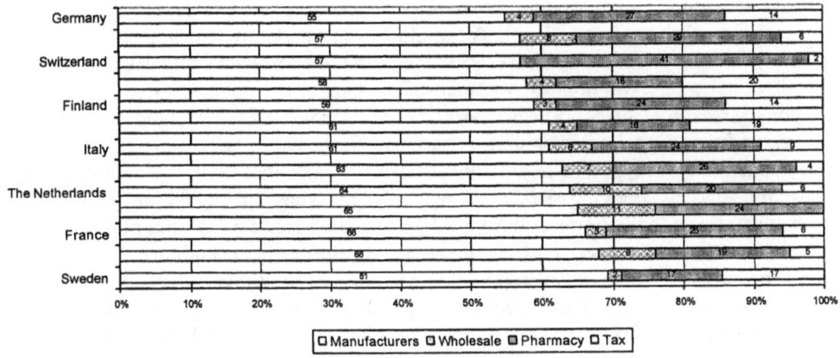

Source: VFA (2004), p.19.

Figure 2: Breakdown of the Final Price for Retailed Pharmaceuticals (2002), in Percent

Figure 2 shows that German manufacturers are obtaining the lowest and Sweden manufacturers are obtaining the highest share in the breakdown of final retailed prices. Beside Ireland and the Netherlands no country allows the wholesalers 10% or more. On average the pharmacists get the second highest share. Also the taxation is rather differently treated.

Second, nations have also incentives to support pharmaceutical firms with respect to their innovation costs by granting them monopoly rights by means of patents for example. Therefore the firms can ask an adequately high mark-up on the marginal cost.[1]

But at least nations try to secure a certain research and development (R&D) level, because anticipating this free-rider problem a drastic reaction by pharmaceutical firms may be the decision not to invest in R&D at all (Danzon (1997b)). The production sector of pharmaceuticals is also an important growth sector in many industrialized countries. Thus, besides health care spending government has to consider also consequences for employment. Therefore, nations are faced with a dilemma. Furthermore the producers of generics as suppliers of unpatented drugs are interested in the research findings of these pharmaceutical firms. Using the information of expired patents puts producers of generics into the position to utilize dearly researched coherences for their production. Therefore, they free-ride on the sunk R&D costs of the researching firms.

Beside the free-rider problem, also a moral hazard can emerge, in particular, on the side of physicians. Physicians for example tend to prescribe more pharmaceuticals than necessary to commit the patients on themselves. Consequently, the amounts of prescriptions are rising and this in turn causes rising expenditures in health care spending. Furthermore, moral hazard exists on the patients' side in the form of excessive consuming. Patients try to hoard as many medicaments as possible aiming at compensating for their insurance payment.

---

[1] According to Danzon (1997b) marginal cost pricing would only cover 30% or less of the total cost.

2.2. Cost Structure of Drugs

R&D costs account for 30% of total costs because the drug development process is risky, time-consuming and heavily regulated. These global joint costs are necessary to develop and in the end to bring the drug to the market, i.e. they can not be properly classified as belonging to any individual drug. Additionally, these costs are sunk at the point of price fixing or price negotiations (Danzon (1997a)). Furthermore, the ratio between sunk costs (sc) and marginal costs (mc) increases over the life time of a pharmaceutical.

This can lead firstly to types of regulation that are reducing incentives for innovative R&D and pushing towards copying R&D or secondly to types of regulation which benefit pharmaceutical firms in the home country. Still, it is a challenge for national policy to create a system that mediates between curbing down the health care expenditures and providing sufficient incentives for innovative R&D leading to optimal health care.

Patents for example can be such a mediator to promote innovations. Patent rights secure the innovator or innovative firm a price above the marginal cost for the life time of the patent as long as the patent prevents competition from close substitutes (Danzon (1997a)).

3. Price Regulations

3.1. Objectives of Price Regulations

First and foremost the aim of price regulation is to control rising health care expenditures. Health care payers can either concentrate on the demand (volume) or the supply (price) or on both sides. Figure 3 shows a possible division of demand and supply side measures. In the following subsections some of these various demand and supply side measures are discussed and evaluated.

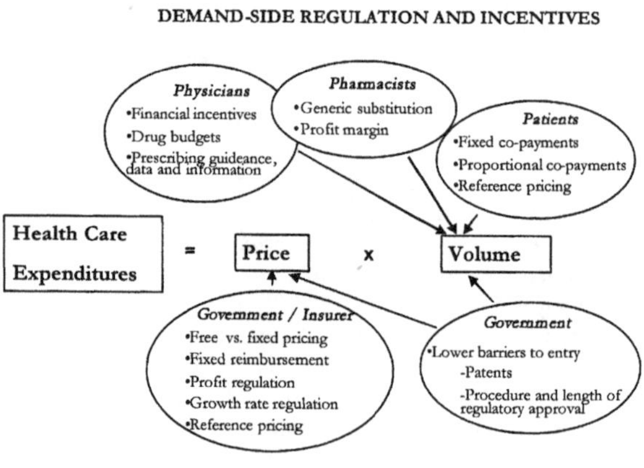

Source: Mrazek (2002), p. 455 and author's own compilation

Figure 3: Regulatory framework for pharmaceutical markets

As mentioned above the second aim of price regulation in the pharmaceutical market is to support industrial policy goals of home investment, employment, and international competitiveness. Italy or France for example allows higher prices for pharmaceuticals if they are produced in the home country. In the U.K. the rate of return on capital within the country is the crucial factor. In this way domestic investment is promoted but these kinds of regulations could also distort productive efficiency (Danzon (1997a)).
As the drug costs become a gradually increasing element of the health care spending, economic evaluations can be used to inform governments and health care organizations to supplement clinical evidence on safety and efficacy. This information can be used for reimbursement negotiations, resource management, and temporary regulation and price control (Smith (2002)).
These regulation schemes include certain norms that have to be fulfilled by existing drugs. Governments have different views with regard to the strictness of these regulations. The USA started with the Pure Food and Drug Act of 1906. For a certain period the United States had the strictest drug testing prerequisites in the world, but today the United Kingdom and Germany have caught up (Scherer (2000)).
A new European system for approval of new drug has come into effect in January 1995. It offers two ways to approve medical products. One way is a more 'centralized' form, which has been implemented by creating the European Medical Products Evaluation Agency (EMEA). The second is a 'mutual acknowledgement' procedure in the EU member states selected by the applicant and then by mutual acknowledgement of national market approval.[2] Through this European reform a platform of introducing new drugs has been created.
The decision-makers' problem is to find the best solution between making a Type I error of supporting a drug which is not truly safe or effective and a Type II error of withholding a drug which is truly effective and safe. Intuitively comprehensible, governments are particularly concerned not to commit Type I errors, to avoid political disasters caused by pharmaceuticals that lead for example to cancer or malformed babies. To reduce this risk, the size of necessary clinical trials has been increased and also the availability of new drugs has been retarded (Scherer (2000)).

3.2. Types of Supply-Side Price Regulations

3.2.1. Reference Price Limits on Reimbursement

Reference pricing is a basic concept. Drugs are classified into clusters according to particular criteria or rather the degrees of similar therapeutic effects. Government or the insurer determines a reference price for each cluster on the basis of a relative lower priced drug within the cluster (Danzon and Ketcham (2003)).
Germany was the first country to introduce reference pricing in 1989 together with the Health Reform Law ('Gesundheitsreform-Gesetz (GRG)'). The aim of this law was to induce more intensive competition in order to contain drug expenses.[3]
Reference price limits usually have been established using a two-step procedure. In the fist step it is defined which drugs can be clustered. These clustered drugs may be described by the

---

[2] For detailed information see Regulation 2309/936 and Directive 93/41/EEC.

[3] The reference price limits on reimbursement regulation applies on the demand and supply side of the pharmaceutical market. The demand side is affected because patients do not receive full reimbursement for the pharmaceuticals whose prices are higher. The supply-side is concerned because of increased price competition.

same chemical entity (or molecular entity),[4] or with comparable therapeutic effects.[5] This clustering guarantees that the therapeutically possibilities have not been restricted, and therefore physicians have the opportunity to prescribe alternative compounds. In the second step the prevailing reference price limit is determined. Here, the price have to fulfil certain criteria, e.g. to guarantee a sufficient, suitable, economic and quality enhancing medical care (BGA (2004)). The patients have to carry the cost above the reimbursement price in Germany; physicians are obliged by law to point out this fact.

The price elasticity is much higher if patients have to pay this difference by themselves, therefore manufacturers tend to adapt to the reference prices (Danzon (1997a)). Reference price reimbursement systems have been also launched in Denmark, New Zealand, and Canada.

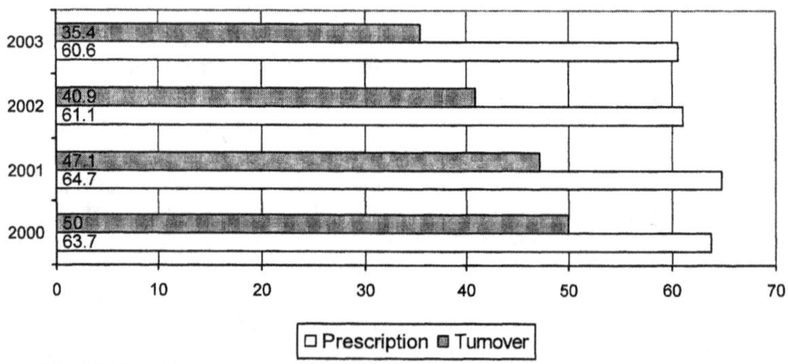

Source: VFA (2004), p.63

* Values are taken on January 1st each year and 2003 are preliminary values.

Figure 4: Share of Reference Price Limits in Germany (2000-2003*)

3.2.2. Patents and Parallel Imports

The idiosyncratic subject matter of patents is to guarantee the holder the exclusive right to use his invention with regards to produce industrial products and putting them into circulation for the first time. This can be done by the patent holder either directly or by granting licenses to third parties. The aim of patents is to reward the creative effort of the invention.

In the European Union the patent protection lasts for 20 years and normally assigns the power to discriminate prices between countries. The cost structure of pharmaceuticals is characterized by high R&D sunk costs.[6] One basic aspect of this share of the global joint costs is that they are constant independent of the number of future consumers or countries that will

[4] The distinction between chemical entities (CE) and molecular entities (ME) is small. CE are new molecules or compounds not tested in human before. ME are used to describe compounds.

[5] In Phase 1 of the German system and also most of the Medicaid programs in USA usually generically equivalent products and drugs, where the patent rights have been lost, are clustered in the same group. Phase 2 includes clustering of drugs with related chemicals, for example benzodiazepines or H2 antagonists. In Phase 3 also drugs with therapeutic comparable effects are grouped together.

[6] DiMasi, Hansen, and Grabowski (2003) find that the total R&D costs per new drug are about US$ 802 million in 2000 Dollars. A critical assessment is given by Frank (2003).

use the drug. Obviously, R&D and the resulting inapplicability of marginal cost pricing is not only a problem for the pharmaceutical market. The goal of patent protection is to find a solution for this problem. This normally enables the patent holder to price discriminate between countries, primarily because the holder enjoys in each country unregulated distribution rights, including parallel imports (European Commission (2003a)). The European Court of Justice can constrain the manufacturer's patent rights by decreeding the patent holders' rights. The patent holders' rights are exhausted throughout the EU once a product has been placed on the market in any EU country. The effect is to nullify the patent holder's rights in the importing country (Danzon (1997b)).[7]

The value of patent protection is further bounded in most European countries by price regulation and other forms of regulation because of the government's role of insurer. In Europe, different governments have important functions, either as a monopoly provider of national health insurance, as e.g. in UK or Italy, or as regulator of the social insurance health funds, as e.g. in Germany, France or the Netherlands (Danzon (1997b)).

The limitations of the patent protection have significantly influenced the decisions concerning parallel imports or trade. The European Commission defines parallel trade as trade in products which takes place outside the official distribution system established by a particular firm. The own distribution system of the firm may cause differences in prices for different countries, utilizing national differences in the behaviour of consumers (price discrimination). Parallel traders buy products in countries where they are sold at lower prices caused e.g. by price regulation and sell them in high-price countries with less or no interventions. The flow of products thereby created is called parallel trade (European Commission (2003b)).

In principal parallel imports are about goods or property rights on goods which are traded beside and therefore parallel to a contractually agreed distribution network. Parallel imports come into a country not by the producers' intentionally designated ways of selected sales dealers or single importers etc. Reimportations however are goods exported from the home country to foreign countries and which are imported back to the home country (Freytag (2001), p. 17).

Legalization of parallel imports implies a decision with respect to the possible form of price discrimination. On the one side, the possibility to discriminate prices is restricted, because the producers can not sell unaffected any longer the same goods for different prices. On the other side, parallel imports are only possible because of intercountry price differences (Goate, Rhys, and Gerner (1999)). But these intercountry differences are usually based upon national pricing policies and different national interests. Supposing that parallel trade operates as an important stimulating force for market integration where there are given price differences between Member States, it is only one kind of importing national pricing policies. If an European harmonized pricing policy for pharmaceuticals would exist parallel import could not exist. But harmonization of the European pricing policies can not be a goal if there are different national costs and different national interests.8

---

[7] For details see judgements of the European Court of Justice: Merck vs. Primecrown C-267 and C-268/95 (1996) ECR I-6285. Parallel imports of pharmaceuticals is a lawful kind of trade within the Internal Market based on article 28 of the Treaty and subject to the impairment in view of the protection of human health and life and the protection of industrial and commercial property, regulated in article 30 of the Treaty. The European Court of Justice defines the European Union as a single market consisting of different European countries.

[8] Maybe parallel imports could be seen in sense of a Pareto optimizing game. An outcome of a game is Pareto optimal if there is no other outcome that makes every player at least as well off and at least one player strictly better off. To describe the existing situation with a Pareto optimal outcome is inadequate, because the price

Recent literature points out that government have a rational motivation to free ride on the sunk costs of innovative pharmaceutical firms. Thus, the question is whether this free rider problem can be solved by parallel imports. The health expenditures can be reduced by setting the drug price ceiling as low as possible. Before a new drug can be brought onto the market high investments are necessary. The problem with these investments is that they are already sunk cost when national drug price ceilings are determined. Within a static perspective sunk costs are not taken into account when deciding on the optimal price. However, these sunk costs amount to 30% of the total costs (Danzon (1997b)). Providing them patents seems to be a rational procedure, because pharmaceutical firm incur high costs in developing new drugs: One major cost driver is R&D expenditures to cover investigations in compounds that have been dropped (so called 'dry holes'). The other major cost driver are the tied up capital costs, because the process to invent and to bring NCE to market takes at least one decade.[9]

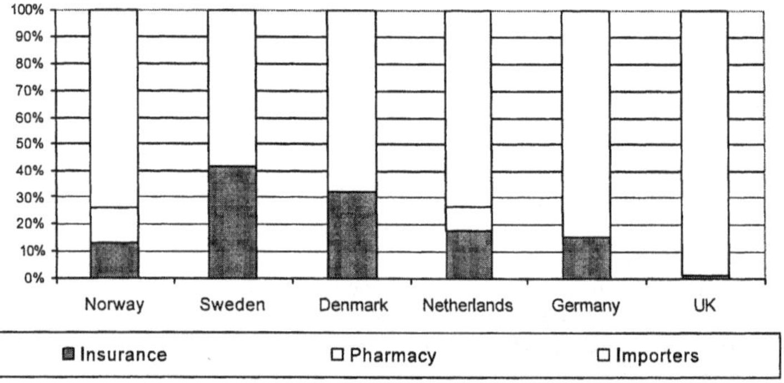

Source: IMS Health Data. For detailed information see Kanavos, Costa-i Font, Merkur, and Gemmill (2003)

Figure 5: Savings by Reimportation in different European Countries (2002)

Figure 5 shows the savings in different European countries that could be made by reimportation. These dates have been presented together with a stakeholder analysis by Kanavos, Costa-i Font, Merkur, and Gemmill (2003) which aims at examining the impact of parallel imports. They demonstrate that the profits from parallel imports flow for the most part to third-party firms that buy and resell patented pharmaceuticals.

3.3. Types of Demand-Side Price Regulations

3.3.1. Drug Budget Regulations for Physicians

There are three categories of regulations to influence the prescribing behaviour of physicians. The most basic category is the restriction of potentially prescribable drugs by introducing so

discrimination of the patent holder is worse off and the volume of sales that are not parallel imported goods decreases.

[9] See DiMasi, Hansen, and Grabowski (2003) for the difference between average out-of-the pocket costs of an new chemical entity (NCE) and the average cost of an NCE (including capital costs): 403-802$. But these costs reflect the outcomes of profit-maximizing choices and are not useful parameters to evaluate the value of an investment.

called positive l[10] or negative lists[11]. The second more general possibility is to give comprehensive guidelines, which are mainly based on therapeutic considerations, and monitoring of prescribing practices. The guidelines stipulate which drugs can be prescribed and in some countries they even specify how prescriptions are written. The third category, drug budget regulation for physicians, includes measures to provide incentives for physicians to consider cost differences between alternative treatments.

Probably one of the most powerful demand side measures to regulate drug spending is to place physicians directly at risk for the financial consequences of their prescribing practice (Danzon (1997a)). It is often argued, that physicians do not directly benefit from prescribing drugs but indirectly be securing repeated visits by patients.

After launching drug budgets in Germany in 1993 two different types containing varying degrees of governmental regulation have been used. On the one hand, spending caps for all physicians of a region were defined, putting all of them into responsibility for any excess of the region's aggregated drug budget. On the other hand, target volumes for individual classes of physicians were defined (Schreyögg and Busse (2004)).

The chronology of the physicians' drug budgets is shown in Table I. As it became clear that collective liability was not very successful target caps with individual liability were introduced in 1998. These target volumes were accompanied by an early information system given to the physicians. Since 2000 each physician receives information about the aggregate prescription volume of his specialist class in his region and about his own prescription volume. In 2002 the liability for negotiated target volumes for individual practices have been statutory determined. The statutory cap for overstepping and repaying is 125% over the individual target (§106(5a) German Social Law, SGB V).

Table 1: Development of Physician Drug Budgets with individual and collective liability in Germany (1989-2003)

	Spending caps (collective liability)	**Target volumes (collective liability)**
1989 to 1992	No spending caps required	Target volumes legally required but not implemented due to lack of data
1993	Legally set national spending caps	
1994 to 1997	Negotiated regional spending caps	
1998	No spending caps required	Negotiated target volumes for individual practices (lack of legal liability)
1999	Legally set national spending caps	
2000 to 2001	Negotiated regional spending caps	
Since 2002	No spending caps required	Legal liability for negotiated target volumes for individual practices

Source: Schreyögg and Busse (2004), p.5

(The darker the shading, the more strictly the regulation is.)

[10] A positive list is a compilation of in principal permitted drugs which are provided within the scope of health care insurance systems and therefore the costs are reimbursed. Patients have to pay for drugs that are not listed.

[11] A negative list is a compilation of drugs where the prescription at the expense of the statutory health insurance funds is not permitted.

3.3.2. Generic drugs

After a regular patent duration of 20 years and loss of patent rights, producer of generic drugs (imitation) can be admitted into this part of the drug market. The share of the generic drugs is around 70% of the prescriptions of the German health insurance funds. In the last 12 years a clear trend towards prescribing generics appears. This tendency to prescribe more generics can be seen in the increasing share of prescribed generics as a percentage of the total prescriptions. Often enough pharmaceutical firms with patent protected drugs loose considerable market share within a few months.

Just after the introduction of drug budgets in Germany the market share of generics increased by 3.7% in 1993 and in the following by 1.3% each year. In 2002 the market share of generic prescriptions exceeded the market share of original compounds (see Figure 6). In 2002, a scheme for generic substitution has been launched in Germany. Under the well known 'aut-idem regulation' pharmacists are asked to substitute non-patented pharmaceuticals above a certain reference price limit by other compounds. Physicians still have the possibility to avoid this by explicitly indicating on the prescription that they do not want the pharmacists to substitute the drugs. The effect of the aut-idem regulation was not strong and therefore cancelled at the end of 2003, but it should be kept in mind while interpreting the data (Schreyögg and Busse (2004)).

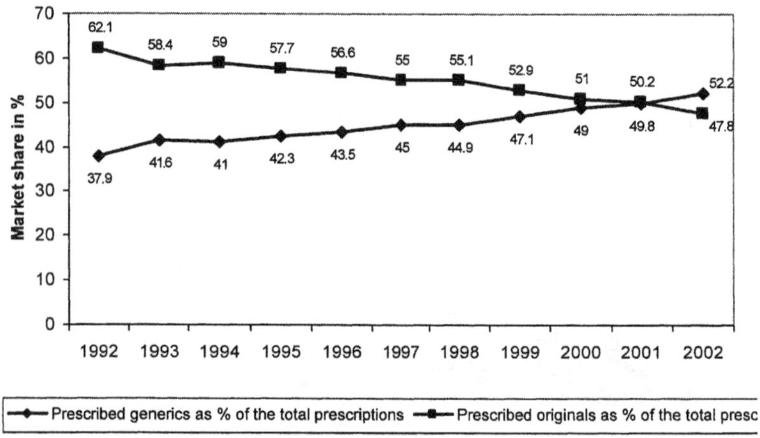

Source: Research Institute of general regional sickness funds (WIdO)

Figure 6: Market share of generic versus original prescriptions in the German Statutory Health Insurance scheme

4. Evaluation of Price Regulations

4.1. Evaluation of Supply-Side Types

4.1.1. Reference Price Limits on Reimbursement

Following the simple two country model of Königbauer (2004) explaining the effects of parallel imports a static two class product model will be introduced in order to analyze reference pricing.[12] Using a sequential price-setting process it can be shown that, applying marginal cost pricing for drugs clustered within Phase 1, welfare can be increased.

Researching pharmaceutical companies produce patent protected drugs *i* in the home country *H*. Beside researching companies generic drug producing companies exist. The researching companies are confronted with large sunk R&D costs *RD* and marginal costs *c*. The generic drug producing companies manufacture generic drugs *j* and are only confronted with the average costs of production which are assumed to correspond to the marginal costs *c*. The drugs *i* and *j* can be freely traded with a corresponding market approval. Demand for patent protected drugs in unregulated markets is $q_i(p_i)$, $i = 1, ..., n$ Demand of generic drugs in unregulated markets is $q_j(p_j)$, $j = 1, ..., m$. Demand of patent protected and generic drugs in markets with reference price limits depends on current reference prices of a certain cluster. The structure of the model is as follows.

In the first stage, the firm decides whether or not to be in the market regulated by reference price limits of reimbursement. The decision depends on the resulting profits. The resulting profits have to be at least as high as the launching costs of the drug. If expected profit is too low the firm will not be in the market. The researching pharmaceutical company will set a price above or equal to the reference price, therefore the patent rights expired drug price is as follows $p_i = p_{rp}$.[13]

In the second stage, the government sets a reference price p_{rp} which determines the maximum reimburseable price.[14] The optimal reference price p^*_{rp} maximizing welfare in home country *H* where welfare is composed of consumer surplus:

$$S_H(p_{rp}) = \int_{p_{rp}}^{q^{-1}} q_{rp}(p)dp,$$

the researching pharmaceutical firm's profit in the unregulated market is $p_i(p_i) = (p_i - c)q_i(p_i)$, and the generic producing pharmaceutical firm's profit in the unregulated market is

$p_j(p_j) = (p_j - c)q_j(p_j)$:

$$max\ S_H(p_{rp}) + p_i(p_i) + p_j(p_j) \qquad (1)$$

In the third stage, the generic producing pharmaceutical firm sets a price below or equal to the reference price, therefore the generic drug price is as follows $p_j = p_{rp}$.[15] It can be assumed that

---

[12] In this static consideration the sunk R&D costs have no effect for the optimal price regulation.

[13] Caves, Whinston, and Hurwitz (1991) analyzed price effects that followed patent expiration and subsequent entry of generic drugs from 1976 to 1987. They found that brand-name drug prices decreased by 4.5% following the entry of generic drugs into previously uncontested markets. But these effects were not significantly different from zero.

[14] In Phase 1 government will set the reference price equal to the marginal costs c because Phase 1 contains cluster with generically equivalent drugs, where the patent rights have been expired.

the researching pharmaceutical firm and the generic drug producing firm will set prices as near as possible or equal to the current reference price. The researching pharmaceutical firm will also lower its prices for the patent rights expired drug in order not to loose market shares but will still set the price above the reference price hoping that a certain reputation and brand loyalty will secure a consumer commitment to pay the corresponding co-payment.[16] It can be shown that if in home country the prices will be set approximately equal to marginal cost the reference price will correspond to the marginal costs.[17]

$$\frac{d[S_H(p_{rp}) + \pi_i(p_{rp}) + \pi_i(p_{rp})]}{dp_{rp}} = -q_{rp}(p_{rp}) + q_{rp}(p_{rp}) + (p_{rp} - c)q'_{rp}(p_{rp}) = 0$$

$$\Rightarrow p^*_{rp} = c$$

Due to resulting reference price the generic drug producer will also set the prices equal to the reference price and generic drug price is as follows, $p_j = c = p_{rp}$.

By setting the reference price equal to the marginal costs welfare can be increased without free riding on the sunk R&D cost of the researching firm because the patent protection has expired. As generic drugs tend to enter into the market at whole sale price of 40 to 70 percent of those prevailing before the patent protection expired, the question can be asked, why generic drug competition is not stronger, considering that generic drug producers have no R&D costs.

Figure 7 shows the price development of drugs which are clustered within the reference pricing. Drugs are clustered accordingly to the two step procedure of reference price limits in Phase 1 and Phase 2. With the introduction of the Statutory Health Insurance Modernization Law ('GKV Modernisierungsgesetz (GMG)') in January 2004 a modified drug prescribing enactment has been established. This usually causes a reduction of prescribing higher priced drugs and an increase of drugs which are fully reimbursed within the reference price limits. The change of the indices between the actual period and prior periods are not comparable if new reference priced drugs have been introduced into the market. In the sub-markets the actual market share has been considered, this means the change of the indices is based on current market conditions.

---

[15] The assumptions that generic drug producer price is equal or below and researching pharmaceutical firms price is equal or above the reference price are reasonable. Caves, Whinston, and Hurwitz (1991) state that generic drugs tend to enter into the market at whole sale prices 40 to 70 percent of those prevailing before the original drug's patent expired.

[16] The accepted price difference between the reference price and the price of the out of patent drug that will be paid depends on the price elasticity of demand.

[17] This procedure causes no free rider problem because reference pricing in Phase 1 includes only drugs where the patent rights have been expired.

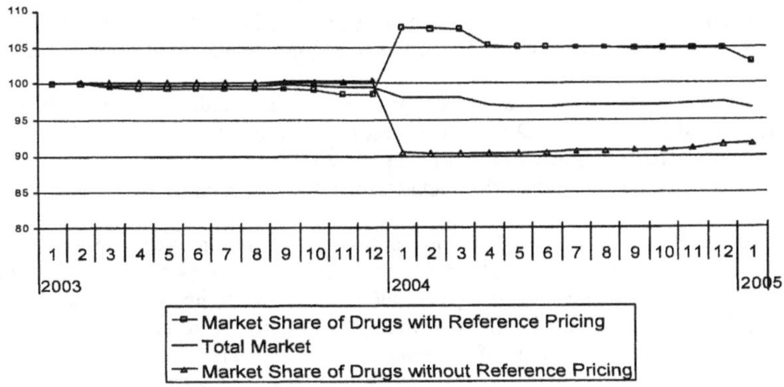

Source: Nink (2005), p.10

Figure 7: Price Indices According to Different Market Segments (January 2003 to January 2005)

The main advantage of reference price limits on reimbursement lies in the enhanced competition between products within a certain cluster. A disadvantage is that the competition below the reference price is reduced or rather completely eliminated. In unrestricted industries, manufacturers have to all intents and purposes an incentive to reduce prices if demand is elastic so that a price reduction creates an equivalent increase in volume. But in the German pharmaceutical market the demand is still rather inelastic at prices below the reference price. However, demand is elastic at prices above the reference prices but only between the ranges of the corresponding co-payments.

Prior experiences in Germany and other countries with reference price limits on reimbursement showed that patients have high price elasticity for pharmaceuticals with co-payments and are therefore strongly interested to avoid co-payments. Thus, reference pricing as a demand side regulation is efficient and introduces an effective measure to influence the volume of demand for pharmaceuticals. As consequence pharmaceutical producers have to adapt their pricing to reference limits if their products are clustered in order to prevent a loss of market share (IMS Health (2004)). An essential feature is that the results are different according to the particular assumptions made regarding the availability of information to the potential buyer and their response to it (Lu and Comanor (1998)). Lu and Comanor (1998) found pharmaceutical pricing behavior is a mixture of skimming and penetration strategies[18]: if pharmaceutical firms are launching a significant innovation they will use the skimming strategy and if me-too products are introduced the penetration strategy will be used. Obviously, with the introduction of a reference price limit on reimbursement the use of penetration strategies will be discouraged. In large, the me-too producer would probably loose the most. Arguing that imitative products induce pharmaceutical price competition after the

[18] Skimming is a strategy of setting a high initial price and then lowering over time; penetration is a strategy of launching a new product at a low price and then raising it over time.

patent protection or during the patent duration if clustered in Phase 3, one could suggest that without the entry of close substitutes the launching price of innovative drugs will be higher and will have a slower decreasing rate because of a lacking comparability (Lu and Comanor (1998)).

Lu and Comanor (1998) found additionally that drugs contributing important therapeutic gains were introduced at prices 3.2 times the level of substitute drugs in equivalent dosages. Drugs which achieved only modest gains were priced at 2.17 times the average for substitutes; those making little or no gain were priced approximately at the same level as substitute drugs that exist before.

Around two-thirds of all prescriptions are drugs out of the reference price limits on reimbursement clusters and which are therefore indirectly regulated (see Figure 4). The share of these drugs has not changed much since 2000, while the turnover of these drugs has dropped significantly from ca. 60% in 2000 to 35.4% in 2003. A necessary consequence of these adjustments is the reduction of turnovers, which indicates that the saving effect is mainly financed by the producers. According to VFA (2004)[19] the health insurance companies saved around 2.4 Mill. Euros in 2004.

The results for the German experiences are exactly monitored by the companies because if they are successful in the largest European Market this kind of price regulation could be adapted in other European countries as well.

4.1.2. Patents and Parallel Imports

Economic theory considers patent protection as a second best solution to pay for R&D. The first best solution is the marginal cost pricing. With the large fixed cost of R&D the first best solution is not feasible. Marginal cost pricing provides no adequate returns to maintain a certain innovation level unless government subsidizes R&D. Therefore, patents deliver the patentees an opportunity for pricing above marginal costs and are the best attempt to finance R&D.

Given monopoly pricing then differential pricing according to the Ramsey principle, postulating prices are inversely related to demand elasticities, is consistent with the criterion of economic efficiency and general norms of equity. From this point of view price differences are not optimal if parallel imports and external reference pricing occur. A solution here could be a managed care approach where payers, normally social insurance funds or government, use their monopsony power and negotiate contracts with pharmaceutical companies that include confidential rebates and allowances. The point is that differential pricing alone can not tackle the problem of generating incentives for R&D to develop new innovative drugs and should therefore be not emphasized one sided.

But the determination of the best patent duration is still unclear. If governments try to take into account the cost to identify prices for pharmaceuticals the conclusions will be distorted in different directions. First, the complete costs of an R&D project comprise investments made over 10-15 years ago and the opportunity costs of the fixed capital. Second, the complete costs of discovering and developing a new drug also include the foregone failures or `dry holes' (DiMasi, Hansen, and Grabowski (2003)). Third, the share of global joint cost is hard to measure. Fourth, pharmaceutical companies have no real incentives to reveal their effective costs. Rather they have in fact a reason to overestimate their R&D cost in order to have a more advantageous standpoint via government or social insurance funds while negotiating for

[19] VFA is the German Association of Research-Based Pharmaceutical Companies.

prices of new pharmaceutical compounds. The question in dispute is whether the rate of returns in the pharmaceutical market is adequate or suboptimal, but this question can not be answered immediately because of incomplete and biased information.

Parallel trade has been argued to be consistent with principles of free trade and to lead to specific effects for patients, welfare, and the parties thereto. Firstly, as a cross-country effect the parallel trades generates in the long run uniform prices and the arbitrage will result in more efficient market operations. Secondly, a general destination country effect combined with an aggregate welfare effect will be an increased price competition that lowers the prices for pharmaceuticals which is again advantageous for patients and payers. Thirdly, patients will benefit of access to innovative new and low-priced pharmaceuticals. Fourthly, parallel imports are assumed to have only marginal effects on the pharmaceutical industry but would enhance the potential to innovate and hence improve the efficiency of this sector (Kanavos, Costa-i Font, Merkur, and Gemmill (2003)). Indeed in the short run there may be savings from lower foreign prices for patients and payers, but still the potential impact on the industry are losses of business in destination countries from the conduct of parallel trade, and decreases of producer profitability without essentially increasing social welfare. Additionally, deadweight welfare losses are possible. The authors point to the conclusion of rather low savings to health insurance institutions through direct (price) and intra- or inter-country competitive effects. Some benefits to pharmacies and marginal benefits to patients occur but parallel trade is most advantageous to parallel traders.[20]

Arguing that parallel trade is consistent with the principles of free trade then it must be noted that the fundamental condition for an efficiency gain from trade is not given, i.e. a lower foreign price does not mirror a lower social cost of production. One possible reaction of manufactures to parallel imports may be to try to set rather high uniform prices for new pharmaceuticals in all countries of the European Union. This strategy will probably fail because of different national regulations.

4.2. Evaluation of Demand-Side Types

4.2.1. Drug Budget Regulation for Physicians

The aim of prescription budgets is to encourage physicians to consider cost when selecting treatments, while allowing them prescribing expensive treatments in individual cases. Examining the data of German health care market the use of drug budgets seems to be an appropriate and effective measure to induce a reflected prescribing behavior.

Figure 8 shows longitudinal data of prescriptions on account of sickness funds in Germany. The data is provided by the WIdO and portrays the development of total number of prescriptions to the number of prescribed drugs with undisputed effectiveness.

The longitudinal data disclose the change in the development of the number of prescriptions after the introduction of physicians' drug budgets in 1993. The range between the total number of prescribed and the number of drugs with undisputed effectiveness has become obvious and this reduction becomes particularly clear after the introduction of drug budgets in 1993. This is due to the increase of prescribed drugs with undisputed effectiveness, whereas the level of the total number of prescribed drugs remains more or less on the same level.

[20] See Figure 5: Savings by Reimportation in different European Countries (2002) for detailed information.

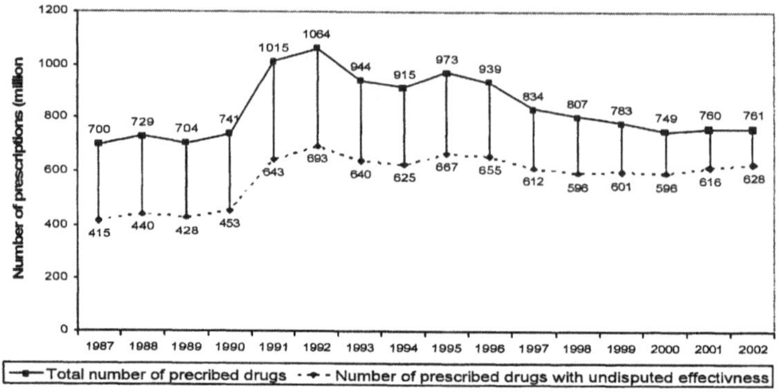

Source: Research Institute of general regional sickness funds (WIdO)

Figure 8: Development of prescriptions in the German Statutory Health Insurance Scheme

Figure 9 demonstrates that the change in the prescribing habit of physicians leads to a totally different expenditure pattern of the German Statutory Health Insurance scheme. Since 1992 the expenditures for prescribed drugs with disputed effectiveness has dropped by 62% and the prescription of drugs with undisputed effectiveness has risen by 69%.

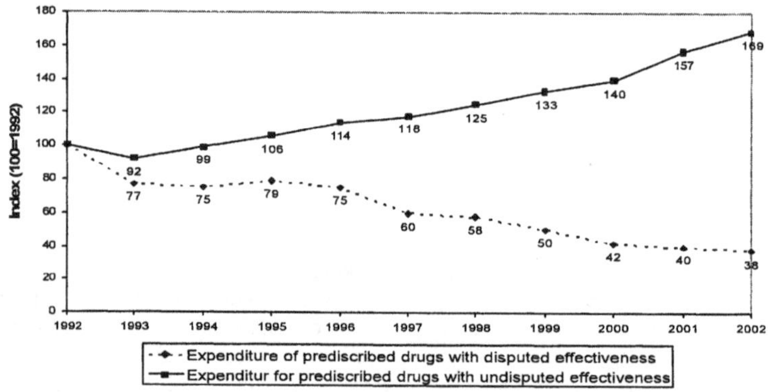

Source: Research Institute of general regional sickness funds (WIdO)

Figure 9: Development of prescriptions in the German Statutory Health Insurance scheme

Considering the development of these time series it is obvious that the physicians have significantly changed their prescribing habits towards more effective prescriptions. But since the total drug costs of the Statutory Health Insurance in Germany raised it can be assumed that the savings are probably used to replace old drug therapies by innovative and more expensive ones.[21] According to Schreyögg and Busse (2004) referrals to specialists particularly for treatments of chronically ill patients increased and also caused raising total drug costs years after the introduction of drug budgets. Given the prescribing restriction of physicians by the introduction of drug budgets the behavior of referral to specialists appears rational.

4.2.2. Generic Drugs

Danzon and Furukawa (2003) found that countries with strict price regulation have lower generic penetration than less regulated markets. The underlying idea is that regulation tends to reduce competition. Accordingly, in this analysis total generic share of unit volume is lower in the relatively high price-regulated markets of France (28 percent), Italy (34 percent), and Japan (40 percent), and higher in countries with less restrictive pricing policy as in the United Kingdom (49 percent), the USA (58 percent), and Germany (61 percent). The high generic share in Canada despite of high price controls is due to other regulative controls which enhance the use of generics.

In the United States the generic sector is dominated by unbranded compounds, but the total generic share of 58 percent of unit volume is confronted with only 18 percent of sales indicating relative low generic prices. In Germany the total share of 61 percent of units is confronted with 34 percent of sales, showing relatively higher generic prices. But the relative higher prices of generics in Germany are due to the reference price limits on reimbursement (Danzon and Furukawa (2003)).

The expected new form of competition after the expiration of patents varies widely from country to country caused by legal obstacles, incomplete information, reimbursement regulations hence the price elasticity of patients, pharmacy dispensing margins and different preferences of the prescribing physicians for the original brand versus generic drugs. As the case may be, the lower the price of generic drugs the higher the health care cost savings will be. Considering these many influencing factors the incentives to subsidy original brand drugs by generic drugs have to be well-thought out. Reference pricing as applied in Germany is expected to increase the prescription of generic drugs because reference prices are usually based on rather low priced products in each class without regarding the actual patent situation. Alternatively, if the pharmacy dispensing margins are more favorably and the drug budgets for physician are fixed, the probability of generic prescription will also increase. In general, complete unregulated pricing is not given but rather a range of price regulations are applied and therefore the different interactions have to be taken into account with regard to the desired outcome.

5. Implications and Conclusions

In the past most regulative measures to contain health care expenditures have been targeted primarily to supply-side measures; however this is changing into a more sophisticated regulative construct. But, supply-side regulation on its own does little to control the rising

[21] To make more reliable statements it would be necessary to analyze the structure of the different prescribed therapies regarding their innovative level and to their respective costs.

expenditures. Without simultaneous use of demand-side incentives and volume controls, pharmaceutical expenditures probably can not be reduced effectively.

What makes the German pharmaceutical price regulation effective is the combination of demand side regulation with physicians' drug budgets, proportional co-payments with upper and lower caps, and the usage of reference price limits on reimbursement. Opponents of current national pharmaceutical price regulation argue that one principle problem occurring in systems of controlling health care expenditures is that much of the pharmaceutical expenditures are spend regardless of the quality of the medicine or treatment reduction.

The standard argument that the R&D location is in the country where the highest profits can be made is not correct. It can be observed that national firms do not research in the country with the highest turnovers, rather they research where the research circumstances, in terms of innovative regional clusters, are the best. Proponents of standard international trade theory often support parallel trading as a way for enhancing competition and in consequence reducing drug prices. But usually standard trade theory is led by the assumption that prices reflect efficiency in production or high or rather low input prices. Considering the drug prices, the situation appears more difficult. Low drug prices in several countries reflect severe governmental price regulations (Danzon (1997b)).

As a matter of principle, national governments have to decide what socio-political goals to follow. Designing different scenarios the point of departure could be intergenerational fairness, meaning that the present generation leaves its successors sufficient wealth so that persons deciding behind a veil of ignorance would be indifferent as to whether they want to be born today or tomorrow.

References

BGA (2004), Glossar: Festbeträge, Glossar, Gemeinsamer Bundesausschuss, Siegburg, http://www.g-ba.de/cms/front_content.php?idcat=32(14.11.2004)

Caves, R. E., Whinston, M. D. and Hurwitz, M. A. (1991), Patent Expiration, Entry, and Competition in the U.S. Pharmaceutical Industry, in: *Brooking Papers on Economic Activity. Microeconomics*, 1-66.

Danzon, Patricia, M. (1997a), *Pharmaceutical Price Regulation: National Policies and Global Interests*. The AEI Press, Washington, D.C.

Danzon, P. M. (1997b), Price Discrimination for Pharmaceuticals: Welfare Effects in the US and the EU, in: *International Journal of the Economics of Business*, 4(3), 301-321.

Danzon, P. M. and Furukawa, M. F. (2003), Prices and Availability of Pharmaceuticals: Evidence from Nine Countries, in: *Health Affairs*, Web Exclusive - 29 October 2003, 521-536.

Danzon, P. M., and Ketcham, J. D. (2003), Reference Pricing of Pharmaceuticals for Medicare: Evidence from Germany, the Netherlands and New Zealand, *Working paper*, NBER, Cambridge, http://www.nber.org/papers/w10007.

DiMasi, J., R. W. Hansen, and H. G. Grabowski (2003), The price of innovation: new estimates of drug development costs, in: *Journal of Health Economics*, 22, 151-185.

European Commission (2003a), Commission Communication on Parallel Imports of Proprietary Medicinal Products for which Marketing Authorisations have already been granted, *Communication from the Commission of the European Communities*, COM/2003/0839 final, 1-17.

European Commission (2003b), "Parallel Trade", Glossary, European Commission, Brussel, http://europa.eu.int/comm/competition/general_info/p_en.html.

Frank, R. G. (2003), Editorial: New estimates of drug development costs, in: *Journal of Health Economics*, 22, 325-330.

Freytag, C. (2001), *Parallelimporte nach EG- und WTO-Recht: Patente und Marken versus Handelsfreiheit*. Duncker und Humbolt, Berlin.

Goate, P., Rhys, J. and Gerner, F. (1999), *The Economic Consequences of the Choice of Regime of Exhaustion in the Area of Trademarks*, Final report, Executive Summary of the Final Report for DG XV of the European Commission, London. http://europa.eu.int/comm/dg15/intprop/tmstudy.htm.

IMS Health (2004): *Pricing and Reimbursement: Review 2003*. Cambridge Pharma Consultancy, Cambridge.

Kanavos, P., Costa-i Font, J., Merkur, S. and Gemmill, M. (2003), The Economic Impact of Pharmaceutical Parallel Trade: A Stakeholder Analysis. Key Study Findings, *Working paper*, The London School of Economics and Political Science, London, http://www.lse.ac.uk/collections/pressAndInformationOffice/newsAndEvents.

Königbauer, I. (2004), The effect of parallel imports on the pharmaceutical price regulation, *Working paper*, University of Munich, Munich.

Krämer, W. (1996), Hippokrates und Sisyphus - die moderne Medizin als Opfer ihres eigenen Erfolges, in: *Rationierung im Gesundheitswesen*, Kirch, H. and Kliemt, W. (eds.), 389-393. Roderer Verlag.

Lu, Z. J. and Comanor, W. S. (1998), Strategic pricing of new pharmaceuticals, in: *The Review of Economics and Statistics*, 8(1), 108-118.

Mrazek, M. F. (2002), Comparative Approaches to Pharmaceutical Price Regulation in the European Union, in: *Croatian Medical Journal*, 43(4), 453-461.

Nink, K. (2005), *Price Development in the Pharmaceutical Market until 2005 – German Index*. Research Institute of general regional sickness funds (WIdO), Bonn.

Scherer, F. M. (2000), The Pharmaceutical Industry, in: *Handbook of Health Economics*, Culyer, A. and Newhous, J. (eds.), 1297-1336, Elsevier.

Schreyögg, J. and Busse, R. (2004), Physician Drug Budget in Germany: Effects on Prescription Behaviour, *Discussion paper*, Department of Health Care Management, Faculty of Economics and Management, Berlin.
http://www.dh.gov.uk/PublicationsAndStatistics/PressReleases/PressReleasesNotices/fs/en?CONTENT_ID=4093244&chk=3b4R7Y.

Smith, S. R. (2002), Multinational economic evaluations of pharmaceuticals, in: *The Lancet*, 360, 816.

VFA (2004), *The Pharmaceutical Industry in Germany*. Verband Forschender Arzneimittelhersteller e.V., Berlin.

TEACHERS' SALARIES IN ARGENTINA AND OTHER LATIN AMERICAN COUNTRIES*

Mariana De Santis, Héctor R. Gertel and Verónica Herrero

IEF – Facultad de Ciencias Económicas,
Universidad Nacional de Córdoba
hgertel@eco.unc.edu.ar

1. Introduction

The low level of teachers' salaries relative to other professional workers ignited in the nineties an intense debate in Argentina as well as in other Latin American countries that stimulated new research work on how personal characteristics and remunerations of teachers are connected. The debate took place in the context of a wave of reforms aimed at improving the quality of education in which, the role of the teacher, was considered to be central in advancing the reforms. Yet, it was not clearly stated the level of teachers' salaries and other incentives that would be necessary to introduce in order to meet the challenge.

The purpose of this paper is to apply a comparative perspective to comment new results on the salary of the teachers and other workers, in eight Latin American countries, where educational reforms have been introduced in the last few years. The comparative perspective will give emphasis to the analysis of the returns to education once personal characteristics of teachers and comparative workers are controlled. In fact, teacher's organizations have been claiming, for a long time, that the remuneration of their associates was lagging behind the wages of other workers that embodied a similar amount of human capital. Were the claim confirmed by statistical analysis, and were markets adjusting smoothly, it follows that the teaching profession could be loosing every year a bigger portion of the cream of the class, seduced by better salaries and more attractive work compensation packages offered to professional workers elsewhere. If confirmed, these are clearly worrying news for those interested in rising the quality in teaching in Latin America. The paper concludes that the teachers′ organizations claims may be, at least in certain cases, right, but for the wrong reasons. Thus, in guiding educational reform implementation, it is suggested, a more careful analysis of the relative salary of the teachers and its determinants should be performed by each of the countries′ educational authority.

Comparative analysis of teachers' salaries in Latin America have now been facilitated by the existence of a number of contemporary research, which make use of similar sources of data (household surveys) where Mincer's equations to link remunerations to workers' characteristics are estimated following similar procedures.

This paper is organized in six sections: the following section comments the results on Mincer equations of teachers' salaries that recent research have reported for Argentina, Bolivia,

* To be read at the IV International Arnoldshain Seminar, Córdoba, march 2005. The research was partially financed through the National University of Córdoba-Secyt Research Grant N° 107/04

Brazil, Chile, Mexico, Paraguay, Peru and Uruguay. Next, the structure of educational systems, which helps in assessing differences across countries in the level and modality of the institutions where students are trained for the teaching profession, is briefly presented. Section IV introduced the comparative analysis of results on salaries and returns to education and other characteristics of teachers relative to comparative workers. The comparative analysis of the income equations is done in Section V. Finally, the last section summarizes the most important findings in the paper.

2. Recent Studies about Teachers' Salaries in Latin America

Within the set of studies on teachers' remunerations performed in Latin America countries (LAC) during the nineties, there are two main groups: first, those analyzing mainly the empirical relation between income, stock of human capital and its return for teachers and for other comparable counterparts and, second, those works where the estimated income differential is additionally broken down into two parts, one explaining the proportion of the difference in income between teachers and comparable professions due to characteristics of individuals (level of schooling, age, experience, and similar) and the other, attributed to market discrimination. Comparable data is only available for the first type of studies based on the application of Mincer's equations.

In a seminal paper, Psacharopoulos, Valenzuela and Arends (1996) reported data for 1989 and 1979 on teachers´ participation on total labor force, average years of schooling and hours worked per week for teachers in 11 Latin American countries (Argentina, Bolivia, Brazil, Colombia, Costa Rica, Chile, Ecuador, Honduras, Panama, Peru, Uruguay and Venezuela). The work also presented the mean earning ratios of teachers and comparable counterparts (non-agricultural workers), and concluded that, in most of these countries, between 1979 and 1989 the relative salary of teachers decreased. The work is not clear about the definition introduced for "teacher", and "salary" is meant to be "average salary", calculated from the aggregate, as the mass of remuneration divided by the total number of teachers, in each country in the sample. Disaggregated data was only presented for Chile, where an OLS Mincerian income equation was then estimated. In this exercise, a dummy variable was introduced to distinguish the teachers from the other workers in the sample and the coefficient to this variable indicated that, the teachers obtained a higher return relative to the average worker in the economy. Corrections for selectivity bias were not included.

In Liang (1999), descriptive data of the characteristics and income of teachers and their comparable counterparts (matching the stock of human capital) was reported for 12 Latin American countries (Bolivia, Brazil, Chile, Colombia, Costa Rica, Ecuador, El Salvador, Panama, Paraguay, Uruguay and Venezuela). The study additionally provided some estimates of the returns to education by applying independent multivariate regression equations of the natural logarithm of the hourly-wage for the two groups, teachers and non-teachers. Corrections for selectivity bias were not included. Control variables included workers' characteristics and hours worked per week and the results suggested that teachers were not underpaid, except in Brazil. Additionally, a specific correction is introduced to take into account that teachers have a more extended vacations' period than comparable workers, and the difference in average salaries increased in favor of the teachers. It should be noticed, however, that the "comparable group of workers" was empirically chosen in each country, constrained by data availability, limiting the value of Liang's conclusions that were based on the comparability of relative wages of teachers in the selected sample of countries.

Vegas (1999) studied teachers' salaries in one country, Brazil, but produced comparable estimates for three regions (Northeast, Center-North and South). OLS estimates of a multivariate hourly wage equation for wage earners was applied to data on individuals who declared to be working more than 20 hours per week in the household survey developed in 1997, the teaching condition is identified by means of a dichotomic variable; also, the differential effect of gender over income is captured through a dichotomic variable. Liang's finding about Brazilian teachers being underpaid was only confirmed for the Northeast and Center-North regions while in the South, the opposite result holds: Vegas, linked this new result to the fact that being a teacher in the South implied higher levels of human capital than in the rest of the country and this explained the higher returns found for the teachers in the South relative to the rest of the country. Returns to "being a teacher" in the South reflected in this specific region a labor market behavior now closer to those reported for other Latin American countries. The work is supplemented with an analysis of the likelihood of participating in the labor market, in each of the regions. Yet this analysis is carried on with independence of the previously commented Mincer's equations.

For Argentina, Vegas, Pritchett and Experton (1999), collected data from the household surveys of 28 Metropolitan areas in October 1997 to analyze the income of teachers relative to that of a comparable group of workers. OLS estimates of a multivariate hourly wage equation for wage earners was applied to data on individuals who declared to be working in the household survey, the teaching condition is identified by means of a dichotomic variable; also, the differential effect of gender over income is captured through a dichotomic variable. Other variables considered were schooling level attained, being a teacher, female teacher condition, and continuous variables indicating years of experience and weekly hours worked. The work concluded that the relative income of teachers appears to be inversely correlated with city size: it appears to be higher than that of a comparable group of workers in some Metropolitan areas (those of a smaller size) while lower in the bigger ones; and that men earn more than women in all occupations and in all the cities. The value of the contribution of experience to remuneration is, as anticipated in the literature, in all cases, increasing at a decreasing rate until the age of 60, approximately.

Briefly, Saavedra Chanduví (2000) analyzes the labor situation of teachers in relation to other professionals in Peru estimating with OLS a multivariate hourly wage equation, which includes a dummy variable to capture the effect of being a teacher, and another to capture the effect of gender. The rates of return obtained for teachers are 7% higher than those of comparable counterparts, while this advantage exceeds 25% if teacher's work is adjusted to 38 working weeks per year. López Acevedo (2002) in a work on teachers' incentives and school professional development in Mexico divides the total number of wage earners of the sample in four groups, namely: teachers in public schools, teachers in private schools, government workers, and private workers. For each group, the determinants of hourly wage were studied through the estimation of an OLS equation. The work suggests that returns to schooling for public Mexican teachers are of 5.8%, and for government and private workers of 13% and 17%, respectively. Each year of experience would contribute to public teachers with a constant increase of about 3% per year. For the other workers, she observes that the effect of experience on income grows at a decreasing rate.

The second subset of studies includes those research works where the income differential between the two groups (teachers and non-teachers) is decomposed into two or more independent effects, which help in identifying the relative contribution of each of them to explain the log-difference in income. The simplest way of doing this is the one proposed by Blinder and Oaxaca in the early seventies, in which the log-difference in income between two groups of wage earners is separated into endowments and discrimination effects. Piras and Savedoff (1998), working with Bolivian data, estimated through OLS, a Mincerian equation of the total sample of wage earners, where the "teacher" and "non-teacher" groups were independently identified, and where "non-teachers" is a summary concept meaning the rest of the urban workers in the job market. The average rate of return to schooling was of 8% and 10% respectively, for the teachers and for the non-teachers workers. On the basis of these equations, log-difference in income, between teachers and non-teachers, was computed, and then the Oaxaca-Blinder decomposition method applied. The study reported that, in explaining the sources of the wage differential in Bolivia, the relative weight of discrimination, in favor of the teachers was found to be lower than that of endowments, meaning that the average teacher embodied a higher amount of human capital relative to the average worker in the economy. Mizala and Romaguera (2000), in their study of Chile, applied Mincer equations and Oaxaca decomposition procedures to analyze data on salaries and workers′ characteristics for teachers and non-teachers from the CASEN 1998 survey. Corrections for selectivity bias were not included in the estimation of the Mincer equation. The work concluded that the average return to schooling was for the teachers (that possessed 15 years of schooling, on average) of 2.5% per year, or about one quarter of the returns to education exhibited by the comparison group, with 9.6 years of schooling, on average. Then, a simple Oaxaca-Blinder decomposition into endowments and discrimination effects was applied. Similar to Bolivia, the average hourly wage of a teacher was higher than that of a non-teacher (i.e. a summary concept meaning the rest of the urban workers in the job market); and, the endowment effect was stronger than the discrimination effect in explaining remunerations' differences. Herrero, De Santis and Gertel (2003), presented results from estimation of a multivariate regression function of the hourly wage of teachers and non-teachers in Argentina, using data from the 1998 household survey. The work try to solve some of the puzzled associated with the definition of a "comparable group" which were discussed before by introducing three alternative standards of comparison: first, a comparative analysis between the "teacher" and non-teacher" group meaning "all the rest of the workers" as in the work of Bolivia and Chile already discussed is provided to facilitate international comparability of results. Additionally, two other control groups are introduced, as follows: a group of individuals having at least some tertiary level of studies completed, that would exhibit, on average, a similar number of years of schooling (about 15 years) relative to that required for a teacher diploma, and, finally, a more selected group composed only by those workers holding a university degree (about 17 years of study) against whom the teachers prefer to be compared, at least in Argentina. The conclusion is that teachers earned more per hour than the general average in the economy, there was still a small prize in their favor in relation to other graduates with higher education, but their hourly wage was lower that of other workers with a university degree. The average salary of a teacher resulted to be higher than that of the average worker, similar to that of other workers with 15 years of schooling, but lower that those of a worker holding a university degree. The exercise included the calculation of the classical Oaxaca-Blinder decomposition in the three cases, obtaining different results in each comparison. The difference in endowments explained only 40 per cent of the advantage the teachers had in relation to the mean remuneration of individuals employed (the rest would be attributable to the higher relative returns teachers obtained in the market), thus, the beneficial effect for teachers of having more education than the average worker appears to be, in Argentina, lower than in the cases of Chile and Bolivia already commented. Let's turn now to the newly introduced groups of comparison: if the control group included all of the workers with an average of 15 years of schooling, income differences were almost non-existent; instead, the endowments of the control group became the determinant factor in explaining the income gap (now against the teachers!) when this group is compared to workers holding a university degree.

To sum up, the issue of teacher's pay in Latin America has been analyzed in several recent works. All of them have in common the use of data coming from regularly collected urban household surveys. Only Brazil and Peru included rural populations in the regular surveys and the Vegas and the Saavedra Chanduví works included analysis of the rural teacher. In all cases OLS regression analysis of a Mincerian multivariate equation were reported. The returns to schooling for teachers were lower than those of an average worker in other markets. A limited number of works measured the impact of market discrimination and endowments in accounting for income differentials between teachers and non-teachers. In general, it was the lack of endowments, not market discrimination that best explained the poor performance of teachers in Latin America.

3. The Structure of the Education Systems: Locating Teacher Training Institutions in Latin America

Most of LAC introduced deep reforms in theirs educational systems during the nineties. These reforms focused on system organization, administrative and budget decentralization and provisions to extend compulsory education up to age 15.

In Argentina, reforms were implemented through several steps: in 1992, the Federal Government transferred primary and secondary schools to the provincial level. Starting in 1993, the provinces began a process that extended compulsory education from age 12 to age 15.

Today, the education system in Argentina is divided as follows[93]:

- **Preschool**: this first level is compulsory for children at age 5, and it is optional for children from 3 to 4 years old.
- **Basic General Education (EGB)**, divided into three cycles of 3 years each, compulsory for children aged 6 to 14;
- **Multimodal Education**, EGB diploma required, duration of 3 years, it includes 5 options: Natural Sciences, Economy and Management of Institutions; Humanities and Social Sciences, Production of Goods and Services; and Communications, Arts and Design. A diploma of secondary school termination is issued.

[93] The Federal Law of Education (N° 24.195) introduced transformations of the academic organization of levels and cycles.

- **Post Secondary Education:** includes both, the non-university sector (where teaching and technical formation constitute two differentiated modalities) and the university sector. Universities remained under the National Administration while the non-university sector is in the jurisdiction of the Provinces.

The structure of educational systems is in Argentina, Paraguay and Uruguay quite similar (K-9-3). On the other hand, Chile, Brazil and Bolivia exhibit in common that the preschool level is non-compulsory, a general basic education whose duration is of 8 years and an upper secondary education of 4 years (8-4). Peru followed a 6+5 structure while Mexico established a 9+4 and a 9+2 structure where students may be able to choose.

All countries reviewed have established as compulsory the general basic education up to age 15. Some of them include in this category the preschool at age of 5.

The following table synthesizes some relevant aspects concerned with the structure that the educational systems acquired after the reforms of the nineties and the place of teaching training.

Table I: The Place of Teachers Training after the Reforms in Several Latin America Countries

Country	Preschool	General Basic Education	Upper Secondary Education	Higher Education	Laws of Educational Reforms	The Place of Teaching Training
Argentina	For children between 3 to 5 years. Compulsory at age of 5.	Duration: 9 years. For children about 6 to 14 years old. Compulsory.	Duration: 3 years. Non-compulsory. Required for superior studies.	Non-university sectors (teaching training colleges and Technical schools). University sectors (Teacher training among several topics – Arts, Humanities, Chemist, and others) and Academic Schools.	1992. Decentralization of Primary, Secondary and Superior non-university level. 1993. Federal Educational Law. 1995. Superior Educational Law.	Preschool and GBE teachers are trained in Non-University Training Institutes. Teachers for Upper Secondary are trained both in the Non-University sector and in the University.
Bolivia	For children between 0 to 5 years. Non-compulsory.	Duration: 8 years. Compulsory.	Duration: 4 years. Non-compulsory. Required for superior studies.	Non- university (Teaching training institutes and Technical Education) and University sectors	1994. Educational Reform.	Training is concentrated in non-university institutes.
Brazil	For children between 0 to 5 years. Non-compulsory.	Duration: 8 years. Compulsory.	Duration: 3 years. Non-compulsory. Required for superior studies.	Non- university (Teaching training institutes and Technical Education) and University sectors	1988. Federal Constitution. 1996. Amendment of Constitution. 1996. New Law of	Minimum qualifications demanded by law: secondary teaching diploma for fist grades of primary education, and

Country	Preschool	General Basic Education	Upper Secondary Education	Higher Education	Laws of Educational Reforms	The Place of Teaching Training
					Guidelines and Basis of National Education.	tertiary degree for higher grades.
Chile	For children between 0 to 5 years. Non-compulsory.	Duration: 8 years. Compulsory.	Duration: 4 years. Non-compulsory. Required for superior studies.	Non- university (Professional institutes, Technical and Professional Programs) and University sectors	1990. Starting some programs related to Educational Reform.	University training with diploma in Pedagogy since 1973.
Mexico	For children between 4 to 5 years. Non-compulsory.	Duration: 9 years. Compulsory.	Duration: 2 to 4 years. Non-compulsory. Required for superior studies.	Non- university (Teaching training institutes and Technological Education) and University sectors	1992. Federalization of education (include transfer of UPN's units to states). 1993. General Educational Law	University training at the National Pedagogical University (UPN) or in tertiary institutes.
Paraguay	For children between 3 to 5 years. Compulsory at age of 5.	Duration: 9 years. For children about 6 to 14 years old. Compulsory.	Duration: 3 years. Non-compulsory. Required for superior studies.	Non- university (Teaching training institutes and Technical Education) and University sectors	1995. Educational Reform	Training takes place at non-university institutes.
Peru	For children between 0 to 5 years. Non-compulsory.	Compulsory. Duration: 6 years.	*Duration: 5 years (2 basic and common years, and 3 for specialization). Non-compulsory.* Required for superior studies.	Non- university (Teaching training institutes and Professional Programs) and University sectors		Training takes place at non-university institutes.
Uruguay	For children between 3 to 5 years. Compulsory at age of 5	Duration: 9 years. For children about 6 to 14 years old. Compulsory.	Duration: 3 years. Non-compulsory. Required for superior studies.	Non- university (Teaching training institutes, Centers of Industrial Design and Military Schools) and University sectors	1996. Educational Law	Training takes place at non-university institutes.

The Table shows that only Chile and Mexico require some sort of training at the university to acquire a teaching diploma. In the rest of the countries, specific non-university Teacher Training Institutes predominate or remain the only option.

Teachers training in Mexico: In the past, preschool, primary, secondary, physical and special education teachers were trained in Teacher Colleges in the non-university sector. In 1979 the National Pedagogic University (UPN) was created to stimulate competency and increase quality. It was intended to provide in-service training (upgrading skills at this institution provided an additional premium to the salary) and offer a university diploma for secondary school graduates who liked to embrace the teaching profession but disliked the non-university option provided by the existing colleges of education. After thirty years, still there is debate as to the merits of the UPN in contributing to raise the quality of teachers in Mexico.

Teachers training in Chile: Until the sixties, teaching training took place at specific secondary schools (escuela normal). In 1967, requirements for teacher training were raised and post-secondary Teachers Colleges were created. In 1973, all teachers colleges were removed out of the system and replaced by a new system of teacher training provided by the University (who offer a degree on Pedagogy after 4 years of study).

4. Characteristics of Teachers and the Rest of the Labor Force

Some common aspects related to teachers' personal characteristics have emerged from the commented reports and are summarized in Table II:

Teaching is a predominant female activity. In all countries reported, the majority of teachers are females.

The percentage of teachers being married or cohabiting and that of the married non-teachers is similar in all the countries, except in Bolivia, where the proportion of married teachers exceeds that of the non-teachers.

The percentage of teachers who are reported head of household is lower than the average in the labor force. This tends to confirm that teachers in the Latin American countries are predominantly secondary earners.

Concerning the size of the place of residence, in Argentina, it was found that the proportion of teachers in the labor force decreases with city size. The Bolivian data indicates that the proportion of teachers in the labor force does not change with city size. In Brazil, cities are classified as having or not having a favorable environment and it came that almost 9 of 10 teachers live in favorable areas.

Table II: Demographic characteristics

Country	% Female		% Married		% Heads of household		% Living in big cities	
	Teachers	Non-teachers	Teachers	Non-teachers	Teachers	Non-teachers	Teachers	Non-teachers
Argentina	85	36	60	60	30	50	60	70
Bolivia	69	41	73	63	44	62	58	61
Brazil	84	37	77	75	13	13	89	97
Chile	70	31	NA	NA	36	52	NA	NA
México	72	32	NA	NA	NA	NA	NA	NA
Paraguay	85	25	NA	NA	20	49	NA	NA
Peru	60	42	57	58	NA	NA	72	NA
Uruguay	76	38	NA	NA	32	47	NA	NA

Source: (a) Herrero, De Santis y Gertel (2004). (b) Piras and Savedoff (2002). (c) Liang (1999). (d) Mizala and Romaguera (2000). (e) López Acevedo (2002) (f) Saavedra Chanduví (2000). NA: Non-available.

Table III shows the age, schooling and hourly-income of teachers and non-teachers in a selected sample of Latin American countries.
Teachers have about 15 years of schooling in most of the countries. Brazil is an exception, and reports 11.4 years of schooling in the teaching force. Argentina and Chile are the countries whose labor force shows the highest average level of schooling (above 10 years).

Table III: Other characteristics and differences in average wages

Country	Average age		Average Schooling		Difference in average hourly income (teachers – non teachers)	
	Teachers	Non-teachers	Teachers	Non-teachers	Dif. in mean hourly wage	Hourly wage premium of being a teacher[94]
Argentine (a)	36.5	37	15	10.6	+42%	NA
Bolivia (b)	38.1	35.7	15.4	8.6	+29%	NA
Brazil (c)	26.4	21.8	11.4	8.4	NA	-7%
Chile (d)	40.0	38.0	15.7	9.6	+48%	NA
México (e)	39.0	34.1	14.1	8.9	+200%	NA
Paraguay	34.4	32.9	14.5	8.7	NA	NA
Peru (f)	35.4	36.6	15.2	8.9	+13%	NA
Uruguay	41.8	38	13.4	8.7	NA	+10%

Source: (a) Herrero, De Santis y Gertel (2004). (b) Piras and Savedoff (2002). (c) Liang (1999). (d) Mizala and Romaguera (2000). (e) López Acevedo (2002) (f) Saavedra Chanduví (2000). NA: Non-available.

The teachers in LAC are, on average, oldest than the rest of the workers. In Argentina, both groups are of a similar age. Hourly wage for teachers were systematically found to exceed

[94] The estimation was obtained using a dummy variable for teachers in a Mincerian equation for all income earners.

that of an average worker, except in Brazil, where teachers earn on average less than an average worker.

Table IV informs the number of hours worked by teachers and non-teachers in the selected countries.

Table IV: Average Hours Worked Per Week.

Country	Teachers	Non-teachers
Argentina (a)	23.1	44.4
Bolivia (b)	23.9	49.7
Brazil (c)	28.7	40.9
Chile (d)	39.0	52.0
Mexico	29.4	46.0
Paraguay	35.8	48.0
Peru	27.8	43.0
Uruguay	31.1	45.1

(a) Herrero, De Santis y Gertel (2004).. (b) Piras and Savedoff (2002). (c) Liang (1999). (d) Mizala and Romaguera (2000). (e) López Acevedo (2002). (f) Saavedra Chanduví (2000).

Teachers were systematically reported to work fewer hours per week than the average worker. Argentina and Bolivia are the countries where the work effort of teachers is shown to be the lowest (equivalent to a half time job).

5. A Comparative Analysis of Studies on the Returns To Schooling and Other Personal Characteristics of Teachers in Latin America

The previously reported work on teacher salaries presented estimates of the returns to schooling, experience and other characteristics of teachers and non-teachers using OLS regression analysis of a Mincer equation that allows us to discuss these findings from a comparative perspective.

The model of teachers' remunerations

The Mincer's income equation is applied in all of the reported studies to estimate the returns to schooling, experience and a number of additional personal characteristics that affect employability and wage determination.

The following equation resumes the model:

$$W = X\beta + u \qquad (1)$$

Where W is a vector of hourly wage, X is the matrix of the human capital variables observed (schooling, work experience, etc) and personal characteristics identifying the individuals (gender, marital status, place of residence, being a teacher, etc.), ß is the vector of returns to those variables, and where u is the error term.

The Results: a Comparative Overview

Table V summarizes the average rate of return to schooling, experience, marital status, gender, place of residence that resulted from estimation of Mincer equations of the log hourly-wage of teachers in Argentina, Bolivia, Brazil, Chile, Mexico, Peru, Paraguay and Uruguay.

Table V: Teachers' income determinants obtained from different studies from LAC.

Countries	Constant	Years of schooling	Potential experience	Square potential experience	Married	Male	Big cities
Argentina (a)	0.5315	0.0568	(a)	-	0.1122	-	0.0216
Bolivia (b)	0.970	0.078	0.03	-0.0006	0.0046	-0.049	0.1343
Brazil (c)	-	0.16	0.02	-	-	-	0.26
Chile (d)	6.704	0.024	-0.003	0.0003	0.073	0.088	-0.002
México (e)	1.2715	0.058	0.033	-0.0004	-	0.083	-0.1233
Paraguay (c)	-	0.05	-	-	-	0.25	-
Peru (f)	0.47	0.054	-	-	0.02	0.067	-
Uruguay (c)	-	0.03	0.04	-0.0007	-	-	0.12

(a) Herrero, De Santis y Gertel (2004). Estimation obtained only for women, using a model with double correction for selection bias. Relation between hourly wage and age is increasing. (b) Piras and Savedoff (2002). (c) Liang (1999). Monthly income equations are been estimated, and number of hours worked was an explanatory variable. (d) Mizala and Romaguera (2000). (e) López Acevedo (2002) Teachers in primary public schools vs. workers mixed-skilled. (f) Saavedra Chanduví (2000).

Returns to schooling were found to be similar in most of the countries in the sample and close to 5% per year. The lowest returns were those of Chile and Uruguay (2% and 3%, respectively). The highest returns of schooling were reported for the Brazilian teachers (16%) who possessed the lowest stock of education in the Region (11 years).

Each additional year of potential experience would contribute to increase the level of earnings in 3% approximately, except in Chile where the effect of additional experience on earnings is negative.

The coefficient of "square experience" (as a proxy for declining of experience's benefits) has a negative sign, as expected, but statistically it is non significant. In fact, only few countries reported results for this variable.

Married teachers were reported to get higher hourly remunerations in all the reported countries. The value of the premium is, however, quite variable across countries (ranging from 1% to 11%).

In Chile, Mexico, Paraguay and Peru, male teachers were reported to get higher hourly remunerations.

The "place of residence" was captured in different ways: in Argentina, Chile and Uruguay the metropolitan areas where separated in groups according to size, in Bolivia, metropolitan areas were grouped into those that belong to the three more important departments or provinces and the rest of the cities included in the survey, in Brazil and Mexico the sample of metropolitan areas were divided according to economic development indicators. In general, the reported studies found that the salary of the teachers was higher the more developed the place of his/her residence is, except for Chile, where no differences were found and Mexico, where teachers earn more in deprived areas.

6. Summary of Conclusions

The most relevant feature related to teachers remunerations in Latin America that this comparative exercise has shown is, perhaps, that the market for teachers operates in a similar manner across countries.

Some methodological warnings are, however, in place: first, in most countries, the data source refers to urban workers, surveyed only in a few metropolitan areas that exceed a certain population size. Additionally, Mincer's equations throw biased estimations of the returns to schooling, experience and personal characteristics that were not corrected in the commented studies. Thus, the reported estimates were overestimated by the application of this method.

In general, evidence taken from recent research on the remuneration of teachers in Latin America has served to illustrate that across Latin America, teachers earn more than the average worker in the economy. Questions arise, however, as to whether "the average worker" is a sensible unit of comparison. Teachers have, on average, some 15 years of education while the typical worker has about 8.5-11 years of schooling. Experience also differs: teachers are older than the rest of the workers, but unlike other workers, for teachers, age is a poor proxy for experience, because rotation is high. Teaching is predominantly a female profession, but men who choose to teach would typically earn a higher salary. The more developed urban areas tend to attract the best and more experienced teachers, who, consequently will obtain a higher salary relative to those colleagues working in the more deprived areas, except for Mexico. Finally, the comparative exercise has shown that teachers are predominantly secondary earners in their household. To earn a diploma in teaching would typically takes 15 years of study; in most of the countries, at a college of education within the non-university sector of Higher Education. Only Chile and Mexico offer a mix of institutions for training teachers in and outside the university. The role of the university for training teachers is, nonetheless, under debate across the Continent. The returns to schooling among teachers from the different countries in the sample seems to converge to a common value of about 5 per cent per year. This is a lower value than the obtained by any comparable worker with no less than 15 years of schooling who to work in any alternative job market.

References

Herrero, V., De Santis, M. and Gertel, H. R. (2003), El ingreso de los docentes en Argentina: Es alto o bajo? In: *ANALES XXXVIII AAEP,* (www.aaep.org/anales).

Herrero, V., De Santis, M. and Gertel, H. R. (2004), Un examen empírico del empleo y la remuneración docente en las escuelas de Argentina en 1998 y 2002 aplicando ecuaciones de ingreso corregidas por selectividad. In: *ANALES XXXIX AAEP* (www.aaep.org/anales).

Liang, X. (1999), Teacher pay in 12 Latin American Countries: How does teacher pay compare to other professions, what determines teacher pay, and who are the teachers? *LCSHD Paper Series N° 49*, Human Development Department, The World Bank.

López-Acevedo, G. (2002), Teachers' Incentives and Professional Development in Colleges in México, *LCSPE Paper Series*. The World Bank.

Mizala, A. and Romaguera, P. (1998), Remuneraciones al Pizarrón, in: *Revista Perspectivas*, Departamento de Ingeniería Industrial, Universidad de Chile.

Piras, C. and Savedoff, W. (1998), How Much Do Teachers Earn? *Mimeo, IADB.*

Psacharopoulos, G.; Valenzuela, J. & Arends, M. (1996), Teacher Salaries in Latin America: A Review, in: *Economics of Education Review,* Vol. 15. No. 4, 401-406.

Saavedra Chanduví, J. (2000), La situación laboral de los maestros respecto de otros profesionales: Implicancias para el diseño de políticas salariales y de incentivos. In: *Informe Final del Grupo de Análisis para el Desarrollo*, Lima.

Vegas, E., Murnane, R. and Willett, J. (2001), From High School to Teaching: Many Steps, Who Makes It? In: *Teachers College Record*, 103 (3), 427-449.

Vegas, E., Pritchett, L. and Experton, W. (1999), Cómo Atraer y Retener Docentes Calificados en la Argentina: Impacto del Nivel y la Estructura de la Remuneración. *LCSHD Paper Series,* 385 (April), The World Bank.

A REVIEW OF INCOME POLARIZATION: CONCEPTS AND APPLICATIONS

Paula Palacios, M. Florencia Ruiz Díaz,
Hector R. Gertel and Roberto F. Giuliodori
Instituto de Economía y Finanzas
Facultad de Ciencias Económicas
Universidad Nacional de Córdoba
palacios@eco.unc.edu.ar

1. Introduction

The concept of polarization was coined to explain certain changes in the distribution of income that were not correctly grasped by the usual measures of inequality.

We say that society finds itself polarized when it can be divided in at least two significant groups, such that members of the same cluster possess similarities in terms of some characteristic or attribute but still kept differentiated from members of the other cluster. These similarities are said to generate a feeling of identification among the members of the same group, while creating alienation between both groups. Such separation or division of population generally appears associated to the existence of social tensions, and depending on the attribute that is selected to divide that population; in some cases it could help explaining rebellions, civil wars, quarrels, or simply mayor violence among the different social groups. That is to say, the greater polarization, the greater the probabilities of the start of social conflicts.

Even though this concept is found closely related to the notion of inequality, as we mentioned before, its development emerged as a result of some dissatisfaction in the inability of standard inequality measures to deal with the formation of antagonist groups in society. As Wolfson stressed, "This concept ['disappearing middle class'] is typically equated with the concept of increased income inequality. However, such an equation entails a fundamental conceptual error". The difference between the measures of inequality and polarization emerges when the distribution of income or wealth of individuals tends to form clusters around local means instead of converging to the global mean.

This paper is structured as follows: first we develop briefly the concept of polarization together with its main axioms, underlining its differentiation in relation to traditional inequality measures. Secondly, we make a brief description of the results presented by several recent papers that measure income polarization in Argentina. Next, we analyze the evolution that polarization has had on others countries. Finally, we present the conclusions.

2. Polarization

2.1. Concept

While measures of inequality analyze the existing dispersion related to a central value, the notion of polarization refers to distance between homogeneous clusters that antagonize with each other.

Following Esteban and Ray (1994), the polarization of a distribution in individual attributes must exhibit three basic features:

- There must be a high degree in homogeneity within each group (identification).
- There must be a high degree in heterogeneity across each group (alienation).
- There must be a small number of significantly sized groups. In particular, groups of insignificant size carry little weight.

The similarity between groups can be associated to the concurrent objectives of its members, which creates a feeling of identification between them and it allows them to form a strong unity. Meanwhile the larger the differences are between the groups, the larger the feeling that will exist of alienation or conflict between them. However, it is necessary for the groups to be sufficiently large, because small groups do not possess a significant roll in the development of the conflict.

Intuitively, a higher identification and a higher alienation would raise polarization. It is worth noting that polarization can increase when inequality decreases (and vice versa). For instance, some transfers from the middle class to the poor and the rich can lead to lower inequality and higher polarization (see Esteban and Ray, 1994 and Wolfson, 1994). Thus, the analysis of income polarization is complementary to that of income inequality. The three basic features presented above, permits us to differentiate the index of polarization from the measures of inequality. A lower intra-group homogeneity increases the inequality, while it decreases polarization. At the same time if one cluster of individuals could capture most of the income, polarization decreases and inequality increases. Additionally lets suppose that the attribute we are about to analyze is the income, and that initially it possess a homogeneous distribution as we can see in figure A. Later (figure B), the income was concentrated in only two points (3 and 8). In this example, that could easily represent a situation of middle class disappearance, the inequality measured by any indicator consistent with the Dalton Principle of Transfers, decreased, however polarization increased because there is a higher intra-group identification (feature 1) while heterogeneity did not change between the two new groups.

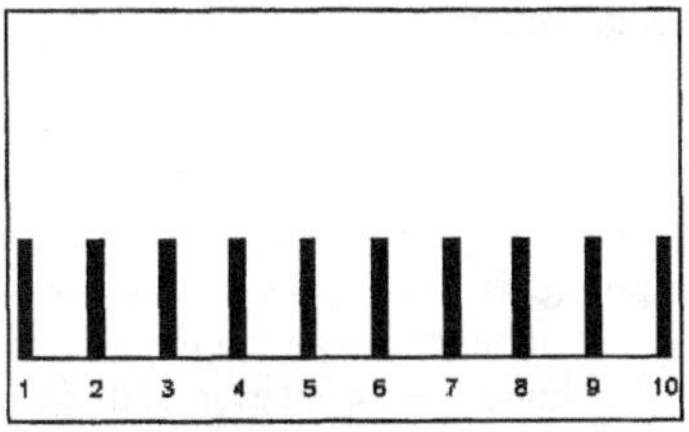

Figure A

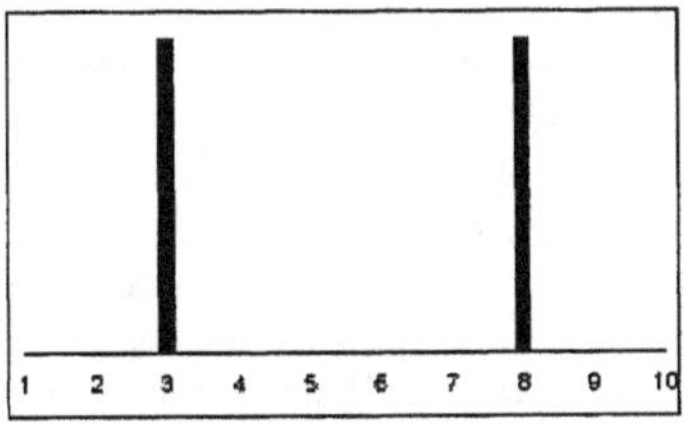

Figure B

Let us suppose now that the group with lower income becomes more poor and that the group with a higher income becomes richer (see figure C). The homogeneity within the each group was kept constant but, on this case, the heterogeneity between groups (feature 2) increased. Inequality and polarization moved in the same direction, which means that these measures not always go in the opposite way or same way, but it they can coincide or not depending on the situation.

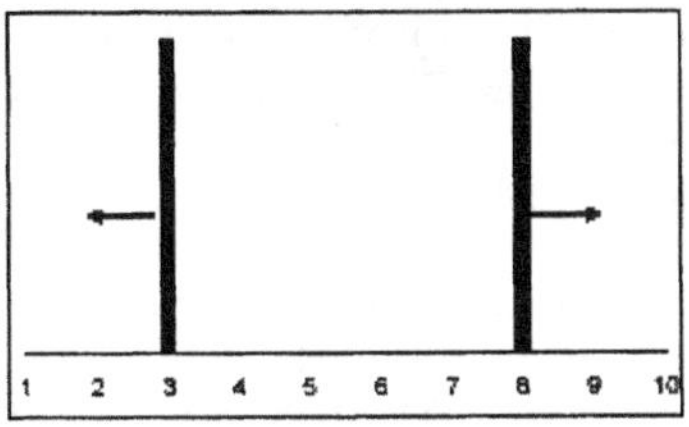

Figure C

Suppose now that the population is distributed according to a three-point distribution, with income spaced equally. It can be shown that when the central and the right-hand masses are being of approximately the same size and the left hand mass is the smallest, introducing a small shift of population in the left hand mass from the left extreme to the right, the shift creates a greater tendency towards forming two sharply defined groups, the left mass may well be instrumental in creating part of the social tensions that do exist, and the net effect is far from clear. However, if the left mass is very tiny indeed compared to the other two then the initial contribution of this mass is vanishingly low and there is more polarization.

2.2. Measurement

To measure polarization, Esteban and Ray (1994), define, first, a function of antagonism such as *T(I,a)* where *a* is the feeling of alienation, *I* the feeling of identification and *T* an increasing function from both arguments.

Specifically ER is the same as:

$$ER(\alpha, \rho) = \sum_{i=1}^{k} \sum_{j=1}^{k} p_i^{1+\alpha} p_j |y_i - y_j| \qquad (1)$$

Where α means the measure of sensibility with respect to polarization
y is average income of each group
p the weight of each group

When the index of polarization is defined for discrete groups, the treatment of continuum variables such as income, consumption, etc, generate two problems: on one hand, changes in polarization are not captured in a continuum way, because the index distribute the population, by the researcher, in a discrete number of points. On the other hand, the population is divided in a few relevant groups and there is no reason to believe that the grouping of income data will conveniently conform to the psychological demands of group identification.

Esteban, Ray and Gradín (1999) suggested a new statistical approach to measuring polarization which extends ER in such a way as to deal with distributions not necessarily pre-arranged in groups. This new measure is:

$$P(F;\alpha;\beta;\rho) = ER(\alpha,\rho) - \beta\varepsilon(F,\rho) \tag{2}$$

Where the second term represents the approximation error committed in ER by dividing the population in K groups (given that the groups are not perfectly homogeneous) and it can be estimated as the difference between the Gini of the original distribution and the Gini of the portioned distribution in groups.
ß is a free parameter which measures the weight attached to the measurement error (or lack of identification).
The quantity of groups in which the population is divided is chosen deliberately, or taking into account the characteristics of the distribution. The size of each group comes from minimizing the term of error, so as to build the most homogeneous groups as possible.

In a more recent paper, Esteban, Ray and Duclos (2002), analyzed rigorously the concept of polarization, giving mathematical form to the intuitive ideas of the concept.

3. Polarization Measurement in Argentina

Polarization was recently analyzed in Argentina by few many researchers with the objective to extend the traditional analysis of income distribution.

Beccaria, Esquivel and Maurizio (2001) applied the ERG index to estimate bipolarization of income in Metropolitan Area of Buenos Aires (GBA), from 1974 to 2000, and for the rest of the country, from 1991 to 2000, using information of family income per adult equivalents for EPH. In GBA, it was found that bipolarization increased along the period, although at a variable rate of increase. The highest rates were found during the second half of the 1980s. The behavior of the polarization index and that of the Gini Coefficient was similar between the early 1970s and the late 1980s indicating that both social antagonisms increased and income distribution deteriorated. In the 1990s the Gini Coefficient increased more rapidly than the bipolarization measure, thus, meaning that the principal phenomenon during those years was income deterioration.

Figure 1.1 shows the evolution of the bipolarization (P) index in GBA 1974-2000. The figure also shows the evolution of its two components: the ER measure and the error introduced by Esteban- Gradin-Ray as shown in (2).

The trend of the ER measure is increasing in all the period but at different rates. It has been increasing at a moderate rate during 1974-1985, a strongly rate during 1986-1991 and it seems to decelerate since 1992.

The lack of identification (error) showed a growing trend all along the period of different growth rates.

Indeed, increasing bipolarization almost always corresponds to periods of increasing polarization between the groups (ER), but partially offset with periods of stable and decreasing identification.

The reason of why polarization increases so much since the second half of 1980s is that during that period the ratio of extreme incomes increased from 3.5 to 4.2 due an increase in the top group average income together with the decline in the mean of the bottom group as figure 1.2 shows. The population shifted from the top towards the bottom group, which increased from 67.1% to 70.2% of households according to table 5 and figure 1.3. This fact diminishes social tensions because the small high-income group does not posses a significant role in the development of conflict.

The moderate increase of the bipolarization on the first half of 1990s was due to opposite factors. On one hand, income distance slightly increased. On the other hand, both effects, the increases the lack of identification within the groups and the size of the bottom group have caused a decrease in the polarization measure, partially compensating the above effect. However, both factors contributed to the increase of inequality.

At the end of the decade, the distance of the mean income continues to rise. It was due to a fall on the average income of the bottom group and an increase of the average income of the top group, which had remained stable until 1991.

In the Rest of the Country, the evolution of polarization showed a similar behavior than in Great Buenos Aires from the first half of the 1990s. This was caused by the increase of the ratio average income between both groups without a variation in their sizes, together with a decrease in the terms of error; which backed the intra-group homogeneity, and along with it, polarization. Contrary to GBA, the biggest identification within the groups, and not the increase in alienation, was the force that produces the increase of polarization. From 1994, polarization kept growing as a consequence of the raising differential of mean income between the groups due to a fall of the bottom group average income as the corresponding increase for top group that comes to its peak on the year 2000. During this period, intra-group homogeneity kept constant and did not contribute to the growth of polarization. This is illustrated in figures 2.1, 2.2 and 2.3

Olivieri and Horentein (2004) made an application of the new calculation methods applied to polarization of income developed by Duclos- Esteban- Ray (2002) in Argentina between 1998 and 2002. They proved that despite deceleration of the growth of inequality, polarization rates increased year after year in the whole country and in every region. The increase in social crisis was generated by two effects: the increase of homogeneity within the low-income group and the increase of heterogeneity between this group and the others. Low-income population provided the higher contribution to polarization.

In order to be able to determine the possible causes of polarization, Beccaria and Olivieri-Horentein (2004) carried out a micro-decomposition of polarization index. Beccaria used education and job eligibility as parameters in Buenos Aires and the rest of the country. He showed that the level of education of people is a determining factor of polarization in Buenos Aires, since it explains, in average, more than half the polarization of the last years. This proportion has been growing up since 1974 by the 41% and it reached the 55% in the year 2000. In the provinces, during the 90's, education systematically presents a lower percentage than that of the Metropolitan area. Only a lower percentage of polarization can be attributed to job qualification if compared to the percentage of education.

Gertel, Giuliodori and Rodriguez (2004) analyzed the effect of the "Plan Jefes y Jefas de Hogar"[95] about the distribution of income for 2002. They used Dagum's calculation method and they studied the DER polarization index in order to complete the first method.

Results, given a=1, indicated that polarization in Argentina decreased from 0.25 under a situation where incomes from PJJH were not computed, to 0.241 when income of PJJH for 1.8 millions recipients were considered, showing a positive effect of the program. However, it should be remarked that this improvement in the polarization measure associated to the implementation of the PJJH is not big enough to restore the observed value of 0.2285 obtained by Horrenstein and Olivieri for 1998. They concluded that the plans diminished both, the inequality and polarization.

4. Polarization measurement in 5 OECD countries

Gradin (1998) and Esteban-Gradin-Ray (1999) observe two basic patterns of income distributions, each showing a distinct polarization level and structure as well as a distinct evolution through the period 1971-1997. One pattern corresponds to the US and the UK and the other to Germany, Canada and Sweden.
The authors try to answer three main questions:

- How were the trends in polarization and inequality in each country?
- Was increasing polarization due to higher alienation between the groups or increasing homogeneity within them?
- Was increasing polarization result of an increasing gap between the extreme groups or the result of extreme groups becoming larger?

For the empirical work both authors made use the data from the Luxembourg Income Study (LIS) database. From the sample of household surveys they compute the EGR Index in a 3-group partition using information of family income per adult equivalents.

In *United States,* polarization follows a U-shaped trend according to figure 3. For the 1970s, a similar decreasing tendency is observed for inequality and polarization. Polarization and inequality strongly increases for the first half of both 1980s and 1990s, remaining stable for

[95] Government job plan for unemployment family heads

the rest of those periods. However, polarization increased more persistently than inequality in this decade.
The trend of polarization between the groups (ER) exhibits the same behavior of the polarization at all. It has been strongly increasing since 1978 but it seems to decelerate at the end. This behavior was partially offset by increasing lack of identification as figure 4.1 shows.
The increasing separation between extreme groups, rather than the declining size of the middle group, explains the increasing polarization between the groups since 1979.
The population share of the low- income group has increased by at the entire expense of the high-income group. The relative size of the middle group does not show a dynamic behavior and remains stable. It has diminished between 1974 and 1991, but not by a significant amount, from 39% of all households to 37.9%, and since 1991 increases coming close to 38% of the households. The size of the bottom group increases, from 39% of households in 1974 to 43% by 1997 and the size of the top group decreases from 21% of households to 18%. This is illustrated in figure 4.2. These changes have made group sizes more uneven, reducing polarization.
At the same time, income distances have spread out as show figure 4.3. They find an increase in the top group average income together with the decline in the mean of the bottom group. The ratio of mean incomes of the two groups has increased 21% during the period. However, the income of the middle group has remained steady around the global mean. This increase in inter- group distances has been so significant that it has overridden the effect of an increased unevenness in the group population shares.

In *United Kingdom,* polarization has been increasing since 1974 with the strongest intensity during the last half of 1980s, as figure 3 shows.
During the second half of 1980s it was a strongly increase in polarization between groups, not compensated for by the very small increase in the lack of identification. This makes polarization increase more sharply than in the first half of the decade, when both terms grow with similar intensity.
As figure 5.1 presents, polarization starts to increase in 1974, while inequality begins in 1979. The discrepancy occurs because during the 1974-1979 periods the higher intra- group identification more than compensated for smaller polarization between the groups.
The reason of why polarization increases so much since the second half of 1980s is that during that period the ratio of extreme incomes increased from 3.5 to 4.3 shown in figure 5.3 and the middle group size diminished 2.6% However, at the first half of 1980s, polarization remains stable because while the income ratio increased, the size of the middle group also increased significantly (5%).
Along the period, the population shifted from the middle and top towards the bottom, which increased from 41.4% to 43.8% of households according to figure 5.2 and table 2.

In the case of Sweden, polarization follows a U-shaped trend according to figure 3. A decreasing tendency is observed for the second half of the 1970s and for the 1980s, polarization started to increase.
The increase in polarization was due to a large increase in polarization between groups for the first half of 1980s, but this effect was lessened by lower identification within the groups, as is shown in figure 6.1.

This increase in polarization was mostly explained by the relative income distance which significantly increase at about 17% from 2.3 to 2.7 in the period 1981-1987 illustrated in figure 6.3. According to figure 6.2, the relative sizes of groups have been quite stable during the episode of high increase in polarization, with the middle group accounting for almost 40% of households. Between 1987 and 1992 there was a transfer of households from the top and middle towards the bottom.

In *Germany,* polarization was declining but progressively stabilizing because both the polarization between groups and identification within them were decreasing at a decelerating rate as it shown in figure 7.1.
For the last period a slight increase in polarization between groups can be observed which did not lead to increasing polarization because the groups also felt less identified. In contrast, inequality increased in this period.
The decreasing polarization between the groups was due to decreasing distances between extreme groups as figure 7.3 shows. The income ratio diminished a 3% from 3.33 in 1973 to 3.23 by 1994. A fall of 10% between 1973 and 1984 was partially offset by an increase of 7% until 1994. There weren't significantly population movements between the groups. But there is evidence of movements from the extreme groups to middle group, reported in table 2.

Canada, presents a depolarizing trend since 1971, due especially to decreasing polarization between the groups at a decelerating rate, with identification remaining almost constant. This id illustrated in figure 8.1
The decreasing polarization between the groups was due to decreasing distances between extreme groups. This approximation between extreme poles occurs with more intensity in Canada than in Germany. According figure 8.3 and table 3, in Canada the ratio fell 30% (from 4.9 to 3.4) while in Germany the ratio diminished 3 % in the same period.
There weren't significantly shifts of population towards the bottom and top groups between 1971 and 1994.

To conclude, two types of income polarization patterns have emerged. On one hand, the US and the UK have a more uneven structure of group sizes, with large low- income groups and small high- income groups. On the other hand, these countries have a large and increasing income distances between high and low income groups. While the first characteristic tends to reduce polarization, the second tends to increase it. The net effect of these opposite forces is driven by the significant size of the differences in income distances across countries. Both US and the UK have increases polarization, while the others countries have stability or decreases. Among this set of four countries, changes in the distance between extreme groups explain most changes observed in polarization either increasing or decreasing.

5. Conclusions

Study of income polarization arises as a response to the questions generated by the analysis of inequality using the Gini method, among others. This complementary nature of both studies helps to better understand the dynamics of distribution of income along time.

Studies carried out in Argentina by Beccaria- Esquivel -Maurizio (2001) and Oliveri-Horentein (2004) show that inequality rates and polarization had a tendency to increase since 1970 and, during the last decade of the 90's, polarization increased to a higher rate. This phenomenon of higher polarization is similar to the one present in other countrie s like US and UK.

The increase of polarization corresponded to a higher heterogeneity between groups: the rate of income increased as a result of a fall of income of the poorer group and a rise of income of the richer group Through the income micro-decomposition technique it can be shown that the level of education of a person is determining factor of polarization.

In studies carried out by Gradín (1999) and Duclos- Esteban- Ray (2002) for five OECD countries (1971-1997), the authors found that there are two types of groups. One of them corresponds to US and UK with increasing levels of inequality and polarization. The other one corresponds to Sweden, Germany and Canada with decreasing levels of inequality and polarization.
Similar to Argentina, the factor that contributed more to the dynamics of polarization was polarization between sectors (alienation) instead of identification within them. Relative high/low income rate had an increasing tendency for the first group of countries and a decreasing tendency for the second group.

References

Esteban, J. and Ray, D. (1994), On the measurement of polarization, in: *Econometrica*, Vol 62, No. 4.

Esteban, J., Gradín, C. and Ray, D. (1999), Extensions of a measure of polarization, with an application to the income distribution of five OECD Countries, *Working Paper* N°24, Instituto de Estudios Económicos de Galicia -Pedro Barrié de la Maza.

Gertel, H. R., Giuliodori, R. F. and Rodríguez, A. (2004), Analysis of the Short Term Impact of the Argentine Social Assistance Program "Plan Jefes y Jefas" on Income Inequality Applying the Dagum Decomposition Analysis of the Gini Ratio. Mimeo presented at *"International Conference in Memory of Two Eminent Social Scientists: C. Gini and M.O.Lorenz: Their impact in the XX-th Century Development of Probability, Statistics and Economics"*. Università degli Studi di Siena, Italy, May 23-26.

Gradín, C. (1999), Polarization by subpopulations in Spain: 1973-91, *Working Paper No*. 9906, Departamento de Economía Aplicada, Universidad de Vigo.

Gradín, C. (1998), *Polarization and Inequality: An International Comparison*. II Encuentro de la Red de Centros de Economía Social en América Latina, San José, Costa Rica.

Duclos, J. Y., Esteban, J. and Ray, D. (2002), Polarization: Concepts, Measurement, Estimation, *Working Paper* No.335, Maxwell School of Citizenship and Public Affairs, Syracuse University.

Beccaria, L., Esquivel, V. and Mauricio, R. (2001), *Desigualdad y polarización del ingreso en Argentina,* Universidad Nacional de Gral. Sarmiento, Argentina.

Horenstein, M. and Olivieri, S. (2004), Polarización del Ingreso en la Argentina: Teoría y Aplicación de la Polarización Pura del Ingreso, *Working Paper* No. 15, CEDLAS, Universidad Nacional de La Plata.

Gasparini, L. Income Inequality in Latin America and the Caribbean: Evidence from Household Surveys, *Working Paper* No. 2, CEDLAS, Universidad Nacional de La Plata.

Schimdt, A. (2000), *Statistical Measurement of Income Polarization. A Cross-National Comparison*, University of Cologne, Germany.

Wolfson, M.C. (1994), When Inequality Diverges, in: *American Economic Review* N°84, 353-358.

Tables and Figures

Table 1: Extended Polarization P(a=1.6, ß=1) in a 3- Group Partition

	P	ER	Error	Gini
U. S.				
1974	0,0558	0,1044	0,0486	0,3478
1979	0,0544	0,0992	0,0448	0,3311
1986	0,0593	0,1073	0,0480	0,3563
1991	0,0601	0,1080	0,0479	0,359
1994	0,0646	0,1166	0,0520	0,3841
1997	0,0669	0,1206	0,0537	0,3903
U. K.				
1974	0,0487	0,0875	0,0388	0,2871
1979	0,0481	0,0844	0,0363	0,2769
1986	0,0485	0,0927	0,0442	0,3078
1991	0,0622	0,1087	0,0465	0,3495
1995	0,0597	0,1073	0,0476	0,3462
Sweden				
1975	0,0361	0,0690	0,0329	0,2331
1981	0,0290	0,0584	0,0294	0,2011
1987	0,0322	0,0682	0,0360	0,2359
1992	0,0343	0,0704	0,0361	0,2413
Germany				
1973	0,0457	0,0862	0,0405	0,2877
1978	0,0450	0,0840	0,0390	0,2780
1983	0,0450	0,0815	0,0365	0,2690
1984	0,0420	0,0795	0,0375	0,2640
1989	0,0408	0,0792	0,0384	0,2648
1994	0,0430	0,0829	0,0399	0,2778
Canada				
1971	0,0607	0,1104	0,0497	0,3673
1975	0,0526	0,0971	0,0445	0,325
1981	0,0508	0,0935	0,0427	0,3122
1987	0,0499	0,0921	0,0422	0,3066
1991	0,0475	0,0893	0,0418	0,2992
1994	0,0482	0,0896	0,0414	0,2993

Table 2: Group Population Shares (% Households) in a 3- Group Partition

	Bottom	Middle	Top
US			
1974	39,24	39,06	21,70
1979	37,92	38,74	23,34
1986	39,28	37,90	22,83
1991	39,31	37,86	22,83
1994	40,89	38,01	21,10
1997	42,94	38,81	18,25
UK			
1974	41,37	37,60	21,03
1979	41,11	35,66	23,23
1986	41,60	37,39	21,01
1991	43,84	36,40	19,76
1995	43,76	37,16	19,08
Sweden			
1975	36,58	37,04	26,37
1981	32,54	39,52	27,94
1987	32,82	39,89	27,29
1992	34,94	40,33	24,74
Germany			
1973	39,54	39,16	21,30
1978	40,75	38,74	20,51
1983	40,60	39,08	20,33
1984	40,19	38,70	21,11
1989	38,73	40,18	21,09
1994	38,75	40,20	21,05
Canada			
1971	39,18	38,01	22,81
1975	37,91	38,54	23,55
1981	38,99	37,62	23,39
1987	39,80	37,34	22,85
1991	39,16	37,78	23,06
1994	39,74	37,15	23,11

Table 3: Relative Income Ratio High/Low Income Groups in 3- Group Partition

	Ratio
US	
1974	4,43
1979	4,16
1986	4,61
1991	4,66
1994	5,21
1997	5,36
UK	
1974	3,3
1979	3,1
1986	3,55
1991	4,32
1995	4,27
Sweden	
1975	2,60
1981	2,31
1987	2,70
1992	2,73
Germany	
1973	3,33
1978	3,19
1983	3,01
1984	3,00
1989	3,03
1994	3,23
Canada	
1971	4,9
1975	4,01
1981	3,09
1987	3,57
1991	3,46
1994	3,44

Table 4: Extended Polarization in Argentina P(a=1, ß=1) in a 2 Group Partition

	P	ER	Error	Gini
GBA				
1974	0,1570	0,2600	0,1030	0,3630
1980	0,1680	0,2830	0,1150	0,3980
1986	0,1800	0,3010	0,1210	0,4420
1991	0,2060	0,3360	0,1300	0,4660
1994	0,2130	0,3490	0,1360	0,4850
1997	0,2270	0,3620	0,1350	0,4970
2000	0,2330	0,3720	0,1390	0,5110
Rest of the Country				
1991	0,194	0,33	0,136	0,466
1994	0,223	0,34	0,117	0,457
1997	0,236	0,353	0,117	0,468
2000	0,248	0,37	0,122	0,492

Table 5: Group Population Shares in Argentina (% Households) in a 2-Group Partition

	Bottom	Top
GBA		
1974	63,9	36,1
1980	65,7	34,3
1986	67,1	32,9
1991	70,2	29,8
1994	70,7	29,3
1997	69,4	30,6
2000	69,6	30,4
Rest of the Country		
1991	66,6	33,4
1994	66,8	33,2
1997	67,4	32,6
2000	68,3	31,7

Table 6: Relative Income Ratio High/Low Income Groups in 2- Group Partition

	Ratio
GBA	
1974	2,9
1980	3,2
1986	3,5
1991	4,2
1994	4,3
1997	4,6
2000	4,8
Rest of the Country	
1991	3,9
1994	4,1
1997	4,4
2000	4,7

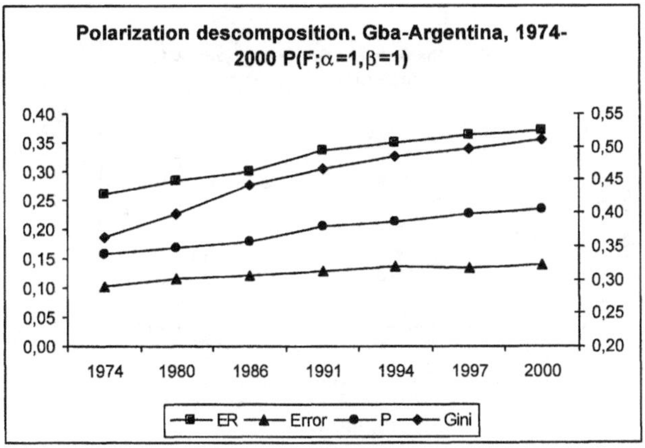

Figure 1.1

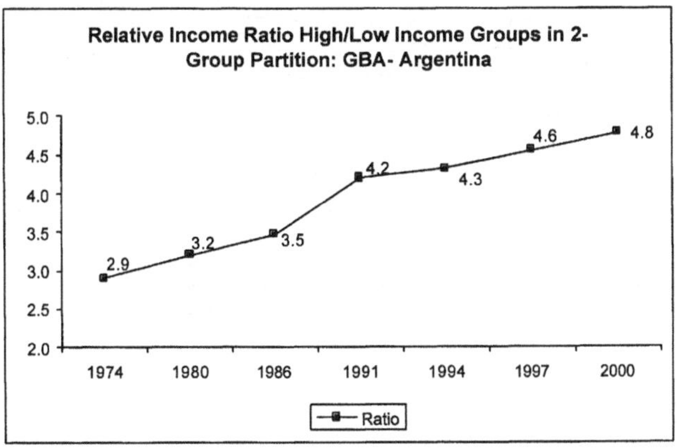

Figure 1.2

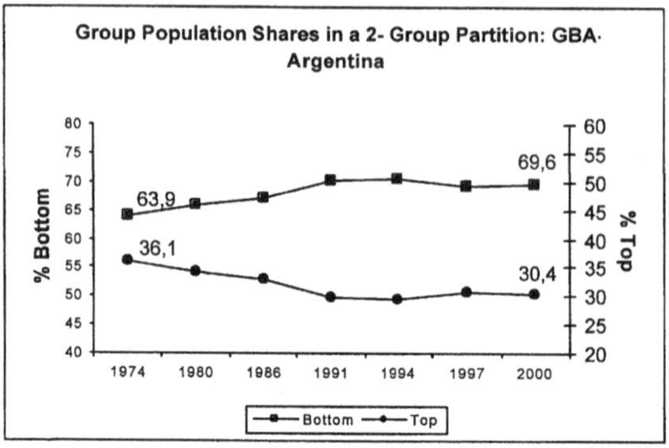

Figure 1.3

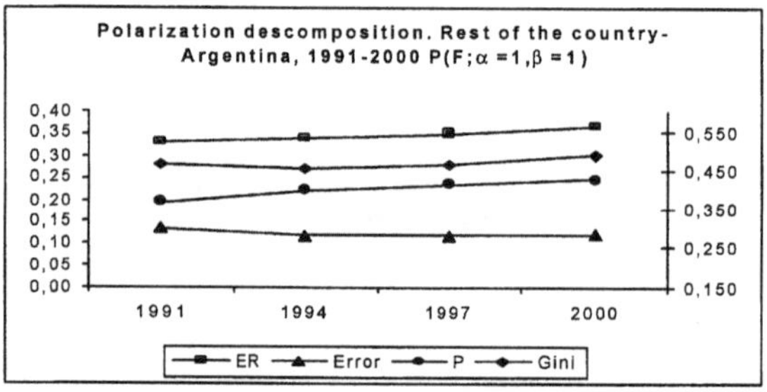

Figure 2.1

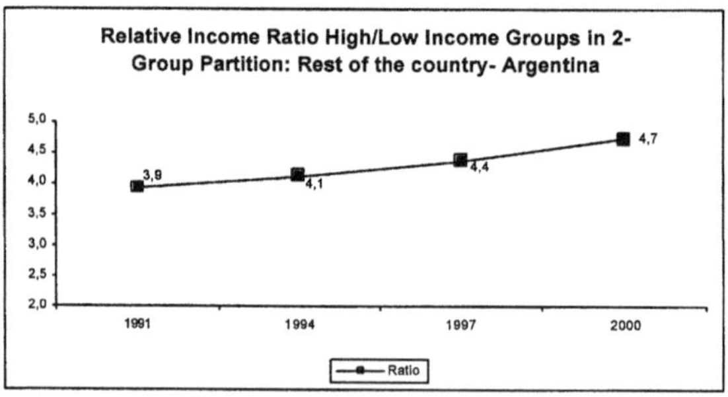

Figure 2.2

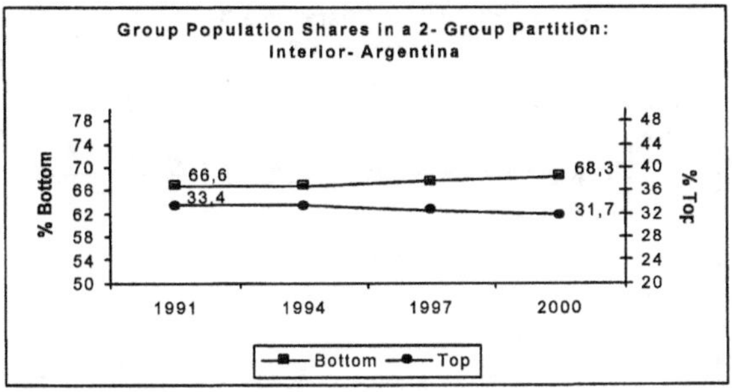

Figure 2.3

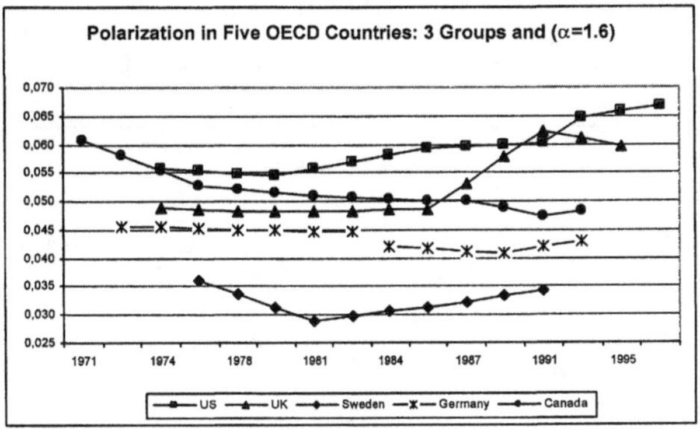

Figure 3

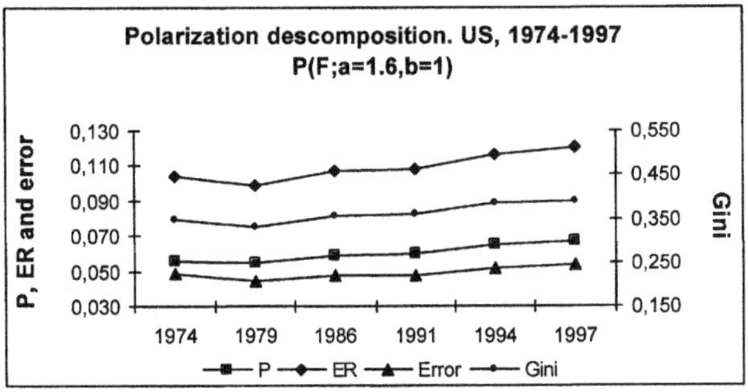

Figure 4.1

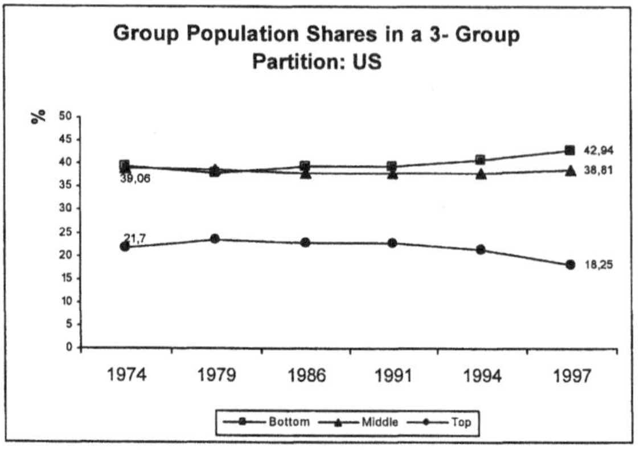

Figure 4.2

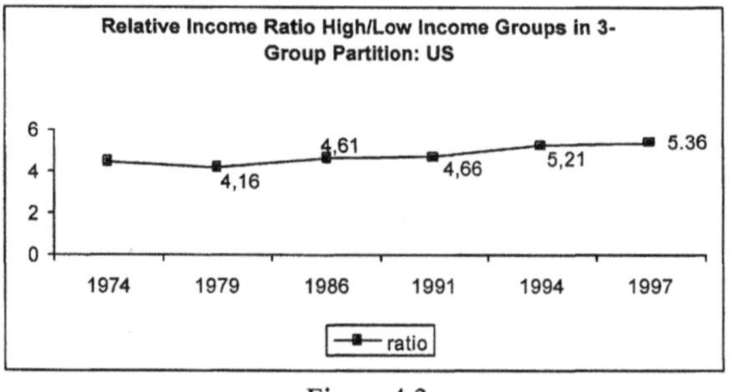

Figure 4.3

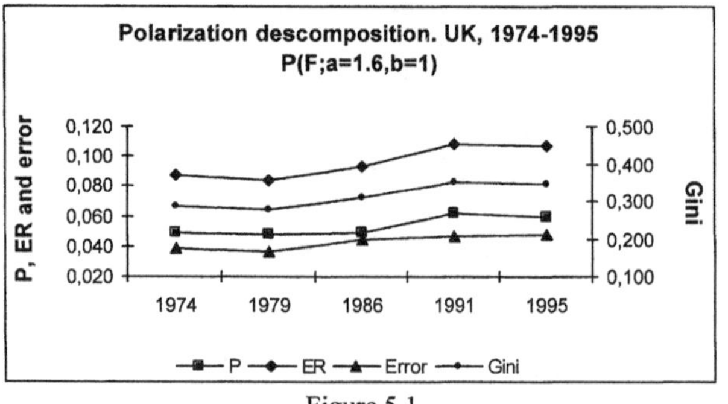

Figure 5.1

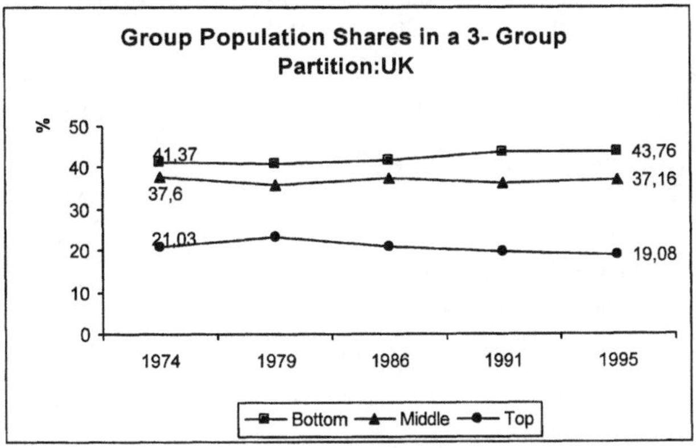

Figure 5.2

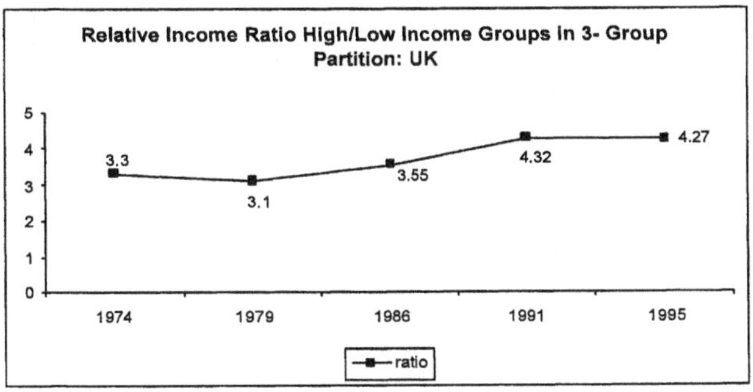

Figure 5.3

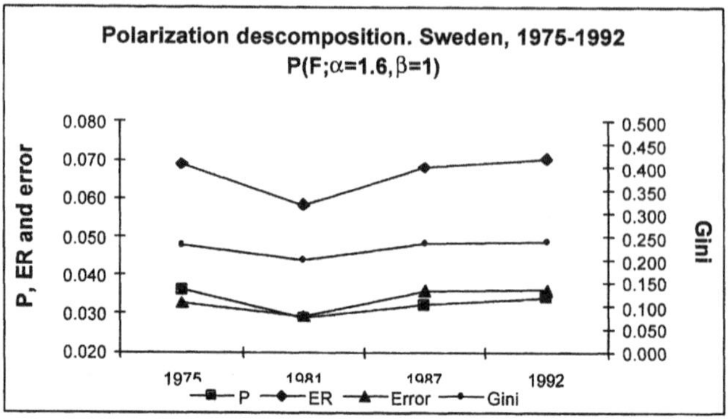

Figure 6.1

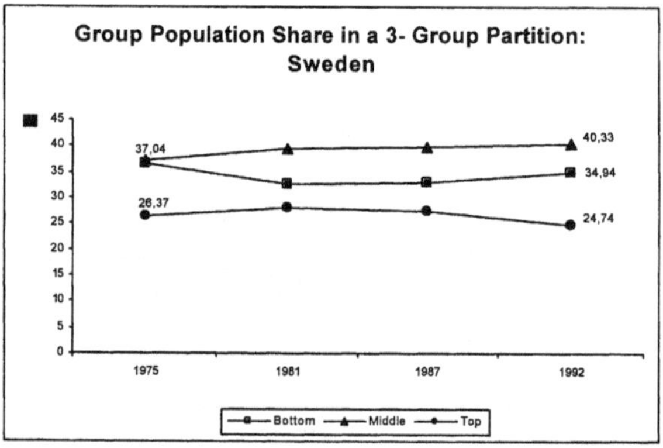

Figure 6.2

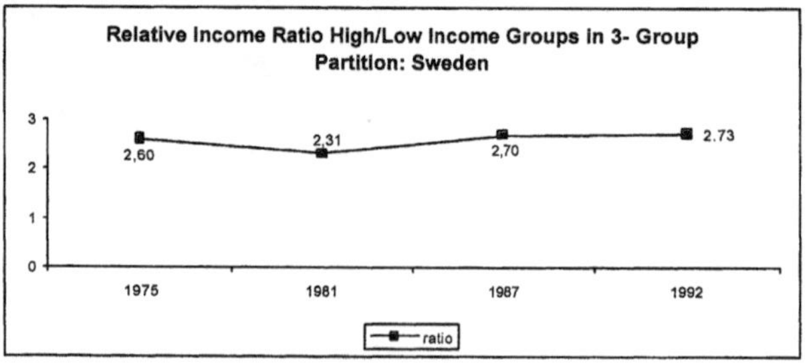

Figure 6.3

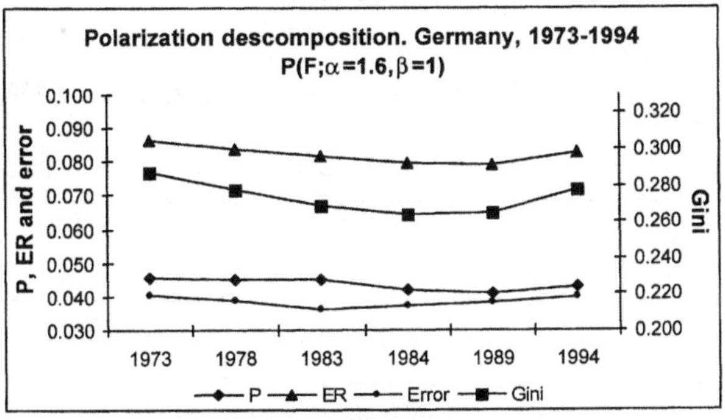

Figure 7.1

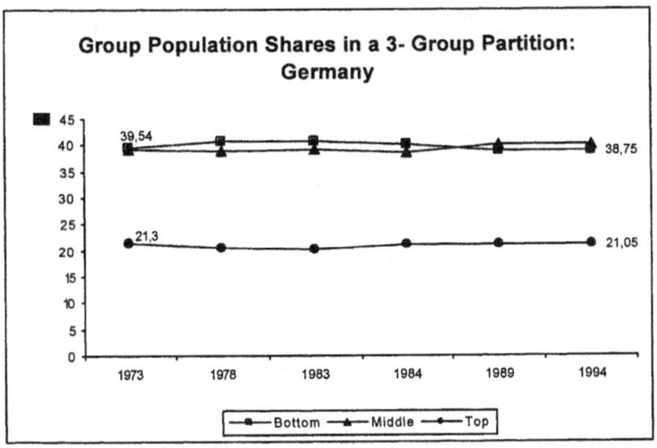

Figure 7.2

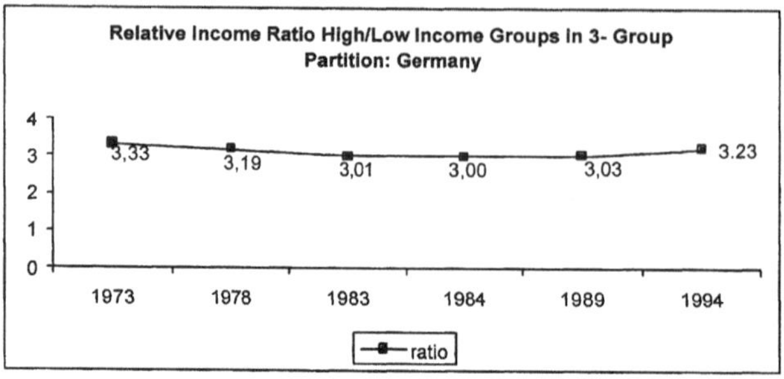

Figure 7.3

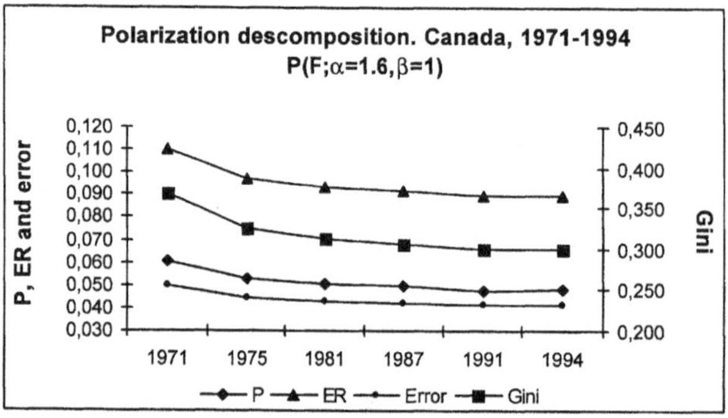

Figure 8.1

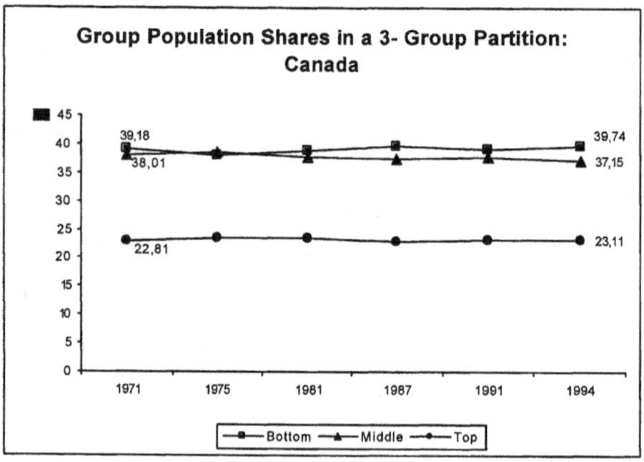

Figure 8.2

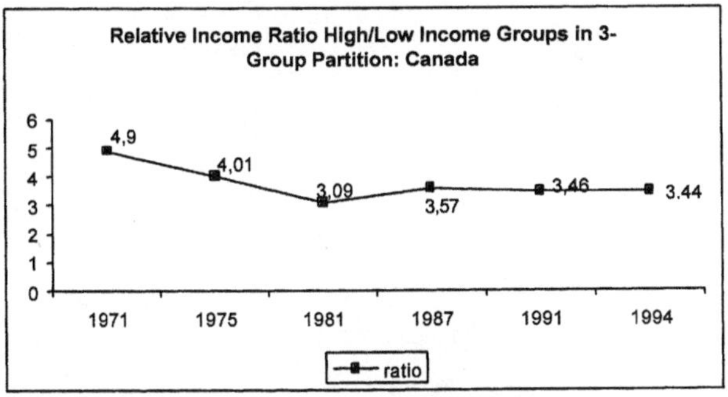
Relative Income Ratio High/Low Income Groups in 3-Group Partition: Canada
6
5
4
3
2
1
0
4,9
4,01
3,09
3,57
3,46
3.44
1971
1975
1981
1987
1991
1994
ratio

Figure 8.3

METHODOLOGICAL FOUNDATIONS OF COMPARATIVE ANALYSIS IN ECONOMICS: THE VIEW OF CRITICAL REALISM

Eugenia Perona[a]

1. Introduction

The methodology of economics is an area of research that has traditionally received little attention. However, in the last twenty years or so, this situation has been changing. Nowadays there are a few specialised journals and groups of scholars who work actively to produce interesting methodological research on various fields within economics.

One of those contributors is Tony Lawson, whose pioneering work on Critical Realism and Economics is today well known by methodologists all over the world. His last book, *Reorienting Economics* (2003), was received with great expectations by the relevant community and a few months after being published it has already become a classic.

My objective in this brief essay is to show how methodology and, in particular, the approach systematised as Critical Realism, can help us to make the case for comparative analysis. I believe this is important because it seems to me that comparative research in economics has usually proceeded in a pretty much *ad-hoc* fashion.

In effect, it is quite common to find that syllabuses of courses focusing on comparative economic studies do not devote any time to discussing the methodological foundations of comparisons as a method of research. The same is true in the case of specialised journals, like the *Journal of Comparative Economics* or the new *European Journal of Comparative Economics*: they usually do not address the issue of comparisons explicitly, in an editorial note or otherwise. In other words, whilst those courses and journals encourage comparative research, they do not make sufficiently clear: a) what a comparison is and/or involves, b) how it relates to alternative research methodologies, c) what sort of phenomena are better dealt with using comparative analysis, and d) what are the advantages and limitations of comparative studies.

I find that such an omission is rather unfortunate. Had the methodological underpinnings of comparative research in economics been explicitly pointed out, the case for making comparisons would be more sound and powerful than it presently is.

In the following pages I shall attempt to start filling this gap. First I will devote some time to explain how methodology can make the difference, i.e. how it can help us to understand reality and to carry out research in economics. Second, I will briefly examine the view of Critical Realism on the nature of economic reality as well as its criticism of traditional (mathematical-deductive) methods when applied to the social realm. Third, I shall discuss the defense that Critical Realism makes of comparative analysis, as an alternative and perhaps more relevant research methodology for economics and the social sciences. The last section concludes with a few reflections on the methodology of comparative research.

[a] Department of Economics, University of Cordoba, Argentina (*eperona@eco.unc.edu.ar*).

2. What is methodology and how can it help us?

There are two accepted definitions of 'methodology of economics' (Lawson 1994). The first one states that methodology is the study of specific techniques or methods of research in economics. The second one – the one that concerns us here – is more comprehensive and essentially views methodology as philosophy of science applied to economics. According to the latter, in addition to dealing with particular methods of research, the methodology of economics is also concerned with *ontology* (i.e. the nature of economic phenomena) and *epistemology* (i.e. the question of theories, models, and different ways of understanding economic phenomena). Figure 1 summarises the main categories associated with methodological analysis from the point of view of the second definition.

Figure 1

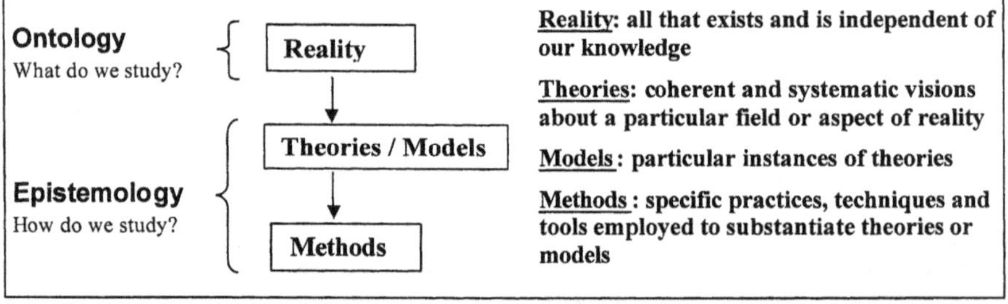

By investigating the philosophical foundations of sciences, methodology stands above the theoretical level (that is, it takes place at a higher level of abstraction than that of theory), in the same way that the theoretical level stands above the applied or empirical level. Thus methodological research provides us with a powerful tool which we can use to assess the validity and relative strength of various theories, models and methods within a discipline.

Nevertheless the attitude of most economists towards methodological reasoning has always been of indifference when not of open hostility. Frank Hahn, for instance, is famous for his advice to "ignore cries of 'economics in crisis'... avoid discussion of 'mathematics in economics' like the plague, and... give no thought at all to 'methodology'" (1992, p.5). More recently, Partha Dasgupta has also expressed his opposition to methodology in the following terms:

> Most economists I know have little time for the philosophy of economics as an intellectual discipline. They have even less patience with economic methodology. They prefer instead *to do* economics.... Some have told me I waste my time worrying about... [some criticisms coming from the methodology of economics]. But worry I do... [because] cumulative criticism can erode the confidence the lay public should have that such a large enterprise as modern, and largely academic, economics does have..." (2002, p.57-59).

As I and others have argued elsewhere (see e.g. Lawson 1992, Backhouse 1997, Perona 2005b), most (if not all) the arguments raised against methodology are not sound. Perhaps the main reason explaining why so many economists have followed Hahn's suggestion of "giving no thought at all to methodology" has been a generalised and persistent, though not always recognised, commitment to defending the current (positivist) methodological position in which modern economics is rooted.

Methodology, however, can be positively defended on several grounds and it is today a fast-growing field of study within economics[96]. First and most important, is the fact that the adoption of a methodological position is unavoidable. This is the main contention of Backhouse who, in his reply to Hahn, writes:

> The most powerful answer to Hahn... is to point out that even economists who, like him, deprecate methodology, are continually making methodological statements. Methodology is unavoidable, and should be made explicit so that it can become the subject of rational discussion (1992, p.4).

Second, since methodology can be regarded as the 'theory of theories', it can help us to understand where we stand, pointing out problematic areas in our theories and/or methods and in many cases telling us how to proceed. In particular, methodology deals with the *connections* between the various categories shown in Figure 1, i.e. the connections between phenomena of a certain type, and the theories and methods used to explain them.

In short, methodology can help us to answer the questions: a) which methods are appropriate or relevant to analyse a given economic problem?, or b) what sort of reality does method 'X' presuppose? As I shall discuss below, this property of methodological thinking is crucial to examine the nature and scope of comparative analysis. For only from a methodological point of view can we pose the question: why is comparative research particularly suitable for carrying out research in the social realm, or at least certainly more suitable than other (alternative) methods?

3. Critical Realism and its criticism of traditional research methodologies

The sort of methodological argument or line of reasoning posited above has been systematically defended and practised by supporters of Critical Realism in economics. Critical Realism uses a 'trascendental' argument, asking what reality should be like for science to be possible (Lawson 2003). To put it differently, it inquires into the nature of economic phenomena as well as the sort of reality presupposed by economic methods.

It is not my intention here to discuss the position of Critical Realism in detail. I would like, however, to focus on one of its most important remarks, namely the conclusion that *modern economics is characterised by a sharp inconsistency between methods and reality* (ibid.; see especially Ch.1). In other words, the sort of methods traditionally employed in economics – i.e. mathematical-deductive modelling, including econometric modelling – entail the presupposition that economic phenomena are of a certain kind, which is in fact at odds with the way economic phenomena *really* are. It is because of this mismatch between models and reality (and the repeated failure to see such an inconsistency as a problem), that traditional methods have often failed and economics as a discipline is now said to be in 'crisis'. Let me elaborate.

Essentially, mathematical models presuppose a reality of 'closed' systems, i.e. systems characterised by the injunction 'whenever x, then y' (ibid., p.5). Closed systems are deterministic systems where endogenous sources of novelty do not play any role. In addition,

[96] Two recent periodicals specialising in methodological discussions are the *Journal of Economic Methodology*, and the online *Post-Autistic Economics Review* (www.paecon.net).

by positing an additive relationship between the 'micro' and 'macro' levels of a system, mathematical-deductive models in economics are reductionist, presupposing a reality that is non-structured. Finally, such models rely on a restrictive conception of dynamics, thus implicitly assuming that reality is both reversible and ahistorical.

Economic reality – that is, economic facts, phenomena and problems – is very different though. New products, methods of production, financial instruments and the like, are created every day, suggesting that novelty and human creativity are vital engines of change. Emergence of new institutions, societal spirits, irrational individual choices, rule-breaking behaviour, unexpected earthquakes, are also common currency. All this comes down to the conclusion that economic (and social) reality is indeterministic in a fundamental way. The human mind on the one hand, and the environment in which societies are embedded on the other, give rise to a reality that is inherently *open* and therefore cannot be adequately and/or fully captured by *closed* system methodologies.

In the same fashion, economic phenomena and actors are structured: macro levels have their own ways and properties that are dependent upon, but not reducible to, those of micro levels. The economy is continually transformed and renovated by the acts of human agents, which are in turn shaped and conditioned by macro outcomes. Additionally, economic reality is clearly historical and irreversible, in a way that is not sufficiently taken into account by traditional models.

To sum up, Critical Realism is highly critical of the (methodologically unsound) insistence by economists on the use of mathematical methods and models which are in many cases just *not appropriate* for dealing with the sort of reality economic phenomena presuppose, namely a reality of open, structured, and historically dynamic systems. Nevertheless critical realists are always careful to point out that they do not oppose mathematical modelling *per se*:

> In this I do not suggest that formalistic methods be excluded for the methodological options on offer. But I do insist that methods of mathematical-deductivist reasoning (like any other tools) have limits to their usefulness, and that this be recognized and respected. However, I see this as a pro-, rather than an anti-, mathematics position (Lawson 2004, p.339).

The criticism to formal modelling raised by Critical Realism has also been contested by other methodologists and heterodox economists sustaining a more conciliatory attitude. In a number of responses to Lawson's recent book (2003), several commentators suggest that there are potentially useful applications for mathematical models in economics. Hodgson (2004), for instance, believes that mathematical models are not problematic by themselves. In his opinion, the real problem is the insufficient development of adequate 'interpretative contexts' (i.e. links between models and the objects they represent), due to the fact that most economists tend to prioritise technique over substance. In addition, Hodgson mentions heuristics and internal critiques as likely good uses for mathematical models. In the same vein, Van Staveren (2004) and Caldwell (2004) regard econometrics as an important tool for exploratory (though not explanatory) research.

If we side with Critical Realism and accept that formal modelling might not be an appropriate method for dealing with many economic issues, then it is a legitimate question to ask what sort of tools or instruments would be apt for understanding systems that are open, structured and inherently dynamic. In contrast to traditional economics whose main concern is with method, the main concern of Critical Realism is with *ontology* i.e. with the nature of economic phenomena. It is only after having elaborated and defended a particular ontological position, that critical realists move on to the epistemological level to discuss feasible research strategies.

In other words, whilst mainstream economics focuses on method – thereby conditioning the sort of theories and models they work with and presupposing a reality of a certain type (illustrated by the bottom-up arrow in Figure 2) – Critical Realism proceeds the other way round: it begins with a discussion about the nature of reality underlying economic phenomena, and then goes on to offer some general guidelines on theorising and method (top-down arrow in Figure 2).

Figure 2

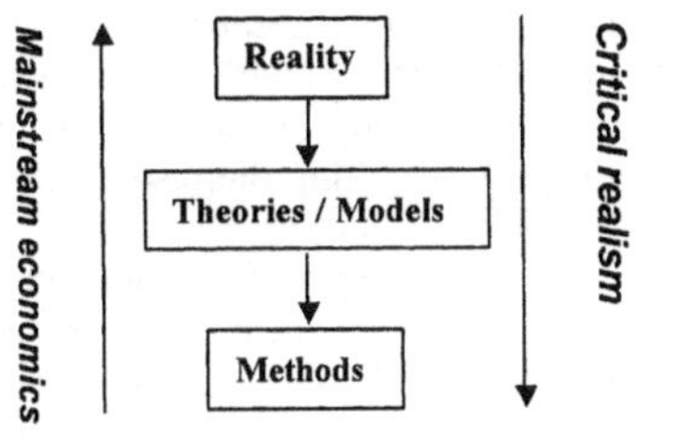

4. A (methodological) defense of comparative analysis

So what sort of methods does Critical Realism support? Following its central thesis about the open nature of economic reality – i.e. a world where innovation, creativity, random mutations in the environment, and human free will play a central role – it is apparent that scientific explanation cannot be carried out by means of controlled experiments. Therefore economics (and social science in general) faces a serious disadvantage relative to the natural sciences. In particular, Lawson (2003, p.81) points out three fundamental problems or aspects that social science needs to address:

1.- How or where is research to be initiated?
2.- Provided research could be initiated, how is it possible to identify causal explanations in the social realm, given that social phenomena are often determined by a multiplicity of (transient) variables and mechanisms?
3.- Even if plausible explanatory arguments could be identified, how can we choose among competing hypotheses?

In answering these questions, Critical Realism puts forward an interesting methodological device: comparative analysis or, to use the critical realist terminology, 'contrastive explanations' (ibid.; see Ch.4). Science is, in effect, inherently comparative. An experiment poses a comparison between two situations: pre- and post-experiment. An exercise in theorising can be seen as a comparison between an object of study and the abstract model or idea created to represent it. In a similar fashion, an empirical study may involve a comparison between the performance of a model in an idealised situation and its performance when applied to the actual economy. And so on and so forth.

In which sense is it then comparative research particularly suitable for studying social phenomena? In short, the answer is that comparative analysis allows the social scientist to cope with the three questions or problematic aspects mentioned above.

First, it is usually a contrast (or a comparison) between an observed situation and our prior expectations, that marks the beginning of an explanatory project. In other words, research is usually initiated when we are struck by an event that is substantially different from what we would have expected. For example, why has a certain region within a country performed systematically better than other regions with similar characteristics? Why do individuals belonging to certain social groups buy goods of similar quality but higher prices, when this is at odds with rational economic behaviour? It is thus a so-called 'surprising contrast' that triggers research in economics (and social science), and in this sense it is not very different from experimental research in the natural sciences. The main difference is that whilst the former is backward-looking, i.e. the social researcher *observes a contrasting result* and endeavours to find plausible explanations or mechanisms responsible for such an outcome, the latter is forward-looking, i.e. the natural researcher *designs the contrast* knowing the mechanism that is in operation (and under her control) but ignoring the result following her intervention (Lawson 2003, p.90).

Second, once a research project is initiated, contrastive explanation facilitates the identification of mechanisms or causes explaining those phenomena of interest. If a researcher can come up with a relevant and interesting comparative framework, then it is likely that she will have a hint on which factors or forces may be in operation. However, as Lawson points out, the process of finding causal hypotheses often follows "a logic of analogy and/or metaphor, and rest usually upon ingenuity as well as luck" (ibid., p.80). The capacity of making good comparisons together with the scientist's background and experience are of great importance in determining the outcome and direction of research in the social sciences.

Third, if there are two or more competing explanations, then comparative analysis will also help to choose among them. According to Lawson (ibid., p.97), the selection will be based on relative explanatory power, meaning that those hypotheses which are capable of accounting for a wider range of facts or a larger number of cases will be (provisionally) accepted as better explanations.

To sum up, Critical Realism offers a coherent and persuasive defense of comparative research as a legitimate method of analysis for the social sciences. Such a conclusion follows not from a blind acceptance of contrastive explanation *per se*, but from an ontological inquiry into the nature of social (and hence economic) objects and phenomena. To put it differently, given the nature of social reality, contrastive explanation seems to be an appropriate instrument for analysing it. Choice of methods is based on the nature and type of problems we intend to study, and not the other way round.

5. Further research on the methodology of comparative analysis

In the previous section I have reviewed the position of Critical Realism and its defense of comparative analysis on methodological (and more specifically, ontological) grounds. In brief, Critical Realism asserts that: i) economic facts, objects, relations and problems are social phenomena and as such, are characterised by an *open system* nature; ii) on the contrary mathematical models, i.e. the traditional sort of model employed in economics, presuppose a reality of *closed systems*; iii) therefore there is a sharp inconsistency or contradiction between models and methods employed by economists on the one hand, and the nature of the objects they intend to describe on the other. Moreover, given the (open) nature of economic systems, iv) contrastive explanation (comparative thinking) stands out as a particularly suitable and potentially fruitful research methodology for the social sciences.

In consequence, Critical Realism makes an important contribution to the epistemology of economics which should be taken into account (or at least not ignored) by supporters of comparative analysis. As I mentioned in the introduction to this note, comparative studies often lack appropriate methodological grounding, e.g. there is often no explicit justification as to why comparative reasoning is a relevant method of research, and/or which elements are (should be) involved in making comparisons. Thus the critical realist position provides an interesting point of departure for investigating the extent to which comparisons could be used to examine economic issues.

However, Critical Realism is far too general in its defense of contrastive explanations as a method of research[97]. First, it shows little elaboration with respect to the details of carrying out contrastive explanation in practice. There is no discussion, for instance, about how to find relevant contrast spaces, or the number of comparisons needed to make inferences. Second and most important, it only focuses on *one* of the functions of comparative analysis, namely *causal explanation*. Comparisons have other important functions though, including classification and policy selection (Perona 2005a).

Hence Critical Realism offers an interesting point of departure and serves as a general guideline for pursuing comparative research in economics. There is, however, much scope for further research and I believe it is at this point that comparatists can positively contribute to the discussion. In other words, I am convinced that economists working on comparative studies can benefit a lot from hearing what methodologists, and especially, critical realists, have to say on comparative methods. At the same time, comparatists can use their expertise and pragmatic knowledge (i.e. know-how) of comparisons, to enhance the defense that Critical Realism makes of contrastive explanation in a more substantive direction. In this way the arguments for defending comparative analysis in economics may become more sound and better grounded than they currently are. As Lawson concludes, the most important thing, after all, is "to be successful in our social-explanatory endeavours" (2001, p.390).

[97] This is acknowledged by Lawson, who is aware that his main objective is methodological elaboration at a general or more abstract level. For instance, in his chapter 4 of *Reorienting Economics* the author affirms: "In the current chapter I have sought to draw out and systematise those matters I think will often be central to the process of explanatory endeavour in open systems... [nevertheless] the concrete details will doubtless be significantly dependent on the context of explanatory study" (2003, p.108-9).

References

Backhouse, R. E. (1992), Should we ignore methodology? In: *Royal Economic Society Newsletter* July, 4-5. Reproduced in the paper for the *Workshop on Realism and Economics*, Univ. of Cambridge, 4th Jan 2002.

Backhouse, R. E. (1997), *Truth and progress in economic knowledge*. Edward Elgar, Cheltenham.

Caldwell, B. (2004), Some comments on Lawson's Reorienting Economics: same facts, different conclusions, in: *Post-Autistic Econ Review* 28, article 3. (http://www.btinternet.com/~pae_news/review/issue28.htm).

Dasgupta, P. (2002), Modern economics and its critics. In: *Fact and fiction in economics*, Uskali Maki (eds.), 2002. Cambridge University Press, Cambridge.

Hahn, F. (1992), Reflections, in: *Royal Economic Society Newsletter* April, p.5. Reproduced in the paper for the *Workshop on Realism and Economics*, University of Cambridge, 4th Jan 2002.

Hodgsonm, G. C. (2004), On the Problem of Formalism in Economics, in: *Post-Autistic Economics Review* 28, article 1. (http://www.btinternet.com/~pae_news/review/issue28.htm).

Lawson, T. (1992), Methodology: non-optional and consequential, in: *Royal Economic Society Newsletter* October, 2-3. Reproduced in the paper for the *Workshop on Realism and Economics*, University of Cambridge, 4th Jan 2002.

Lawson, T. (1994), Methodology in economics. In: *The Elgar Companion to Radical Political Economy*, Arestis, P. and Sawyer, M. (eds.), Edward Elgar Publishing, Aldershot and Brookfield.

Lawson, T. (2001), Economics and explanation, in: *Revue Internationale de Philosophie* 217(3), 371-393.

Lawson, T. (2003), *Reorienting economics*. Routledge, London and New York.

Lawson, T. (2004), Reorienting Economics: On heterodox economics, themata and the use of mathematics in economics, in: *Journal of Economic Methodology* 11(3), 329–40.

Perona, E. (2005a), The comparative method: its applications to economics, in: *XI Jornadas de Epistemología de las Ciencias Económicas*, University of Buenos Aires, 6-7 October.

Perona, E. (2005b), Why is it important and what should be taught in a course on methodology? In: *Round table on Methodology of Economics, XL Reunión de la Asoc. Arg. Econ. Política (AAEP)*, University of La Plata.

Van Staveren, I. (2004), Feminism and realism - A contested relationship, in: *Post-Autistic Economics Review* 28, article 2. (http://www.btinternet.com/~pae_news/review/issue28.htm).

The role of information technology in the globalized world

E - GOVERNMENT INFRASTRUCTURES – A COMPARATIVE ANALYSIS

Alexander Elsas
Institute for Information Systems,
Johann Wolfgang Goethe-University Frankfurt,
Germany

elsas@wiwi.uni-frankfurt.de

1. E-Government

The overwhelming success of the Internet technology as the foundation for e-commerce and e-business applications has caused considerable pressure on the public sector to modernize administrative processes and implement interaction with the citizens via the World Wide Web (Ndou, 2004, p. 2).

The so-called e-government applications range from information-offering static web sites to sophisticated transaction-oriented applications, supporting the administrative processes and interaction with the citizens. The degree of sophistication of those applications can be categorized in four levels:

1. Static web sites providing information.
2. Web sites with interaction.
3. Support of internal and external workflows of the administration.
4. Integration with other e-government or even e-commerce applications.

According to the *United Nations Online Network in Public Administration and Finance* (UNPAN) another classification of the state of development of e-government is (UNPAN, 2001, 2003, p. 2, p. 13):

1. **Emerging:** A government web presence is established through a few independent official sites. Information is limited, basic and static.
2. **Enhanced:** Content and information is updated with greater regularity.
3. **Interactive:** Users can download forms, contact officials, and make appointments and requests.
4. **Transactional:** Users can actually pay for services or conduct financial transactions online.
5. **Seamless / Networked:** Total integration of e-functions and services across administrative and departmental boundaries.

The dimensions of e-government can be described by categorizing the involved partners:

- **Government-to-government (G2G) or administration-to-administration (A2A)**: relating to internal processes of the administration.

- **Government-to-business (G2B) or administration-to-business (A2B):** interactions between governmental organizations and commercial or business organisations are possible, e.g. to pay taxes.
- **Government-to-citizen (G2C) or administration-to-citizen (A2C):** interactions between governmental organisations and citizens, e.g. to register vehicles or to organize marriages.

Most countries are engaged in various e-government projects on different levels of administration and sophistication. The reasons for the implementation of e-government applications are based on efficiency and cost developments. Most projects make use of proprietary, often self-developed, standards for communication and interaction. The problem is a lack of coordination and joint efforts between the different projects, which might lead to incompatibilities and integration or coordination problems.

An important prerequisite for the implementation of e-government applications is the existence of an appropriate infrastructure. This infrastructure as viewed here consists of three parts:

1. Telecommunication (T): An appropriate telecommunications infrastructure is the *condition sine qua non* for establishing a successful e-government. Factors like availability of PC, internet connectivity via telephone or broadband connections, the internet infrastructure with servers, and especially the associated costs are relevant.
2. Communication between distributed applications (C): The development of e-government typically begins with isolated, non-compatible task-specific applications (e.g. taxes, car registration, etc). Data compatibility and information exchange between those applications has to be implemented.
3. Composition of distributed applications into a workflow system to support the processes (P): To reach the state of seamless or networked e-government it is necessary to support the entire processes from within the administration to the interface to the citizen.

Figure 1 gives a graphical overview over these 3 levels of infrastructure and associated technologies and protocols.

The second part of this paper discusses the differences in telecommunication infrastructures and degree of development of e-government between South America and Europe. Within the focus and restrictions of this paper, the communication and composition levels of infrastructure can not be detailed. A suitable solution is the *Web services framework*, which allows for the communication and composition of distributed applications (Elsas, 2004).

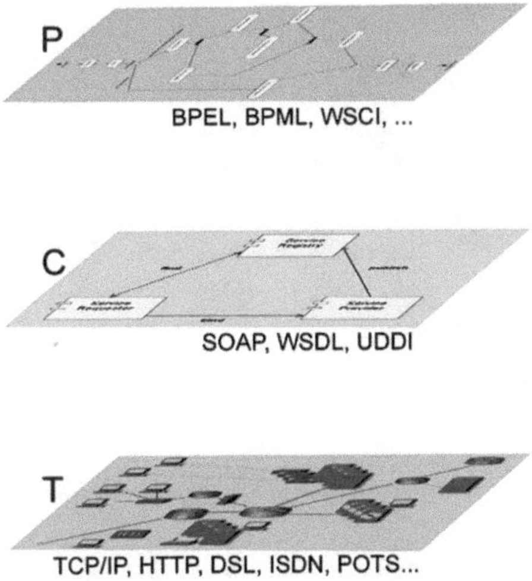

Figure 1: Infrastructure levels and technologies.

2. E-Government in South America and Europe

2.1. Brown University Studies

The *Center for Public Policy* of Brown University (Providence, Rhode Island, USA) conducts regular surveys with the objective to assess the state of development of e-government by analyzing the respective web sites.

The surveys evaluate websites for "the presence of various features dealing with information availability, service delivery, and public access." (West, 2005). For the overall ranking a 0 to 100 point index is created and applied to every website, the average for every nation is computed as percentages. The aggregated values for the different regions are calculated then. Table 1 shows these percentages (%) and the overall ranking (#).[99]

[99] For details cf. (West, 2005).

Table 1: Regional results according to Brown University.

Region	2001		2002		2003		2004		2005	
	%	#	%	#	%	#	%	#	%	#
North America	51,0	1	60,4	1	40,2	1	39,2	1	47,3	1
Asia	34,0	3	48,7	2	34,3	2	31,6	2	37,3	2
Western Europe	34,1	2	47,6	3	33,1	3	30,0	3	29,6	3
Pacific Ocean Islands	30,6	7	39,5	8	32,1	5	29,9	4	27,9	4
Middle East	31,1	4	43,2	5	32,1	4	28,1	5	27,4	5
Eastern Europe	--		43,5	4	32,0	6	28,0	6	27,1	6
South America	30,7	6	42,0	6	29,5	8	24,3	8	25,9	7
Russia/Central Asia	30,9	5	37,2	9	29,7	7	25,3	7	25,0	8
Central America	27,7	8	41,4	7	28,6	9	24,1	9	24,1	9
Africa	23,5	9	36,8	10	27,6	10	22,0	10	22,0	10

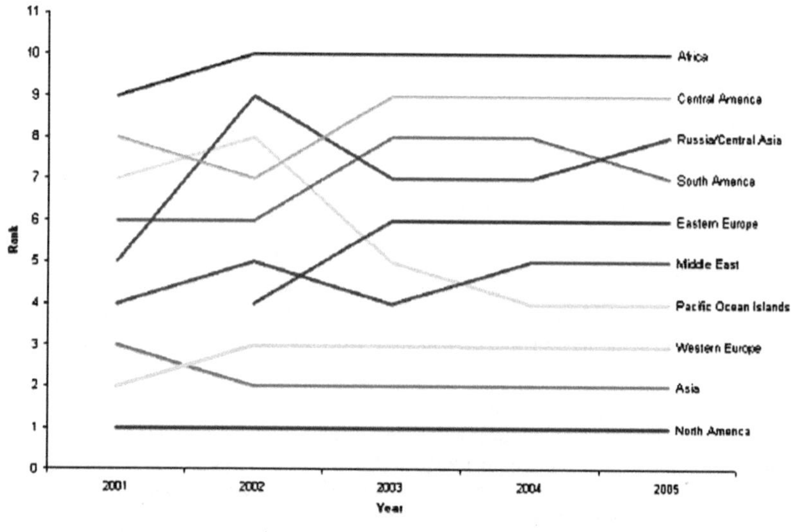

Figure 2: Regional development according to Brown University.

Table 1 and Figure 2 summarize the findings for the regions of the world since 2001 (West, 2001, 2002, 2003, 2004, 2005): the global leadership of *North America* has been unchallenged for all the surveys, *South America* made an improvement in 2005. The Brown University surveys have been criticized for their methodology (Di Maio and Kreizman, 2001). An important point of this criticism, not to take into account the availability and actual use of the IT and communication infrastructure, is addressed in the UNPAN studies.

2.2. UNPAN Studies

The UNPAN surveys since 2001 rank countries and regions with an index and use a more complex methodology than Brown University (UNPAN, 2003, 2004). In addition to measure the degree of sophistication of web sites (the *Web Measure Index*, WMI) UNPAN calculates a *Telecommunication Index* (TI) and a *Human Capital Index* (HCI). As a weighted average of these 3 indices the *E-Government Readiness Index* (EGRI) is calculated for the individual countries and regions of the world.[100] The surveys add another index in addition to the EGRI, the *E-Participation Index* (EPI). It's a qualitative assessment of the degree of participation in public policy making, it "assesses the quality, usefulness and relevancy of the information and services and the willingness of countries to engage citizens in public policy making through the use of the e-government programs." (UNPAN, 2004, p. 18). Within the focus of this paper it is omitted here. Table 2 shows the results for the regions of the world in 2003 and 2004. The grey cells represent the regions below the world average.

The significant better ranking for South America in comparison to the Brown University surveys is evident.

Table 2: EGRI in 2003 and 2004 for the regions of the world.

Region	RID	2003 WMI	2003 TI	2003 HCI	2003 EGRI	2003 #	2004 WMI	2004 TI	2004 HCI	2004 EGRI	2004 #
North America	NA	0.8820	0.7380	0.9800	0.8665	1	0.9365	0.7190	0.9700	0.8750	1
Europe	EU	0.4180	0.4215	0.8345	0.5580	2	0.5044	0.4159	0.8395	0.5867	2
South East Asia	SEA	0.3545	0.1969	0.7580	0.4365	4	0.4050	0.2057	0.7700	0.4603	3
South Central America	SCAM	0.3793	0.1232	0.8226	0.4417	3	0.4056	0.1214	0.8405	0.4558	4
Caribbean	C	0.1915	0.1676	0.8445	0.4011	6	0.1923	0.1787	0.8608	0.4107	5
West Asia	WA	0.2410	0.2039	0.7844	0.4098	5	0.2451	0.1846	0.7982	0.4092	6
South Central Asia	SCAS	0.1953	0.0347	0.6458	0.2918	8	0.2554	0.0362	0.6723	0.3214	7
Oceania	O	0.2169	0.1378	0.5817	0.3122	7	0.2342	0.1401	0.5275	0.3007	8
Africa	A	0.1369	0.0365	0.5650	0.2461	9	0.1450	0.0360	0.5776	0.2528	9
World					0.3997					0.4127	

Compared with the original version in the study of 2003, the different results in this paper for the region of *Oceania*[101] are noteworthy (UNPAN, 2003, p. 37, 67, 98): $EGRI_{2003}$ for the country of *Micronesia* is wrongly given as 0.52, resulting from an obvious wrong value of 1.422 for the HCI_{2003}. HCI_{2003} for *Micronesia* has been corrected to 0.04 within the research for this paper - this is consistent with the HCI_{2004} of 0 for *Micronesia*. This correction results in less regions under the corrected world average of 0.3997 vs. 0.4020 (calculated on the basis of the individual countries) in 2003.

UNPAN finds positive correlation coefficients between the key access indicators (represented as TI) and the EGRI.

[100] All indices are noted as $INDEX_{year}$ (e.g. $EGRI_{2004}$ for EGRI in 2004) if necessary.
[101] $EGRI_{2003}$=0.3510 for *Micronesia* in the original study.

Table 3 shows those coefficients for 2003 and 2004. The light grey lower half of the matrix represents the correlations for 2003, the dark grey upper half the correlations for 2004.

Table 3: Correlation coefficients in 2003 and 2004.

2004 / 2003	WMI	TI	HCI	EGRI
WMI	1.000000	0.749628	0.548479	0.898745
TI	0.710141	1.000000	0.440498	0.836352
HCI	0.506342	0.451304	1.000000	0.807065
EGRI	0.866388	0.839266	0.808236	1.000000

As can be seen from the table the correlation coefficient TI - WMI is high, indicating a strong relation between the telecommunication infrastructure and the quality of the web sites. The weaker coefficient HCI - WMI could be resulting "perhaps because it is not the total educational level but the technology related skills which are of greater importance in the educational content." (UNPAN, 2004, p. 94).

Figure 3 gives a graphic representation of the correlations TI - EGRI and HCI - EGRI in 2004. It is noteworthy that in the original UNPAN publication the captions of the axes have been mixed up (UNPAN, 2004, p. 94).

The conclusion can be drawn, that generally a country's website development is positively linked to the key access indicators, represented by TI. This leads to a *Global Access Divide*, as the poorer regions suffer from the underdevelopment of their communications infrastructure.

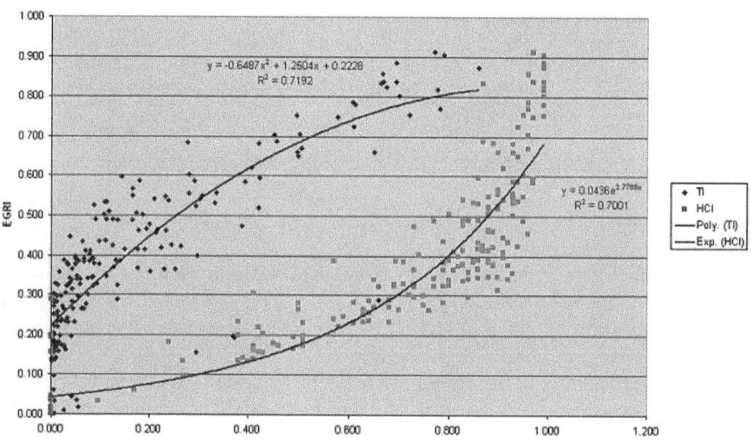

Figure 3: Correlations TI - EGRI and HCI – EGRI.

Table 4 and Figure 4 show this Global Access Divide in 2004.

Table 4: Global Access Divide in 2004 (RID = Region ID).

Region	RID	TI	EGRI	TI / EGRI
North America	NA	0.7190	0.8750	0.82
Europe	EU	0.4159	0.5867	0.71
South East Asia	SEA	0.2057	0.4603	0.45
South Central America	SCAM	0.1214	0.4558	0.27
Caribbean	C	0.1787	0.4107	0.44
West Asia	WA	0.1846	0.4092	0.45
South Central Asia	SCAS	0.0362	0.3214	0.11
Oceania	O	0.1401	0.3007	0.47
Africa	A	0.0360	0.2528	0.14

This divide can be interpreted in two ways:

- Regions with a good infrastructure (e.g. NA, EU) benefit for their e-government from their well developed infrastructure.
- But even regions with a not so well developed infrastructure (e.g. SCAM, SEA) show good relative results. Table 4 calculates the ratio TI / EGRI: within the above average regions in the world, South Central America leads with a ratio of 0.27 (= 1/3.75) for 2004.

The regional results are now broken down to selected countries within South America, Europe and for comparison the global leader USA. The focus is the Telecommunication Index TI, as the previous results suggest a strong correlation between TI and EGRI.

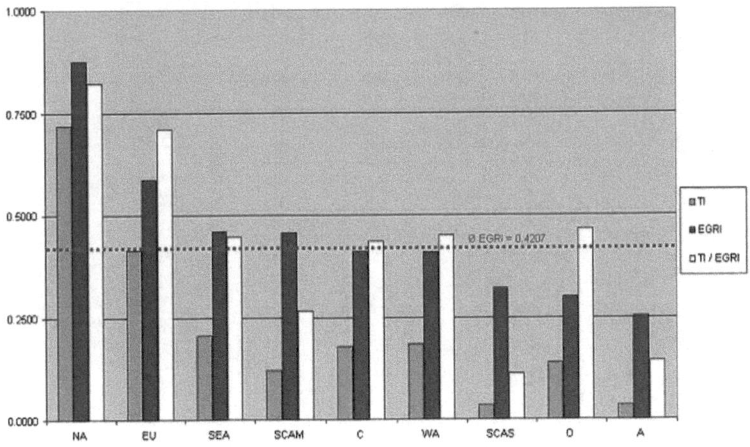

Figure 4: Global Access Divide.

Table 5 therefore shows the components of the telecommunication infrastructure in 2003 (UNPAN, 2003; Worldbank, 2004), Figure 5 and 6 give a graphic representation of Table 5.

Table 5: Telecommunication components and Internet costs

Country	ISO		PC	Internet	Online	Telephone	Mobile	TV	Internet Costs	Internet Costs
		Year	2002	2002	2002	2002	2002	2000	2003	2003
		Unit	/1000	/1000	/1000	/1000	/1000	/1000	$	% GNI per capita
Argentina	AR		82.0	112.0	103.8	218.8	177.6	293	13	3.9
Brazil	BR		74.8	82.2	68.4	223.2	200.6	343	28	11.8
Chile	CL		119.3	201.4	200.2	230.4	428.3	242	22	6.1
Mexico	MX		68.7	45.8	33.8	146.7	254.5	283	23	4.6
USA	US		625.0	537.5	597.5	658.9	488.1	854	15	0.5
France	FR		347.1	313.832	262.8	568.9	647	628	14	0.8
Germany	DE		434.9	423.729	344.9	650.4	716.7	586	14	0.7
Spain	ES		168.2	193.103	184.3	459.8	822.8	368	21	1.7
UK	UK		366.2	406.174	553.2	587.4	844.9	661	24	1.1
Slovenia	SI		300.6	400.802	311.3	406.5	835.2	368	25	3.1
Ukraine	UA		18.3	11.929	15.4	212.1	44.2	456	17	26.0

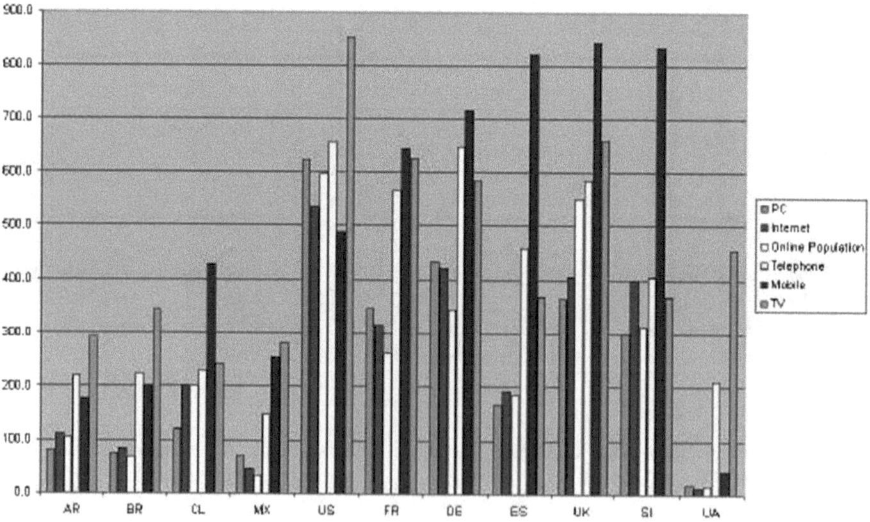

Figure 5: Telecommunication components

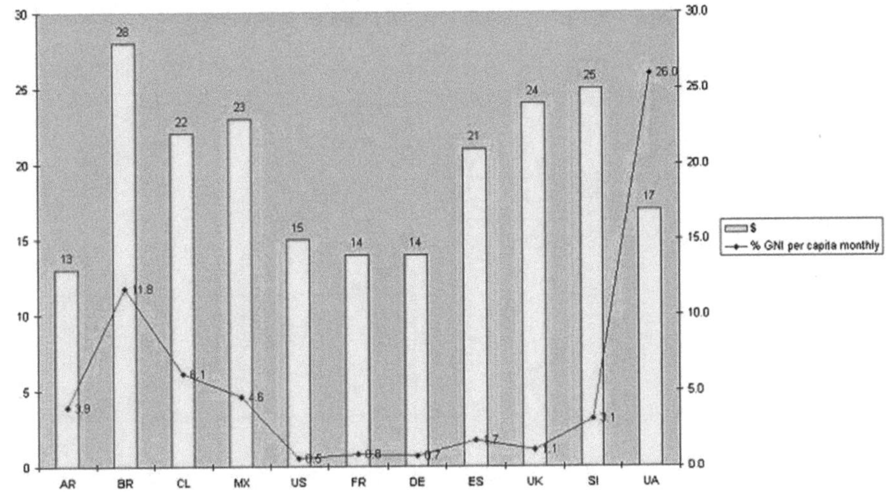

Figure 6: Telecommunication costs

Table 6 shows WMI, TI, HCI, EGRI, TI / EGRI, and rankings for the selected countries in 2003 and 2004.

Table 6: Indices in 2003 and 2004 for selected countries.

		WMI				TI				HCI		EGRI				TI / EGRI	
Country	ISO	2003		2004		2003		2004		2003	2004	2003		2004		2003	2004
			Rank		Rank		Rank		Rank				Rank		Rank		
Argentina	AR	0.624	15	0.643	22	0.187	63	0.179	62	0.92	0.94	0.577	31	0.5871	32	0.32	0.30
Brazil	BR	0.576	21	0.637	24	0.174	66	0.165	67	0.83	0.90	0.527	41	0.5675	35	0.33	0.29
Chile	CL	0.838	2	0.884	6	0.275	44	0.276	45	0.90	0.89	0.671	22	0.6835	22	0.41	0.40
Mexico	MX	0.808	4	0.784	11	0.132	72	0.143	71	0.84	0.86	0.593	30	0.5957	30	0.22	0.24
USA	US	1.000	1	1.000	1	0.801	3	0.770	5	0.98	0.97	0.927	1	0.9132	1	0.86	0.84
France	FR	0.570	22	0.541	36	0.529	20	0.505	20	0.97	0.96	0.690	19	0.6687	24	0.77	0.76
Germany	DE	0.683	11	0.795	10	0.632	16	0.607	18	0.97	0.96	0.762	9	0.7873	12	0.83	0.77
Spain	ES	0.428	41	0.390	60	0.409	32	0.393	31	0.97	0.97	0.602	29	0.5844	34	0.68	0.67
UK	UK	0.777	5	0.973	2	0.675	10	0.693	8	0.99	0.99	0.814	5	0.8852	3	0.83	0.78
Slovenia	SI	0.441	39	0.514	44	0.513	23	0.498	22	0.94	0.94	0.631	28	0.6506	27	0.81	0.77
Ukraine	UA	0.349	56	0.556	32	0.116	83	0.112	81	0.92	0.93	0.462	54	0.5326	45	0.25	0.21

The left hand part of Table 7 shows the most significant winners and losers for all countries in 2003 and 2004, the right hand part of Table 7 shows the changes in ranking for the countries of South and Central America between 2003 and 2004, finally Table 8 presents the overall top 40 countries in 2003 and 2004.

Table 7: Worldwide winners and losers and South and Central America rankings.

	Country	Rank 2004	Rank 2003	Δ
1	Kyrgyzstan	66	111	45
2	**Venezuela**	56	93	37
3	Uzbekistan	81	115	34
4	Samoa	92	121	29
5	Mongolia	75	103	28
6	Bosnia and Herzegovina	93	118	25
7	Belarus	58	80	22
8	Swaziland	101	123	22
9	Pakistan	122	143	21
10	SierraLeone	161	180	19
1	Tajikistan	189	119	-70
2	Libya	187	125	-62
3	Zambia	191	132	-59
4	Nauru	178	126	-52
5	Equatorial Guinea	181	140	-41
6	**Paraguay**	109	74	-35
7	Oman	127	97	-30
8	Algeria	118	89	-29
9	United Arab Emirates	60	38	-22
10	Haiti	184	165	-19

	Country	Rank 2004	Rank 2003	Δ
1	Venezuela	56	93	37
2	Honduras	113	129	16
3	Colombia	44	56	12
4	Panama	54	61	7
5	Uruguay	40	46	6
	Brazil	35	41	6
7	Ecuador	82	84	2
8	Suriname	105	105	0
	El Salvador	79	79	0
	Guyana	71	71	0
	Mexico	30	30	0
	Chile	22	22	0
13	Peru	53	52	-1
	Guatemala	111	110	-1
	Argentina	32	31	-1
16	Belize	76	70	-6
17	Nicaragua	121	113	-8
	Costa Rica	73	65	-8
19	Bolivia	88	76	-12
20	Paraguay	109	74	-35

Venezuela is leading the progress in South and Central America and it is the country with the second largest step forward on a world wide basis. The reason for this progress can be seen in the implementation of the new national web portal (http://www.gobiernoenlinea.ve) and significant improvements of the online education services (http://www.me.gov.ve) (UNPAN, 2004, p. 36).

Table 8: Top 40 countries in 2003 and 2004 in EGRI.

	2003	2004		2003	2004		2003	2004		2003	2004
1	USA	USA	11	Netherlands	Netherlands	21	Austria	Malta	31	Argentina	Portugal
2	Sweden	Denmark	12	Singapore	Germany	22	Chile	Chile	32	Poland	Argentina
3	Australia	United Kingdom	13	Republic of Korea	New Zealand	23	Belgium	Israel	33	Philippines	Hungary
4	Denmark	Sweden	14	New Zealand	Iceland	24	Israel	France	34	Lithuania	Spain
5	United Kingdom	Republic of Korea	15	Iceland	Switzerland	25	Luxembourg	Italy	35	Bulgaria	Brazil
6	Canada	Australia	16	Estonia	Belgium	26	Portugal	Luxembourg	36	Czech Republic	Greece
7	Norway	Canada	17	Ireland	Austria	27	Malta	Slovenia	37	Greece	Slovakia
8	Switzerland	Singapore	18	Japan	Japan	28	Slovenia	Czech Republic	38	United Arab Emirates	Romania
9	Germany	Finland	19	France	Ireland	29	Spain	Poland	39	Croatia	Latvia
10	Finland	Norway	20	Italy	Estonia	30	Mexico	Mexico	40	Slovakia	Uruguay

2.3. Efficiency Model

A first step for research beyond the scope of the UNPAN studies, is to check for the overall consistency of the Brown University studies and the UNPAN studies. This can be achieved by calculating the correlation between the results of the different studies. The correlation between $EGRI_{2004}$ and BI_{2004} is 0.5860, between WMI_{2004} and BI_{2004} it is 0.5871, which supports the overall consistency of the different studies.

Calculating the correlations between EGRI and GDP and population (POP) leads to the results shown in Table 9.[101] To account for marginal decrease size effects the correlations between EGRI and the logarithmised values of POP (logPOP) and GDP (logGDP) have been calculated.

Table 9: Correlation with GDP and population.

2004	logGDP	logPOP	GDP/POP
EGRI	0.61563	0.24645	0.74702

There seems to be a strong correlation between the logGDP and the EGRI, which is plausible: richer countries can afford the investment into e-government.

The correlation between the grade of *economic freedom*[102] (econfreed) and EGRI is 0.7109: with more economic freedom (as a proxy for freedom in general) the demand for e-government rises.

These results can be used to formulate a first economic model regarding the efficiency aspects of e-government investments. The model uses a microeconomic approach.

A hypothesis regarding the relation of e-government development and general administration costs is, *that there should be a negative correlation between these two factors: a well developed state of e-government should save costs.*

To investigate this hypothesis further, an econometric OLS analysis with White standard errors[103] between:

- General government expenditures[104] (gov_exp), measured as percentage of total expenditures, therefore acting as a proxy for efficiency (required resources per output unit),
- the E-Government Readiness Index EGRI as an indicator for the development of e-government,
- logarithm of population (logpop) as a control variable for general heterogeneity and
- egecon as a measure of economic freedom, which is econfreed * EGRI, to measure the interaction effect between the two factors,

has been calculated for the world, South Central America and Europe.

Table 10 shows the global result, computed with Stata 7 (http://www.stata.com).

[101] For GDP and POP cf. (CIA, 2004).

[102] For economic freedom cf. (Gwartney and Lawson, 2004).

[103] White standard errors are robust against heteroscedasticity, cf. (Greene, 2003).

[104] For general government expenditures cf. (Gwartney and Lawson, 2004).

Table 10: OLS with White standard errors for the world.

Regression with robust standard errors

Number of obs =	119
F(4, 114) =	22.99
Prob > F =	0.0000
R-squared =	0.3645
Root MSE =	6.3175

gov_exp	Coef.	Robust Std. Err.	t	P>|t|	[95% Conf.	Interval]
egri	.4906931	.1580647	3.10	0.002	.1775682	.803818
logpop	-1.280557	.2991192	-4.28	0.000	-1.87311	-.6880045
econfreed	2.442755	2.061342	1.19	0.238	-1.640748	6.526258
egecon	-.046168	.0256707	-1.80	0.075	-.0970215	.0046856
_cons	16.73118	11.31483	1.48	0.142	-5.683422	39.14577

The result is contrary to the savings hypothesis: EGRI costs 0.491 for every unit of government expenditure (which reduces the efficiency of government), but this effect gets weaker with greater economic freedom (egecon = -0.046). This result seems not too surprising: all e-government activities or projects are still in their early stages and represent an investment into the future (they cost additional money), the payback is still in the future.

Table 11 shows the same analysis for Europe only, the result is the same. Due to the small number of samples within South Central America (n = 19), the result here (Table 12) does not have statistical significance, but points into the same direction.

Table 11: OLS for Europe.

Regression with robust standard errors

Number of obs =	33
F(4, 28) =	14.44
Prob > F =	0.0000
R-squared =	0.5716
Root MSE =	3.9267

gov_exp	Coef.	Robust Std. Err.	t	P>|t|	[95% Conf.	Interval]
egri	1.212328	.4538657	2.67	0.012	.2826265	2.14203
logpop	-.7824546	.5477758	-1.43	0.164	-1.904523	.3396132
econfreed	2.938199	4.141348	0.71	0.484	-5.544969	11.42137
egecon	-.1089352	.0637601	-1.71	0.099	-.2395419	.0216715
_cons	-11.94681	29.10344	-0.41	0.685	-71.56251	47.66889

Table 12: OLS for South Central America.

Regression with robust standard errors

Number of obs =	19
F(4, 14) =	2.06
Prob > F =	0.1407
R-squared =	0.2816
Root MSE =	5.0851

gov_exp	Coef.	Robust Std. Err.	t	P>|t|	[95% Conf. Interval]	
egri	2.181835	1.192126	1.83	0.089	-.3750197	4.73869
logpop	-1.488066	1.09809	-1.36	0.197	-3.843235	.8671031
econfreed	13.62244	9.390004	1.45	0.169	-6.517121	33.76199
egecon	-.2917941	.1778245	-1.64	0.123	-.6731898	.0896016
_cons	-61.4052	64.87501	-0.95	0.360	-200.5483	77.73785

The developed model does not take into account the different structures of general government expenditures in different countries and it follows a microeconomic approach only, these issues will be dealt with in further research efforts.

3. Summary

After a short introduction into the concept of e-government, this papers followed the UNPAN studies to assess the state of development of e-government. A first result is, that the telecommunication infrastructure of a country has a high impact on the development of e-government - investments into telecommunications are likely to improve the state of e-government.

South America is quite successful in implementing e-government, establishing itself above the world average with the best ratio between infrastructure and EGRI.

The overall promise of cost savings and efficiency gains through e-government, here formulated in hypothesis, can not be supported by the findings of this paper. The conducted OLS analysis shows the investment structure of e-government: the initial expenses for establishing e-government are on their way - the payoffs are still in the future.

To foster further economic research in this field, the author has implemented an online database, which provides the raw data of the mentioned studies. The complete data sets can be downloaded from http://www.elsas.de/papers as an SQL file, http://www.egov-is.org provides the online database.

References

CIA: *The World Factbook* 2004. URL http://www.cia.gov/cia/publications/ factbook/ and http://www.cia.gov/cia/publications/factbook/ (6.2.05).

Di Maio, A. and Kreizman, G. (2001), *E-Government Ranking Survey Is Meaningless*. URL http://www3.gartner.com/resources/101800/101888/101888.pdf (8.2.05).

Elsas, A. (2004), E-Government in Germany: Status Quo and Perspectives, in: *Journal of Systemics, Cybernetics and Informatics*, 2(2).

Greene, W. H. (2003), *Econometric analysis*. Prentice Hall, 5th edition.

Gwartney, J. and Lawson, R. (2004), *Economic Freedom of the World: 2004 Annual Report.* The Fraser Institute, Vancouver. URL http://www.freetheworld.com/2004/2004dataset.xls (15.2.05).

Ndou, V. (2004), E-Government for Developing Countries, Opportunities and Challenges, in:*The Electronic Journal on Information Systems in Developing Countries*, 18(1): 1–24. URL http://www.is.cityu.edu.hk/research/ejisdc/vol18/v18r1.pdf (8.2.05).

UNPAN (2001), *Benchmarking E-government: A Global Perspective.* URL http://pti.nw.dc.us/links/docs/ASPA_UN_egov_survey.pdf(8.2.2005).

UNPAN (2003), *UN Global E-government Survey 2003*. URL http://unpan1.un.org/intradoc/groups/public/documents/un/unpan016066.pdf(4.2.05).

UNPAN (2004), *United Nations Global E-Government Readiness Report 2004 - Towards Access For Opportunity.* URL http://unpan1.un.org/intradoc/groups/public/documents/un/unpan019207.pdf (4.2.05).

West, D. M. (2001), *WMRC Global E-Government Survey, October, 2001*. URL http://www.insidepolitics.org/egovt01int.html (7.2.05).

West, D. M. (2002), *Global E-Government, 2002*. URL http://www.insidepolitics.org/egovt02int.PDF (7.2.05).

West, D. M. (2003), *Global E-Government, 2003*. URL http://www.insidepolitics.org/egovt03int.pdf(7.2.05).

West, D. M. (2004), *Global E-Government, 2004*. URL http://www.insidepolitics.org/egovt04int.pdf(7.2.05).

West, D. M. (2005), *Global E-Government, 2005*. URL http://www.insidepolitics.org/egovt05int.pdf(16.9.05).

Worldbank (2004): *The information age*. URL http://www.worldbank.org/data/wdi2004/pdfs/Table5_11.pdf (7.2.05).

IMPLEMENTATION OF IT GOVERNANCE IN GLOBAL FINANCIAL ENTERPRISES- CHALLENGES, BENEFITS AND THE IMPACT OF GLOBALISATION

Kerstin Herhaus
Institute for Information Systems,
Johann Wolfgang Goethe-University Frankfurt,
Germany

herhaus@wiwi.uni-frankfurt.de

1. Introduction

In the absence of good corporate governance companies are having to comply with new rules and regulations created by regulators. This is because of a whole series of events caused by inadequate control systems. In some cases a leak in adequate control systems can lead to collapse. A prominent example is the ruin of Andersen due to the fact, that the American audit practice of Andersen was accused of malpractice in regard to the ENRON breakdown. This and other cases like Parmalat, Flow Tex etc. are the reason that governance has become a critical topic for regulatory boards like the SEC. Missing or inadequate internal control systems, fraud, threats and vulnerabilities in corporate governance are the reason for new regulatory requirements like Sarbanes Oxley Act[105] (SOX) and Basle II[106]and the reason that governance is now being mire and more imposed by regulation.

Regulatory Governance can only be achieved by a high level of transparency in a companies financial reporting and process transparency. This forces a company to expose critical parts of their business and can lead to short term decision making by management.

In an age of globalisation, regulatory governance imposes an even greater burden on those companies operating in different jurisdictions. In the financial sector, banks must not only consider domestic banking regulations like German banking act (KWG), but also international requirements like SOX and any other regulations in countries where the bank has subsidiaries. This means if the bank has subsidiaries in 100 countries, at the very least 100 different compliance requirements need to be met as well as any international regulatory acts.

All of these regulations represent a major burden for organisations and impose new responsibilities, especially for financial institutions where regulations are even tighter than other industrial sectors.

Companies now need to define and incorporate governance bodies into their organisational structure. These governance bodies are not only for Corporate Governance (regulatory Governance) and Enterprise Governance, but also for IT Governance as IT penetrates the

[105] In July of 2002, U.S. Congress passed the Sarbanes -Oxley Act (SOX) mandating that all public companies (SEC registrants) make changes to the way their financial results are reported. The Sarbanes -Oxley Act contains two Sections (302, 404) dealing with management responsibility for controls.

[106]New Basel Capital Accord; Basel II puts a strong focus on operational risk and Governance.

heart of an organisation thru its financial systems. These three main streams of Governance are explained in the table below:

Tabel 1: Comparison of Governance Streams

Table 1—Comparison of Corporate, Enterprise and IT Governance Characteristics

	Corporate Governance	Enterprise Governance	IT Governance
Primary Proponent	OECD (Organisation for Economic Co-operation & Development)	None	ISACA (Information Systems Audit and Control Association)
Refers to the workings of	• Board of directors • Executive team • Shareholders	• Board of directors • Executive team • Rest of organization	• Board of directors • Executive team • Rest of organization
Core Principles	• Shareholders' rights • Independence • Accountability and disclosure • Board roles and responsibilities	• Strategic direction • Accountability and disclosure • Organization's roles and responsibilities • Alignment	• Align with corporate strategy • Provide good IT value • Manage IT risks
Intent	• Ensure integrity of accounting and financial reporting systems • Include independent audit • Have appropriate controls for: – Financial control – Monitoring risk – Compliance with laws and regulations	• Ensure integrity of financial and nonfinancial reporting systems • Inclusion of independent audit • Have appropriate controls for: – Financial control – Monitoring risk – Compliance with laws and regulations – Operations – Communications— internal and external – Integrated strategic planning and alignment	• Ensure integrity of IT systems • Inclusion of independent audit • Have appropriate controls for: – Monitoring IT risk – Controling IT assets – Compliance with laws and regulations – Records management • Enable the enterprise by exploiting opportunities and maximizing benefits of IT • Ensure IT resources are used responsibly
Factors Driving	• Growth in complexity of the organization • Globalization • Rapid advance of technology • Accelerated decision making • More proactive boards • Shareholder activism • Increased news coverage • Increased competition • Recent scandals	Same factors as corporate governance plus: • Increased emphasis on accountability • Need to manage the management process • Need for meaningful communication • Focus on organizational capital, value and balance	Same factors as corporate and enterprise governance plus: • Expanding role of IT – Corporate/enterprise governance support – Strategic initiatives – Knowledge management – Privacy/security/continuity • Proliferation of technology "solutions"
Key Elements	• Majority of independent directors • Use international accounting standards • Independent audits • Responsive to requests for information	• Management of mgt. processes: – Strategic planning and alignment – Comprehensive control framework – Clear and well-managed operations – Financial management	• IT strategic planning • IT control framework • IT project management • IT asset management • IT policies/standards/processes – Corporate – Business units – Information Services

Source: Stacy Hamaker (2003).

The focus of this paper lies with IT Governance, but to understand the focus and intent of IT Governance it's crucial to understand all three forms of governance. As table 1 clarifies, IT Governance is driven by the same factors as Corporate and Enterprise Governance but also includes additional IT related factors. The objective of all three streams looks slightly different, but the purpose is always the same: the integrity of systems and a stable internal control environment.

2. Evolution and Definition of IT-Governance

IT Governance is not a new topic. It is now seen more in the context of regulatory requirements but in fact should be seen as a result of a long development process, which started with Infrastructure Management (ITIM), followed by IT Service Management (ITSM) and IT Risk Management (ITRM) and has now reached his highest level in IT Governance. The role of IT departments has also changed from a Technology Provider to a Service Provider to a Strategic Partner. It is one of the most important factors in a successful business.[107]

2.1. IT-Management vs. IT Governance

Figure 1 shows the evolution from a pure Technology Provider to a strategic business partner and integral part of the business.

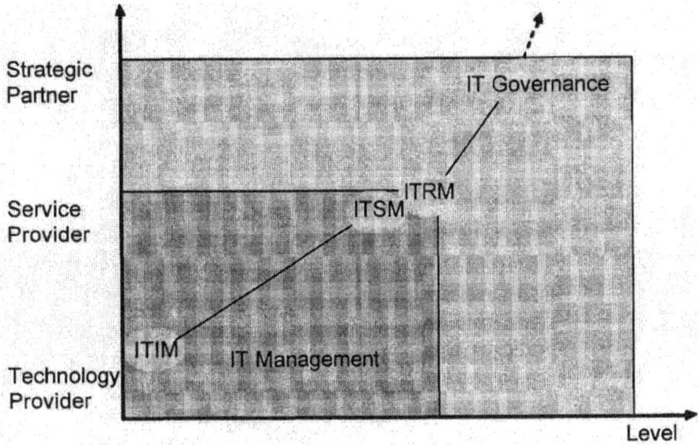

Figure 1: Evolution of IT understanding and role of IT.

Source: Mathias Sallé (2004), p.1

The main difference between IT Governance and previous evolutions can be described as followed: "Whereas the domain of IT Management focuses on the efficient and effective supply of IT services and products, and the management of IT Operations, IT Governance faces the dual demand of (1) contributing the present business operations and performance, and (2) transforming and positioning IT for meeting future business challenges".[108]

In other words IT Governance focuses on the implementation of measurable IT Governance processes, described in Control Objectives and the implementation of a permanent improvement process.

[107] cp.: Mathias Sallé, IT Service Management and IT Governance: Review, Comparative Analysis and their Impact on Utility Computing, Hewlett-Packard Company 2004, p.1

[108] R. Peterson, Integration Strategies and Tactics for Information Technology Governance, in Strategies for Information Technology Governance, Ed. Wim Van Grembergen, Idea Group, 2003.

2.2. Definition of IT Governance

Different scopes and definitions of IT Governance have been published (cp. ISACA, Peterson etc.). Peterson's (see p. 4) focuses on the contribution to the business and also future improvements. COBIT's definition is based on relationships and control processes: "A structure of relationships and processes to direct and control the enterprise in order to achieve the enterprise's goals by adding value while balancing risk versus return over IT and its processes." [109]

This paper will use the following definition of IT Governance:

IT Governance encompasses a structure of relationships, activities and processes to direct and control the enterprise while contributing to the business in order to achieve, maintain and improve the enterprise's goals by adding value while balancing and controlling risk and ensuring compliance versus return over IT and its processes.

Consequently IT Governance must be understood as a lifecycle which deals with a permanent improvement of both, IT Processes and Business Processes as well as the compliance with internal and external requirements.

3. Implementing IT Governance

Financial Institutions always had particular legal and regulatory requirements, as they were regulated by different control boards. Therefore Compliance departments already exist, but mainly deal with corporate and enterprise governance. The Implementation of IT Governance is still a challenge and not yet solved. The reason for this often lies with the wrong positioning of IT-Governance or missing objectives or even the wrong motivation (i.e. just to satisfy outside regulations).

Figure 2: Three dimensional Governance Model

109 COBIT Control Objectives 3rd. edition, released by the COBIT Steering Committee and the IT Governance Institute, July 2000, page5.

Several IT Governance Models exists, like COBIT™ from the Governance Institute™ or eSCM®[110] from the Carnegie Mellon University but none of these give advice for achieving IT Governance in global financial institutions. COBIT™ considers control processes and management of IT Governance while the eSCM® considers the implementation of IT Governance for service providers. COBIT which is based on a maturity model is often used in banks internal audit departments to structure the IT processes and set control points for auditing while the eSCM model is a capability model. Both of these models are only one dimensional. The author of this paper believes three dimensions need to be considered to implement a highly valuable governance model.

These dimensions must encompass the service view as well as the process view in conjunction with control objectives and the tools and resources to achieve the governance goals.

3.1 The three Dimensions of a Governance Model

Following three dimensions describe IT Governance:

1. The processes view including the definition of the right control objectives (maturity model)
2. The Service view including the compliance with internal and external requirements and risk management (capability model)
3. The Tools and Resources to incorporate in the IT Governance Model.

Add.1 The implementation of a maturity model ensures efficient process quality and support the measurement of the outcome

Following levels will be defined:

<u>Maturity Level 1:</u> Non existent: recognisable Processes are not existent. Risk are not identified

<u>Maturity Level 2:</u> Ad hoc: Risks are identified and will be solved on an ad hoc basis, with ad hoc processes (not standardised)

<u>Maturity Level 3:</u> Standardised: Standard processes exists, processes are documented and monitored

<u>Maturity Level 4:</u> Processes are measurable, gaps can be identified and a permanent improvement takes place

The most common fault in the implementation of IT-processes in a governance model is to disregard the underlying governance process. The governance process does not necessarily mean to implement operational control – this is part of the IT process like e.g. the

[110] Hyder Elaine B., Heston, Paulk, Mark C., The eSCM-SPv2: The eSourcing Practice Capability Model for Service Providers, Carnegie Mellon University, 2004

authorisation, test etc. in a change management process[111]. The governance process ensure that base activity is being performed and control (operational) is being executed appropriately (evidence). With other words – the governance process gives us the evidence that the base activities like the change management is being performed and also the operational controls like the authorisation; tests etc. are done as part of the IT-process. Governance has to ensure that these controls are being performed in a traceable and measurable way and could be evidenced at every time. The figure below shows the difference components of the operational IT Process (high level process view) and the related governance functions. The governance functions are showing the evidence that the IT Process is executed according to the internal policies and external laws and regulations (e.g. segregation of duties, 4 eyes principle etc.).

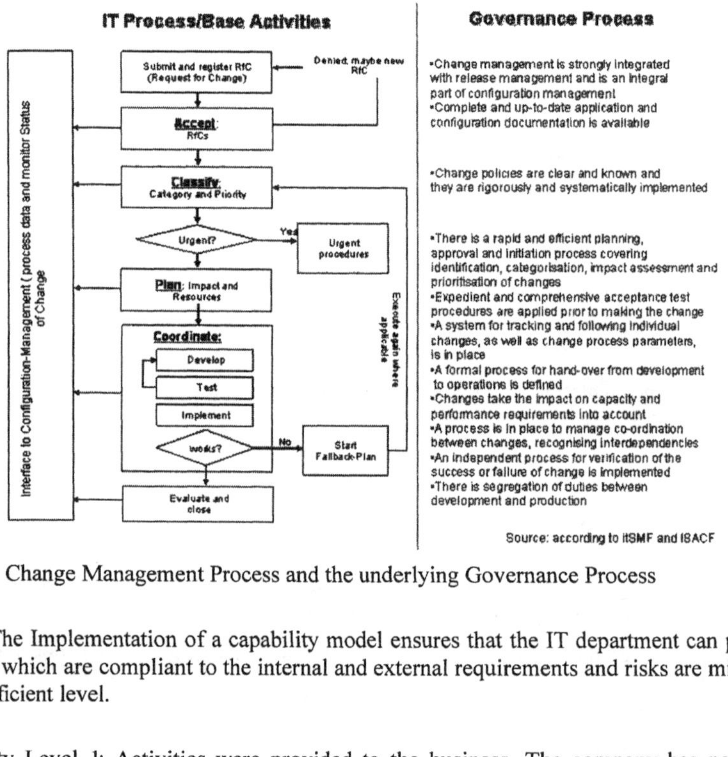

Figure 3: Change Management Process and the underlying Governance Process

Add 2: The Implementation of a capability model ensures that the IT department can provide Services which are compliant to the internal and external requirements and risks are mitigated to an sufficient level.

Capability Level 1: Activities were provided to the business. The company has not even recognised that there is a compliance or risk issue

Capability Level 2: Compliance and Risk Issues are identified, Services are provided

---

[111] The goal of the Change Management process is to ensure, that only authorised changes, improvements, and standardised methods are being performed with a minimum of disruption of the service quality. As an example the Change Management process from the itSMF (IT Service Management Foundation) could be used.

Capability Level 3: Services are reconciled with Compliance Requirements and potential risks are known and monitored

Capability Level 4: Services are compliant to the internal and external requirements, business goals are met and risks are managed. Change management is implemented communication is set up, solutions and improvements are provided.

Add 3: Tools and Resources: Existent policies, standards and procedures for business and it processes and the respective Subject Matter Experts (SME´s).

While the process maturity is about the growth in the process capability and about building one set of processes to establish a higher maturity set of processes[112] (improvement of all processes in a specific time range), the capability describes the range of expected results (services) that can be achieved (range of achievements independent from the status quo, measured per service). This means the achievement of a particular stage of capability does not necessarily mean to start with capability level one but to implement practices from different levels simultaneously[113]. The maturity model is the basis for formulating IT department's processes the capability in this context means the translation into understandable Services provided to the business. But the maximum improvement can only be reached by combining maturity, capability, tools and resources.

3.2. Motivation for Implementing IT Governance

The most common motivation for implementing IT Governance is the legal or regulatory pressure, but this might give the false impression, that Governance is only an Instrument to meet legal or regulatory requirements or has only a marketing or reputational function. This is a misinterpretation of the full scope and power of Governance. The correct use of governance helps to achieve standardisation, reduction of complexity, risk mitigation and the avoidance or reduction of audit issues. All these goals result in major cost savings and quality improvement.

IT-Governance enables financial institutions to structure their processes in a way that are traceable, standardised, and controlled. This means that all IT-Processes have an underlying control process which helps to evidence process performance, process gaps and encourages permanent improvement. COBIT defined 34 high level control objectives with various detailed controls. These processes are a useful foundation and should be considered when implementing IT-Governance. It lies with the financial institution to adjust these processes to their individual needs. The challenge is to find the right approach for implementing IT Governance and make the framework fit for purpose.

The scope of an implementation project depends on the motivation and goals which should be achieved with IT Governance.

---

[112] Hyder Elaine B., Heston, Paulk, Mark C., The eSCM-SPv2: The eSourcing Practice Capability Model for Service Providers, Carnegie Mellon University, 2004, p. 76.

[113] Hyder Elaine B., Heston, Paulk, Mark C., The eSCM-SPv2: The eSourcing Practice Capability Model for Service Providers, Carnegie Mellon University, 2004, p. 76.

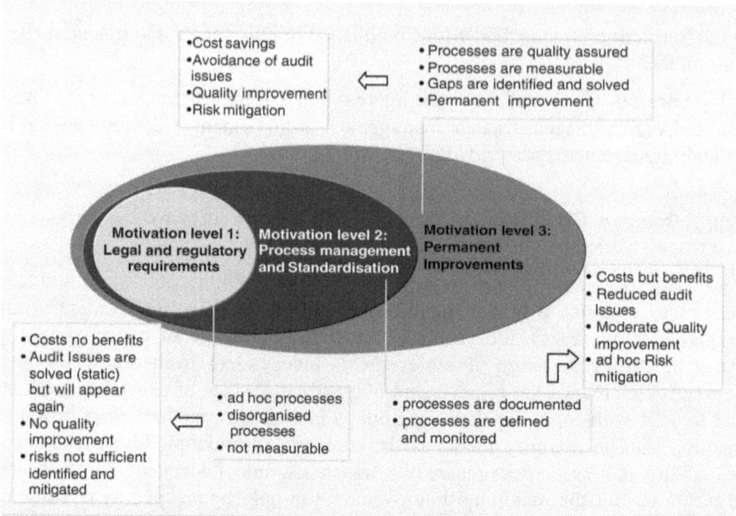

Figure 4: Motivation for Implementing IT-Governance.

As shown in figure 3 the most basic approach deals with the fulfilment of legal and regulatory requirements (motivation level 1(includes maturity level 1 and 2)) and can be characterised by additional costs but low or missing benefits. Controls are implemented, but process or performance weaknesses are not considered, processes can almost be considered as ad hoc processes.

The next stage (motivation level 2, maturity level 2 and 3)) includes processes definition, monitoring and documentation – but advantages are not measurable in terms of quality and quantity.

A holistic approach (motivation level 3 maturity level 4) encompasses the implementation of controls, Key Performance Indicators, Key Goal Indicators and Critical Success Factors. These are traced permanently and are the key to success measurement. Gaps are identified and processes consequently improved to achieve business goals, process quality and cost savings.

3.3. Holistic Approach for Implementing IT Governance in global Financial Institutions

To implement IT-Governance in global Financial Institutions, the following questions need to be considered:

1. Is the board/executive team involved in the IT-Governance process?
2. Are the respective governance bodies involved in implementation and maintenance?
3. Are data centres and IT Departments located in several countries or does only one centralised data centre/IT Department exist?

3.3.1. *Management Responsibility*

The first question is also the "root" of IT Governance. It is essential to have the awareness of the board / executive team to ensure an overall implementation of IT Governance. As mentioned above, IT Governance is an integral part of Enterprise Governance. IT strategy has to be in line with the enterprise strategy, because of the high impact of IT on the business. Therefore IT Governance needs the attention of all relevant board members, because the degree of management attention mandates and optimises the use of resources.

3.3.2. *Organisational Involvement in IT Governance*

The second question deals with the most common fault when implementing IT Governance and is a result of the missing attention by the board members: IT Governance is implemented as a "silo". This means, the Financial Institution either has implemented an isolated IT-Governance Department or it is organised within the IT Department only. But to have an effective and efficient IT Governance Model in place, the Financial Institution has to involve all relevant governance bodies. These governance bodies should encompass:

- The IT Department (IT infrastructure, engineering, operations, development, architecture etc.) as the operational body of IT Governance
- The IT Security Department (could also be included in the IT Department). IT Governance means also having a secure, reliable and confidential environment.
- The legal Department to ensure all legal requirements are met and to support the IT Department regarding the controlling of third party contracts.
- The Compliance Department to be aware of the regulatory requirements, especially banking regulations.
- The Controlling Department. IT Governance includes also includes financial controlling and must ensure that the value of IT is in line with the costs of IT (internal cost allocation)
- The Operational Risk Department to build an Operational Risk Management approach
- Business representatives to ensure that the business needs are met.
- Furthermore the Department for physical/corporate security should be involved.

3.3.3. *Organisational placement of IT Governance in global Financial Institutions*

The third question deals with the structure of IT. Due to the growing globalisation of financial institutions new aspects have to be considered. IT processes are a subject of standardisation while most banking applications and data centre hosting are regulated by the different control boards of several countries. Therefore the room for standardisation is limited by the regulators. E.g. if the IT Department/data centre is located in one country for the whole company the laws and banking regulations of all other involved countries need to be considered and the underlying IT processes must comply with all these regulations. If the IT Departments or data centres are located in different countries the financial institution has to ensure that, besides laws and regulations a common framework is also implemented, which directs the different locations and supports the standardisation of the IT processes as much as possible. As mentioned in section 3.2.2 not only the IT department is responsible for ensuring IT Governance but several other departments are also responsible. If we now assume that we have a global financial institution with one centralised data centre and we have to fulfil the regulatory and internal requirements for e.g. 45 countries we have to multiply each involved department with 45 countries. For example: 10 departments are involved in 45 countries (from the IT Department to the compliance department) and each of these departments has three specific requirements than we would have to consider 1350 (10x3x45) different local and internal requirements and incorporate them into one consistent global IT Governance Model for the respective financial institution. In other words, the financial institution could have 1350 variables which are dependent and x combinations are possible.

All these topics deal with the complexity of implementing IT Governance. The establishment of an overall organisational framework generally fails because of weak knowledge about regulatory requirements in the different countries and misunderstanding of IT Governance. IT Governance in global financial institutions creates a lot new responsibilities, but it is still the question, how to manage these new responsibilities effectively and by whom. It is crucial to know that IT-Governance is not only a responsibility of IT. It should be seen as a broad approach which impacts the whole financial institution. Each governance body has to consider the main themes of governance: accountability, transparency, compliance, independence, disclosure and control effectiveness.

Therefore metrics or objectives must be defined for each respective governance body to orchestrate all efforts in a manner which ensure a permanent and consistent support of IT-Governance to gain maximum value.

3.4. Benefits of Implementing IT Governance

As mentioned before, Governance is often seen as a "must" to satisfy the regulators or auditors. The basic economic parameters also do nothing to encourage IT Governance. But this is a very short sighted thinking. Information Technology is one of the biggest costs in financial institutions, but the governance over this costs is mainly poor. All attempts to provide a transparent and consistent IT-Controlling which allows seeing the single cost driver are useless, unless the processes behind are not clearly defined, managed and measurable. Week and inadequatly controlled IT Systems and insufficient Business Continuity Approaches can cause major breakdowns in all industries. IT in banks has grown above average in comparison to other industries. Banks also depend more on IT, than other industries do.

3.4.1. Realisation of Cost Savings

A holistic IT Governance approach helps to achieve major cost savings while defining Key Performance Indicators, Key Goal Indicators and Critical Success Factors to measure the outcome of each IT Process and to reveal Gaps. With the implementation of these three Governance Key Drivers the necessary transparency for measuring IT costs and therefore the establishment of an effective IT-Controlling is made possible.

Key Performance Indicators:

These are measures that tell management that an IT process is achieving its business requirements by monitoring/measuring the performance of the enablers of that IT process.[114] They are key figures to show the current achievement of IT processes. Examples are[115]:

- Number of non-compliance reportings
- Increased quality and innovation
- Service availability and response times, etc.

Key Goal Indicators:

The KGIs display the interface to the business. Usually they are defined for Service Level Agreements (SLA). A KGI is a measurable indicator of the process achieving its defined goals, often defined as a target to achieve.[116] It is the key figure in tracking back the measurement of business oriented achievements caused by IT processes. Examples are[117]:

- Number of customers and cost per customer served
- Number of standardised processes
- Reduced IT risks
- Productivity improvements etc.

Critical Success Factors:

The CSF´s are the most important Factor for implementing IT Governance. This key Indicator provides management information and guidance for the management with regard to implementing control over IT and its processes[118]. This key figure helps to identify the strategic, technical and organisational elements for controlling IT Processes. Examples are[119]:

- IT processes are defined and aligned with the IT strategy and the business goals
- IT performance is measured in financial terms, in relation to customer satisfaction, for process effectiveness and the future
- Capability. IT management is rewarded based on these measures.
- Control practices are applied to increase transparency, reduce complexity, promote learning, provide flexibility, scalability
- and avoid breakdowns in internal control and oversight.

[114] COBIT Management Guidelines Released by the COBIT Steering Committee and the IT Governance Institute TM, 3rd edition, June 2000, page 20.
[115] COBIT Management Guidelines Released by the COBIT Steering Committee and the IT Governance Institute TM, 3rd edition, June 2000, page 19.
[116] COBIT Management Guidelines Released by the COBIT Steering Committee and the IT Governance Institute TM, 3rd edition, June 2000, page 17.
[117] COBIT Management Guidelines Released by the COBIT Steering Committee and the IT Governance Institute TM, 3rd edition, June 2000, page 20f.
[118] COBIT Management Guidelines Released by the COBIT Steering Committee and the IT Governance Institute TM, 3rd edition, June 2000, page 14.
[119] COBIT Management Guidelines Released by the COBIT Steering Committee and the IT Governance Institute TM, 3rd edition, June 2000, page 16.

The combination of these three key indicators is the key to an efficient and effective IT-Governance model and provides the necessary control over IT processes and their value as presented to the senior management of both the IT department and the Business as the clients of the IT department.

4. Conclusion

IT Governance could simply be seen as an instrument to satisfy the regulators and legal requirements. Most of the companies see in governance no more than this and handle Governance as a necessary effort without achieving any benefit. Furthermore IT Governance is often seen as an extension of the internal IT audit department. But while internal audit is focussed on a reference date or small time frame in which the audit need to be performed, IT Governance is focussed on a continuous life cycle consisting of a strong structure of relationships and processes to direct, measure and control IT in order to achieve the business goals. The internal and external auditor has the responsibility to ensure that the implemented governance model is compliant with the regulatory and legal requirements. But they do not deal with the cycle of improvements, a holistic IT Governance Model can provide.

The obvious disadvantages of Governance like the disclosure of financial reports and the big efforts can not be avoided off as long as the financial institution has the wrong motivation for implementing an IT Governance Model. Governance provides transparency over the performed tasks, the people who operate the business and the effectiveness of senior management. This means not only the processes are measurable but also the involved parties. But transparency should not only be used as a factor to apply pressure on the involved parties it's purpose is to improve financial benefits by enabling an end to end control starting with the underlying IT and ending with the efficiency of the related business process.

Even if the bank is globally organised the efforts to implement IT Governance and to fulfil all domestic and international requirements are so high, that most of the financial institutions fail in their attempt to implement an IT Governance model. Lack of management attention and wrong motivation are other factors in failing to implement an IT Governance model. Only a holistic governance approach achieves the desired results by providing measurable, controlled and reliable processes which support the business and mitigate risks by concentrating all efforts in a comprehensive manner.

References

Banking Committee on Banking Supervision (2001), *New Basel Capital Accord.*

Hamaker, S. (2003), Spotlight on Governance, in: *Information Systems Journal*, Volume 1.

Herhaus, K. and Woell, P. (2001), Ohne Kostentransparenz keine wirtschaftliche IT, in: *Computerwoche* 39/2001, 58.

Herhaus, K. (2002), Implementierung einer effizienten und effektiven IT-Leistungsverrechnung. In: *Zukunft der Netze - Die Verletzbarkeit meistern*, Knop, J. and Haverkamp, W. (eds.), Köllen Druck & Verlag GmbH, Bonn.

Hyder, E. B., Heston, P. and Mark, C. (2004), *The eSCM-SPv2: The eSourcing Practice Capability Model for Service Providers*, Carnegie Mellon University.

Peterson, R. R. (2004), Integration Strategies and Tactics for Information Technology Governance, in *Strategies for Information Technology Governance*, Wim Van Grembergen (ed.), Idea Group.

Sallé, M. (2004), *IT Service Management and IT Governance: Review, Comparative Analysis and their Impact on Utility Computing*, Hewlett-Packard Company IT Governance Institute TM (2002): COBIT Control Objectives 3rd. edition, released by the COBIT Steering Committee and the IT Governance Institute, July 2000.

IT Governance Institute TM (2002), *COBIT Management Guidelines*, released by the COBIT Steering Committee and the IT Governance Institute, 3rd edition, June 2000, page 16.

ITSMF (IT Service Management Foundation): *Service Delivery Set* CD-ROM, English, ISBN 0113308930.

THE COMPLEXITY PROBLEM OF HIGH PRODUCT VARIETY IN GLOBAL DISTRIBUTED VALUE CHAINS

Peter Langner
Institute for Information Systems,
Johann Wolfgang Goethe-University Frankfurt,
Germany
langner@wiwi.uni-frankfurt.de

1. Motivation

Today's manufacturing companies are faced with a steadily increasing dynamic business environment which is characterized by globalization, shorter product life cycles, new competitors and a shift from a make-to-market to a make-to-order or assembled-to-order approach. This has great impact on a company's production-related and product-related decisions. Classically two poles in the environment of production systems can be discerned. At one extreme, mass production, with the goal to produce as cheaply and efficiently as possible. This leads to standardized mass products normally for consumer markets. At the other extreme engineer-to-order production with the goal of offering products which are individualized to customers needs [Garud / Kotha 1994]. These products can normally not produced as cheaply and efficiently as mass products and belong classically to the field of industrial production. In recent decades both strategies have dominated the industrial world. However, in the recent years customers have become more critical and selective. On both sides, customer orientation is becoming an important phrase for many companies leading to new strategies like mass customization. Mass Customization is characterized by customer individualization while trying to realize the scale effects of mass production and the scope effects, which can be realized by the use of modern product concepts and platforms [Pine 1993; Piller 1998].

The overall effect is increasing product variants - and due to that - an increasing complexity of products and production-related processes (e.g. controlling, coordination and planning processes) [Meffert 2000; Blecker / Abdelkafi 2004]. Through this, the dilemma between flexibility and productivity emerge, which mainly address the production system and supply management.

On the one hand the achievable product individualization degree is mainly determined by product and production flexibility. Production flexibility refers to the rapidity with which a production system can deliver end-products when required. Product flexibility refers to the assortment size of products and the inherent degree of customization [Helberg 1987; Garud / Kotha 1994]. On the other hand the efficiency of manufacturing and assembling products in highly flexible production environments is noticeably determined by those evolving costs, which result from increasing complexity.

Overall, flexibility and simultaneously productivity in development, manufacturing and supply management become extremely important for the success of global corporations. Against this background the question arises: How can companies develop products and services for worldwide markets and reach the necessary flexibility and speed in product

design and manufacturing under the restriction of low production costs and customer satisfaction?
This is the main question ask by this paper. It attempts to address the complexity, which arises because of high product variety. One of the first tasks therefore is to examine the complexity dimensions of producing variants. Complexity can be roughly categorized in product and process complexity. The first kind of complexity emerges from product parameters in a logical viewpoint and from subassembly in a physical viewpoint. In contrast, process complexity can be seen in aspects of supply planning, coordination and control as a result of product complexity. Both complexity dimensions are interdependent, what means, that high product complexity will cause high process complexity.
For reasons of complexity causes, two product views are differentiated in the paper. Namely a customer and a more technique-oriented product view. In line with the customer product view customizable product parameters and within the scope of the technical view the assembly of products and bill of materials (BOM) comes to the fore. In this, the customer view of products will give us in principle the overall cause of increasing complexity, but on a closer look complexity will mainly result from the number, heterogeneity and variability associated with the pre-assembly of products.
The last section of this paper will focus on the effects of high product variety on the value chain. With this, complexity affects mainly customer integration on the one hand side and coordination and controlling supplies in partner networks on the other hand side. The complexity results here from the high flexibility and the dynamic, which is needed in value chains for offering highly customizable products. But there is still one major problem to achieving high flexibility in value chain networks namely assuring trust. Distrust in global supply chains can be seen as one of the most cost-triggering factors in B2B-Transactions. The need and possibility of reducing costs because of distrust form the basis of further research and are reserved for further analysis.

2. Product variants and their dimension of complexity

So far, the term "complexity" has no generally admitted definition. Often it is discussed in conjunction with system theory. Basically a system consists of elements, which are processes, fine grained objects or again subsystems, as well as their existing relationships. The complexity of systems can be normally expressed by three complexity variables: the number, the heterogeneity, the variability of system elements and their relationships [Blecker / Abdelkafi 2004; Meffert 2000]. Based on this definition it is possible to differentiate between a structural and dynamic dimension of complexity. Whereas the dynamic dimension represents the ability to change system configuration over the course of time, the structural dimension describes the system structure at a defined point in time. For example, by considering the solution space of an industrial lot production that consists of individualized product variations, the assembly units are normally fixed in time of customer order and consequently determine the structural complexity of the unit assembly system. In contrast customer-specific bills of material are normally created by a product configuration system at the time of order entry. Thus these bills of material depend on the variability of the construction kits in a long term and the degrees of freedom different product variants may be configured. This circumstance describes the dynamic dimension of complexity [Maroni 2001;

Meffert 2000]. *Figure 1* summarizes the conception of complexity in the understanding of this paper.
With the complexity provoked by many product variants, the main goal is to cope with complexity in a reasonable way, which means to reduce complexity without restraining product individualization and control the rest of complexity which cannot be reduced [Adam 1997]. To archive that, two actions are possible. First of all, complexity reduction which aims at simplifying structures e.g. eliminating the variety of components and assemblies in the product structure by designing more modularized construction kits. Secondly, complexity control and prevention, which tends to deal the rest complexity efficiently, e.g. developing methods and rules for product classification, product configuration and product abstraction [Meffert 2000].

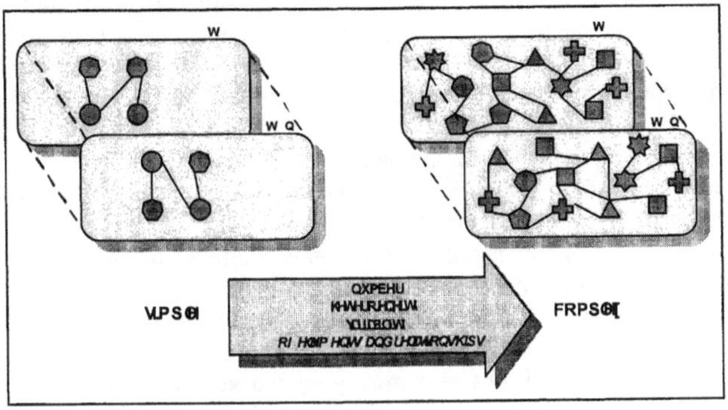

Figure 5: Complexity and causing variables

In the underlying case of high product variety, the provoked complexity not only affects the composition structure of products, but also the planning, control and coordination processes within the scope of customer integration, manufacturing and supply chain management [Adam / Rollberg 1996]. The first complexity type will be named as product complexity, the second as process complexity. Usually the product and process complexity resulting from highly individualized product variants affects many systems in production environment. Here the cause of complexity in the so called "product composition system" and "supply management system" form the main attention of this paper:

- Product composition system: Within this scope, two product views are distinguished, namely a technical view and customer view. The technical view describes the bill of materials (BOM) and routings of products and construction kits. In the customers' or sales' point of view, products are mainly specified in terms of functionality, including common features, optional features and selection constraints [Du et al 2003]. The complexity dimensions of the product composition system will be analyzed in *chapter ?* .
- Value chain system: In a value chain mainly two kind interfaces can be distinguished, namely to customers and to suppliers. In a production environment with high diversity of variants the interface to customer is normally established by product configuration and/or selection systems (e.g. product catalogs). They are often represented by software-based expert systems. The task is to ensure that customers receive individual specified and correctly-priced products by transforming the customer requirements into technical

product-related data. Normally the transforming process of the customer's individually chosen product features is based on rules or decision tables [Schwarze 1996]. Configuration and selection systems mostly consist of front-end and backend systems. The front-end covers the user interface and is needed for analysis tasks of configuration. It serves as the starting point for deriving structural descriptors from the functional specification of a "virtual" product which up to now does not exist physically. The backend includes the product logic and serves for the synthesis phase of product configuration. Tasks like design, configuration, feasibility tests, scheduling and so on, are typical for this phase. Customer integration on the basis of product configuration will be briefly discussed in *chapter 4.1*.

The second interface is represented by a supply chain management system. Supply chains consist of networks formed by cooperating partners. Companies which are facing markets with highly individual customer demands are confronted with steadily increasing complexity of business processes and turbulent production environments. As a result of that, business processes have to be highly efficient and need to provide the necessary scope and speed flexibility to be able to react to short-term changes of customer's demands and unforeseen events during fulfillment. One phenomenon is the so-called bullwhip effect, which is mainly caused by a multiplication of fluctuating demands in the supply chain. In addition the planning process of material resources is hampered by the non-willingness of companies to reveal their production data in the supply chain particularly when potential competitors are present [Frey et al. 2003]. Except for the fact, that supply chain partners are on equal terms or rather not forced to reveal there data, mechanisms to ensure trust have to be implemented. All in all, the complexity of managing supply chains with highly individualized goods results in interdependent tasks such as planning, execution and control of production, transportation and warehousing process. Complexity will further increase, if supply chains are global-oriented. The integration of suppliers in the value chain is one main topic of the paper. The different types of integration will be analyzed in detail in *chapter 4.2*.

3. Complexity dimensions in the product composition system

3.1. The dimensions of structural complexity from the vantage point of customer-oriented product variants

From the customer or sales viewpoint, neither the product itself nor the composition of product in terms of BOM structures stands at the centre of interest, but the ability of the product to solve specific customer requirements. The companies' ability to solve problems arises firstly from customer noticeable product functions and parameters and secondly from product related services like warranty or financing. In this view a product variant is an individualized product attributable to customer-specific needs and requirements and aims to increase customer satisfaction [Maroni 2001].

A product variant represents itself as a bundle of product parameters and functions. Thus, in this perspective the usability of the product comes to the fore. For example, the frame of an off-road bicycle may consist of carbon or aluminum. From the view point of production both kinds of material provoke different manufacturing processes, which will result in different product variants. From the customer's perspective, the customer will see both bicycle types as variants if and only if he is able to associate different functional uses because of the different frame types [Kestel 1995]. Overall, different functional and physical product parameters normally result from changes in the product composition structure, the product construction and from the manner in which a product function is generated, as well as to dependencies between product parameters [Meffert 2000].

From the customer view of the product composition system the possible number of producible end-products is determined by the degree of individualization and thus by the number of customizable product parameter and their values. Individualization should be accomplished by product configuration and not by product design engineering [Firchau / Franke 2002]. Product parameters can refer to a wide repertoire. For example in case of gearmotors, the range of parameters is spanned from prime cost, ease of maintenance and field of environment to more technical parameters like speed, torque or gear-size. The producible number of end-products through this is often called "external variety" [Ringsletter / Kirch 1991].

As mentioned before, the number of system elements can be seen as one major reason for increasing complexity. In addition to this, a high external product variety can be considered as an indicator of a high product and process complexity. For example, an end-product consists of four obligatory variable equipment attributes, whereas one possess five, another one possess six and each of the last two attributes possess three possible attribute values. Based on the formula

$$\Phi(P) = \prod_{m=1}^{M} Dom(M_m),\ m \in \square$$

with:

with:	$\Phi(P)$	=	combinational quantity of the possible variants,
	$Dom(M_m)$	=	domain of the obligatory attribute *m* (attribute values),
	M	=	quantity of the obligatory attribute.

an external variety of 270 can be calculated. The complexity in this example results fom the multitude of combination dependencies between the variable attributes and their attribute values. Against the background of material requirement planning and if each attribute value is for reason of simplification represented by a part, each of the dependencies has to be evaluated.

3.2. The dimensions of structural complexity from the vantage point of manufacturing-oriented product variants

In contrast to the customer view, the technical view sees product variants as component structure based on construction kits. Product variants are defined as functionally similar items with almost identical bills of material. In this perspective product variants are based on construction kits and product platforms. Product platforms and construction kits embodies mechanisms of variety fulfillment [Du et al. 2003]. Thus, product variants do not represent completely developed products, but are built up from a pool of existing product components like parts, construction sets or even platforms.

From this point of view we can define variants, if firstly different products have at least one similarity in a functional, physical or technological product parameter and secondly, if their bills of material predominantly comply [Scheer et al. 1991; Lingnau 1994]. Variations may appear anywhere in the whole product composition system and not only on the level of end-products. In the case that variations show up on a sub level – i.e. variants in variants exist - the number of possible variations is described by the so called "internal variety" of parts.

In the before described customer-based view the number and heterogeneity of product parameters and values as well as their manifold relationships were crucial for the degree of complexity. In the technical view the variety of end-products is generally predetermined by the targeted marketing orientation. From this point of view, the internal variety of components and relationships are in the first place responsible for the structural complexity. This does not mean that internal and external varieties are not related. In general the internal variety will depend on external variety. A higher external variety will cause a raised probability of increasing number and heterogeneity of components and relationships in the technical product composition structure. Here it will be seen, that the kind of relationship will have an influence on complexity.

Generally relations between parts can be represented as disjunctions or conjunctions. While disjunctions indicate optional relationships, conjunctions indicate obligatory relationships between parts or parameters [Lingnau 1994; Montau 1996; Kurbel 1999]. Furthermore, two different relationships may be distinguished in case of disjunctions, namely either OR-relations or XOR-relations. OR-relations indicate choices to use or not to use a part or parameter in the product model (e.g. a fog lamp). In contrast XOR-relations characterize mandatory one to many relationships, where one and only one element in a set must be chosen (e.g. a producer-specific water pump for a car). For manufacturing purposes, the variety of part-of-relations is normally fulfilled by the following generation methods [Du et al. 2003]:

- Attaching: Modules, containing certain additional functions and attributes, can be attached to a base product to create a new product variant.
- Removing: The opposite of attaching is removing. In this case new product variants can be derived by removing certain modules with special functions.
- Swapping: Swapping can be seen as a combination of removing and attaching. This method is mostly used by products with different performance levels for a range of same functions.
- Scaling: Like swapping, a range of different parameter values for certain product parameters can be changed without altering the fundamental technology or system structure of the product. Due to the fact that the product structure remains unchanged, these products are well suited for self-customization by the customer (e.g. the rotation speed of a drilling machine) [Piller 1998].

Normally these methods are not bound to the level of product platforms or base products. But for complexity reasons, variations should be as close as possible to the end-product level [Helberger 1987]. Advantages that accrue are manifold. The product complexity is reduced, due to the modular design of construction kits and platforms. The main objective of modularization can be seen in generating various product variants out of a small pool of parts. Through this, it is possible to reduce process complexity by manufacturing these parts in batches and gain efficiencies by economies of scale. Furthermore the product quality rises as product exceptions are identified more easily and quicker. In addition potentials for outsourcing and supplier integration arise because of well-defined and standardized parts [Mayer 1993; Feitzinger / Lee 1997].

For example, a car consists of six variable components, each of which can be realized by one of six construction kits (e.g. engine, ABS, headlights, air condition, seats and sound system). Each of those components can be build up in different way by different sets of parts. Thus, so called "variants in variants" exists within the product composition structure. The product composition structure and the differentiated types of relationships of this example are shown in *Figure 2*. Based on the formulas [Anderl 2005, 43-45]:

$$\Phi(P) = \prod_{i=1}^{n} (h_i^{T})$$

with:

$T \in \{F, K, M\}$, F = fixed, K = optional (OR), M = mandatory (XOR)

and:

$$h^{F} = \prod_{i=1}^{n} h_i^{T} \quad \Rightarrow \text{frequency of the subtree for fixed components}$$

$$h^{K} = 1 + \prod_{i=1}^{n} h_i^{T} \quad \Rightarrow \text{frequency of the subtree for variable (OR) components}$$

$$h^{M} = \sum_{i=1}^{n} h_i^{T} \quad \Rightarrow \text{frequency of the subtree for mandatory (XOR) components}$$

216 possible product variants are feasible.

$$\Phi(P) = \prod_{i=1}^{6} h_i^{T} = h^{M}_{engine} * h^{F}_{ABS} * h^{F}_{headlights} * h^{K}_{air\ condition} * h^{M}_{seats} * h^{K}_{soundsystem}$$
$$= 6 * 1 * 2 * 2 * 3 * 3 = 216$$

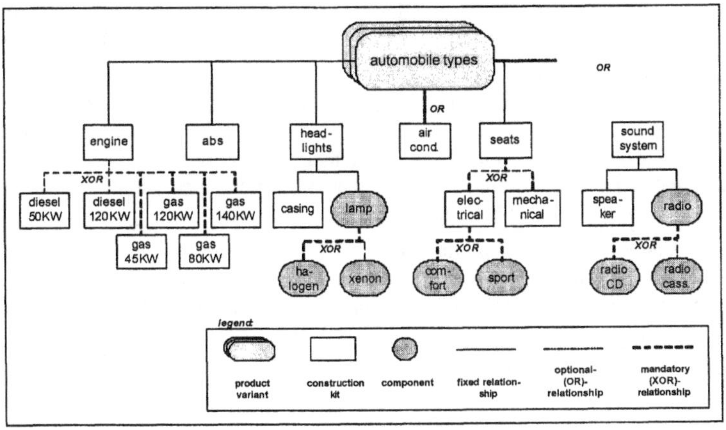

Figure 6: Complexity due to XOR-, OR- and fixed-relations

It seems to be clear, that if the component, which forms the product attributes, consists on a lower product level furthermore of several parts (e.g. comfort seats with or without seat heating), the internal variety and complexity will increase accordingly. By means of modularization, it will be possible to significantly reduce the complexity of subassembly structures, represented by the number, heterogeneity and variability of parts. Therefore, it is particular important for technical reasons, that the interfaces of parts, components and construction kits are standardized. Only then is the opportunity provided to establish that combinational variety, which is needed for assembling highly individualized products. This means also that decreasing internal variety and respectively product complexity thru modularization and standardization, tends to result in higher controllability of external variety on customer side.

To control and prevent complexity for data management and planning purposes, product variants are aggregated to base products or product families. These product abstractions are usually based from a logical viewpoint on technical issues like aggregations of non-variable parts that comply with the utilized classifications in manufacturing (platform, construction kit). But often, especially for planning purposes, there also exist synthesized abstractions for base products that cannot be assembled (e.g. ABC-classifications based on the average lead time of construction kits) [Winter 1991].

Against this background, the degree of product standardization and the customer influence on product creation makes up the product-spectrum, of which four main product categories are distinguished [Schomburg 1980; Schönsleben 2002]

- Customer specified products (engineer-to-order): These products are customer order-related. Each product is produced as units and is significantly different from existing ones. Standardization of parts and components are barely possible. Typical customer specified products are products in the range of plant engineering and construction.
- Standard products with customer specified product variants (make-to-order): These are mainly configurable products, which consist of a set of predefined components and the knowledge of how components can be connected. On a small scale, components can be adapted to customer requirements and assembly is based on construction kits. Products of this kind are primarily located in the engine / machine building industry, e.g. drive gears.
- Standard products with factory specified product variants (assemble-to-order): In contrast to the last product category, this variant program is fully specified by the producer. Because of a high degree of prefabrication customer influence on product construction is limited. Due to this fact, customer requirements are only provided through equipment components on the end-product level by the above mentioned variation methods. Typical products are computers, automobiles, standard software etc.
- Standard products without product variants (make-to-stock): These products are fixed, which means that these products cannot be modified. This product category is predestined for mass production. Examples are washing machines, TV sets and Hi-fi systems.

The following figure shows the different product categories, and the way customer influence on product creation leads to complexity. The customer and factory specified product variants covered by are highlighted.

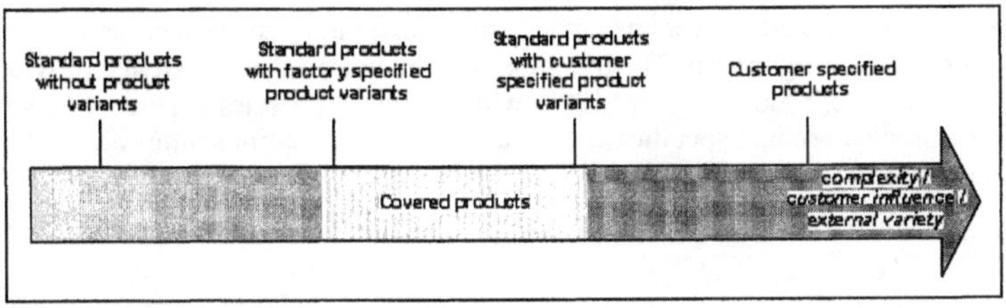

Figure 7: Differentiated product categories depending on customers' influence on product creation

Recapitulating, it has been pointed out that complexity mainly results from the number of product variants because of increasing external variety. But external variety is not the direct cause for complexity. It is rather the effect on the number and heterogeneity of parts, components, construction kits - and so basically the internal variety - which tends to result in high complexity. Classification, standardization and modularization are for different production tasks well suited to reduce the complexity.

4. Reducing and controlling complexity provoked by product variants in the value chain system

The effect on the variability of system relations - more precisely - in case of the customer-oriented view on parameter structures and in case of the technical viewpoint on the BOM structure, has not been researched up to now. The next section will briefly introduce possibilities to control and prevent complexity, which is related to customer provoked variability on product structures.

4.1. Handling complexity by means of product configuration

In the context of order processing and product configuration or selection respectively, two phases can usually be distinguished, namely product specification and (technical) product configuration. The specification phase is always needed, when the customer or the sales person does not directly possesses sufficient technical knowledge for product configuration [Sinz 2003]. In this case, the initial information about product configuration is the customer's functional product specification. According to the customer view of product variants, the customer thinks mostly of the operation and/or use of a product for a certain application. In the phase of product specification the client specifies what he intends to use the product for. The customer is considered as a "co-producer" as well as a "co-designer" [Blecker / Abdelkafi 2004; Piller 2003]. In this situation, functional product requirements are likely to be subjective. The complexity of transforming customer specifications into technical specifications rises when the product knowledge of the customer is vague, especially when the client describes the product's functionality by words like "often", "sometimes", "never" or by quality inputs like "big", "cheap", "fast" etc. In such cases, it depends on how the sales expert interprets the functional requirements and how he is able to transform these specifications in technical data [Schwarze 1996].

In the scope of mentioned viewpoints, specification mapping can be seen as first task in the process of product configuration. The intention is to transform the knowledge provided by the customer during order processing - possibly with the help of a sales expert - to a structurally concrete and precise product specification. In this stage major complexities arise when

- uncertain, rough and tacit knowledge has to be used and
- the input data does not have a fixed format, but varies widely in appearance [Schwarze 1996].

Depending on the product complexity and need for product specification respectively, the complexity of the product configuration process can be decreased if specification mapping can be done automatically e.g. over internet-based product configuration systems with proper customer front ends. In case, that the customer has the ability to directly specify the technical product parameters like speed torque, voltage, engine power etc., there is no need for specification mapping at all. If so, technical configuration is the first step in configuration process.

Technical product configuration can be seen as an interface between the customer and technical product view. The objective of this stage is to find one or several possible configuration solutions and to detect contradictions. Just as in the process of specification mapping, technical product configuration is normally covered by a (software-supported) rule-based or decision table-based configuration system. Unlike specification mapping, the availability of formalized data is characteristic during this stage. The covered tasks on this stage are in particular product visualizing and dimensioning, feasibility testing, finding consistent combinations of components, generating bills of material and price calculation [Schwarze 1996; Piller 1998].

The complexity in the process of generating consistent bills of material on the basis of product parameter specifications depends on the number and heterogeneity of parts and relationships and thus on the underlying product model. For this purpose different configuration approaches exists [compare for further reading Weigel / Faltings 1999; Gzara / Rieu / Tollenaere 2003; Felfernig et al. 2001]:

- Production rule-based: This type of configuration is based on logical "if-then-else" expressions. A rule expresses the relationship between parts or components and the conditions under which the rule is applicable.
- Constraint Satisfaction Problem (CSP): The idea behind a CSP is to assign values to certain variables without breaking predefined constraints (like a system of equations). Constraints between different variants like restrictions and completeness of configuration are defined by relationships, whereas each relationship restricts possible variable values in a domain.
- Graph-oriented: As a rule, parts and components are represented as nodes. The nodes constitute a tree-like graph, and the relations between the nodes are represented as disjunctions or conjunctions (*see Figure 2*).
- Object-based: A relatively new approach is product configuration based on object-oriented methods. In this context, UML is often mentioned as a graphical description language for configuration problems, because of the similarity to graphical tree-like configuration models. UML provides a set of notational conventions for classification, abstraction or compositions (part-of-relations), which can be used to model configuration problems.

All modeling approaches are mostly based on declarative descriptions of product configurations. This means, that in the majority of cases these approaches only describe valid configurations but not how to obtain them. The implication of this is the need for special search algorithms to generate bills of material from customer specifications [Sinz 2003].
Altogether, configuration systems have the ability to control product complexity on the customer side. But in case of high product variety it becomes more and more difficult or even impossible to store predefined bills of material for each product variant in databases. In such cases, the built-in functionality of BOM explosion, which is normally covered by the backend of the configuration system, is of particular importance.
By now we have analyzed the configuration front-end as an interface to take up the customer's individual wishes and the backend as a kind of transformation system, where customer's specifications are transformed to technical product-related data. ***Figure 8*** summarizes the two differentiated product views and their relation in the understanding of this paper.

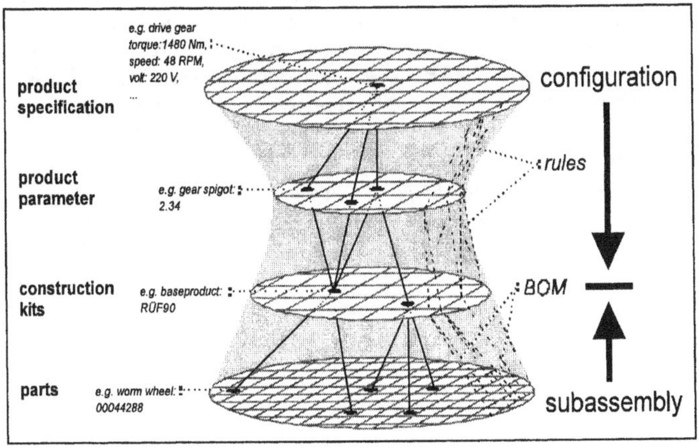

Figure 8: The product composition system

In the next section we will analyze the impact of high product complexity on the interface to the supply chain. Against the background, that an external processing of manufacturing parts or even leasing free assembly capacities from an affiliated company could - under certain circumstances - reduce the complexity, it has to be analyzed, which general conditions must exists to offer the potential for complexity reduction. This in turn will provide the chance to achieve higher product individualization.

4.2. Reducing complexity in supply chains

Productivity arguments on the one hand and individualized products at high cost on the other hand have determined supply and demand in the past. Where the friction loss was too high, the controlling company tends to use insourcing. The result of this is the tendency to large and even multinational corporations or joint ventures with inflexible value chains and an increasing slackness in reacting to changing markets conditions. Due to price-competition suppliers are forced to reduce their costs with the effect that they keep quality and stockpiling to a minimum. As a result of this, the risk of reduced quality, longer delivery times and poor delivery reliability increases significantly [Schönsleben 2000]. But in the last decades, customers are getting more selective and the offered (make-to-market) products do not meet the customers' needs anymore.

In today's production environment, manufacturing companies are looking towards re-engineering their supply chains to reduce cost, drive down inventories and speed their time to market. Companies find that it is not enough to improve processes within their enterprises; they must improve processes across their extended enterprises. In particular modern information and communication systems (ICS) provide the opportunity to reduce process complexity and reach a higher degree of product customization.

4.2.1. Initial position

Against this background the initial position is formed by hierarchically organized production systems. Given the emphasis on productivity, scientific management principles were focused on eliminating variations in the production process thru standardized work designs and specialization of labor [Taylor 1967]. Coordination and control were accomplished thru hierarchies instituted to ensure that employees adhered to a set predefined task that enhances efficiency. Coordination is basically done by directive based on centralized decision making. Characteristic is the poor need for information during manufacturing and formalized communication channels. These principles also had the consequence of creating a trade-off between productivity and flexibility or production cost and product variety in a narrow sense. Due to that fact, either standardized products were produced in a connected line-flow mass production environment, which ensure economies of scale, or customized products were produced at high cost in job shops [Reichwald / Möslein 1997].

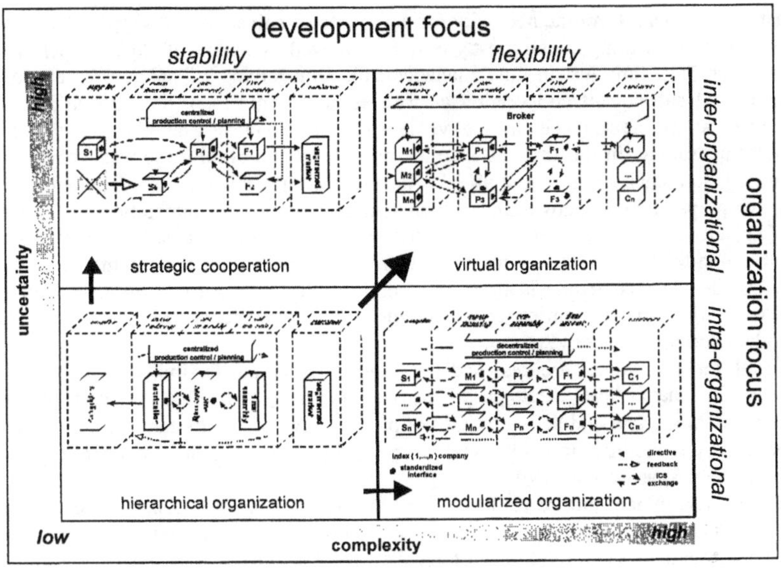

Figure 9: Different partnership strategies

Starting from this background and connected with the innovations in the ICS development three basic organizational strategies come to fore [Reichwald / Möslein 1997]:

- establishment of inter-organizational networks between different corporations (e.g. joint venture, strategic alliances),
- additional modularization of internal business processes and their subsequent intra- and inter-organizational cross-linking (e.g. profit centers, strategic-oriented business units),
- virtualization in terms of dynamic, self-organized, problem-oriented and interconnected, but loosely coupled organizational units within and between organizations.

Figure 9 summarizes these partnership strategies in dependency upon the two dimensions of complexity or product variety and market uncertainty. The arrows in the figure indicate possible trends starting from hierarchical organizations. The main reasons for these different organizational strategies can be seen in [Krystek et al. 1997]:

- realization of flexibility potentials and/or complexity control for opening up room for manufacturing high product variety,
- utilization of comparative transaction cost advantages,
- splitting entrepreneurial risk and
- opening up synergy potentials.

4.2.2. Strategic cooperation as partnership strategy

Increasingly dynamic and uncertain global markets, related distribution risk (e.g. because of cultural distinctions) and the need for shorter delivery times and increasing unreliability on the part of suppliers, form the necessity for new strategic adjustment of supply chains. Shorter delivery times for example, can mostly only be achieved by means of close cooperation with the supplier (e.g. thru just-in-time management). Outsourcing of services to a subsidiary company and subsequent cooperation as well as joint ventures or strategic alliances with companies at different levels in the value chain, are typical examples for this kind of partnership strategy. In the first instance the main objective of all these kinds of partnership strategies is to reduce entrepreneurial risk. As a general rule, this type of cooperation demands extensive preparation of networking, which also assumes a tight integration of the partners' ICS (e.g. electronic data interchange (EDI)). For this reason, strategic networks normally focus on long-term and relationships can usually not be established and maintained with many members. Beside risk diversification, frequently the development of synergy-potentials like the exploitation of economies of scale and scope are crucial for inter-organizational networking too [Schönsleben 2000].

All in all, these strategies are designed for stability. Thus, the flexibility to react to varying customer demand is little. Strategic alliances are normally built up to increase productivity e.g. for fast throughput and delivery times of products. According to this, complexity can only be reduced by reducing external product variety and by enforcement of standards. [Reichwald / Möslein 1997; Krystek et al. 1997].

Problems arise when the controlling company appears as the central decision making authority in the value chain and enforces their decisions on dependent undertaking (e.g. the use of information technology). Therefore, the need for trust is here not such a problem as comparatively to the next organizational type. Furthermore, risks may result from wrong partner choices and changes in crucial conditions on the suppliers' components [Schönsleben 2000].

4.2.3. Modularization as partnership strategy

Modularization is similar to the last mentioned organization type, but is more open, flexible and partner-oriented. The initial position is nearly the same as before. High complexity in the range of services - due to high product variety - customer specific demands as well as the demand for a short time to markets, forms the characteristic organizational environment. In consequence, knowledge and information exchange are extremely important for the success of the partnership. The emergence of modern ICS, like ISDN, LAN and EDI, offers the potential to decrease evolving transaction costs. If transaction costs can be decreased, there are fewer reasons for keeping parts of the value-added chain within the own company, especially if processes are involved which are not seen as core competency. Besides, when product development and manufacturing become more costly due to increasing complexity, then entrepreneurial risk may be more widely distributed.

Reducing time to market demands intensification of intra- and inter-organizational cooperation with co-producer. A co-producer in this sense does not only mean the corporations' supplier, but also the customer [Piller 2003]. As shown above modern ICS enables the possibility to integrate the customer in the process of product development. Furthermore regular information exchange at all hierarchical levels are necessary. Modular organization units are characterized by decentralized decision-making authorities and profit responsibilities. The hierarchy of the corporation is more likely to be flat and the independence of the units is particularly typical for this strategy. Each partner is active within his own area of core competence. Insofar this type of partnership strategy depends on closely integrated but thru open standards loosely coupled information systems and abstains from a

tight inter-organizational coordination thru centralized control [Schönsleben 2000; Reichwald / Möslein 1997; Krystek et al. 1997]. Besides, arrangements for ensuring trust are absolutely necessary. This can be accomplished by installing mechanism for providing trust, e. g. thru an internet-based clearing and certification instance [Keim / Weitzel 2005].
Overall, intra- and inter-organizational collaboration processes provide better product and production flexibility in order to satisfy specific customer wishes.

4.2.4. Virtualization as partnership strategy
The initial position is the drastically increased aspiration level of the customer, the increasing differentiation of customer wishes as well as the growing demand for products and product services as bundle. The entrepreneurial tasks are shaped thru a high variability and a structureless company's environment. It is an environment, which causes therefore high product variety and high complexity respectively. Accordingly, an organizational network is needed, which can be formed temporarily and closely for manufacturing such non-repetitive products that solve a customer's specific problem. The concept of virtual organizations, which was mainly introduced by *Davidow and Malone (1992)*, seems to be a potential answer. Virtualization can be seen as the advantageous combination of the both last described strategies. The concept of virtuality aims to utilize the advantages of inter- and intra-organizational networking as soon as the customer defines its individual needs. Here, the customer becomes definitely a co-producer. The members of the virtual corporation stand as single company to the customer for the duration of contract. After fulfillment the participants will be again separate and may form new virtual organizations.
Against this background, virtual organizations can be characterized as dynamic networks of legally independent companies or persons, which offer their core competencies in the value-added process. Prerequisite is the use of open standards so that loose coupling of different ICS is feasible at any time at low cost. Furthermore virtual organizations normally do not possess decision hierarchies and control instances, except for trust establishing coordination. They are self-organizing systems like project teams or task forces, which exists temporarily for the duration of a project (in terms of manufacturing a problem solution). The strength of virtual organizations can be seen in the ability to form quickly. Practically this means, the members of the network must be familiar with each other and - more important - they must trust each other.
Accordingly, this organizational structure optimally permits a high degree of product and production flexibility, but also assumes a high focus on the partnership [Rittenbruch et al. 1999; Fischer 1995]. The achievable flexibility potential in virtual corporations is basically determined by the [Krystek et al. 1997]:

- degree of specification, which is needed for a cooperation treaty,
- degree of structural and cultural interconnection,
- dimension of slack and redundancy in the network,
- possibility for market research with regard to the partner's competences in order to develop proactive proposals for new products,
- barrier for accessing and leaving the virtual corporation (e.g. friction loss in line with procurement negotiations) and
- existence of mechanisms for establishing trust in the network.

The last point can be seen as one of the biggest problems of virtualization at present. On the one hand virtual organizations must form themselves rapidly and due to that, the company boundaries of the potential co-producers in the network must already be open. On the other hand mutual trust between the members must exist. But the development of mutual trust normally needs time, which seems to be a contradictory to the rapidness of formation. Beside the general principle, that competition within the network must generally ruled out, a neutral broker for rapid formation of network and for ensuring trust is normally required (*see **Figure 9***). The broker might also serve as a center of order processing (i.e. for planning and control) for legal advice and for appropriation of net proceeds (namely as a centrally managed cost center).
Overall, the concept of virtual organization is best suited for controlling process complexity in value chains due to high product variety, if distrust is absent or can be avoided. Theoretically it does not only enable horizontal service exchanges in value chains, but also vertical exchanges e.g. capacity balancing between legally independent assembly facilities in case of capacity bottlenecks.

5. Conclusion and further research

Reducing and controlling complexity is one of the most important tasks in the production environment of high product variety. Complexity reduction can be mainly done by reducing internal product variety thru modularization. But this has to be accomplished in such a way, that external variety and so the degree of product individualization will not suffer from reduced internal variety. Complexity which can not be reduced has to be controlled in reasonable way. First of all the product configuration and selection system provides major potentials to control complexity which results from complex product composition structures. In the scope of product configuration two basic subsystems can be distinguished. Firstly, the system of product parameter which inherently covers the possibilities for fulfilling customers' product specifications on the one side and which form on the other side the interface to the subassembly. Secondly the system of subassembly, at which it is in case of high product variety, as a rule does not allow a BOM for each product variant. Due to the fact, that for planning purposes it is normally not possible to break down BOM on the top level of end-products, single-level BOM for producible or abstract base products build up the highest manageable level.
Complexity control in production planning offers a wide research field and is particular important for the requirement adjustment of materials in global value chains. With increasing bull-whip effects, chain-wide balanced planning requirements become more and more important. Not only the bull-whip effect, but also increasing competition in global markets can be seen reason for well organized supply chains. Opportunities for external processing or outsourcing of value-added processes, due to a lack of core competence or higher production costs compared to competitors, necessitate new collaboration types in manufacturing. Traditional cooperation strategies like strategic alliances or joint ventures with inelastic value chains are not suitable for increasing market demand. Here, from an organizational point view, the concept of virtual organization seems to offer promise for reaching significant flexibility and for reducing process complexity. Virtual organizations attempt to achieve - in a self-organizing way - short-term company cooperation for specific customer orders. An important fundamental for the formation of virtual organizations is the agility of the

companies involved. Agility in this sense does not necessarily mean lean manufacturing, which can be typical met in highly modularized organization forms. Rather, members of virtual organizations are able to remain competitive on the basis of proactive development of knowledge and competence [Schönsleben 2000]. But this in turn, can only be accomplished by the support of modern and open information technology, like EDI or on basis the new web-service technology, and particularly by the support of trust-building systems.

References

Adam, D. (1997), *Produktionsmanagement*, 8. Aufl., Wiesbaden 1997.

Adam, D. and Rollberg, R (1995): Komplexitätskosten, in: *Die Betriebswirtschaft*, 55, 667-670.

Anderl, R. (2005), Produktdatentechnologie B. Produktmanagement. *Skript* zur Vorlesung, Technische Universität Darmstadt, SS 2005, http://eos.dik.maschinenbau.tu-darmstadt.de/projects/pdt_b/deutsch/skript.html.

Blecker, T. and Abdelkafi, N. (2004), A Framework for Understanding the Interdependencies between Mass Customization and Complexity, in: *Proceedings of the 2nd International Conference on Business Economics, Management and Marketing*, Athens / Greece, June 24-27, 2004, 1-15.

Davidow, W. H. and Malone, M. S. (1992), *The virtual corporation*, Haper Collins, New York, 1992.

Du, X., Jiao, J. and Tseng, M. M. (2003), Modelling platform-based product configuration using programmed attributed graph grammars, in: *Journal of Engineering Design*, Vol. 14, No. 2, June 2003, 145-167.

Feitzinger, E. and Lee, H. (1997): Mass Customization at Hewlett-Packard: the power of postponement, in: *Harvard Business Review*, 75. Jg. (1997), H. 1, 116-121.

Felfernig, A., Friedrich, G. and Jannach, D. (2001): Conceptual modeling for configuration of mass-customizable products, in: *Artificial Intelligence in Engineering* 15, 2001, 165-176.

Firchau, N. and Franke, H. J. (2002): Methoden zur Variantenbeherrschung in der Produktentwicklung, in: *Variantenmanagement in der Einzel- und Kleinserienfertigung*, Franke, H. J. et al. (eds.) München, Wien.

Fischer, P. (1995), *Die Selbständigen von morgen; Unternehmer order Tagelöhner?* Campus, Frankfurt/Main.

Frey, D., Stockheim, T., Woelk, P.-O. and Zimmermann, R. (2003), Integrated Multi-agent-based Supply Chain Management, in: *IEEE International Workshops on Enabling Technologies: Infrastructure for Collaborative Enterprises* (WETICE-2003), 24--29; Linz, Austria.

Garud, R. and Kotha, S. (1994), Using the brain as a metaphor to model flexible production systems, in: *Academy of Management Review*, 19, Nr. 4, 671-698.

Gzara, L., Rieu, D. and Tollenaere, M. (2003), Product information systems engineering: an approach for building product models by reuse of patterns, in: *Robotics and Computer Integrated Manufacturing*, 19, 239-261.

Helberg, P. (1987), PPS als CIM-Baustein: Gestaltung der Produktionsplanung und -steuerung für die computerintegrierte Produktion, in: *Betriebliche Informations- und Kommunikationssysteme*, Krallmann, H. (ed.), Bd. 8, Berlin.

Keim, T. and Weitzel, T. (2005), An Integrated Framework for Online Partnership-Building, in: *Proceedings of the 38th Hawaiian International Conference on System Sciences* (HICSS-38); Hilton Waikoloa Village, Big Island, Hawaii 2005.

Kestel, R. (1995), *Variantenvielfalt und Logistiksysteme, Ursache – Auswirkungen - Lösungen*, Wiesbaden.

Kurbel, K. (1999), Produktionsplanung und -steuerung – Methodische Grundlagen von PPS-Systemen und Erweiterungen, in: *Handbuch der der Informatik*, Endres, A., Krallmann, H. and Schupp, P. (eds.) Bd. 13.2, 4, München, Wien.

Krystek, U., Redel, W. and Reppegather, S. (1997), *Grundzüge virtueller Organisationen: Elemente und Erfolgsfaktoren, Chancen und Risiken*, Wiesbaden.

Lingnau, V. (1994), *Variantenmanagement: Produktionsplanung im Rahmen einer Produktdifferenzierungsstrategie*, Berlin.

Maroni, D. (2001), *Produktionsplanung und Steuerung bei Variantenfertigung: eine komplexitätsbasierte Betrachtung*, Frankfurt am Main.

Mayer, R. (1993), *Strategien erfolgreicher Produktgestaltung: Individualisierung und Standardisierung*, Wiesbaden.

Meffert, H. (2000), Marketing: *Grundlagen marktorientierter Unternehmensführung, Konzepte – Instrumente – Praxisbeispiele*, 9. Auflage, Wiesbaden.

Montau, R. (1996), Föderatives Produktdatenmanagement anhand semantischer Informationsmodellierung, in: *VDI Reihe 20: Rechnerunterstützte Verfahren*, Nr. 213 , ETH Zürich, Düsseldorf 1996.

Piller, F. T. (1998), *Kundenindividuelle Massenproduktion: die Wettbewerbsstrategie der Zukunft*, München, Wien.

Piller, F. T. (2003), Von Massenproduktion zu Co-Produktion, Kunden als Wertschöpfungspartner, in: *WIRTSCHAFTSINFORMATIK*, 5/2003.

Pine, B. J. II (1993), *Mass Customization: The New Frontier in Business Competition*, Boston.

Reichwald, R. and Möslein, K. (1997), Chancen und Herausforderungen für neue unternehmerische Strukturen und Handlungsspielräume in der Informationsgesellschaft. In: *Telekooperation und virtuelle Unternehmen - Auf dem Weg zu neuen Arbeitsformen*, Picot, A. (ed.), Heidelberg.

Ringsletter, M. and Kirsch, W. (1991), Varianten einer Differenzierungsstrategie, in: *Beiträge zum Management strategischer Programme*, Kirsch, W. (ed.), München.

Rittenbruch, H., Kahler, H. and Cremers, A. B. (1999), Unterstützung von Kooperationen in einer Virtuellen Organisation. In: *Electronic Business Engineering. 4.Internationale Tagung Wirtschaftsinformatik 1999*, Scheer, A. W. and Nüttgens, M. (eds.), Physika, Heidelberg.

Scheer, A.-W., Mattheis, P. and Steinmann, D. (1991), Konzeptionen, in: *CIM Handbuch*, 2. Auflage, Geitner, U. W. (ed.), Braunschweig.

Sinz, C. (2003), *Verifikation regelbasierter Konfigurationssysteme*, Tübingen.

Schomburg, E. (1980), *Entwicklung eines betriebstypologischen Instrumentariums zur systematischen Ermittlung der Anforderungen an EDV-gestützte Produktionsplanungs- und -steuerungssysteme im Maschinenbau*, Aachen.

Schönsleben, P. (2000), With agility and adequate partnership strategies towards effective logistics networks, in: *Computer in Industry* 42, 33-42.

Schönsleben, P. (2002), *Integrales Logistikmanagement, Planung und Steuerung von umfassenden Geschäftsprozessen*, 3. Auflage, Berlin, 2002.

Schwarze, S. (1996), Configuration of Multiple-Variant Products. Application Orientation and Vagueness in Customer Requirements, in: Forschungsberichte für die Unternehmenspraxis, Schönsleben, P. (ed.), vdf, Zurich.

Taylor, F. W. (1967), *Principles of scientific management*, W. W. Norton & Company, New York 1967.

Weigel, R. / Faltings, B. (1999): Compiling constraints satisfaction problems, in: *Artificial Intelligence* 115, 257-287.

Winter, R. (1991): *Mehrstufige Produktionsplanung in Abstraktionshierarchien auf der Basis relationaler Informationsstrukturen*, Springer, Berlin

Kolibri 360 GmbH
Ferdinand-Jühlke-Straße 7
99095 Erfurt, Deutschland
produktsicherheit@kolibri360.de

Druck:
CPI Druckdienstleistungen GmbH
im Auftrag der
Kolibri 360 GmbH
Ferdinand-Jühlke-Str. 7
99095 Erfurt